# FrameMaker 4: From Desktop to Print Shop

*Yvonne Johnson*

Osborne **McGraw-Hill**

Berkeley New York St. Louis San Francisco Auckland Bogotá Hamburg London Madrid Mexico City
Milan Montreal New Delhi Panama City Paris São Paulo Singapore Sydney Tokyo Toronto

Osborne **McGraw-Hill**
2600 Tenth Street
Berkeley, California 94710
U.S.A.

For information on software, translations, or book distributors outside of the U.S.A., please write to Osborne McGraw-Hill at the above address.

FrameMaker 4: From Desktop to Print Shop



1234567890 DOC 9987654

ISBN 0-07-881970-9



Series Design: Seventeenth Street Studios

*Dedicated to Hunter Taylor*

# CONTENTS AT A GLANCE

## INTRODUCTION TO DESKTOP PUBLISHING



## FRAMEMAKER BASICS



## SHAPING TEXT INTO DESIGN

## USING GRAPHICS AND COLOR

# IV



## HIGH-POWERED FEATURES

# V



## GETTING TO PRESS

# VI



## SUPPORT AND TROUBLESHOOTING

# VII

APPENDIXES

# VIII

# CONTENTS

# USING GRAPHICS AND COLOR

# IV

## HIGH-POWERED FEATURES IV

# SUPPORT AND TROUBLESHOOTING VII

## APPENDIXES VIII

# Acknowledgments

This book was more challenging to write than a simple "this-is-how-you-use-the-program" book, and it required input from many sources which are credited individually in the text of the book. The list is too lengthy to repeat here, but you know who you are, and you know that I appreciate your help.

I would especially like to thank Sandy Knox from Frame Technology, Inc., who contributed Chapter 12, and all the technical support representatives from Frame who answered my questions about the program. In addition I would like to say that Frame Technology, Inc., was one of the most cooperative and helpful software companies that I have ever worked with to produce a book.

At Osborne/McGraw-Hill I would like to thank my editor, Bill Pollock, as well as Bob Myren, Mark Karmendy, and Kim Torgerson. I would also like to thank Fred Lass for the technical review and suggestions.

# Introduction

*FrameMaker 4: From Desktop to Print Shop* is not your ordinary book on how to use a desktop publishing program. Instead of focusing solely on the FrameMaker 4 program, this book discusses FrameMaker 4 in the larger context of desktop publishing issues in general.

The book is divided into eight sections: Introduction to Desktop Publishing, FrameMaker Basics, Shaping Text into Design, Using Graphics and Color, High-Powered Features, Getting to Press, Support and Troubleshooting, and Appendixes. Users of all levels will benefit from the topics in this book as well as the many hands-on exercises designed to walk you through some of the more advanced features.

In the first section you will learn about the history of desktop publishing. In the second section you will learn how to use FrameMaker 4 to create documents. In section three you will learn how to format documents. Section four explains the drawing and color features of FrameMaker 4. Section five discusses more complex documents and hypertext. Section six gives you tips on how to work with a printer and a service bureau. Section seven is particularly valuable because it contains support and troubleshooting information obtained directly from Frame Technology, Inc. In the appendixes you will find a glossary of terms, FrameMaker installation information, helpful how-to tables, special character tables, and a list of recommended reading.

## CONVENTIONS USED IN THIS BOOK

Many of the desktop publishing terms used at the beginning of this book are not explained in context because the explanation of the term would detract from the point being made. Such terms are found in the index and are explained in the glossary (Appendix A).

When referred to in text, hotkeys for menu options or buttons (that have hotkeys) are underlined to help you make selections using the keyboard.

However, it is assumed that most users are making menu selections with a mouse instead of the keyboard. You will find that not all items on a FrameMaker 4 menu or in a dialog box have hotkeys, so it is more convenient to use a mouse in these cases.

Additional information and interesting tidbits are scattered throughout the book. These items are boxed like this:

> **FrameMaker 4: From Desktop to Print Shop**
>
> *You will find this to be the most informative book written on FrameMaker 4. It covers many features, such as hypertext, that other books only mention. We are sure that you will find this book a solid investment.*

Many of the chapters have hands-on exercises. When a step in an exercise requires you to type text, the text is bold like this:

1. Type **Welcome to the company.**

Non-typing keys like the Enter key and the Tab key are represented in text like this: ENTER and TAB. Keys that are pressed together are represented like this: CTRL+ENTER. Keys that are pressed one at a time are represented like this: ESC, p, z. And, as in the last example (ESC, p, z), keys that must be pressed are case sensitive, so be sure to use the case that is indicated.

# I

# Introduction to Desktop Publishing

# 1

# What is Desktop Publishing?

DESKTOP publishing (DTP) is the newest way to produce crisp, clean, professional-looking letters, memos, newsletters, books, brochures, flyers, posters, etc., right at your own desk. Desktop publishing replaces the traditional method of publishing which uses many outside sources like typesetters to produce a printed product. Conceivably, using desktop publishing technology, you should be able to accomplish all the steps to publish a product without using any outside sources.

A DTP program like FrameMaker 4, a computer, and a printer (usually a laser) are the basic tools of desktop publishing. New tools like scanners, light pens, and drawing pads are being added to the toolkit everyday.

*Research shows that professional-looking documents, that is, documents that are typeset, are easier to read, demand more attention, and are more believable.*

Desktop publishing has revolutionized the publishing/printing industry as much as Gutenberg's printing press did in the fifteenth century. This new leap in publishing has been a long time in coming. Gutenberg's original movable type concept was still being used in the early 1900s.

*The term* desktop publishing *was coined in 1985 by Paul Brainerd, the founder of Aldus Corporation, a Seattle-based company. Brainerd developed the inexpensive page-makeup software package called PageMaker for the PC.*

Since desktop publishing has established itself, there has been an explosion of printed material. Because many of the expensive processes like typesetting and paste-up have been eliminated by desktop publishing, more and more people are producing printed materials to get their messages out to the public. The good news is that more information is available to more people. The bad news is that much of the DTP material is atrocious looking!

One purpose of this book is to keep you out of the bad-news category. No matter how well-intentioned you are or how worthy your message is, if the printed piece is poorly designed and executed, it simply becomes "paper clutter" that gets filed in the proverbial "round file." To keep your printed pieces from ending up in the round file, you will need to learn how to use FrameMaker 4 effectively, and you will also need to learn the principles of good layout, techniques of design, how to select the correct typestyle, what kind of paper to use, and so on.

Before you plunge head-long into desktop publishing, you should be warned that DTP is addictive. Once you start on a project you can spend hours experimenting, fine-tuning, and polishing, especially if you have perfectionist tendencies. Unlike hacking away at the keyboard for hours at a time with a word processing program or crunching numbers with a spreadsheet, DTP is not boring or monotonous. The time goes by very quickly when you are using a desktop publishing program.

DTP is a process that gets the creative juices flowing (and don't think you don't have any just because you can't draw a straight line—and by the way, you *will* be able to draw one with FrameMaker 4). The many different tasks and challenges in DTP can hold the interest of even the most hyperactive adult. The finished product also brings more satisfaction than other computer-produced products. Of course, you take pride and satisfaction in producing a well-written and flawlessly typed report, but that pride and satisfaction pale beside the feeling of producing something with style and pizazz.

Like any addiction, DTP can be costly. Once you have the basic tools of the trade you may find that you are lusting after more tools or more powerful tools than the ones you have. You might decide you need a huge library of illustrations. Then you might need to add a CD ROM drive to use the huge library of illustrations that comes on a CD ROM disk. Almost invariably, you will find that you want to move up to a printer that can print special illustrations and special fonts (kinds of type) that are categorized as PostScript.

## THE PUBLISHING PROCESS BEFORE DTP

It will help you understand desktop publishing if you understand the traditional publishing process. In simple terms, publishing is the process of committing an idea to paper and printing it. In between the idea and the final printed product are several steps, as indicated in Figure 1-1.

FIGURE 1-1

*The steps of the publishing process*

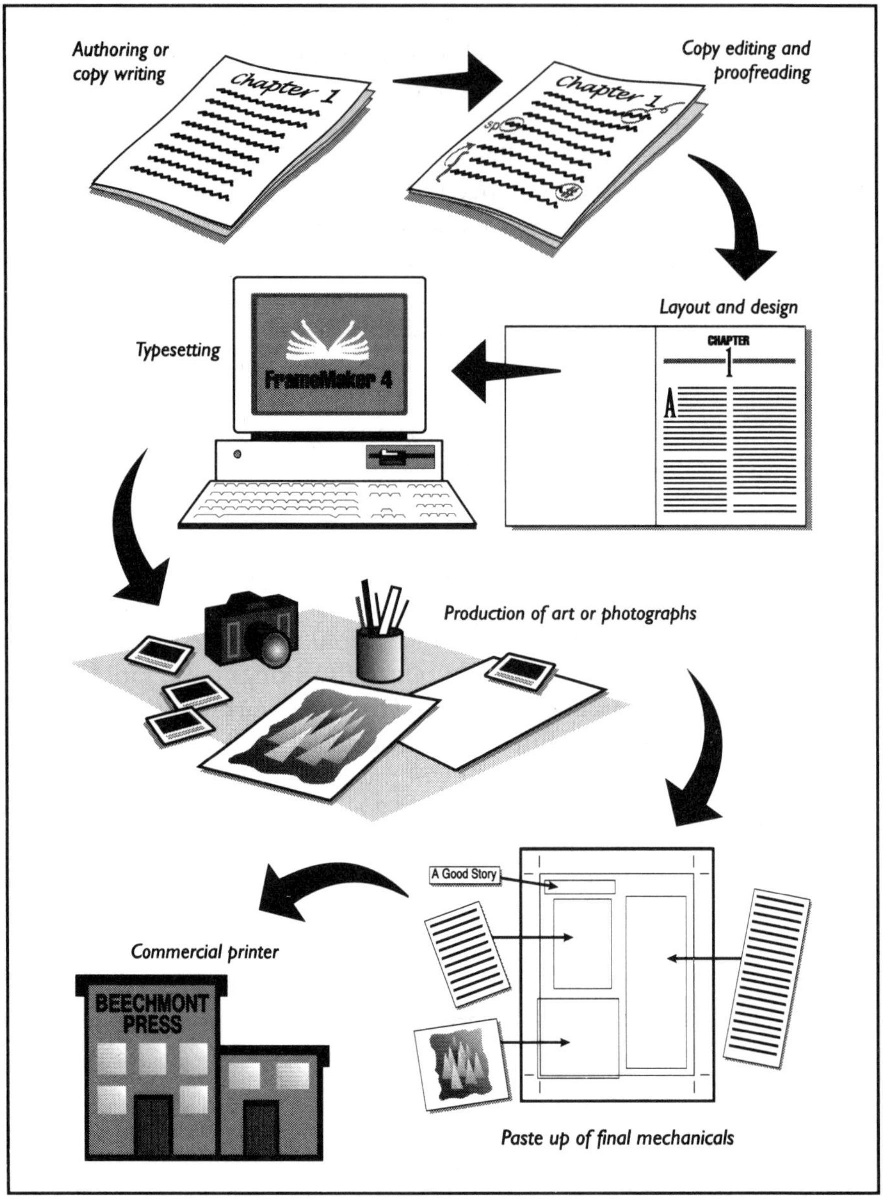


When these processes are completed, the final piece, often called a *mechanical* or *camera-ready copy* is taken to a commercial printing company (normally referred to as *the printer*) where the final product is produced. The camera-ready copy is photographed (thus the name camera-ready) and made into *plates* for a press. Copies are printed and, if necessary, trimmed to size and bound with a cover.

*A publisher is usually not a printer, and a printer is rarely a publisher.*

## Writing and Proofreading

Traditionally copy or manuscripts were written by hand or typed on a typewriter. Now writing copy is usually done with a word processing program or with the DTP software itself (although there are still holdouts who continue to use typewriters or yellow legal pads).

Although proofreading and editing can be done on the screen, many people feel that it is still better to print the copy and proofread from the printed copy. It seems that mistakes are more easily overlooked on the screen. Proofreading is one of the processes that has not been incorporated in DTP, and it is doubtful that a really good proofreading type of program is forthcoming any time soon.

## Layout and Design

The layout and design of a printed piece must be determined early in the process. Layout influences the amount of copy that must be prepared, the type specifications, and the number and size of photographs and art that must be prepared (see Figure 1-2).

Traditionally, the work of the layout artist is done on layout boards (also called bristol boards) which are preprinted with special grids that aid in the placement and alignment of text, photographs, and artwork. These boards, made of heavy paper (usually card stock), are used during the design process and finally in the paste-up process when the copy and artwork are pasted on the boards to produce the mechanical for printing.

Other tools of the layout artist include colored pens, pencils, markers, White-out, scissors, X-acto knives (very sharp, scalpel-like tools used for precision cutting), rubber cement or waxers (equipment that melts and applies wax to the back of anything that must be "glued" to the layout board), cellophane tape, straight edges and Bezier curves, rub-on letters, border tapes for making lines and boxes, and so on. Layout artists usually work on drawing tables, called paste boards, so-called because the artist pastes copy and artwork to the board so that it does not get lost.

**NOTE:** *You may be wondering how copy or artwork can be used if it is already pasted to the paste board. Remember, however, artists use rubber cement or wax not Elmer's glue. Rubber cement and wax do not create a permanent attachment. Almost anything that has been glued with rubber cement or wax can be carefully removed and reattached some place else.*

**FIGURE 1-2** *The layout and design are determined early in the process*

The work of the layout artist is still very much the same in DTP, but the paste board, the layout boards, and the grids are electronic. Unlike the physical layout boards, electronic layout boards allow the artist to change the grids and thus are more flexible. The X-acto knives, scissors, and glue have been replaced by the cut and paste commands. The border tapes have been replaced by electronic line drawing and box drawing tools and a selection of line patterns. Almost all of the artist's tools have been replaced with electronic equivalents.

**NOTE:** *Many artists are of the opinion that DTP lacks precision and has other shortcomings which outweigh its flexibility. But improvements in the artistic area of DTP are descending in a torrent and artists may have few complaints in the near future.*

## Typesetting

Typesetting has evolved over the years through three stages. In the initial stage, individual metal characters, referred to as a *slug of type*, were set by hand—thus the terms *setting type* and *typesetting*. In the second stage, the linotype machine set up casting molds (via a keyboard) for each character required and poured hot metal into the forms to produce a single line of type. After the type was used, the slugs were melted and the metal was reused. In the third stage, just before the advent of DTP, phototypesetting was used.

This process used a clear plastic font strip or disk with negative images of the characters.

*For the first 400 years of printing, typesetting meant literally setting individual pieces of metal molded in the mirror image of numbers, letters, punctuation, or special characters. Typesetters selected individual characters one by one from storage cases to form words and lines, inserting thin spaces of metal where required so that all lines came out even at the end. (The capital letters were kept in upper storage cases and all other letters were kept in lower storage cases, thus the terms* uppercase *and* lowercase*.) When the typesetter finished setting the type, he would lock down all the characters in a special frame called a* chase*. Printers would then roll a layer of ink on the characters in the chase, after which they would press a blank piece of paper on top of the inked type to transfer the ink to paper.*

When copy was taken to a phototypesetter, the copy had to be retyped by the typesetter. As the characters were keyed, the font disk rotated very quickly moving back and forth across a photo-sensitive paper. When the disk was in just the right place on the paper, a light would flash and a lens would focus the image of the selected character on the page (see Figure 1-3). Later improvements in phototypesetting used digitized type instead of photo negatives of type. This improvement in phototypesetting really opened the door to DTP. Once type was digitized, it was a small step to the PostScript definition of type which is the standard in DTP today.

**FIGURE 1-3**

*How a phototypesetter works*

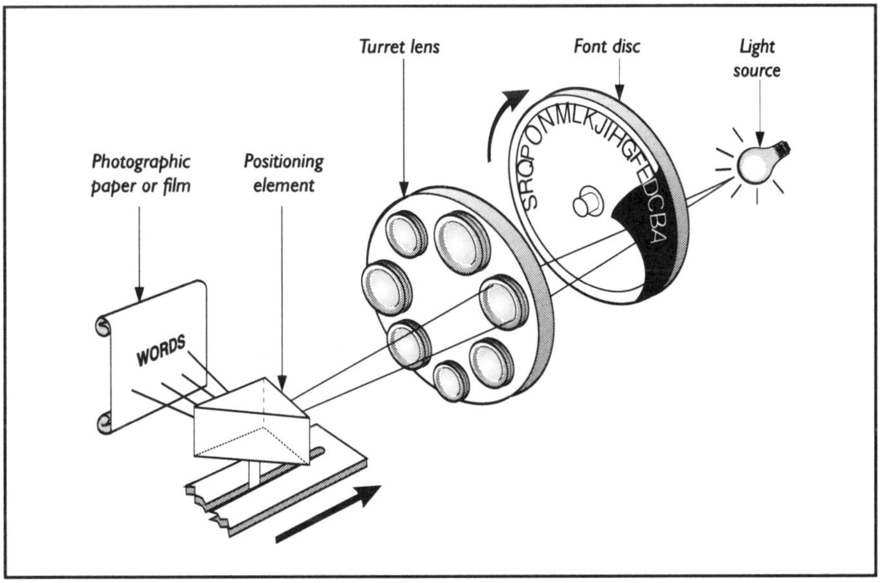

When the typesetting was finished, the paper was run through a developing solution and then out the machine. After a brief drying period, the paper, called a *galley*, was ready to be proofread. Mistakes were marked and returned to the typesetter for correction. Corrections were made, and another galley proof was run out and proofread again. This process continued until there were no errors in the galley proof. The spell checking features of computer software provide an obvious advantage over this method, but do not completely eliminate proofreading.

Regardless of the typesetting method, before the copy can be typeset, someone has to *spec the type*, that is, determine the type specifications. The typesetter has to know which typeface and size to use, how much space to use between each line, and how wide to set the type. Type specifications are very much dependent on the layout and design of the printed piece, which is one of the reasons the piece must be designed early in the process.

Typesetting in DTP involves many of the same principles as phototypesetting, but it is not always necessary for the typesetter to type the copy. The copy can be given to the typesetter in a file, and the file can be imported into the publication. Then the type specifications can be applied to the text. However, it is still possible for the typesetter to type the copy directly in the publication or edit copy that has been imported.

With FrameMaker 4, copy can be typed directly in a publication or it can be imported from word processing programs such as Ami Pro (referred to as Ami Professional in FrameMaker documentation); DisplayWrite (DCA/RFT); Microsoft Word for DOS, Windows, and the Macintosh; and WordPerfect for DOS and the Macintosh. Additionally, FrameMaker 4 can import files from Ventura Publisher (versions 1.0 through 4.0). If you use FrameMaker 4 to type copy, you will find that it has many word processing features including a spell checker and thesaurus, find and replace commands, footnotes, autonumbering, cross-references, generated tables of contents and indexes, and conditional text.

Type specifications can be changed more quickly and easily in DTP than they can be when using the traditional typesetting method. Although DTP typesetting is more flexible than the traditional method, it is a bit ironic to note that the output of traditional phototypesetting was as much as twenty times faster than the output of sophisticated DTP imagesetters. Speed of output was traded for speed of input, but the overall savings in time comes out on the side of DTP.

*The original phototypesetting, produced with photo negatives, became the standard against which digitized and PostScript type were measured. After improvements were added to the PostScript definition of type, PostScript type became the standard.*

## Paste-up

As mentioned earlier, layout boards were traditionally used for paste-up. Once the galley copy was finalized, the layout artist cut the desired portions of the copy and pasted them on the layout boards in the proper places. Often the copy would be either too long or not long enough to fit the design. In such cases, the artist might be able to cut out portions of the copy if it was too long or, if the copy was not long enough, fill the space with something else. Many times though, copy had to be reset to fit the space of the design. Naturally the copy editor had to be consulted when changes were made.

Although *copy fitting* is still one of the layout artist's major problems, DTP has made the problem much easier to resolve. The text can be shortened or lengthened to fit the layout space during the electronic paste-up process. Since the copy is visible on the PC screen, there is never any question about how much to delete or add for the perfect fit.

The ability to experiment with paste-up is one of DTP's major advantages. Prior to DTP, there was usually not enough time to experiment with paste-up once the copy was set, and experimentation was also costly because it could result in additional typesetting charges. With DTP, paste-up is quick, simple, and clean. Copy is never ruined by too much moving around and handling. Type specifications can be changed easily and blocks of copy can be made to fit in a different design from the one originally intended.

## Production of Artwork and Photographs

The traditional means of producing artwork and photographs are still alive and well, but DTP has much to offer in this area too. Many software programs such as Aldus Freehand, CorelDRAW!, and Micrografx Designer are available for creating electronically produced art that would otherwise be drawn by hand. Computer clip art is also available from many sources.

Although PCs have not replaced the function of the camera for taking pictures, scanners make it possible to include a photograph as a graphic file in a DTP publication. The quality is not as good as the conventional means of using a photograph and making a halftone, but technology is closing the gap. Using scanned images in FrameMaker 4 is discussed in more detail in the next chapter and in Chapter 8.

Even color photographs and drawings can be scanned and included in a publications. Color processing (both spot color and four-color work) has been the area of greatest development in DTP in the last few years. Later in this book, you will see how FrameMaker 4 can print publications on a laser printer in such a way that the commercial printer can use the output to produce color in the final piece.

## BENEFITS OF USING DTP

Obviously, the benefits of DTP are great or no revolution in publishing would have taken place. DTP benefits you in the following ways:

- saves you money
- saves you time
- gives you more control over production
- insures the confidentiality of your work
- lets more people read what you publish

### DTP Saves You Money

One of DTP's biggest money- and time-saving advantages is the ability it affords to experiment with page make-up. Change and experimentation are very costly if copy is typeset in the traditional way. Typesetters might charge anywhere from $30 to $100 per page (depending on the complexity) for the typography and mechanical art necessary for an ordinary 8 1/2×11-inch newsletter. If you then alter this newsletter, your last-minute type changes—and the necessary fast turnaround, can add 10 to 30 percent more to the typesetting costs. Overnight turnaround can double or triple these charges.

Desktop publishers, on the other hand, report per-page costs as low as $6 to $9. Some users report paying off equipment costs within a couple of months with the savings garnered. For the most part, double-time and rush charges disappear. (Remember, the truly addicted desktop publisher will stay up all night for free!)

*For five years, Wherehouse Entertainment, Inc., the largest music and video chain on the West Coast, had produced* The Entertainer, *a monthly 20-page newsletter. Production delays would cause a backlog of up to five weeks in the "monthly" turnaround.*

*Then the Wherehouse installed desktop-publishing equipment. With two days' training, the staff comfortably took over production of* The Entertainer. *Turnaround for an issue was cut to five days; cost for 5,000 copies fell from $7,600 per issue to $3,400.*

DTP also saves money in illustrations and other artwork. With DTP, you have access to inexpensive electronic methods of obtaining and processing artwork. As already mentioned, computer clip art is readily available and reasonably priced. You can even get free art work from electronic bulletin boards and services like CompuServe. Scanning is another way to obtain art, but be careful that you do not violate copyright laws by scanning copyright protected art. If you are artistically inclined, you can create your own artwork. FrameMaker 4 has very good drawing tools and graphic features, and it will import art that is created in other programs like CorelDRAW!.

## DTP Saves You Time

DTP saves you time in several ways. One big timesaver is the ability to import text that has already been typed in a word processing program. As already mentioned, FrameMaker 4 can import files from several of the most popular word processing programs. Importing art is another timesaving feature.

Using a modem, you can instantly send or receive files for text, art, charts, graphs, photographs, and so on. This instantaneous transmittal of data shortens the time between the concept for a publication and its delivery to readers.

*Just one week after the November 1992 elections, a lobbying organization mailed more than 100,000 copies of a DTP-produced fund-raising mailer questioning president-elect Clinton's stand on Social Security.*

## Maintaining Control and Confidentiality

With DTP, you have the opportunity to keep all aspects of the production of a publication job *in house*. This control is especially important if you are on a tight deadline, since you are not at the mercy of an outside supplier's schedule.

Further, if the content of the piece is confidential—a new product introduction or a financial disclosure, for example—you can control who has access to the information. If any part of the job is sent out, you have no control over who sees (and talks about) the information.

## DTP Lets More People Read What You Publish

In many ways, desktop publishing has brought the tools of publishing to the masses. Because it is so much cheaper and faster to produce a publication, lots of people are doing it. Many works are being published in small print runs that just five years ago could not sustain themselves. The downside to DTP stems from precisely the same fact: because publishing is now so much quicker, cheaper, and easier, there is much more printed material out there. This means that it is harder for good materials to get the attention they deserve.

FrameMaker 4 has a feature called hypertext that facilitates "online distribution" of publications with a companion product called FrameViewer. By distributing documents electronically you save the expense of printing, mailing, and manual distribution. Documents can be printed on demand by viewers. The hypertext feature embeds commands in documents that allow the viewers to interact with the information. Publications that are distributed electronically can be updated quickly so information is never out of date.

## DIS-ADVANTAGES OF USING DTP

As wonderful as the new technology of DTP is, it still has its weaknesses and drawbacks. In fact, some of the advantages of DTP can be disadvantages in disguise.

### Multiple Platforms

One drawback is the existence of multiple platforms. Most DTP software is made to run on only one or two platforms. For example, a program may run only in Windows or only in Windows and Macintosh. Other platforms, such as Unix, usually cannot use the files created on a Windows or Macintosh platform. This can be a problem if multiple platforms exist in the same organization or if you want to create a publication and have it printed by a service bureau that uses a different platform. With FrameMaker 4, this drawback is minimized. FrameMaker 4 runs on more platforms than any other DTP package including PC/Windows, Macintosh, Sun, Hewlett Packard, and IBM RS/6000.

### Quality of the Output

Another limiting factor in DTP is the quality of the printed output. Most DTP systems use a 300 dpi (dots per inch) laser printer which is not capable of printing as crisp and clean a page as the DTP program is capable of producing. A far better output is produced by a 1,270 or a 2,540 dpi imagesetter, but this type of equipment is very expensive and is usually found only in service bureaus.

Undoubtedly the cost of better quality printers will go down in the future, but for now, most desktop publishers have to take their finished files to a service bureau if they want a really high quality output. Service bureaus can output to paper or directly to film which is used by the printer to make the plates for the printing press.

### Cost

In addition to the obvious costs of DTP—software and equipment—there is the cost of training and the cost of labor. Someone has to do the desktop publishing. Suppose the vice president of the company decides to take on the DTP duties because he enjoys it so much. Now you are using a highly paid individual to do a job that could be done by someone who is paid less, and the vice president does not have enough time to preside over the vice (or whatever it is the vice president does). Obviously, if you assign the DTP work to someone who already has full-time responsibilities, something is not going to get done or that person will be working overtime to get everything done. You may find that it is necessary to hire a new employee, and then you have the added expense of salary and benefits.

## THE USER'S RELATIONSHIP TO DTP

Terms like *user-friendly* and *menu-driven* were coined by advertising copy writers for the purpose of selling software. The big advertising push for DTP programs of all kinds may give the user the mistaken impression that buying a desktop publishing program makes you an instant publisher. This impression could not be further from the truth. You must still learn the principles of typesetting, design, and layout; then you must learn how the program applies these principles.

The purpose of this book is to provide you with knowledge of the fundamentals of publishing and to show you how FrameMaker 4 uses these fundamentals. No book, however, can teach you to be talented and creative. You must look for those qualities within yourself and try to engender them.

If you are feeling a little discouraged at this point, take heart. You probably know more about design and layout than you think you do. After all, you see hundreds of printed pieces every week, and you know what attracts your eye and what doesn't.

If you are a novice at layout and design, it would be a good idea for you to start a collection of printed pieces that you like. Collect pieces from all categories—letterheads, memos, flyers, brochures, newsletters, books, reports, title pages, unique headlines, business cards, advertisements, and so on. Later, you can get ideas from your collection or base your own designs on the designs you like.

Remember that the key to successful design is experimentation—one of DTP's strong points. By applying various designs and layouts to the same page, you will begin to get a feel for what looks good. Keep the designs that appeal to you and get the opinions of others. As you become more experienced, you will find that FrameMaker 4 helps you unlock your creative talents.

# 2

# Mechanical Basics

IN this chapter, you will learn some of the basic concepts involved in putting together a printed piece. Although certainly not a complete treatise on desktop publishing, this chapter provides an overview of a process—a process that cannot be described in any strict order, since many issues come to bear on the project. For example, if you have been given a gift of one ton of lime-green, dull-coat paper stock, the paper will determine the color of ink used and the size of the printed piece. On the other hand, if you have an unlimited budget, you can choose any colors of ink that you want, use any paper you want, and make the piece any size you want.

The mechanics for creating a printed piece involve the following processes, all discussed in this chapter: writing the copy, obtaining a printer, selecting paper, determining the size and binding, and obtaining the art and photographs. The next chapter explores the basics of creating camera-ready copy, which involves design and layout. After reviewing these two chapters carefully, you will be ready to tackle FrameMaker 4.

If you need more detailed information beyond the basics, you can choose among the many excellent books listed in the appendix.

## WRITING THE COPY

In the next few paragraphs, you will learn how to write brilliant technical articles, compelling ad copy, spell-binding fiction, and information-packed news. NOT! Of course, you know that you cannot learn to be a successful writer simply by reading a book, but you can get useful suggestions here to help in your writing practice.

To become a good writer, you have to write and write and write, and then rewrite, rewrite, rewrite. Use a word processing program, and be sure to use your spelling checker, thesaurus, and even a grammar checker. When you think you have achieved the desired result, give your copy to someone who is already a good writer and ask for comments and suggestions. Watch for patterns and bad habits in your writing that you can improve or correct.

*There are many freelance copy editors around. If you find a good one, learn from the experience. Remember, every change a copy editor suggests is not necessarily a good one. When you disagree, talk it out with the editor.*

Another way to improve your writing is to read good writing and notice the style, the wording, the tone, and so on. If you have to write ad copy, read lots of ads. If you have to write technical articles, read lots of technical articles (but not late at night).

When writing, keep your audience in mind. Your goal is to communicate, so try to write specifically to the reader's education, experience, income, and so on. Many writers imagine that they are talking to a specific person when they are writing. If you could stand face to face with the reader, what would you say? Say it—then write it. If you don't know what you would say, then you haven't done your homework. Go back and do some research. Arm yourself with the needed information and face your reader again.

Once you start writing, don't interrupt the creative process; don't stop to tweak things. Just let the words flow. If you can't think of just the right word or phrase, leave a blank spot and go on; you can fill it later.

After you have finished this first stage of writing, go back and edit your work. Read what you have said, and see if you can improve it. You'll find that you can fill in the blanks more easily the second time around because you are in an analytical mode rather than a creative mode. Make sure the writing is understandable and follows a logical order. Try reading each sentence out loud or in your head. This will help you find the rough spots because you will be able to "hear" your mistakes. You will be able to detect sentences that are too short and choppy or too long and involved.

When the piece is rewritten, let it sit for a while. When you read it again, you will have a fresh perspective. Make your final improvements, and then, if possible, let a typical reader read the piece. For example, if you are working on a health care brochure for senior citizens, let your grandmother read it. See if she understands everything and has any questions. Remember, the writer usually has more information about the subject than the reader. Because of this perspective, the writer may inadvertently leave out some information that the reader needs.

*Recently my publishing company sent out a brochure about a software convention where attendees could go to three seminars a day. Three seminars were given simultaneously at each session, so attendees had to choose a seminar from each session. The schedule was printed like this:*

| | | |
|---|---|---|
| | *Opening Session address by Bob Hamilton* | |
| *Creating Relational Databases* | *Word Processing Basics* | *Using Enable on a Network* |
| *Using the Popup Command* | *Using Fonts* | *Spreadsheet Tips and Tricks* |
| *Using Memo Fields* | *Creating Newsletters (with emphasis on fonts)* | *Linking Spreadsheets* |
| | *Dinner and Keynote Address by Don Payne* | |

*The reader's dilemma was, "Do I select a seminar from each row or from each column?" Adding identifying heads and specific instructions would give the reader the information needed for action.*

## SELECTING A PRINTER

When you have a firm idea about the specifications of your printed piece, it is time to select a printer. Most printers are selected on the basis of cost and turnaround time (the length of time it takes to deliver the finished piece to you). When seeking a bid from the printer, you must provide the printer with the following information:

- Quantity to be printed
- Paper that will be used
- Number of pages
- Whether the pages are printed on one side or two
- Number of ink colors
- Number of photographs
- The finished size of the piece
- Whether full-color photographs or other artwork will be used

The size, number of pages, and whether the job involves full-color art usually determines the printers that you can go to for a bid. Quick copy shops often use expensive copiers rather than presses, which limits what they can produce. Small print shops generally use medium-size offset presses that can print 8.5×11 inches, 8.5×14 inches, and 11×17 inches. Offset presses can print multiple colors and even full-color work, but the more expensive presses give higher quality for full-color jobs. Commercial printers (sometimes called trade printers) can print just about anything. They have very expensive presses that print all sizes and high-quality, full-color printing. Some commercial printers have special presses called *web* presses, which print from paper on a roll, called a web. Web presses are used for large print runs, as for newspapers and catalogs. It costs less per printed piece to print on a web press than on a press that uses cut sheets, but web presses cannot use as high a quality of paper as cut-sheet presses.

When selecting a printer, be aware that the printer who offers the lowest bid and the fastest turnaround time may not be your best choice, particularly if the printer cuts corners on quality and fails to meet your deadline. The middle-priced bid is probably a better and more realistic bid.

Printing deadlines can slip, with last-minute changes, unanticipated delays, or jobs getting shuffled. To play it safe in planning your project, always allow extra time for the printer and don't be unreasonable in your expectations. For example, don't expect a printer to run 100,000 four-color pieces with a letter fold in one day. Using multiple colors of ink may require running the paper through the press multiple times (depending on the press). The ink must have sufficient time to dry between press runs and before folding.

*W. C. Walter, who owns ABC Printing in Louisville, Kentucky, uses this logo:*

**YOU WANT IT WHEN?**

*This logo could be interpreted two ways: Printers are notoriously late, and customers want their jobs yesterday. To help keep peace, always plan ahead to give your printer ample time to meet deadlines.*

Once you have selected a printer, sit down with the printer and discuss your job in more detail. Get the printer's recommendations on paper and ink colors. The printer knows what looks good, what runs through the presses well, what folds well, what costs less, and so on. Use the printer's experience to your advantage.

*Print runs of 500 or less are not cost-effective. Consider copying or laser printing. Printing becomes cost-effective at quantities of 1,000 or more. Two-color printing is more expensive, but not twice as expensive as one-color printing. Three-color printing is not cost-effective, and you might as well use full-color printing (four colors) so you can print color photographs.*

## PAPER

The look and feel of the paper on which a publication is printed conveys a message to the reader, so select paper—or stock, as it is called in the printing industry—carefully. Considerations in selecting paper include the grade, size, color, texture, finish, and weight.

*Paper takes it name from the word papyrus, a reed used by the ancient Egyptians in the making of writing material. Beginning in about 200 BC, parchment made from animal skins gradually replaced papyrus. Paper similar to our modern paper was invented in China in 105 AD by Ts'ai Lun. The paper industry was established in Baghdad in 795 AD after the Arabs' capture of several Chinese papermakers.*

## Grade

Paper is graded by use. These are the most common grades of paper:

COVER used for covers, business cards, invitations, menus, and posters

BOND used for stationery, forms, flyers, and resumes

TEXT used for booklets, brochures, and flyers

BOOK used for books, catalogs, and directories

OFFSET used for general, low-cost printing

Paper with the same color and texture may come in different grades. This allows you, for example, to use the same type of paper for the cover of a booklet as you do for the inside pages.

## Size

Most grades of paper come in reams (500 sheets) of standard sizes called *parent* sizes. Cover stock is usually 20×26 inches; bond is 17×22 inches; text, book, and offset are 25×38 inches. Other sizes for each grade are also available, but the size your particular printer uses is determined by the size of the press that will run the job.

## Color

Paper comes in a spectacular array of colors, including pastels, basic colors, and bright fluorescents. Paper is even available in gradient color and two-tone color.

*The first paper mill in America was established in 1690 near Philadelphia.*

Colored stock generally costs more than white paper, but the effect it can produce may be worth the extra cost. Be careful, however, not to detract from the printed message with an overpowering color stock. Also, be aware of the fact that colored stock changes the appearance of the ink that is used to print the piece. Basically, ink is transparent, and the color of the stock will "show through" the ink changing the color of the print.

White or light colored stock is generally best for most printed materials because it provides maximum contrast, not only for the printed text, but for color and artwork. Even white stock comes in a myriad of shades, such as Winter Frost, Alpine White, Bright White, Pillar White, Willow White, Formal White, and Pebble White. If you could compare paper in each of these shades of white, you would readily see the differences. Some white paper has a yellow cast, some a blue cast, and so on. When selecting a white paper, make certain that the white is compatible with the other colors used in the printed piece.

Colors of stock are not standard, by any means. They are determined and named by the paper mill that manufactures the paper. Therefore, when selecting a color you must also specify the manufacturer. For example, two popular paper mills, Weyerhaeuser and Hammermill, may produce almost the same color in the same grade of paper and call the colors something entirely different—such as yellow and canary. Therefore, when specifying the paper, you must specify Weyerhaeuser Yellow or Hammermill Canary.

**NOTE:** *Paper mills change the colors, textures, and names of paper frequently. Be sure you know the current name and color of the paper by asking for samples from a printer or the paper mill itself.*

## Texture and Finish

The texture of paper, which is determined by the fibers and processes used to make the paper, spans the range from rough to smooth and glossy. Newsprint, for example, is made from one part chemically treated pulp and three parts groundwood pulp. The chemically treated pulp gives the paper strength; the woodpulp costs little and has good printing properties.

High-quality writing papers are made of pulp from bleached cotton rags. Glossy papers are coated with a mixture of starch solution and clay and then polished.

Choose a texture that reflects the printed piece. For example, the Cracker Barrel Restaurant chain prints its menus (featuring country cookin') on rough brown paper that is similar in texture and weight to the paper used in grocery bags. The restaurants are decorated like primitive, country cabins with burlap curtains on the windows and oil lanterns on the tables. The stock used for the menus, as well as the wording and types style, fits the motif of the restaurant. (See Figure 2-1.)

For stationery and formal documents, use bond paper with a linen, wove, or laid finish, preferably with at least 25 percent cotton rag content. Elegance can be added by using a paper with a watermark. Certificates and diplomas are often printed on a parchment texture. Books and magazines that use a lot of color are usually printed on a coated stock with a high gloss or a matte finish. This type of paper holds the different colors of ink better and makes a sharper image, giving a very professional look to the printed piece. Coated stocks are more expensive than uncoated stocks.

*A small book publishing firm prepared a very professional-looking mailer on high-gloss stock. The stock showed off the colors that were used, but the mailer contained an order blank. Since it is impossible to write on high-gloss paper with a ball point pen without smudging, the choice of paper caused frustration for the person who filled out the order blank and also for the order processor who had to read it. The next mailer was printed on dull-coat stock with much happier results.*

## Weight

The weight of paper is measured in pounds, specifically the number of pounds that a ream (500 sheets) of standard-size paper weighs. This is called the *basis weight*. (Remember that the standard size varies by grade.) Common copier paper is typically 20-pound bond. A better grade of copier paper is 24- or 28-pound bond.

Do not confuse weight with thickness. For example, a piece of 28-pound bond paper is equivalent to the thickness of a piece of 70-pound text, and a piece of 67-pound cover stock is thicker than a piece of 70-pound text. Remember that the weight of cover stock is determined by weighing 500 pieces of 20×26-inch paper, whereas the weight of text stock is determined by weighing 500 pieces of 25×38-inch paper.

**FIGURE 2-1**

*The Cracker Barrel menu printed on brown-paper-bag-type paper*

*Here are three ways to save money on paper:*

1. *To reduce mailing cost, use a good quality paper of a lighter weight.*
2. *Ask the printer if a stock similar to the one you like exists in a less expensive stock.*
3. *Use house stock—paper that the printer buys in bulk at a better price and keeps in house.*

## Paper Properties

Three properties of paper must also be considered when selecting stock for a printed piece. These properties are ink holdout, opacity, and stiffness.

Ink holdout is a measure of the paper's absorbency. A paper with low ink holdout, such as text stock, allows the ink to soak into the paper, making the ink much darker and less lively. Coated stock has a high ink holdout, which makes it good for printing color for magazines and catalogs.

Opacity is the measure of a paper's translucence. A paper that is very translucent should not be used for printing on both sides of the paper. Material from the other side of the paper will bleed through and distract the reader. If the paper is very translucent, the *bleed through* may actually obliterate copy or images, making it impossible to read or understand the printed piece.

*To compare the opacity of two different papers, use your laser printer to print several lines of type ranging in size from 10 to 36 points. Hold the printed sheet behind the paper to be tested. The paper with more opacity will allow you to read more lines of the smaller type.*

The stiffness of paper makes one paper appropriate for some print jobs and inappropriate for others. Different degrees of stiffness may be desired for different types of printed pieces. For example, a poster would require a stiffer paper than a flyer. If paper is too stiff, it may not fold well.

## Specialty Papers

The desktop publishing revolution has created a new niche in the paper industry especially for laser paper. Companies including Paper Access, Queblo, and Paper Direct (to name a few) have a full range of unprinted and preprinted papers with a finish that is made for laser printers. These papers include graduated-color sheets, full-color graphic design sheets, and paper with special effects such as marble, stippling, granite, metallics, and pinstripes. Matching envelopes, folders, note cards, certificates, and even business cards and tri-fold brochures are also available. See Color plate #1.

*Paper Access offers the Paper Access Kit with over 500 samples for $25. Each sample is preserved in a sheet protector to keep the sample neat and clean while you search through the samples over and over again. Paper Access offers more colors and sizes in comparable papers. You can contact Paper Access at 1-800-PAPER-01.*

*Queblo offers a sample kit with over 250 pieces for $59.85, which includes a 10-percent discount coupon for your first order. You can contact Queblo at 1-800-523-9080.*

*Paper Direct offers a PaperKit and Paper Selector free with your first order over $30 or you can buy the sample kit and selector for $19.95 and receive a $19.95 credit when you place your first order for $30 or more. The PaperKit contains over 100 samples. Paper Direct offers a greater variety of products and accessories. You can contact Paper Direct at 1-800-A-PAPERS.*

*Call any of these companies for a free catalog.*

Most papers in the 8.5×11-inch size can be ordered in quantities of 50 to 500 sheets ranging in price from $6 to $39. Most of the papers offered by Paper Access in its catalog are also available in the 11×17-inch size.

Another type of specialty paper is recycled paper. Great strides have been made in the quality, brightness, and texture of recycled paper as the paper industry has become more committed to environmental care. Although the cost of recycled paper is generally higher than other comparable paper, the price will undoubtedly go down as the paper industry recovers its investment in research and processing equipment.

*To be classified as recycled, paper must contain at least 50 percent paper waste. This waste can be preconsumer or postconsumer waste. Preconsumer paper waste is generated during the manufacture of paper. Postconsumer paper waste is paper that has been used by the consumer and returned to recycling centers.*

## FOLDS, PAGES, AND SIGNATURES

Many printed pieces require folding. Even a simple business letter needs to be folded to fit in a #10 envelope. Letters can be folded in the traditional letter fold or in a Z-fold, as shown in Figure 2-2. If you take your piece to a printer to be printed, the printer can also fold the piece, and you must be careful to specify the kind of fold you want. Folding is an extra charge, so be sure to figure this expense in your budget. If you are printing the pieces on your laser printer, you may still want to take the finished product to a printer or quick copy shop for folding.

If you are producing a multipage piece such as a booklet, the printer will print several pages on one sheet of paper and fold the sheet into a *signature* as shown in Figure 2-3. Then the signature will be trimmed.

The number of pages printed on one sheet depends on the finished page size you want and the paper size that can be run on the press. If your piece has several pages, it may be necessary to have several signatures. When planning your piece, you must know how many finished pages are needed

**FIGURE 2-2**

*Letter folds*

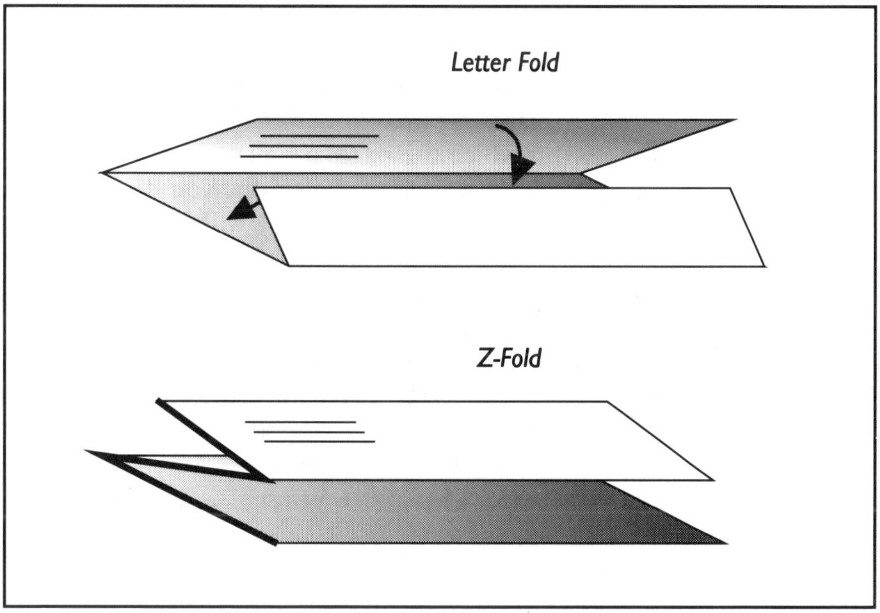

FIGURE 2-3

An 8-page signature

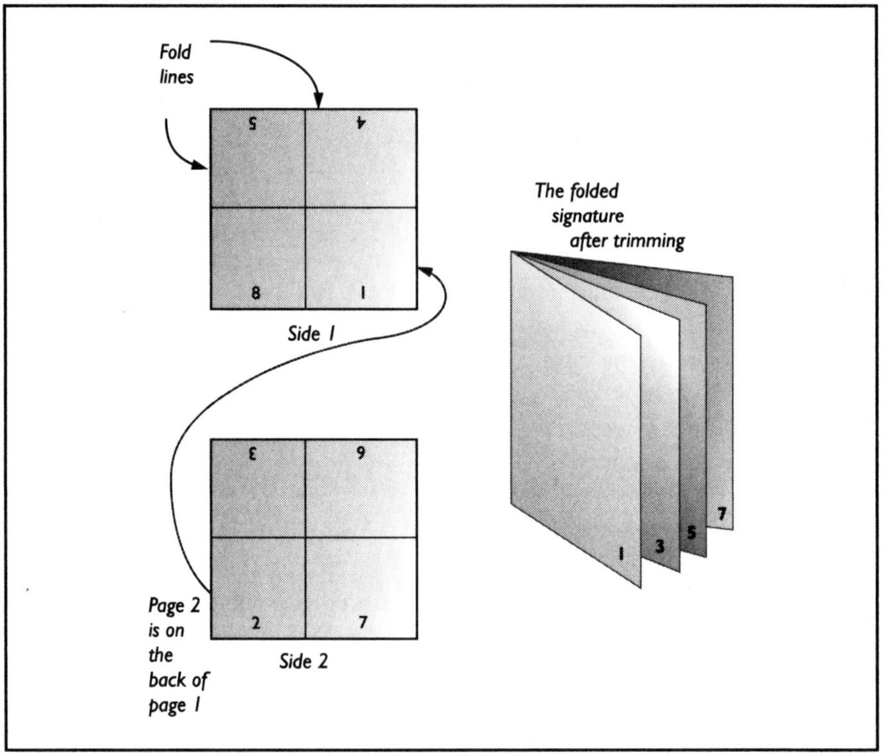


so you can prepare the correct number of pages. For example, you would not want to plan a nine-page booklet.

The way in which the pages are placed on the large sheet of paper for printing is called *imposition*. Generally, you do not have to be concerned with imposition because your printer will arrange the camera-ready pages (called *mechanicals*) before printing. If you work with a service bureau, the bureau may impose the pages using a special imposition program before printing on the imagesetter.

Page imposition will concern you, however, if you want to print color on one side of the sheet. Then you will need to know what pages are on the same side of the sheet, and the number of pages in the signature determines this factor. As you can see in Figure 2-4, a 16-page signature has eight pages on the same side. If you are printing a lengthy piece that uses several

**FIGURE 2-4**

*A 16-page signature*

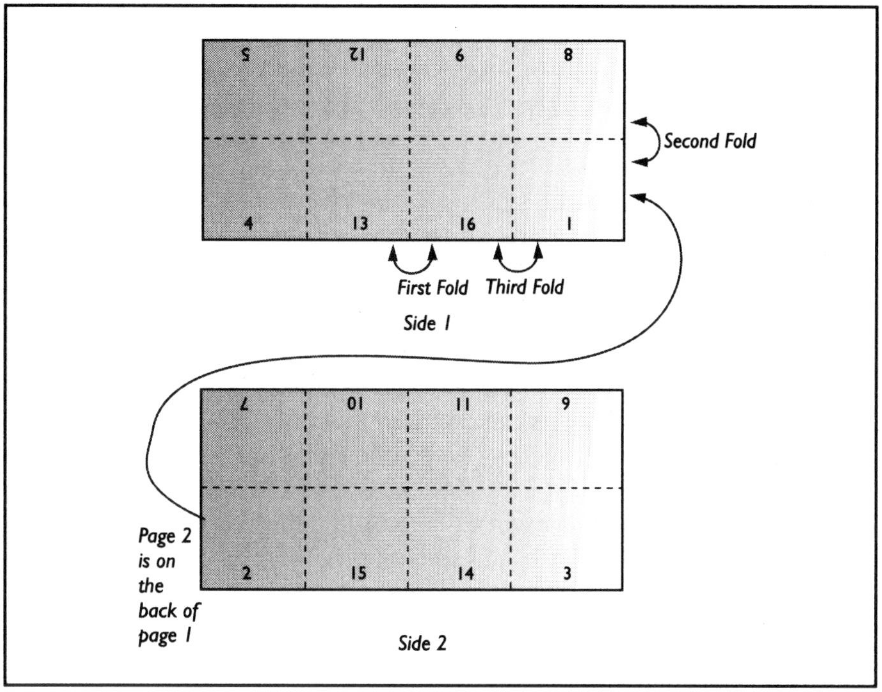


signatures, it may be better to simply ask the printer what pages are on the same side for the signatures that you want to print in color.

## PAPER SIZE CONSIDERATION

The cost of paper can be the greatest expense in producing a printed piece. To reduce cost, work closely with your printer and consider the size paper the printer can use. Using standard sizes will also save you money. For example, if you want a finished size of 8×10 inches, you will have to pay extra for trimming. If you want a finished size of 9×11 inches, the printer will have to use a paper size of 11×17 inches, which is much more expensive than the standard 8.5×11 inches.

**TIP:** *If you simply must have an unusual size, consider running two print jobs on the same piece of paper. The second job would have to fit in the portion of the paper that otherwise would be trimmed and wasted. See Figure 2-5.*

## BINDING

If a printed piece requires binding, be sure to include appropriate margins in the layout of the piece. The binding, like all other aspects of the printed piece, sends a message to the reader, so bindings should be selected with care. Table 2-1 lists the standard types of bindings.

Saddle stitching is recommended for newsletters, magazines, and booklets. This type of binding is fast and inexpensive, and it uses a minimal amount of margin space. Ring binding is good to use for instruction manuals, product books, and so on, because it facilitates adding and removing pages. Mechanical bindings are used for cookbooks, manuals, and documents that need to lie flat when open. Perfect binding is used for paperback books of 100 pages or more. The spine of a perfect bound book is flat, so it can be printed. Case binding, used for hard cover books, is the highest quality, longest lasting, and most expensive binding.

**FIGURE 2-5**
*Printing two jobs on the same sheet*

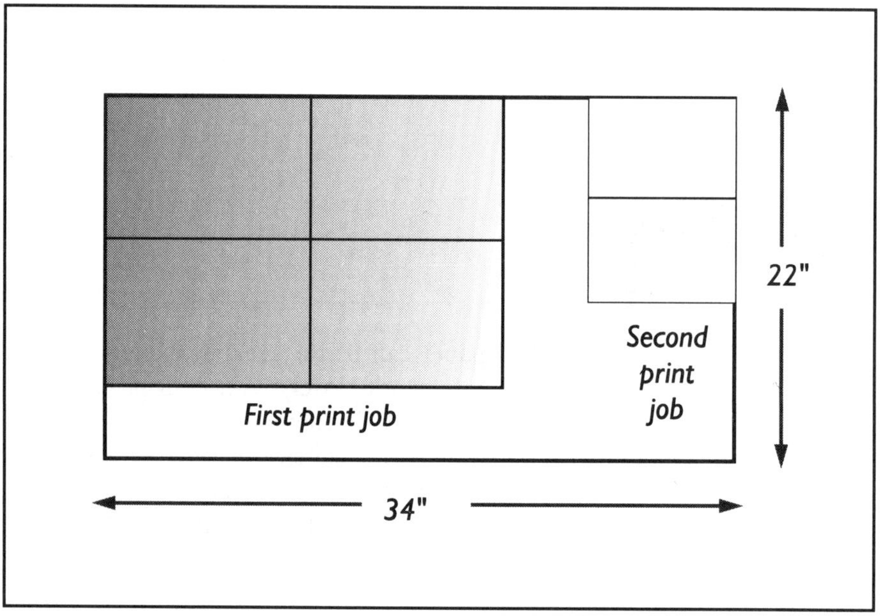

| Types of Bindings | Description |
|---|---|
| Saddle stitching | Wire staples are stapled through the crease of the spine. |
| Ring binding | Holes are drilled in the paper in the locations where metal rings will be inserted. |
| Mechanical binding | A plastic comb or wire spiral is inserted along the spine. |
| Perfect binding | Multiple signatures are glued along the spine. |
| Case binding | Signatures are sewn together and placed in a hard cover. |

**TABLE 2-1** *Standard Binding Types* ■

## VISUALS

All but the most boring printed pieces contain visuals of one kind or another. Visuals, which include art, photographs, scanned images, graphs, maps, and so on, add interest and information to a publication.

### Art

Art can be obtained by hiring a professional artist (the spare-no-expense method), by drawing your own art (the definitely-takes-talent method), or by using clip art (the inexpensive-and-looks-great method). Traditional clip art comes in hard copy and can be cut out and pasted on the mechanical for printing. Electronic clip art is placed in a publication by importing a file that contains the art.

Electronic clip art comes in various file formats including bitmapped, TIFF (Tagged Image File Format), and EPS (Encapsulated PostScript), all of which FrameMaker 4 can import. Images that are imported can be flipped, rotated, cropped, and scaled with FrameMaker 4's tools. More direct modifications of the art itself can be made to many clip art pictures by using a graphics program such as CorelDRAW.

Electronic clip art is easy to find; just pick up any magazine devoted to desktop publishing and look at the ads in the back. The following companies advertised clip art products in an 80-page magazine. They represent just a few of the many options you have for acquiring clip art.

3G Graphics, Inc.
1-800-456-0234
Offers six EPS product categories including Accents and Borders 1 and 2, Business 1, Graphics & Symbols 1, People 1, and Places & Faces 1. All six products are available on CD-ROM.

Metro ImageBase, Inc.
1-800-525-1552
Offers 18 categories with 100 or more images per category and a 2,000-image CD-ROM.

Techpool, Inc.
1-800-777-8930
Offers the LifeART product, which has professional medical illustrations in the categories of super anatomy, human anatomy, health care, emergency, and dental for PC and Macintosh. Also available on CD-ROM.

Totem Graphics
1-206-352-1851
Offers 18 categories with 96 full-color images per collection.

Alpha Media
1-800-998-8705
Offers the MediClip product, which contains "perfect body parts" in EPS and all major formats for PC and Macintosh.

Cartesia
1-800-334-4291
Offers four volumes of map art for metro areas, the states in the USA, the continents, and global maps.

DS Designs
1-800-745-4037
Offers authentic art and environmental drawings by children and professionally created images of children for PC and Macintosh.

Figure 2-6 shows a sampling of the clip art files from several different sources. As you can imagine, practically any illustration that you want is available.

**FIGURE 2-6**

*Samples of clip art*

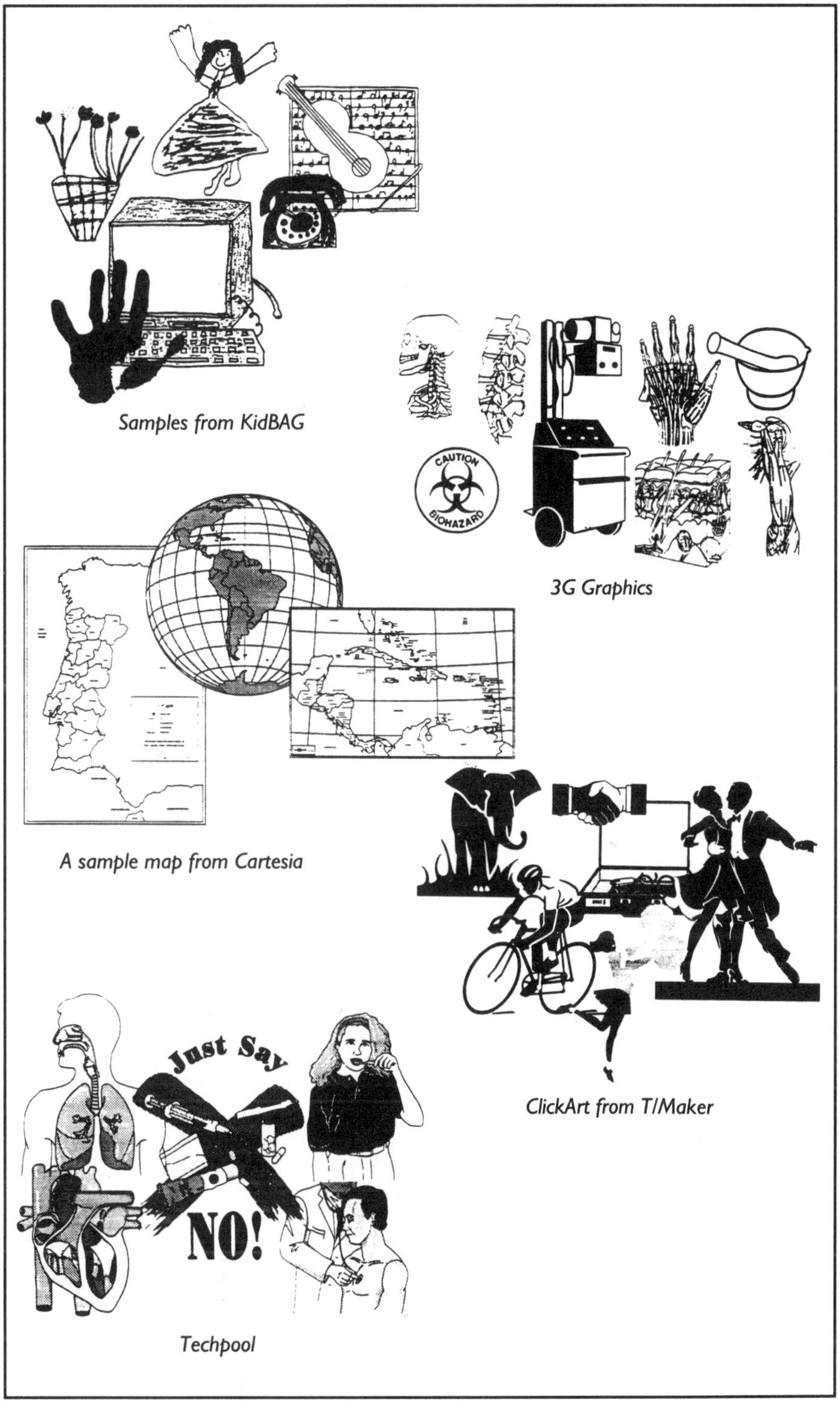


*Samples from KidBAG*

*3G Graphics*

*A sample map from Cartesia*

*ClickArt from T/Maker*

*Techpool*

*DS Designs, founded by Joe and Jane Scarano, began selling KidBAG in October of 1992. All the art work was created by children age 4 through 11. Joe and Jane's two boys, Scott and Jake, along with their friends at Valley Cottage Elementary School in New York and Northwoods Elementary School in North Carolina, drew all the pictures. The children are not paid for their art, but DS Designs contributes 2 percent of KidBAG's gross sales to schools and other nonprofit organizations dedicated to improving the quality of education.*

## Creating Art in FrameMaker 4

If you are up to the challenge of the "definitely-takes-talent method" of creating your own art with FrameMaker 4, you will find the following tools available: straight line tool, arc tool, rectangle tool, rounded rectangle tool, polyline tool, oval tool, polygon tool, and freehand tool. FrameMaker 4 also has fill patterns, line patterns and weights, line ending styles, and a color palette. Even though you can produce some very good drawings with FrameMaker 4, including Bezier curves, for more sophisticated drawings you should use a graphic package like CorelDRAW or Micrografx. Figure 2-7 show a fairly complicated technical drawing that can be accomplished with FrameMaker 4.

## Photographs

Photographs, especially photographs of people, attract readers (and buyers—which is why newspapers and magazines use so many photos of people). You can include black-and-white photographs in a publication in three ways:

- By importing a file that contains a scanned image. Many high-quality photographs are available on disk just like clip art. Scanning is discussed in the next section.
- By having a "paper" halftone made of the photo and pasting the halftone on the mechanical.
- By having a "negative" halftone made and letting the printer strip it into the page, as shown in Figure 2-8.

**NOTE:** *The stripping method produces the highest print quality for photographs.*

Halftones are produced by photographing the photograph through a screen of fine lines. This process produces a dot pattern on the picture that

FIGURE 2-7

*Technical drawing*

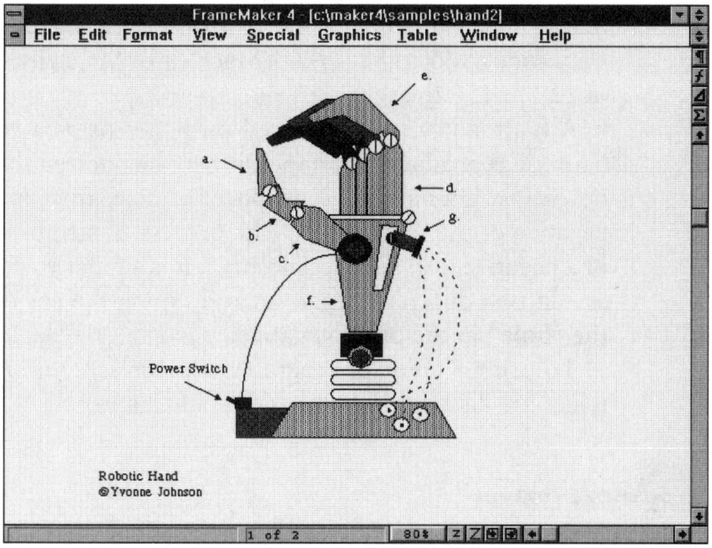


makes it possible to print. A continuous tone, such as the blend of colors or grays in a photograph, is printed as a series of dots. Lighter colors or shades are printed with only parts of each dot and the white paper shows through next to each dot. The viewer's eye mixes the tone.

FIGURE 2-8

*A stripped-in flat*

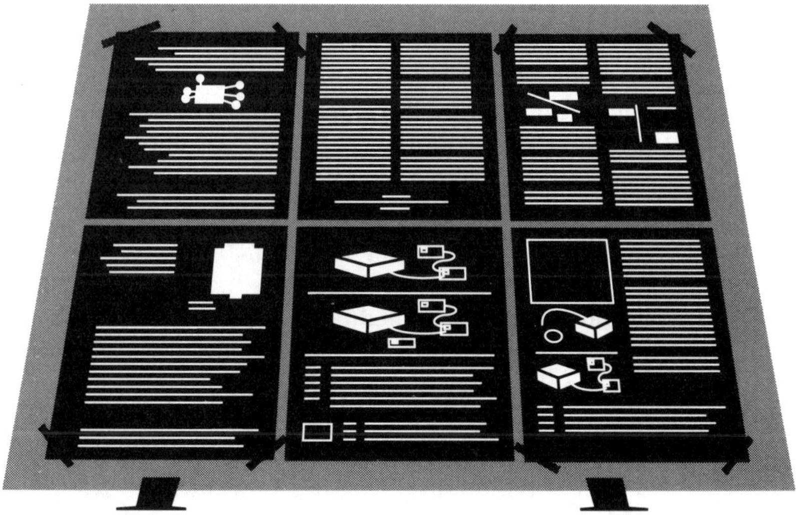

The printed quality of the photograph depends in large part on the screen that is used to produce the halftone. Newspapers typically use a *screen frequency* of 65 to 85 lines per inch (lpi). Magazines use a screen frequency of 120 to 150 lpi.

A halftone can be produced on paper or as a photo negative. When a halftone is produced on paper, it may be referred to as a *PMT*, a *photostat*, or a *velox*. If a halftone is produced as a negative, it will be stripped into the negative of the mechanical. The process of stripping refers to the inserting of a negative into another negative. It is similar to cutting a square the same size in two different negatives and taping the cut-out of one negative into the "hole" in the other negative.

To print a color photograph, a *color separation* must be made. Color issues are discussed in more detail in Chapter 9.

## Scanned Images

A scanner translates "what it sees" into digitized images that can be manipulated by a computer. Hand-held scanners can scan widths of 4 to 5 inches and flatbed scanners can scan 8.5×14 inches. Hand-held scanners range in price from $200 to $500, while flatbed scanners range from $800 for grayscale versions to $1,500 for color models. Figure 2-9 shows two possibilities.

Practically anything can be scanned, but the results may not always be what you expect. Certainly the results will be no better than the original. Creative scanning, on the other hand, can produce some unusual and unique results. Try scanning a piece of colored paper that has been crumpled and then smoothed out—a marbled effect can result. Don't restrict yourself to scanning paper—try scanning suede, wood grain, and wallpaper. With a hand-held scanner, you can really let your imagination run wild.

Most desktop scanners scan at a resolution of 300 to 400 dots per inch (dpi). Dots per inch describes the grid the scanner "looks through" when scanning. This resolution is sufficient for most art, but it does not produce a high-quality photograph. By experimenting with resolution, reducing the size of the photo in FrameMaker 4, and using a high resolution output, a medium quality that might be acceptable in some print jobs can be obtained for photographs. If the scanned photos are not acceptable quality, they can be used for position only (FPO); that is, to show the printer where to strip in the halftone.

Most scanners can scan in black and white or gray scale. Gray scale describes the number of different shades the scanner can differentiate for each dot of resolution. Most scanners offer at least 256 shades of gray, which is about the limit of what the average eye can discern.

**FIGURE 2-9**

*Examples of a flat-bed and a hand-held scanner*

For a black-and-white scan, the scanner moves left to right, top to bottom, evaluating every individual square in its grid. If the square is at least 50 percent black, the scanner turns that whole square black. Such scans are called black and white or high-contrast, since only two "colors" are allowed. The resulting file is called a one-bit file since a bit (binary digit) can have only two possible values—zero or one. Zero represents white and one represents black.

The process of gray-scale scanning is just like the black-and-white process. The scanner looks at the subject through the grid as it did before, and it selects an appropriate shade of gray from white (0) to 50 percent gray (128) to black (256). Files that result from gray-scale scanning are called 8-bit files because eight bits can store up to 256 numbers.

**TIP:** *Scan an image larger than you wish to use and then reduce it in desktop publishing to increase the dots per inch—but be sure the output device has a comparable resolution. For example, if you scan an item at four times the size you want to use on a 300 dpi scanner and then reduce it four times in FrameMaker 4, you have effectively used a resolution of 1200 dpi. Don't bother doing this if you are going to print it on a 300 dpi laser printer.*

Color scanners are also available in 24-bit 300 dpi. The best color scanners on the market today are slide scanners. A 35mm slide can be scanned in 20 to 60 minutes at a resolution of 1,000 lines per inch—a quality almost good enough for four-color process printing.

**TIP:** *If you do not have the inclination to buy a scanner just yet, consider renting one for a day and making all the scanned files that you want.*

# 3

# Basics of Design and Layout

THIS chapter helps you explore the basics of design and layout. As you read, keep in mind that design and layout are subjective processes. Very few hard-and-fast rules apply in every case, but, as you'll see, there are some guidelines and traditions you can follow. Just remember that experimentation and refinement are the keys to success.

## THE DESIGN PHASE

Traditionally, all the steps in a project's design phase were done by hand, on paper. A mock-up was prepared with the type handwritten or drawn to size, colored pens or markers were used to specify the colors that would be used, frames were drawn for pictures or art work to show the locations, and so on. If changes were necessary, it took extensive time and effort to make the desired changes in the hand-generated sketches.

### Designing with FrameMaker 4

With FrameMaker 4, the design phase occurs electronically, making changes almost effortless. You can prepare many more designs for a given project and more quickly and efficiently than you could using traditional methods. Each design can be saved as a different file. You can also build on the same design and save the enhancements as different files. The final design can serve as a *template*—a design saved as a file for repeated use with other similar projects.

### Templates

Templates help you save time. For example, you may have a template for a monthly newsletter. Each month, you would base the new issue on the template. The design might include page numbers, repeating graphics, headline styles, and so on.

You can create your own templates from scratch, use FrameMaker 4's templates, or revise FrameMaker 4's templates to create your own templates. FrameMaker 4 has five categories of templates: book, business, outlines, reports, and special. Chapter 7 explores the use of templates in more detail.

## FORM VS. FUNCTION

Some designers get carried away with the sheer thrill of designing, forgetting that form must always be tied to function. When this happens, design actually becomes a barrier to communicating.

Effective design of a printed piece performs four basic functions:

- Attracts the reader's attention
- Communicates clearly
- Provides for easy and cost-effective production
- Elicits the desired response from the reader

### Attracting Attention with Publication and Page Design

The object of publication design is to grab the reader's interest and make a positive first impression, while the object of page design is to *keep* the reader's interest. No matter how necessary, informative, and interesting the text may be, if it is not presented in a logical, easy-to-follow manner, it may never be read. Compare the designs in Figure 3-1. The design on the left looks long and boring. The design on the right is more inviting because it breaks up the text in chunks that look more interesting and nonthreatening.

One way to keep a reader's interest is through the consistent use and placement of text and design elements. For example, place page numbers

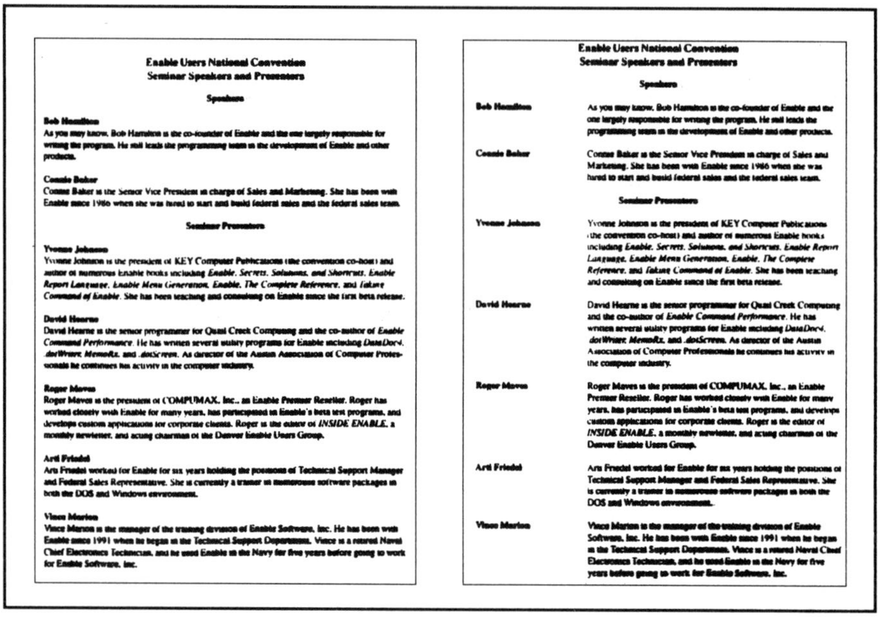

**Enable Users National Convention**
**Seminar Speakers and Presenters**

**Speakers**

**Bob Hamilton**
As you may know, Bob Hamilton is the co-founder of Enable and the one largely responsible for writing the program. He still leads the programming team in the development of Enable and other products.

**Connie Baker**
Connie Baker is the Senior Vice President in charge of Sales and Marketing. She has been with Enable since 1986 when she was hired to start and build federal sales and the federal sales team.

**Seminar Presenters**

**Yvonne Johnson**
Yvonne Johnson is the president of KEY Computer Publications (the convention co-host) and author of numerous Enable books including *Enable, Secrets, Solutions, and Shortcuts, Enable Report Language, Enable Menu Generation, Enable, The Complete Reference,* and *Taking Command of Enable*. She has been teaching and consulting on Enable since the first beta release.

**David Hearne**
David Hearne is the senior programmer for Quail Creek Computing and the co-author of *Enable Command Performance*. He has written several utility programs for Enable including *DataDoc4, .dotWriter, MemoRx,* and *.dotScreen*. As director of the Austin Association of Computer Professionals he continues his activity in the computer industry.

**Roger Maves**
Roger Maves is the president of COMPUMAX, Inc., an Enable Premier Reseller. Roger has worked closely with Enable for many years, has participated in Enable's beta test programs, and develops custom applications for corporate clients. Roger is the editor of *INSIDE ENABLE*, a monthly newsletter, and acting chairman of the Denver Enable Users Group.

**Arti Friedel**
Arti Friedel worked for Enable for six years holding the positions of Technical Support Manager and Federal Sales Representative. She is currently a trainer in numerous software packages in both the DOS and Windows environments.

**Vince Marion**
Vince Marion is the manager of the training division of Enable Software, Inc. He has been with Enable since 1991 when he began in the Technical Support Department. Vince is a retired Naval Chief Electronics Technician, and he used Enable in the Navy for five years before going to work for Enable Software, Inc.

**Enable Users National Convention**
**Seminar Speakers and Presenters**

**Speakers**

| | |
|---|---|
| **Bob Hamilton** | As you may know, Bob Hamilton is the co-founder of Enable and the one largely responsible for writing the program. He still leads the programming team in the development of Enable and other products. |
| **Connie Baker** | Connie Baker is the Senior Vice President in charge of Sales and Marketing. She has been with Enable since 1986 when she was hired to start and build federal sales and the federal sales team. |

**Seminar Presenters**

| | |
|---|---|
| **Yvonne Johnson** | Yvonne Johnson is the president of KEY Computer Publications (the convention co-host) and author of numerous Enable books including *Enable, Secrets, Solutions, and Shortcuts, Enable Report Language, Enable Menu Generation, Enable, The Complete Reference,* and *Taking Command of Enable*. She has been teaching and consulting on Enable since the first beta release. |
| **David Hearne** | David Hearne is the senior programmer for Quail Creek Computing and the co-author of *Enable Command Performance*. He has written several utility programs for Enable including *DataDoc4, .dotWriter, MemoRx,* and *.dotScreen*. As director of the Austin Association of Computer Professionals he continues his activity in the computer industry. |
| **Roger Maves** | Roger Maves is the president of COMPUMAX, Inc., an Enable Premier Reseller. Roger has worked closely with Enable for many years, has participated in Enable's beta test programs, and develops custom applications for corporate clients. Roger is the editor of *INSIDE ENABLE*, a monthly newsletter, and acting chairman of the Denver Enable Users Group. |
| **Arti Friedel** | Arti Friedel worked for Enable for six years holding the positions of Technical Support Manager and Federal Sales Representative. She is currently a trainer in numerous software packages in both the DOS and Windows environments. |
| **Vince Marion** | Vince Marion is the manager of the training division of Enable Software, Inc. He has been with Enable since 1991 when he began in the Technical Support Department. Vince is a retired Naval Chief Electronics Technician, and he used Enable in the Navy for five years before going to work for Enable Software, Inc. |

**FIGURE 3-1** *Weak design on the left, with simple improvements on the right*

consistently. Use headlines to indicate main topics and subtopics, and use icons, lines, boxes, and other design elements to identify or emphasize important points or sections. With the use of FrameMaker 4's Master pages, you can ensure consistent placement of elements. Master pages are discussed in more detail in Chapter 7.

## Effective Communication

Consistent use and placement of text and design elements also facilitates good communication. Headings, for example, should use size or design elements in keeping with a hierarchy of importance.

A good design also caters to the way readers read. Most readers do not read sequentially through a publication, but flip through the pages, reading 50 percent or less on the first pass. Therefore, the design should identify logical units of information and logical sequences.

> *Readers typically hold a bound publication by the spine and leaf through the pages, so the outside margins are more visible than the inside margins. Use this fact to your advantage by placing elements to attract the reader in these margins.*

Nontextual elements such as photos and illustrations can also effectively communicate the basic content of a publication with captions. Other elements that can be used for stronger communication are sidebars, boxed text, and use of icons that call attention to particular kinds of text, like notes or tips.

### Easy and Cost-Effective Production

It's a good idea to base the design of a piece on the budget set aside for the entire piece. Designs that require special treatment in the production stage always escalate costs. Special treatments might include cutting irregular shapes into paper using dies mounted to a press (called *die-cutting*), pressing an image into the paper so it is raised (called *embossing*), or printing to the edge of the paper (called *bleeds*). Remember that design can be simple and still be effective.

### Eliciting Reader Response

The goal of most printed pieces is to elicit a response from the reader. You may want the reader to buy your product, request information, learn something, be converted to your point of view, or feel some emotion. Naturally the correct text must be present to elicit the response, but the design of the piece must emphasize the text. You must tell the reader what to do, why to do it, how to do it, and when to do it, and the design of the piece must make these points clear and easy to find. For example, if you want the reader to call you, the phone number must be prominently displayed.

## THE THREE BUILDING BLOCKS OF DESIGN

All designs are based on three elements—page design, text elements, and graphic elements. The page design provides the overall format of the publication. The text elements include such considerations as typeface, typestyle, type size, alignment, line length, and line spacing. Graphic elements deal with rules (lines), borders, white space, and visuals (art, charts, and photographs).

## PAGE DESIGN

Page design includes such elements as:

- Page size
- Orientation
- Number of sides
- Number of columns and the space between columns
- Margins

When creating a new piece in FrameMaker 4, you can select the orientation, and all other page design elements will be selected for you based on default settings. The default settings are 8.5×11 inches for page size, single-sided, one column, and one-inch margins on the top, bottom, left, and right.

If you do not want to use the default settings, FrameMaker 4 allows you to customize the page design. You can select from seven standard page sizes, including letter, legal, and tabloid (11×17 inches) sizes, or you can specify a custom size. If you want the piece to be designed for printing on both sides, select double-sided. You can also specify the number of columns that you want and the gutter space between the columns (called the *gap* by FrameMaker 4).

> *In general, the more columns on the page, the smaller the gap should be.*

In the custom dialog box, you can also specify margin widths. For single-sided documents, the margins are called top, bottom, left, and right. For double-sided documents, the margins are called top, bottom, inside, and outside. If a publication will be bound, the left margin (for single-sided publications) or the inside margin (for double-sided publications) should be slighter wider than the opposite margin.

> *Double-sided documents reduce the number of sheets used by half, thus saving money on paper—one of the major costs of printing. Bulk is also reduced—another money-saving bonus if you are mailing the piece.*

## TEXT ELEMENTS

Type is usually the basic component of a printed piece. Selecting an appropriate type is important, but specifying a readable alignment, line length, and amount of line spacing are equally important.

### Type

Three major factors that contribute to the impact of the type are typeface (also called font), typestyle, and type size.

- *Typeface* refers to the design of the type. Literally thousands of typefaces exist, but two standard fonts, Helvetica and Times Roman, are probably used more than any other.
- *Typestyle* refers to the weight and slant of the type. Typestyles include normal (called *plain* by FrameMaker 4), bold, and italic.
- *Type size* refers to the height of the type, measured in points, from the top of an ascender (like the top of the lowercase "f") to the bottom of a descender (like the bottom of a lowercase "g").

> *Times Roman was originally created for the London Times in 1931. Helvetica was designed by Max Meidinger in 1957.*

#### Typeface

Almost all typefaces can be divided into two classes: serif and sans serif. Serifs are the short lines stemming from the upper and lower ends of the strokes of characters as shown here:

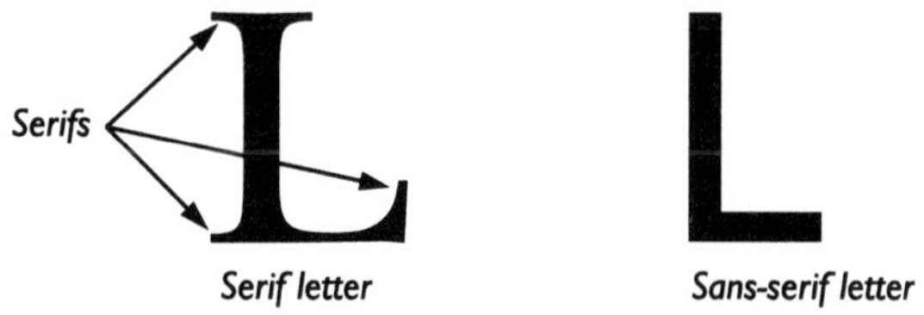

*Studies show that Americans prefer serif type when reading large blocks of text and Europeans prefer sans serif.*

Serif fonts have a more traditional look, and many typographers argue that serifs facilitate the horizontal movement of the reader's eye from left to right. Sans-serif type, on the other hand, is more contemporary looking and will accommodate more letters on the line.

Because so many typefaces are available to desktop publishers, novices sometimes make the mistake of using too many typefaces in the same publication. Usually no more than two different typefaces are needed. It is quite common to use a sans-serif font for headings and a serif font for the body of the text. Variety can be achieved by using bold and italic and different type sizes.

*Serif fonts do not reverse out of dark colors as well as sans-serif fonts, especially in small type sizes as shown here:*

This type is reversed out of a black background.

*A serif font*

This type is reversed out of a black background.

*A sans-serif font*

Typefaces convey definite impressions, so be sure to select a typeface that reflects the "feel" of the piece you're planning. Serious pieces should use body copy typefaces, such as Times Roman, Helvetica, Bookman, Century Old Style, Bodoni, Cooper, Goudy Oldstyle, Garamond, Optima, Palatino, and Souvenir to name but a few. Special fonts classified as *display typefaces* are best used for short passages or headlines because they are not extremely legible for long passages. Popular design typefaces include Aria, Bombay, Calligraphy, Seville, and Paint Brush.

## Popular Fonts

| | | |
|---|---|---|
| | Broadway: | FrameMaker for Windows |
| | Cooper Black: | FrameMaker for Windows |
| | Dom Casual: | FrameMaker for Windows |
| | Exotic: | FrameMaker for Windows |
| | Handel Gothic: | FrameMaker for Windows |
| *Display fonts* | Hobo: | FrameMaker for Windows |
| | Pt Barnum: | FrameMaker for Windows |
| | Schadow Black: | FrameMaker for Windows |
| | Seagull Heavy: | FrameMaker for Windows |
| | Windsor: | FrameMaker for Windows |
| | Zurich: | FrameMaker for Windows |
| | Brush Script: | FrameMaker for Windows |
| | Cloister Black: | FrameMaker for Windows |
| | Embassy: | FrameMaker for Windows |
| *Script fonts* | Formal Script: | FrameMaker for Winsows |
| | Kaufmann: | FrameMaker for Windows |
| | Park Avenue: | FrameMaker for Windows |
| | Ribbon: | FrameMaker for Windows |
| | Zapf Chancery: | FrameMaker for Windows |
| | Avant Garde: | FrameMaker for Windows |
| | Bookman: | FrameMaker for Windows |
| | Charter: | FrameMaker for Windows |
| | Goudy Old Style: | FrameMaker for Windows |
| *Text fonts* | Helvetica | FrameMaker for Windows |
| | New Century Schoolbook: | FrameMaker for Windows |
| | Palatino: | FrameMaker for Windows |
| | Times New Roman: | FrameMaker for Windows |
| | University Roman: | FrameMaker for Windows |

The popular typeface called Zapf Dingbats (named for the designer, Hermann Zapf) is neither a body copy typeface nor a design typeface. It is a collection of nontraditional characters and symbol elements that are used as decorations and text highlights. For example, this character <§> could be used to denote the end of an article in a magazine or newspaper. The dingbat characters include stars, scissors, pointing fingers, pencils, snowflakes, boxes, bullets, arrows, and a variety of other characters. Some of the uses are shown in Figure 3-2. Other character sets, similar to dingbats, may include characters for a specific purpose. For example, the font called Sonata is a music notation font.

The font called DingBrats, made by DS Designs, is a font that looks like a child's writing because that is exactly what it is. This font is actually a collection of clip art made from the writing of children rather than a traditionally designed font in which each letter is defined by exact specifica-

**FIGURE 3-2**

*Examples of Zapf Dingbats include an airplane, scissors, stars, a pointing finger, boxes, and a telephone* ■

## We get letters. . .

*This letter comes from Sadie Hawk. She writes,*

Jed,
We love your magazine *JET Air*. The articles about air travel are so interesting, and the photographs are spectacular. We read it from cover to cover and then give it to the kids. They love to cut out the pictures for school projects. Keep up the good work.✈

Cut on the dotted line
✂- - - - - - - - - - - - - - - - - - - - - - - - - - - - - - - - - - - - - - - - - - -

★ ★ ★ ★ Restaurant features gourmet dining.

☞ Warning: Do not close the file without saving. Data will be lost.

Please specify disk size: ❒ 3.5 ❒ 5.25

☎ Call 1-800-000-0000 to place your order.

tions. Figure 3-3 shows a sample of this font and other unusual fonts available from DS Designs.

### *Typestyles*

The three basic typestyles—regular, bold, and italic—give "color" to the printed page. Regular text can be thought of as the background color. Bold, of course, stands out and calls attention to the text. Italic also calls attention to the text, but in a more subtle way.

> *The word "italic" comes from the same root as the word "Italian" because the style was first used in an Italian edition of Virgil in 1501.*

Bold is used for headings and to give emphasis to a word or phrase. Italic is used for bylines, captions, definitions, and titles of books and other publications.

**FIGURE 3-3**

*Examples of DingBrats and other fonts*

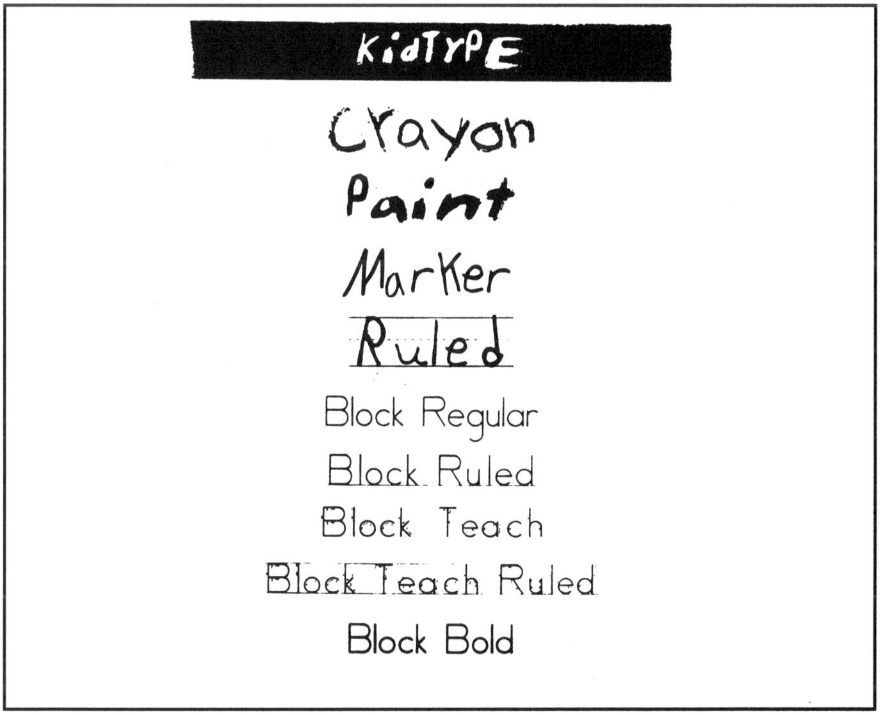

FrameMaker 4 also provides these styles: underline, double underline, strikethrough, overline, change bar, superscript, and subscript. Samples of each are shown in Figure 3-4. Underline and double underline should be used sparingly, if at all, because underlined text is difficult to read. Overline could be used as a design element for headings; change bar displays a vertical line in the left margin to show where revisions and additions have been made; superscript raises the text above the baseline; and subscript lowers the text below the baseline.

**FIGURE 3-4**

*Examples of various type styles*

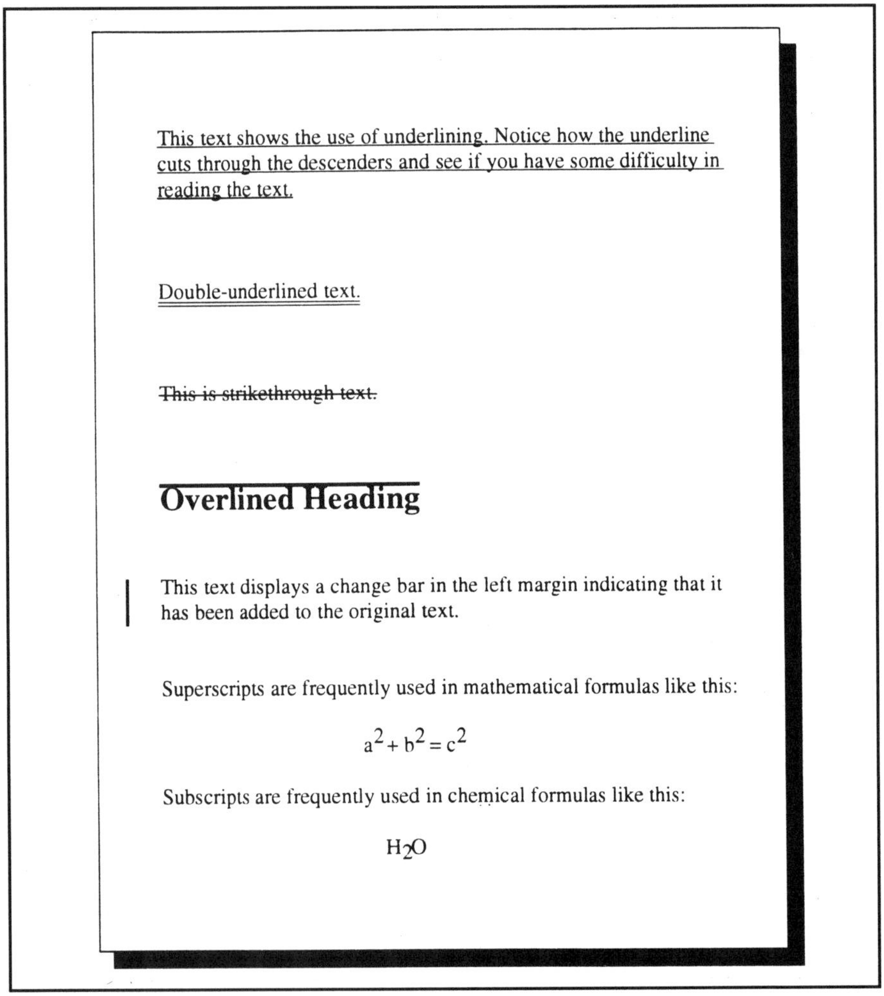

This text shows the use of underlining. Notice how the underline cuts through the descenders and see if you have some difficulty in reading the text.

Double-underlined text.

~~This is strikethrough text.~~

**Overlined Heading**

This text displays a change bar in the left margin indicating that it has been added to the original text.

Superscripts are frequently used in mathematical formulas like this:

$$a^2 + b^2 = c^2$$

Subscripts are frequently used in chemical formulas like this:

$$H_2O$$

## Type Size

As previously stated, the height of a font is measured from the top of an ascender to the bottom of a descender as shown here:

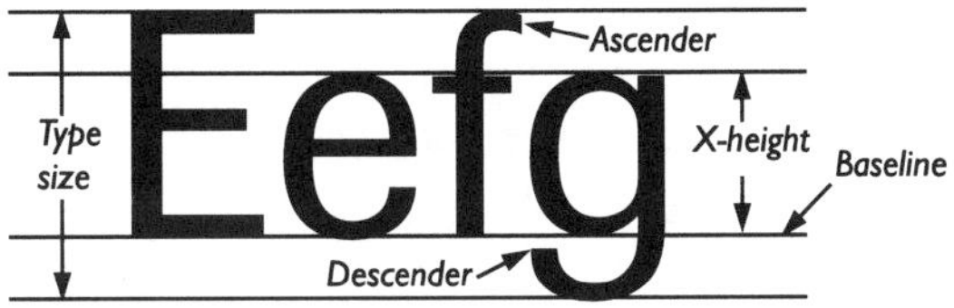


Many users think that a capital letter is the height of the type's point size, but as you can see, the uppercase letter is actually smaller than the type size.

> *A point is 1/72 of an inch. Commercial printers and layout artists usually measure in picas instead of inches. Twelve points make one pica, and six picas make one inch. Some sizes of type are shown here:*
>
> 72 points
>
> 36 points
>
> 24 points
>
> 18 points
>
> 14 points
>
> 10 points

The kind of information being presented should determine the size of type you choose. The following guidelines will help you select type sizes initially, but remember page designs will vary, and an unusual design may call for print sizes outside of these guidelines. You should experiment with what looks best for your piece.

- *Body copy* is usually 8 to 12 points, with 10 point being most commonly used.
- *Subheads* can be the same size as the body copy or several points larger than the body copy.
- *Main heads* are usually in the range of 14 to 20 points.
- *Titles* (such as used on a cover page) are usually 24 to 48 points.
- *Captions, headers, and footers* are usually the same size as the body copy.
- *Page numbers* are usually 2 to 4 points larger than body copy.

In the early days of desktop publishing, you had to buy fonts in different sizes. This was expensive and highly limiting. Fortunately, new font technology has brought *scalable* fonts, that is, fonts that can be scaled to almost any size by the font software.

### Font Types

When using desktop publishing, you must not only be concerned with fonts, but with font types. The most popular types of fonts for desktop publishing are Adobe Type 1 and TrueType. Both are scalable fonts. FrameMaker 4 uses the Adobe Type 1 fonts that are available with the program called Adobe Type Manager as well as TrueType fonts. Adobe is a major font vendor and provides the widest selection of fonts. A popular TrueType font vendor is Bitstream. Some companies still sell bitmapped fonts which are useful for non-PostScript printers, particularly dot matrix printers, but FrameMaker 4 requires a PostScript or PCL printer.

## Alignment

Alignment refers to the way each line of text is placed in relation to the other lines of text in the paragraph. FrameMaker 4 offers these paragraph alignments:

- Left aligned
- Right aligned

- Centered
- Justified

Left alignment aligns the beginning of each line in a paragraph flush against the left margin. The ends of the lines are said to be *ragged right*. Left-aligned text is the easiest to read.

Right alignment aligns the end of each line in a paragraph flush against the right margin, making the left side of the paragraph ragged. This alignment is sometimes used for headlines and subheads to make them stand out from left-aligned body text.

Center alignment centers each line of a paragraph between the margins, making both the left and right margins ragged. Centering is rarely used for body text except in formal invitations or in small amounts in an advertising piece, for example. It is used for titles, introductory information, and headlines.

Justified alignment forces each line to be flush on the left margin and on the right margin, as in newspaper columns. To achieve justification, the program adds extra space between words and characters. This extra white space can form "rivers of white" on the page, especially if the line length is wide. FrameMaker 4 allows you to adjust the spacing that is added between words and letters to control this effect.

## Line Length

The length of a line is a critical element in the readability of text. For 10-point type on an 8.5×11-inch page, a line length of 4 to 4.5 inches is recommended; for larger type sizes, use longer line lengths. A good rule of thumb is to set the line length to whatever measurement will accommodate 65 characters. If the line length is too long, it is difficult for your reader's eye to get back to the beginning of the next line. If the line is too short, too many words will be hyphenated, increasing the reading difficulty.

## Line Spacing

Line spacing, also called *leading*, is measured in points from baseline to baseline. When line spacing is the same as type size, the type is said to be *set solid*. In most cases, however, it is necessary to use a line spacing larger than the type size to increase readability. For example, 10-point body text is usually set on 12-point line spacing. A good rule of thumb for line spacing is to use 1.2 times the size of the type.

> *The term leading comes from the days of setting type with metal slugs. Spacing between lines of type was achieved by inserting "leads" between the lines.*

Leading is often expressed as a fraction, with the type size as the top number and the leading as the bottom number, as in 10/12. The fraction is not read as "ten twelfths," but as "ten on twelve."

## GRAPHIC ELEMENTS

Graphic elements add interest and organization to a printed piece. They may include the following:

- Rules (lines)
- Boxes
- Shading
- White space (unprinted areas)
- Bullets
- Pull quotes
- Dropped shadows
- Dropped caps
- Icons

Rules can be used to separate columns, draw attention to headlines, divide body text, and organize charts. FrameMaker 4 offers many rule patterns and point sizes.

Shading and boxes give emphasis to text or art. When boxes are used to frame photographs, they are called *keylines*. Use boxes with restraint and avoid "boxitis" (like the example in Figure 3-6).

Inexperienced users have a tendency to stamp out white space as if it were an enemy, cramming text or art in every available space inside the margins. Instead, white space should be used generously. It makes a page more inviting and less overpowering to the reader. White space gives text "breathing room" and makes it less intimidating. Like all design elements, white space should be used consistently throughout the publication. For example, white space could be placed at the bottom of each page.

Bullets call attention to items in a list, as in the list of graphic elements referred to at the beginning of this section. FrameMaker 4 allows you to type a bullet by pressing CTRL, +, q, % or you can use a symbol from the Zapf Dingbats as bullets (if this font is installed). Additionally, you can specify a bullet in the Paragraph Designer dialog box. The exact steps for creating bullets in different ways are given in Chapter 6.

Pull quotes are segments of text set in a larger size than the surrounding text and inserted to pique the reader's interest. Pull quotes are usually set off by rules above and below the text.

Dropped shadows give boxes more depth and "drama." They also focus the movement of the reader's eye.

Dropped caps are large first letters used at the beginning of text. Dropped caps may start each new section, be used at the beginning of a callout, be used at the beginning of an article, and so on. Be careful that you do not overdo this design element.

Icons are used frequently to call attention to notes or hints. Publications that provide multiple methods of doing things might have icons to quickly identify the method being referred to in a given section. For example, in computer books, steps are sometimes given for keyboard users and for mouse users. An icon of a keyboard or a mouse helps readers choose the text to read.

## TEN WAYS TO STRENGTHEN DESIGN

Several design mistakes have been alluded to already in this chapter, but they are repeated here for emphasis. By eliminating or minimizing design problem areas, you make your piece stronger and increase the likelihood its message will come through clearly.

**USE IRREGULARLY SHAPED BLOCKS OF COPY SPARINGLY** As you know, readers proceed from left to right. Left-justified text is the easiest text to read; text that forms a shape, is right justified, or wraps around a figure, is difficult to read. Figure 3-5 shows two designs using the same text and graphic. The design at the bottom is an interesting design but it is difficult to read the text. The design at the top shows a better use of white space and still gives the feeling that the ship is sailing through the text.

**FIGURE 3-5**

*The design at the top eliminates the irregular block of text and uses white space more effectively*

REDUCE EXCESSIVE UNDERLINING It's a good idea to avoid underlining more than one or two words together in body copy. Underlining cuts through the descenders and makes text more difficult to read. To emphasize longer blocks of text, use bold or italic instead.

CHECK FOR WIDOW AND ORPHAN LINES Examples of this effect are shown in Figure 3-6. A widow line is the first line of a paragraph that has been split from the paragraph and left at the bottom of a page. An orphan line is the

**FIGURE 3-6**

*A printed piece with many design mistakes*

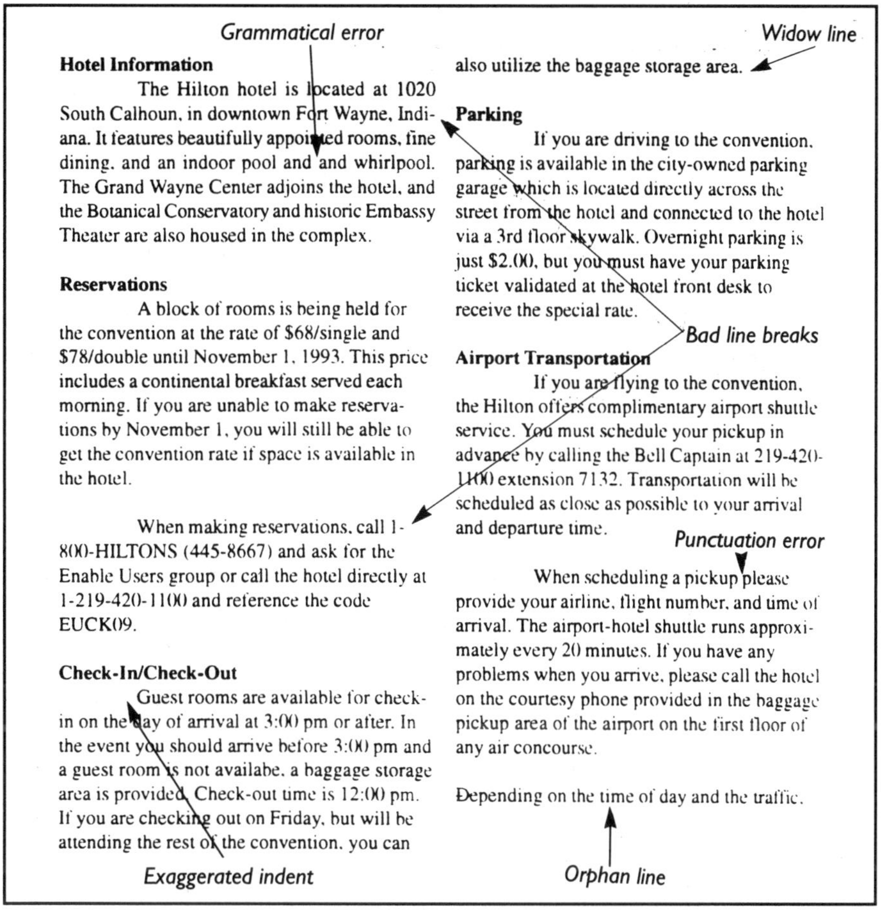
**Hotel Information**

The Hilton hotel is located at 1020 South Calhoun, in downtown Fort Wayne, Indiana. It features beautifully appointed rooms, fine dining, and an indoor pool and and whirlpool. The Grand Wayne Center adjoins the hotel, and the Botanical Conservatory and historic Embassy Theater are also housed in the complex.

**Reservations**

A block of rooms is being held for the convention at the rate of $68/single and $78/double until November 1, 1993. This price includes a continental breakfast served each morning. If you are unable to make reservations by November 1, you will still be able to get the convention rate if space is available in the hotel.

When making reservations, call 1-800-HILTONS (445-8667) and ask for the Enable Users group or call the hotel directly at 1-219-420-1100 and reference the code EUCK09.

**Check-In/Check-Out**

Guest rooms are available for check-in on the day of arrival at 3:00 pm or after. In the event you should arrive before 3:00 pm and a guest room is not availabe, a baggage storage area is provided. Check-out time is 12:00 pm. If you are checking out on Friday, but will be attending the rest of the convention, you can also utilize the baggage storage area.

**Parking**

If you are driving to the convention, parking is available in the city-owned parking garage which is located directly across the street from the hotel and connected to the hotel via a 3rd floor skywalk. Overnight parking is just $2.00, but you must have your parking ticket validated at the hotel front desk to receive the special rate.

**Airport Transportation**

If you are flying to the convention, the Hilton offers complimentary airport shuttle service. You must schedule your pickup in advance by calling the Bell Captain at 219-420-1100 extension 7132. Transportation will be scheduled as close as possible to your arrival and departure time.

When scheduling a pickup please provide your airline, flight number, and time of arrival. The airport-hotel shuttle runs approximately every 20 minutes. If you have any problems when you arrive, please call the hotel on the courtesy phone provided in the baggage pickup area of the airport on the first floor of any air concourse.

Depending on the time of day and the traffic.



last line of a paragraph that has been split from the paragraph and left at the top of a page. FrameMaker 4 allows you to specify the number of lines that can be isolated from the rest of the paragraph.

AVOID UNEQUAL SPACING Readers can intuitively sense inconsistent spacing, which gives a published piece a sloppy and unprofessional look (see Figure 3-8). To avoid inconsistent spacing, be sure that you do not set different line spacing for the same size type. FrameMaker 4 has automatic line spacing default settings for single spacing, one-and-a-half spacing, and double spacing. It also allows you to specify custom spacing.

USE PROPORTIONALLY SPACED TABS AND INDENTS Paragraphs should not be exaggerated too deeply. The indentation space should be proportional to the type size and the line length. Compare the paragraphs in Figures 3-6 and

3-7. Notice that Figure 3-7 has no paragraph indentations so that paragraphs align with the headings. To make the large block of text more interesting looking, headlines were increased in size and a rule was added.

AVOID EXCESSIVE HYPHENATION As stated earlier, a line length that is too short causes excessive hyphenation. FrameMaker 4 has precise hyphenation control. You can specify the number of adjacent hyphenations, the shortest word to be hyphenated, and the shortest prefix and suffix.

**FIGURE 3-7**

*A make-over eliminating design mistakes*

**Hotel Information**

The Hilton hotel is located at 1020 South Calhoun, in downtown Fort Wayne, Indiana. It features beautifully appointed rooms, fine dining, an indoor pool, and whirlpool. The Grand Wayne Center adjoins the hotel, and the Botanical Conservatory and historic Embassy Theater are also housed in the complex.

**Reservations**

A block of rooms is being held for the convention at the rate of $68/single and $78/double until November 1, 1994. This price includes a continental breakfast served each morning. If you are unable to make reservations by November 1, you will still be able to get the convention rate if space is available in the hotel.

When making reservations, call 1-800-HILTONS (445-8667) and ask for the Enable Users group or call the hotel directly at 1-219-420-1100 and reference the code EUCK09.

**Check-In/Check-Out**

Guest rooms are available for check-in on the day of arrival at 3:00 pm or after. In the event you should arrive before 3:00 pm and a guest room is not available, a baggage storage area is provided. Check-out time is 12:00 pm. If you are checking out on Friday, but will be attending the rest of the convention, you can also utilize the baggage storage area.

**Parking**

If you are driving to the convention, parking is available in the city-owned parking garage which is located directly across the street from the hotel and connected to the hotel via a 3rd floor skywalk. Overnight parking is just $2.00, but you must have your parking ticket validated at the hotel front desk to receive the special rate.

**Airport Transportation**

If you are flying to the convention, the Hilton offers complimentary airport shuttle service. You must schedule your pickup in advance by calling the Bell Captain at 219-420-1100 extension 7132. Transportation will be scheduled as close as possible to your arrival and departure time.

When scheduling a pickup, please provide your airline, flight number, and time of arrival. The airport-hotel shuttle runs approximately every 20 minutes. If you have any problems when you arrive, please call the hotel on the courtesy phone provided in the baggage pickup area of the airport on the first floor of any air concourse.

Depending on the time of day and the traffic, the airport is about a 20 minute drive from the hotel.

**ELIMINATE GRAMMATICAL ERRORS** Nothing undermines the printed message more than misspelled words, double words, incorrect grammar, improper capitalization, or incorrect punctuation. Copy should be spell-checked and proofread thoroughly before printing. For example, you would be surprised how often a grammatical error like this gets overlooked:

Protestors Picket the
the Abortion Clinic

**HINT:** *Someone other than the person who wrote the copy should proofread the copy.*

**GIVE VISUALS ADEQUATE ROOM** Graphic images and photographs should be given plenty of room. Remember, graphics should be included in a publication to add interest and emphasis, not to fill white space.

**AVOID USING TOO MANY FONTS** Too many fonts on the same page compete for the reader's attention and make the publication look amateurish and "too busy" to read. Figure 3-8 is a nightmare! It suffers from too many fonts (eleven to be exact) and unequal spacing. It looks like a ransom note put together by pasting text from different sources.

As a general rule, use one font for all body text and use one font in different sizes for headings and subheadings. Figure 3-9 shows the same text with fewer font styles and consistent spacing between paragraphs and headings. Three fonts have been used: Palatino and Palatino italic for the body, and Humanist for the headings. A box has been drawn around all the text to give it a more finished look. Bullets have been used to break up the text and emphasize important points.

**USE WHITE SPACE LIBERALLY** White space has already been discussed in some detail, but suggestions about using white space bear repeating. When white space is used generously, the reader is more likely to read the publication. Even if additional white space causes the page count to go up, the enhanced readability will probably compensate for the added length. The white space in Figure 3-10 makes the design elements stand out and the graphic has plenty of room. Notice that the font chosen for the headline, Windsor, gives the feeling of motion and elegance.

**FIGURE 3-8**

*Too many fonts and unequal spacing make this flyer look amateurish*

## Other Diet Plans vs. DietStyles

It's estimated that *up to 10 million* Americans begin to diet every day! Statistics indicate that most of them will discontinue the diet before achieving their desired weight loss. And of those who stay with the diet and lose weight, 95% of them will regain the lost weight over a period of time. Why does this phenomenon persist? The most prevalent cause is that **dieters tend to return to their former weight-accumulating lifestyles**. The actual reasons given are varied: "too costly," "too much hassle to prepare," "felt hungry all the time," "became moody or depressed," "food was boring or distasteful," "felt weak and trembly," "it was too slow."

**Eradicating the Failure Syndrome**

DietStyles realized that in order to be effective, the ideal diet had to eradicate the basis for the failure syndrome. Therefore, it was determined that the product should include fiber because of its health, nutrition, weight loss, and hunger control characteristics. Also, it was deemed critical that the product taste great, produce quick results, *be reasonably priced*, simple, and exceedingly convenient in order to conform to today's accelerated lifestyles. Finally, DietStyles sought a product that would enable people to maintain weight loss with ease.

*DietStyles has achieved those objectives.*

**Three Phase Program**

Phase I and II are designed to maximize weight loss through maintaining the most efficient fat burning level. Phase I is scheduled for two weeks. Phase II is one week and it increases the caloric intake by 325 calories in order to keep the metabolism functioning at the optimum calorie burning level. Phase III is a maintenance program that allows you to stay slim, healthy, and energized.

## TAKING THE NEXT STEP

With the information presented in Chapters 2 and 3, you're better prepared to start using FrameMaker 4 with confidence. Terms and features used in the menus will make more sense to you, and you will understand why you must do certain things.

**FIGURE 3-9**

*A make-over improving flyer's readability and appearance*

## Other Diet Plans vs. DietStyles

It's estimated that up to 10 million Americans begin to diet every day! Statistics indicate that most of them will discontinue the diet before achieving their desired weight loss. And of those who stay with the diet and lose weight, 95% of them will regain the lost weight over a period of time.

Why does this phenomenon persist? The most prevalent cause is that dieters tend to return to their former weight-accumulating lifestyles. The actual reasons given are varied:

- too costly
- too much hassle to prepare
- felt hungry all the time
- became moody or depressed
- food was boring or distasteful
- felt weak and trembly
- it was too slow

### Eradicating the Failure Syndrome

DietStyles realized that in order to be effective, the ideal diet had to eradicate the basis for the failure syndrome. Therefore, it was determined that the product should include fiber because of its health, nutrition, weight loss, and hunger control characteristics.

Also, it was deemed critical that the product taste great, produce quick results, *be reasonably priced*, simple, and exceedingly convenient in order to conform to today's accelerated lifestyles. Finally, DietStyles sought a product that would enable people to maintain weight loss with ease.

*DietStyles has achieved those objectives.*

### Three Phase Program

Phase I and II are designed to maximize weight loss through maintaining the most efficient fat burning level. Phase I is scheduled for two weeks. Phase II is one week and it increases the caloric intake by 325 calories in order to keep the metabolism functioning at the optimum calorie burning level. Phase III is a maintenance program that allows you to stay slim, healthy, and energized.

**FIGURE 3-10** *Good use of white space and design element arrangement*

Remember to collect samples of layout and design that appeal to you, and use them as a basis for your own designs. If you are unable to find an appealing example, or you are not sure whether the samples are really good or not, go to the library and look for graphic design annuals or magazines. Three good annuals are *Print's Regional Design*, *Communication Arts*, and *Graphis Design*.

# II

# FrameMaker Basics

# 4

# Getting Acquainted with FrameMaker

IF you are a new FrameMaker user, you need to get acquainted with the features of FrameMaker 4 and how they work. There is no better way to get acquainted with the program than by using the online tutorial, and we recommend you do just that. Frame's tutorial is excellent, and it will teach you enough about the program that you will feel comfortable enough to begin creating your own documents. Depending on your previous knowledge and experience, the tutorials can take an average of 45 minutes to two hours to complete. In addition to the help you get from the tutorials, Appendix C provides a quick reference to the basic commands.

The tutorial contains eight lessons which cover most of the basic routines in the program. If you do the tutorial lessons you will learn to:

Start and exit the program
Open, save, and close documents
Change the view
Enter and edit text
Cut and paste text
Use paragraph formats
Use online Help
Change the font family and size
Align objects
Autonumber headings
Set tabs
Create and use character formats
Create and use a template
Use master pages and their formatting elements
Import a page layout
Import a graphic and add text to it
Create a table with shaded rows
Find and change text
Use the thesaurus and spell checker

Print a document
Create and print a table of contents
Create an equation

This chapter reviews basic FrameMaker 4 functions using tables and sample screens. It points out some details you would not discover in the tutorial and contains many helpful tables that do not appear anywhere in the FrameMaker documentation. We recommend you use this chapter as a quick reference and supplement, rather than as a replacement for the tutorial lessons.

## THE APPLICATION WINDOW

When you start FrameMaker 4, the application window is opened as shown in Figure 4-1. As a Microsoft Windows user, you should be familiar with the title bar, the control menu button, the maximize, minimize, and restore buttons, and the menu bar displayed at the top of the screen. Under the menu bar is the QuickAccess bar, a bar of icons that can

**FIGURE 4-1**

*The application window*

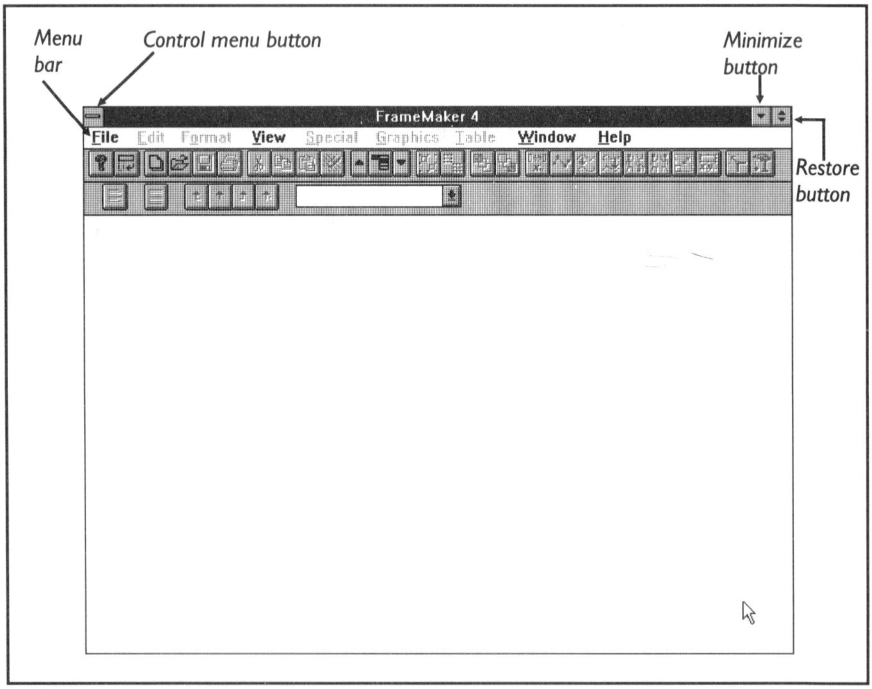

be used instead of menu commands. Below the QuickAccess bar is the formatting bar with icons for alignment, spacing, tabs, and paragraph formats.

When no document is open, the menu bar has only four usable options—File, View, Window, and Help. In addition, very few icons in the QuickAccess bar are usable.

Once the application window is open, you can create a new file or open an existing file. The document window is shown in Figure 4-2.

## THE DOCUMENT WINDOW

The document window also displays the title bar with its control menu and minimize and maximize buttons, the menu bar which has a document control menu button and a maximize button, the QuickAccess bar, and the formatting bar. In addition, the document window displays a vertical and horizontal ruler, a status bar, scroll bars, and additional buttons in the right border and on the status bar (all of these elements are labelled in Figure 4-2). The remainder of this chapter explains the various bars and buttons in more detail.

**FIGURE 4-2**

*The document window*

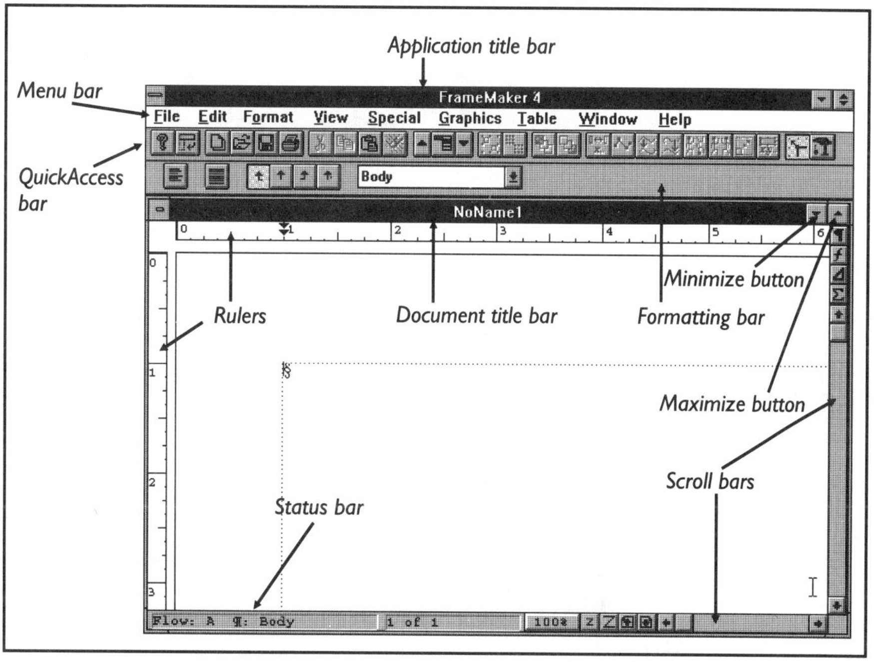

## The Menu Bar

The menu bar in FrameMaker 4 is used just like every other menu bar in a Windows application. You can select an option by clicking it with a mouse, or, if you are using the keyboard, you can press ALT to access the menu bar and type the underlined letter, or press the arrow key to move to the desired option and press ENTER. You can also select a menu option simply by clicking the mouse on the option. For example, to access the File menu, as shown in Figure 4-3, you can either click on it with the mouse, press ALT+F from the keyboard, or press ALT, cursor to File, and press ENTER.

As on the menu bar, simply click on an item in a pull-down menu to select that option. There are several other aspects of pull-down menus that you should know:

- Underscored letters on a pull-down menu represent shortcut keys that activate the option. For example, if you want to save your document, you can either use the mouse to click on the File menu and then click on Save, or without removing your hands from the keyboard you can simply press ALT+F to activate the menu, and S to save the document.
- Several options also can be accessed using control-key combinations that appear to the right of some menu items. Once you learn these shortcuts, you can access the corresponding commands without

**FIGURE 4-3** *Accessing a menu from the menu bar*

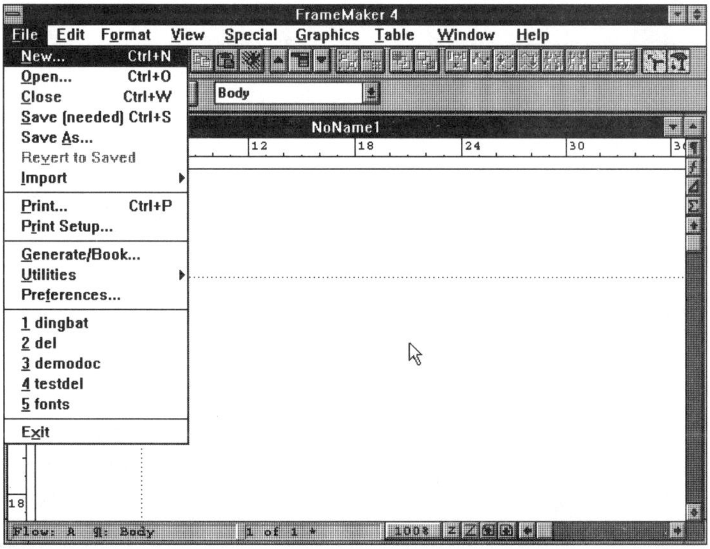

touching the mouse. So, looking at Figure 4-3, you can see that another way to save your document is to press CTRL+S.

- If an option is not available, it is gray. In Figure 4-3, for example, the Revert to Saved option is not available.
- Options that are followed by ellipsis points display a window or a dialog box. To close a dialog box without making any changes, press ESC or select Cancel. To close a window, double click the control menu button in the upper-left corner or press ALT+F4.
- Options that have a small arrow to the far right bring up a submenu with more options. See, for example the Import and Utilities options in Figure 4-3.

A brief summary of each option on the menu bar follows.

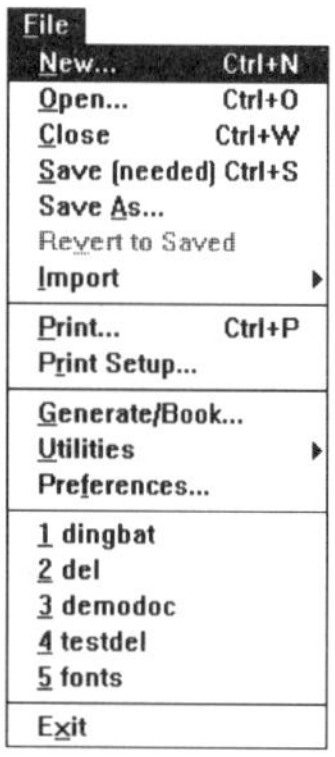


FILE The File menu contains options to create a new document, open and close a document, save a document and revert to the last saved version of a document, import a file, print a document, set up the printer, generate books and other files, perform document utilities (compare documents and do document reports), set preferences, and exit the program. It also lists the last five documents opened in the order in which they were opened. Selecting a document from this list automatically opens the document.

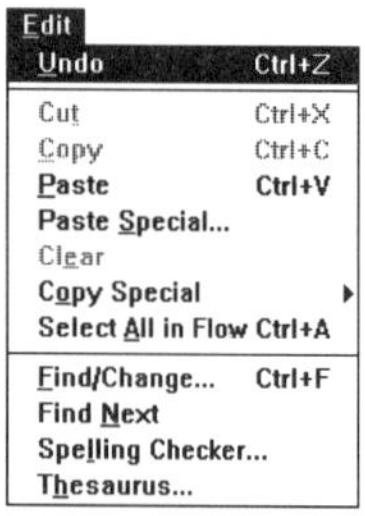


EDIT The Edit menu contains options to undo the last change; cut, copy, and paste text; copy and paste special objects; clear (delete); select all text; find text and find and change text; check spelling; and use the thesaurus.

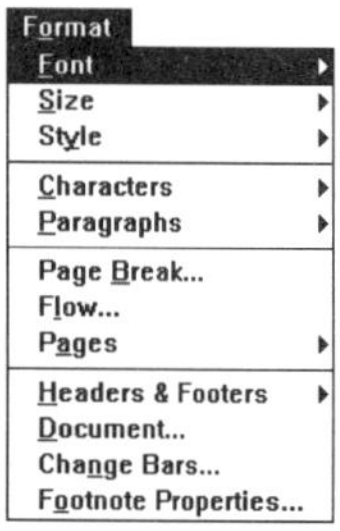


FORMAT The Format menu contains options to select font, size, and style; format characters and paragraphs; set page breaks; set text flow properties; insert variables in headers and footers; set document properties for page numbering and text attributes; set change bar properties; and set footnote properties.

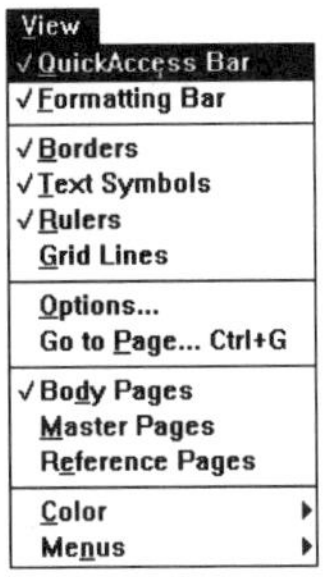


VIEW The View menu contains options that can be toggled on (displays a check mark) or off to display or hide the QuickAccess bar, formatting bar, borders, text symbols, rulers, and grid lines. This menu also allows you to set view options; go to specific pages in the body of the document; go to master pages, body pages or reference pages; set color options; and set menu options.

SPECIAL The Special menu contains options for positioning and sizing anchored frames; entering footnotes; creating cross-references; inserting system variables such as the date or filename; inserting markers (for indexed items, comments, cross-references, and so on); displaying the equation palette; creating conditional text; adding disconnected pages; and deleting pages.

GRAPHICS The Graphics menu contains options to display the graphic tools and toggle gravity and snap features on and off. It also has options to group and ungroup graphic objects; send overlapping objects to the front or back; align and distribute objects; reshape objects; smooth and unsmooth corners and lines; flip and rotate objects; scale objects; set the number of sides for an object; and set object properties. Another option allows you to specify whether or not an object should be printed over or cut out of objects that it overlaps.

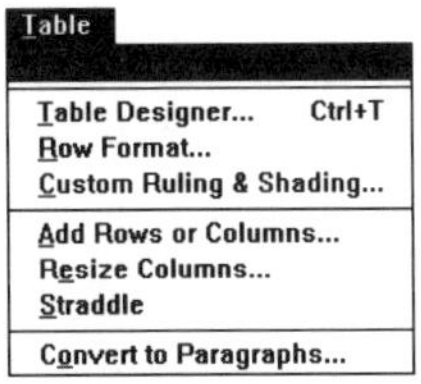


TABLE The Table menu contains options to insert a table; design a table; set row format; specify custom ruling and shading; add rows or columns; resize columns; straddle (combine) cells; and convert text to a table.

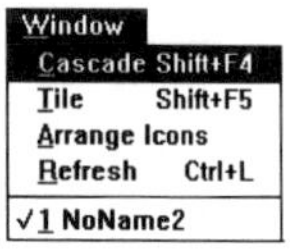


WINDOW The Window menu contains options to cascade or tile open windows, arrange icons, and refresh the screen. It also displays the names of all open windows. Selecting a document name places that document in the current window.

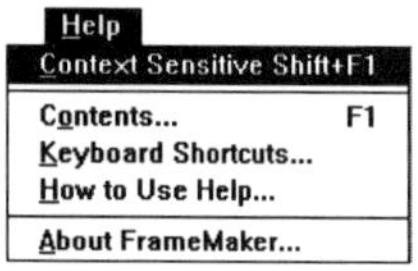


HELP The Help menu contains options to turn on context-sensitive help; display a list of help topics; display a list of categories of keyboard shortcuts; explain how to use Help; and display information about FrameMaker 4.

## The QuickAccess Bar

The QuickAccess bar contains icons that perform menu commands. Clicking an icon (the only way to select an icon) is faster than selecting the command from a menu. The QuickAccess bar, which can be displayed horizontally or vertically, has two sections. The icons on the left or the top are common commands, and they are always displayed. Four sets of icons can be displayed (one at a time) on the right or the bottom. The sets include text editing icons, graphic icons, graphic editing icons, and table editing icons.

To change the display of icons, click the up/left or down/right arrows on the QuickAccess bar. The QuickAccess bar displays the selected set until another set is chosen. When you exit FrameMaker 4 and then reboot, the QuickAccess bar will be just like you set it when you last used it.

Since there are so many icons (one bizillion to be exact), and FrameMaker 4 does not give you a word clue for what the icons do, you may be discouraged from using the icons except for the ones that have the most obvious pictures (such as the scissors). The problem of recognizing and remembering icons is compounded by the fact that all Windows products use so many of them, and there is no standard icon for common icons like cut and paste. Table 4-1 pictures each icon and describes its function. Study this table to find and memorize the icons that would be most useful to you—it's worth the time and effort.

**NOTE:** *Some icon descriptions here may not be clear to you on first reading. Later, after you have read the chapter that pertains to certain tasks, you can refer back to this table and decide which icons suit your needs.*

**Common Commands (available on all QuickAccess bars)**

| Icon | Name | Description |
|---|---|---|
|  | Help | Displays the help topics concerning the QuickAccess bar. |
| 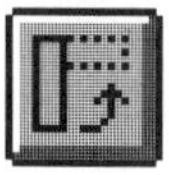 | Flip bar | Changes the position of the bar to vertical or horizontal. When the bar is in a vertical position it becomes a window that can be positioned anywhere on the screen. When the bar is in a horizontal position, it is locked in place below the menu bar. |
|  | New | Displays the dialog box that allows you to create a new document. |
|  | Open | Displays the dialog box that allows you to select an existing file to open. |
|  | Save | Displays the dialog box that allows you to save a document. |
|  | Print | Displays the dialog box that allows you to print a document |
|  | Cut | Cuts selected text or objects and places them on the Clipboard. |
|  | Copy | Copies selected text or objects and places them on the Clipboard. |
|  | Paste | Places text or objects stored on the Clipboard in the document |
| 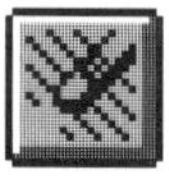 | Undo | Reverses the previous action if it can be undone. FrameMaker 4 alerts you if an action cannot be undone before you perform the action. |

**Text Editing**

| Icon | Name | Description |
|---|---|---|
|  | Plain | Removes text emphasis. |
|  | Bold | Applies bold to selected text. |

**TABLE 4-1** *The QuickAccess Bar Icons* ■

**Text Editing** (continued)

| Icon | Name | Description |
|---|---|---|
|  | Italic | Applies italics to selected text. |
|  | Underline | Applies underline to selected text. |
|  | Increase size 1 pt | Increases the font size of selected text by one point. |
|  | Decrease size 1 pt | Decreases the font size of selected text by one point. |
|  | Lowercase | Changes selected text to lowercase. |
|  | Initial caps | Capitalizes the first letter of each word in the selected text. |
|  | Uppercase | Capitalizes all letters in the selected text. |
|  | Find/change | Displays the Find/Change window in which you can find specified text or find specified text and change it to specified text. |
|  | Spell check | Displays the Spell Checker window used for checking spelling and punctuation errors and for storing and maintaining spelling and hyphenation dictionaries. |
|  | Anchored frame | Displays the Anchored Frame dialog box used to position and size a frame. |
| 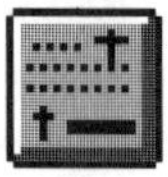 | Footnote | Creates a footnote reference. |
| 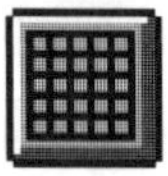 | Insert table | Displays the Insert Table dialog box, which allows you to create and insert a table. |

**TABLE 4-1** *The QuickAccess Bar Icons* (continued) ■

**Graphics**

| Icon | Name | Description |
|---|---|---|
| 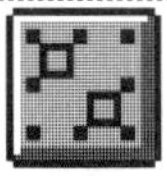 | Group | Groups a number of selected objects into one object that can be manipulated as a single object. |
| 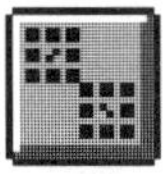 | Ungroup | Splits grouped objects into single objects again. |
| 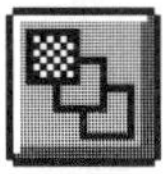 | Bring to front | Positions the selected object in front of all objects that overlap it. |
| 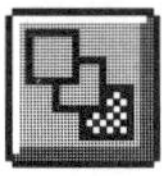 | Send to back | Positions the selected object behind all objects that overlap it. |
|  | Distribute | Displays the Distribute dialog box, which allows you to position selected objects horizontally. Objects can be distributed with equal space between the edges and between the centers. They can also be spaced with a gap value. |
| 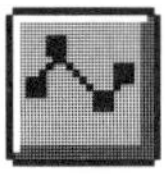 | Reshape | Allows you to change the shape of polygons (many-sided closed figures), polylines (many-sided open figures), arcs, and freehand curves. |
| 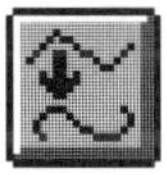 | Smooth | Rounds the corners of rectangles and changes polylines and polygons into a series of Bezier curves. |
| 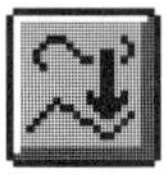 | Unsmooth | Decreases the radius of a rounded corner and changes freehand curves into polylines. |
| 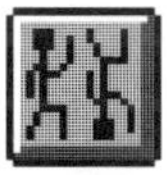 | Flip up/down | Flips a selected object top to bottom (that is, on the horizontal axis). |
| 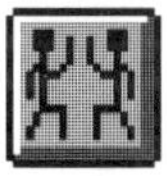 | Flip left/right | Flips a selected object on the vertical axis. |
| 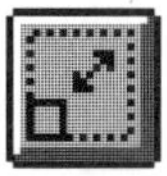 | Scale | Displays the Scale dialog box, which allows you to resize an object to scale so the object is not distorted. |
| 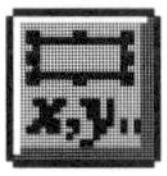 | Object properties | Displays the Object Properties dialog box, which allows you to set various properties for objects. The options displayed in the properties box depend on the type of object that is selected. |

**TABLE 4-1** *The QuickAccess Bar Icons* (continued) ■

**Graphics** (continued)

| Icon | Name | Description |
|---|---|---|
|  | Snap | Toggles the snap feature on and off. When snap is on, objects can be moved or positioned in preset increments only. The objects are said to "snap" to the grid (formed by the preset increment). |
|  | Gravity | Toggles the gravity feature on and off. Gravity is a force of attraction between objects. When one object is moved towards another object, gravity will cause the objects to be joined on the same path. |

**Graphics Editing**

| Icon | Name | Description |
|---|---|---|
| 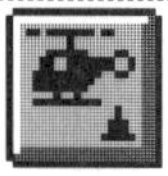 | Move up 1 pt | Moves a selected object up one point. |
| 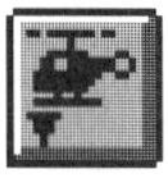 | Move down 1 pt | Moves a selected object down one point. |
|  | Move left 1 pt | Moves a selected object to the left one point. |
|  | Move right 1 pt | Moves a selected object to the right one point. |
|  | Top align | Aligns selected objects at the top. |
|  | Center align top to bottom | Aligns selected objects on their vertical centers. |
|  | Bottom align | Aligns selected objects at the bottom. |
|  | Left align | Aligns selected objects to the left. |
|  | Center align left to right | Aligns selected objects on their horizontal centers. |
|  | Right align | Aligns selected objects to the right. |

**TABLE 4-1** *The QuickAccess Bar Icons* (continued) ■

**Graphics Editing** (continued)

| Icon | Name | Description |
|---|---|---|
|  | Rotate clockwise | Rotates a selected object clockwise. |
|  | Rotate counter-clockwise | Rotates a selected object counterclockwise. |
|  | Solid line | Changes a selected line to a solid line. |
|  | Dash line | Changes a selected line to the pattern set in the dash pattern dialog box. |

**Table Editing**

| Icon | Name | Description |
|---|---|---|
| 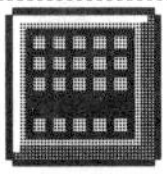 | Select row | Selects the row in which the cursor is positioned. |
| 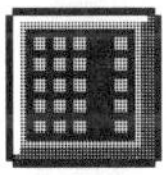 | Select column | Selects the column in which the cursor is positioned including the row that is the heading. |
| 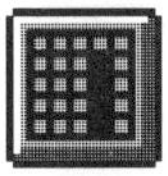 | Select body cells in column | Selects cells in the column where the cursor is positioned excluding the cell in the heading row. |
| 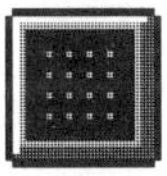 | Select table | Selects all the cells in the table. |
| 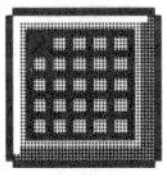 | Move pointer to top left cell | Moves the pointer to the upper-left cell. |
| 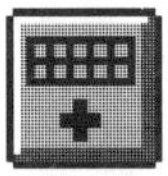 | Add rows below | Adds rows below the pointer position. |
| 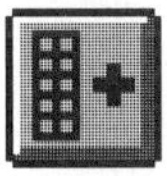 | Add columns to right | Adds columns to the right of the cursor position. |
| 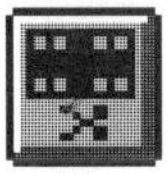 | Cut rows/ columns | Deletes selected rows, columns, or groups of cells. |

**TABLE 4-1** *The QuickAccess Bar Icons* (continued) ■

**Table Editing** (continued)

| Icon | Name | Description |
|---|---|---|
| 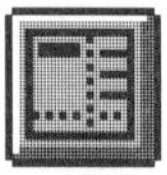 | Top align text in cell | Aligns text in the top of the cell. |
| 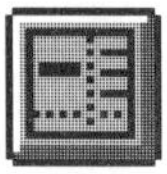 | Middle align text in cell | Aligns text in the middle of the cell. |
| 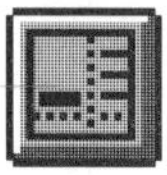 | Bottom align text in cell | Aligns text in the bottom of the cell. |
| 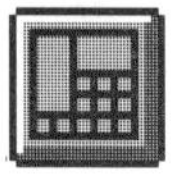 | Straddle/ unstraddle | Combines or splits selected cells. |
| 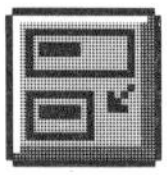 | Shrink wrap | Changes the column width where the cursor is positioned so no paragraphs wrap. |
| 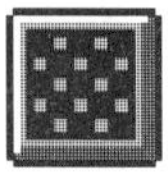 | Custom ruling and shading | Displays the Custom Ruling and Shading dialog box in which you can specify line thicknesses and custom cell shading. |

**TABLE 4-1** *The QuickAccess Bar Icons* (continued) ■

## The Formatting Bar

The formatting bar, like the QuickAccess bar, provides icons and a pop-up menu for faster execution of commands. As indicated by the name of the bar, the icons and menu options all deal with formatting. Table 4-2 pictures all the elements of the formatting bar and describes each one.

## The Rulers

The two rulers, displayed horizontally across the top of a document and vertically on the left side of a document, aid in placement of text and objects. By default, the rulers display inches marked off in 1/8-inch increments.

Since the basic element of most documents is type, which is measured in points (an increment of picas), it makes more sense to display the rulers in picas and points. To change the measuring units of the rulers, follow these steps:

1. Choose View from the menu bar.

2. Choose Options.
3. Click the first Display Units pop-up menu and choose Picas.
4. Click the second Display Units pop-up menu (under the first one) and choose Picas.
5. Click the Set button.

The dialog box looks like this:

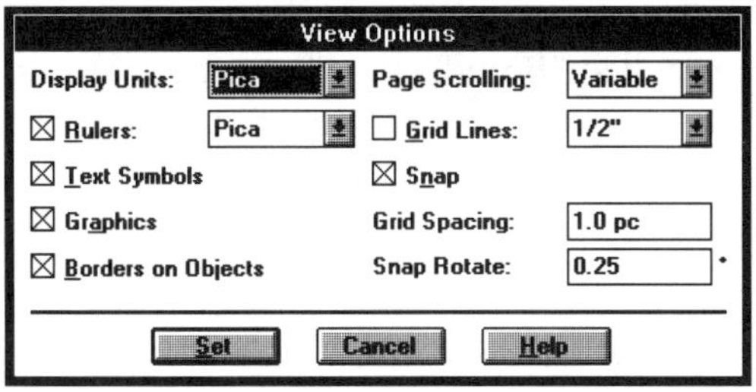


**NOTE:** *You should also change the Grid Spacing option in the View Options dialog box to a pica measurement. One pica is a reasonable number for this option. The Grid Spacing option controls the unit of "snap."*

| Icon | Name | Description |
|---|---|---|
| | Alignment icon | Displays the pop-up menu for aligning the selected paragraph(s). Choices include left, right, centered, and justified. |
| | Spacing icon | Displays the pop-up menu for changing the space between lines in the selected paragraph(s). Choices include single spacing, one and a half spacing, double spacing, custom, and space between. |
| | Tab icons | Sets a left, centered, right, or decimal tab. |
| Body | Paragraph format pop-up menu | Displays the formats in the Paragraph Catalog (a list of named formats with preset attributes). Also has the options to create a new format or update all formats. |

**TABLE 4-2** *Elements of the Formatting Bar* ■

## The Status Bar

The status bar, at the bottom of the document window, displays information about the text of a document, the pages, and the zoom. When the insertion cursor is clicked in the document, the left side of the status bar displays information like these examples:

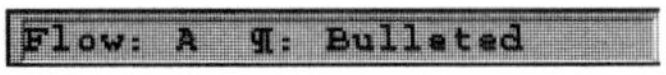


The flow tag in use for both examples is "A." The two paragraph formats are called "Body" in the first example and "Bulleted" in the second example. The next example shows a different flow tag. Flow tags are explained briefly in the box on the next page.

If special emphasis such as italics has been added to a paragraph, the status line looks like this when the insertion cursor is clicked in the paragraph:

The next space in the status bar is the page display, which tells you what page you are on and how many pages the document contains. When you have made changes in the document that have not been saved yet, the page display has an asterisk like this:

To move from page to page, click the up arrow or the down arrow in the status bar or press PGUP or PGDN. To go to a specific page, press CTRL+G or choose View, Go to Page, enter the desired page number, and choose Go.

Next to the page display is the zoom percentage display button. By default, a document is first displayed at 100%—meaning that the document is shown at actual size on the monitor. To the right of the zoom display are the zoom buttons as shown here:

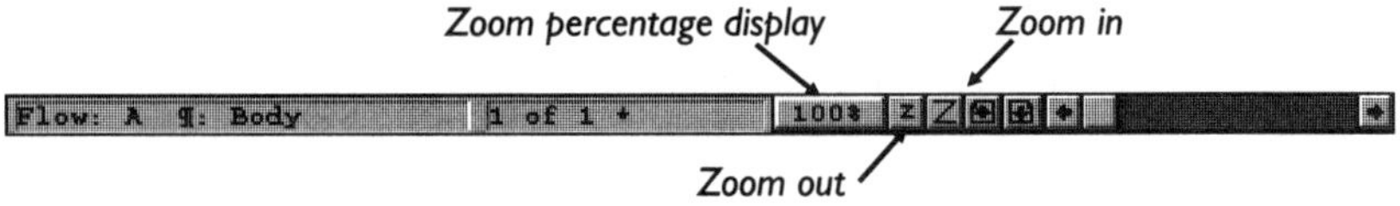

## Flow Tags

*Flow tags control the flow of text through the document. In the following example, flow tag A flows in the first column and flow tag B flows in the second column.*

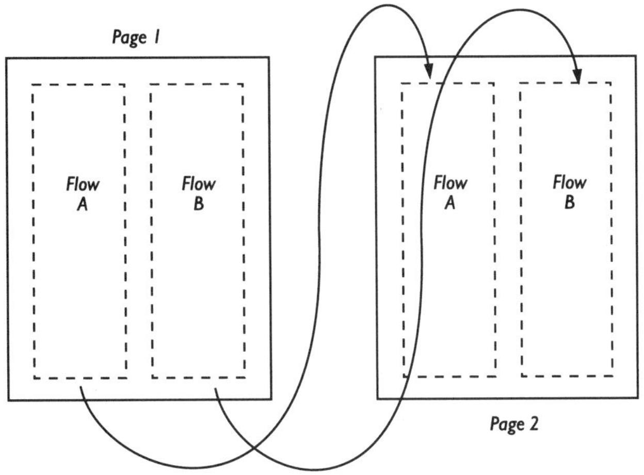


*You will learn more about flow tags and paragraph formats in later chapters.*

If you click the mouse cursor on the zoom percentage display button, a menu like this is displayed:

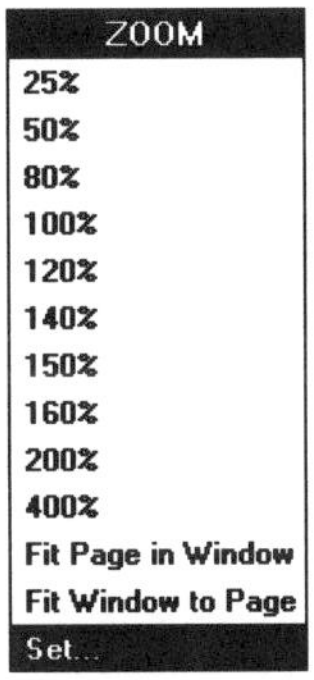


You can select an option from the menu or select Set and display the Zoom Menu Options dialog box where you can define your own percentages.

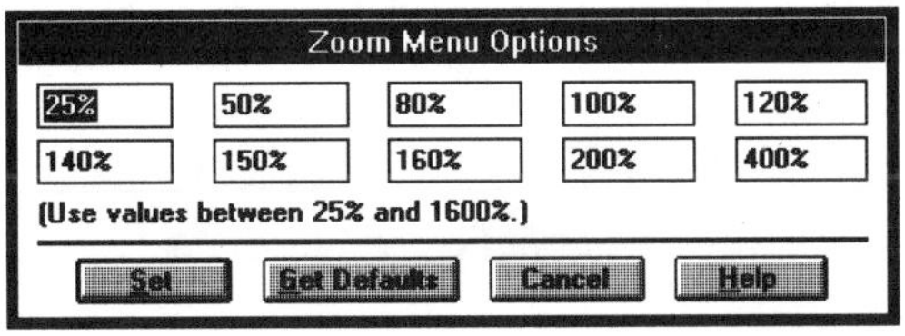

The zoom buttons decrease or increase the zoom one preset percentage at a time. (The preset percentages are 25%, 50%, 80%, 100%, 120%, and so on.)

On the right side of the status bar is the horizontal scroll bar used for scrolling the document window left and right. You probably already know how to use scroll bars. Refer to your Windows documentation if necessary.

### The Right Border

The right border has four icons and the vertical scroll bar (see Figure 4-2). Table 4-3 pictures each icon and describes its function.

#### FRAME SUPPORT

Frame Technology Corporation supports its users in may ways. Registered users receive free technical support for 30 days beginning with the first call. After your 30 days of free support, you may want to look into the technical support plans that the company offers to customers in the United States and Canada. You can also fax your questions to Frame at (408) 433-1928.

Registered users also receive two newsletters, *Frame Footnotes* and *Frame Focus*. These publications provide technical tips, news, and product information.

| Icon | Name | Description |
|---|---|---|
|  | Paragraph catalog | Displays the Paragraph Catalog window, which is used to apply a paragraph format to selected text. |
|  | Format catalog | Displays the Format Catalog window, which is used to apply character formats such as font family, font size, and italic to selected text. |
|  | Graphics tools | Displays the Graphics Tools window (which actually looks more like a palette). Tools include a box drawing tool, line drawing tool, font tool, and so on. |
|  | Equation palette | Displays the Equations window which contains buttons for mathematical symbols, operators, functions, and so on. |

TABLE 4-3 *The Icons in the Right Border*

Another way to get helpful information about FrameMaker 4 is to use your modem and connect with CompuServe or Frame's electronic bulletin board service (BBS). The CompuServe forum called Desktop Publishing Vendors has information about FrameMaker in section 12. If you are a CompuServe user, use GO DTPVEND to browse the forum for useful software information. To reach the Frame electronic BBS, which runs 24 hours a day, use your telecommunications program and call 408-433-4841 if you have a 2400 baud modem or 408-433-4867 if you have a 9600 baud modem.

The FrameFacts help feature offers information by fax. When you call (408) 428-6153, you respond to a voice menu with your fax number and the number of the help document you want to receive. If you do not know the document number, you can listen to an index listing, and then request the document.

# 5

# Entering and Editing Text

TEXT is entered in a FrameMaker 4 document in one of two ways—by typing the text directly in the FrameMaker 4 document or by converting text from other applications. The rules for typing text in FrameMaker 4 are very similar to the rules for typing text in a plain word processing document. To import text in FrameMaker 4, special files called *filters* must be used. These filters are provided by FrameMaker 4 and are copied to the hard disk during installation.

**NOTE:** *If you did not install filters, you can run the installation program again and add them to your hard disk. You can also create filters with Frame Developers Kit—a program that uses Frame's proprietary programming language.*

## TYPING TEXT

When you begin to enter text in a new document, you will notice a special character (called the section symbol) located in the upper-left corner as shown here:

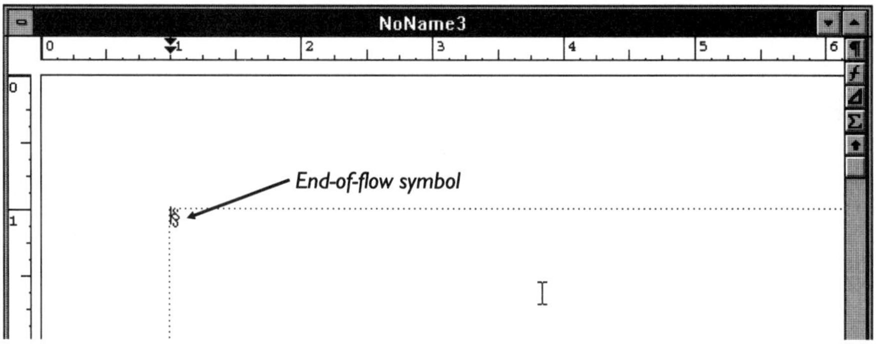

This symbol denotes the end-of-text flow. It is the last character in any FrameMaker 4 file, and the cursor cannot be positioned after (or below) this symbol.

To begin typing, click the cursor in front of the end-of-flow symbol and begin typing. The end-of-flow symbol is pushed along as you type and the text wraps from line to line automatically.

To indent text, press the TAB key. (In a later chapter you will learn how to use an indent feature to indent paragraphs.) Text will be indented to the next tab stop that is set in the ruler. To start a new paragraph or make a blank line, press ENTER. To force a line to break without starting a new paragraph, press SHIFT+ENTER. If you have the option Text Symbols checked (on the View menu), FrameMaker 4 displays a ¶ when you press the ENTER key, < when you press SHIFT+ENTER, and > when you press the TAB key.

When you have filled up a page with typing, just keep typing. FrameMaker 4 automatically adds a new page when it is needed. If you make a mistake while typing, press BACKSPACE to delete the character to the left of the cursor or press DEL to delete the character to the right of the cursor.

## Entering Special Characters

Some characters used frequently in manuscripts are not keyboard characters and must be entered with special keystrokes. These characters and their keystrokes are listed in the following table:

| Character | Keystrokes |
|---|---|
| Em space | CTRL+SHIFT+SPACE |
| En space | ALT+CTRL+SPACE |
| Numeric space | ESC SPACE 1 |
| Thin space | ESC SPACE t |
| Bullet | CTRL+q % |
| Em dash | CTRL+q Q |
| En dash | CTRL+q P |

You will notice that many of the special characters are various kinds of spaces. A space typed with the SPACEBAR is a proportional space; that is, the width of the space is dependent on the characters on either side of the space. To enter a fixed space, one whose width is always the same, use the keystrokes to type an em space, en space, thin space, or numeric space. The em space is equal to the size of the font. The en space is one-half the size of the font. A thin space is one-twelfth the size of the font. A numeric space is the same width as the font's zero character.

**HINT:** *Numeric spaces can be used to align numbers in columns without using tabs. Typically all numbers in a font have the same width; therefore, all numbers take up the same amount of space. If you have a list numbered from 1 to 10, you can precede each one digit number with a numeric space, then all the numbers would be right aligned with the number 10.*

The em dash and en dash have the same width as the em space and the en space, respectively. Use the em dash to denote a sudden break in thought or to give examples and explanations. Use the en dash to indicate a range like 1–4.

## Smart Spaces

Top-notch secretaries would rather be drawn and quartered than end a sentence without two spaces after the punctuation mark. This has been the rule taught in typing classes for years; however, this rule does not apply to typesetting. Only one space should be inserted after end punctuation.

The Smart Spaces option ensures consistent spacing between words and sentences. When this option is activated, it is impossible to type more than one space in a row unless you enter fixed spaces. To activate Smart Spaces, follow these steps:

1. Choose Format.
2. Choose Document.

The Document Properties dialog box is displayed:

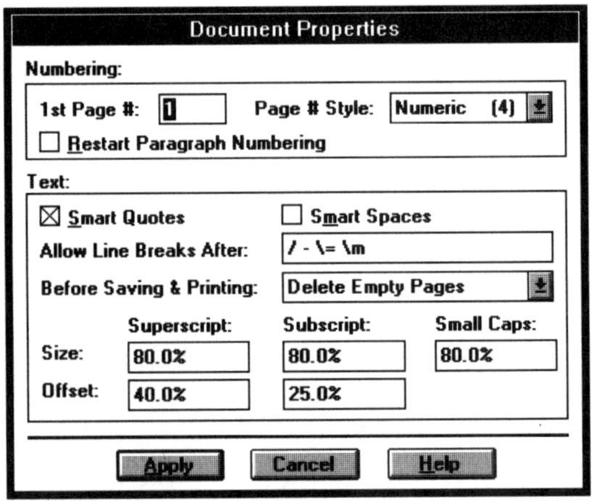

3. Select Smart Spaces and choose Apply.

**NOTE:** *Activating or deactivating Smart Spaces will not change existing spacing, but changes can be made with the Spelling Checker, which is discussed later in this chapter.*

### Smart Quotes

Straight quotation marks and apostrophes (" ,', and ') are not generally used in typeset text except for the inch (") and foot (') symbols. If the Smart Quotes option, seen in the previous illustration of the Document Properties dialog box, is activated, FrameMaker 4 uses curved marks and is smart enough to know whether to use an open or closed mark. For example, when you type **"word"**, FrameMaker 4 uses an open quotation at the beginning and a closed quotation at the end.

**NOTE:** *The apostrophe is always curved whether Smart Quotes is activated or not.*

To activate Smart Quotes, follow these steps:

1. Choose Format.
2. Choose Document.
3. Select Smart Quotes and choose Apply. (If selected, the option has an "x" in the check box.)

**NOTE:** *Activating or deactivating Smart Quotes will not change existing marks, but changes can be made with the Spelling Checker.*

## CONVERTING TEXT

FrameMaker 4 can use text from other sources with the help of filters that convert the formats to one that the program can use. Currently, FrameMaker 4 has filters for these formats:

- Ami Pro (2.0 and 3.0)
- ASCII
- Displaywrite/DCA RFT (4 and 5)

- Microsoft Word (DOS 4.0, 5.0, and 5.5; Macintosh 3.0, 4.0, 5.0, and 5.1; and Windows 1.x and 2.x)
- Rich Text format (0 and 1)
- Ventura Publisher (3.0 and 4.0)
- WordPerfect (DOS 4.2, 5.0, and 5.1; Macintosh 2.0; and Windows 5.0 and 5.1)

If you need to use a file that FrameMaker 4 does not support, you may be able to save the file in a format that FrameMaker 4 recognizes. Many programs save files in multiple formats. Document conversion programs are also available to translate formats.

## Preparing a Document for Conversion

Some formatting features of a document cannot be converted by FrameMaker 4 filters. These include drop caps, equations, and side headings. Before importing a document in FrameMaker 4, follow these suggestions to make the conversion as clean as possible:

- Move a graphic that has text wrapped around it so that the text returns to a regular text block.
- Use only one page orientation if possible.
- When differing column layouts are used, specify the most frequently used format first.
- Change rotated text to regular text.
- Replace spaces used to indent with tabs.
- Delete shading, line drawings, or graphic characters used to create table borders.
- Include page breaks instead of extra lines that force page breaks.

## Converting Text

To convert text that is supported by a FrameMaker 4 filter, you simply open the file by following these steps:

1. Choose File, Open.
2. Choose or type the name of the desired file.

3. Choose Open.
4. Choose the appropriate type from the Convert From list box.
5. Click Convert.

After the file is converted, it can be saved as a FrameMaker 4 document using the Save As command. It can also be copied into other FrameMaker 4 documents.

**NOTE:** *Each application that FrameMaker 4 supports may have specific limitations. For example, soft page breaks are not converted in Microsoft Word for Windows documents and vertical alignment is not supported in Ventura documents. For details on how specific file formats are converted, refer to the online manual* ***Using Frame Filters****, accessible through the Help menu.*

Using the File, Import command is an alternate way of converting a file, but this method is not recommended. This command converts and imports a document in an existing FrameMaker 4 document, placing it at the cursor location. In addition to importing the text, font styles, spacing, and so on, the Import command also imports the page format of the original document, which may not be the same as the page format of the FrameMaker 4 document. Importing multiple page formats could cause formatting problems.

## EDITING TEXT

If you have looked at Appendix C, you have seen the table that lists the steps for many basic functions. Included in the table are most of the editing functions like find, find and change, copy, cut, paste, check spelling, and use the thesaurus. In this chapter, you can learn about some of the finer details of these functions.

### Selecting Text

The selection of text is common to several editing functions and other functions such as formatting. Appendix C lists these methods of selecting text—drag the cursor through the desired text, double click a word, or triple click a paragraph. Additionally you can use one of these two methods:

- Position the cursor at the beginning of the desired text and SHIFT-click the cursor at the end of the text.

- Position the cursor at the beginning of the desired text and hold the SHIFT key while pressing a cursor movement key such as END, DOWN ARROW, PGDN, and so on.

## Copying, Cutting, Pasting, and Clearing Text

Once text has been selected, you can copy, cut, or clear it with the corresponding Edit commands. Text that is copied or cut is stored on the Clipboard and can be pasted in a new location. Once text is pasted, it does not leave the Clipboard. It can be pasted over and over again. When new text is stored on the Clipboard, it replaces the text that was there previously; it is not added to it.

Text that is cleared is not stored on the Clipboard and can only be retrieved with the Undo command, and then only if the Undo command is invoked before another significant action is taken (like using another Edit command). The DEL key performs the same function as the Edit, Clear command.

## Finding and Finding/Changing Text

Using the Find/Change command to find or find and change text is not the only capability of the command. You can also search for formats, cross references, footnotes, tables, automatic hyphens, and other items that you will learn about in later chapters.

The Find/Change window looks like this:

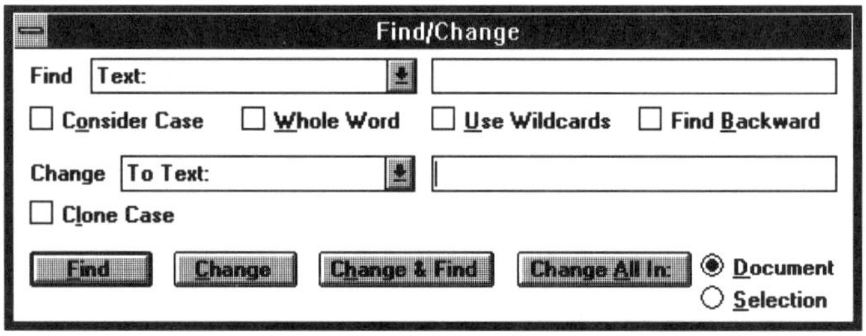


It is displayed by selecting Edit, Find/Change.

When finding text, you can consider the case, look for a whole word, use wildcards, and search backwards from the point of the cursor. If you select Use Wildcards, you can enter text that includes the wildcards * and ? in the Find box. The * stands for any character and any number of characters; the ? stands for any character, but only one character. For example, if you enter **Frame*** in the Find box, select Consider Case and Use Wildcards. FrameMaker would find Frames, FrameMath, FrameMaker, Framework, and so on. If you enter **Frame?** instead, only Frames would be found.

If you are finding text and changing it to different text, you can select Clone Case. This option copies the capitalization of the text that is found when it replaces it with the new text. If you are finding text or another item to change the character format, select To Character Format in the Change list box. This dialog box is displayed:

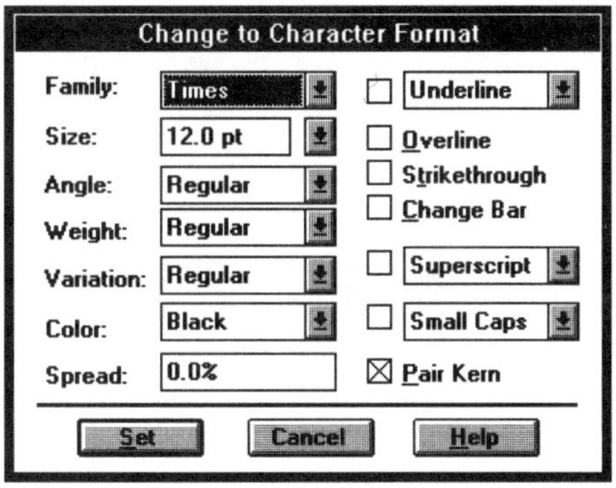


Make the desired selections and choose Set. If you want to change an item in the Find list box with what is on the Clipboard, select By Pasting in the Change list box.

The buttons at the bottom of the Find/Change window include Find, which searches for the text or selected item and highlights it if found; Change, which changes the highlighted text that is found; Change & Find, which changes the highlighted text that is found and looks for the next occurrence; and Change All In, which changes every instance of the found text. Before clicking a button, be sure that the correct option, Document or Selection, is chosen.

When the Find/Change window is open, it can be moved to a new location to display more of the document. It can also be left open while you perform other tasks. For example, you can search for a particular text string and then type a new paragraph. To return to the Find/Change window, simply click the mouse cursor anywhere in the window. Likewise, when the Find/Change window is active, you can click the mouse cursor anywhere in the document window to make it active. The Find/Change window is closed just like any other window.

## Checking Spelling

To check the spelling of a document, choose Edit, Spelling Checker. The following window is displayed:

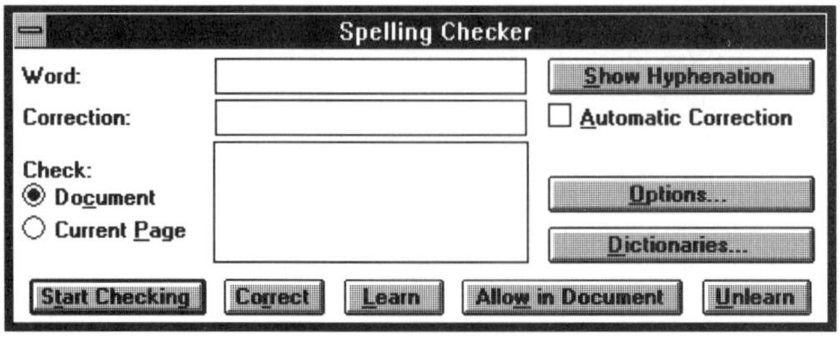


Choose Start Checking. The first word that is not in the FrameMaker 4 dictionaries is displayed in the Misspelling box as shown here:

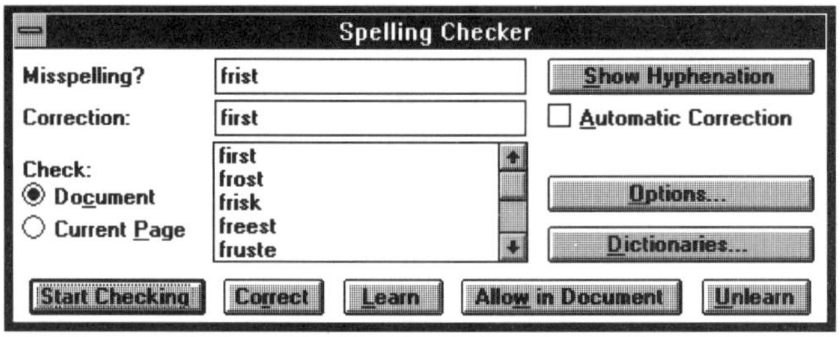


The Correction box displays the first word in the list of suggestions. If this is the correct spelling, you can choose Correct. If one of the other suggestions is correct, select it, and then choose Correct. If none of the suggestions are correct, type the correct spelling in the box and then select Correct. To have FrameMaker 4 automatically correct all future occurrences, select Automatic Correction.

If the word is correct, you can add it to one of two dictionaries or ignore it. To add the word to a personal dictionary, select Learn; to add the word to a dictionary that is attached to the current document only, select Allow in Document. To ignore the word, choose Start Checking again. If the word is spelled correctly and it appears often in more than one document, add it to the personal dictionary by selecting Learn. If the word appears mostly in the current document, add the word to the document dictionary by selecting Allow in Document.

To understand how FrameMaker 4 checks the spelling of a document, keep in mind that four dictionary types are available—the main dictionary, a site dictionary, personal dictionaries, and document dictionaries. The main dictionary contains 130,000 words, and it cannot have words added or deleted. The site dictionary has some technical terms like Ethernet, FrameMaker, Helvetica, LaserWriter, PostScript, and so on. Additional words can be added to the site dictionary by directly editing the file (\maker4\dict\site.dct) and saving it as a text-only file. You can also add words to the site dictionary if you specify it as your personal dictionary.

Then you can add or delete words with the Learn and Unlearn buttons. The main dictionary and the site dictionary are always used by the Spelling Checker.

**NOTE:** *If you are working on a network, it is possible that only the system administrator can make changes to the site dictionary.*

Personal dictionaries can have words added or deleted with the Learn and Unlearn buttons or by directly editing the files. The first time you select Learn, FrameMaker 4 creates a personal dictionary called \maker4\user.dct. Likewise, the first time you select Allow in Document, a document dictionary is created. This dictionary is saved with the file. To remove a word from either the personal dictionary or the document dictionary, enter the word in the Misspelling box and select Unlearn. To remove all words from the document dictionary, choose Dictionaries in the Spelling Checker window and then select Clear from the Document Dictionary pop-up menu.

The features described so far are about the extent of what many spelling checkers accomplish, but the FrameMaker 4 spell checker is much more powerful. The Options button displays this dialog box:

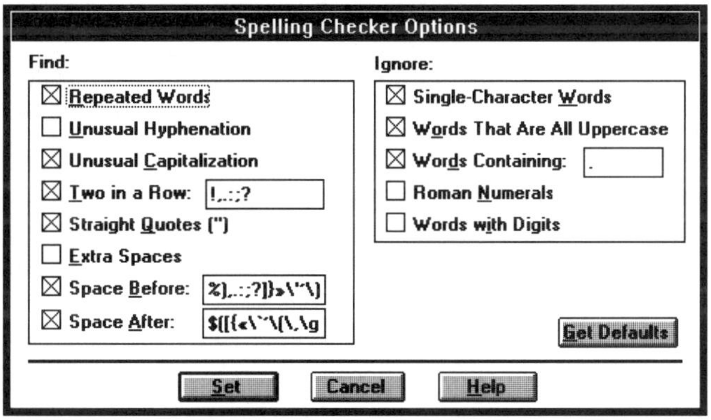


Table 5-1 explains each option.

## Using the Thesaurus

To look up a word in a document either for the purpose of reading its definition or replacing it with a synonym, click the cursor anywhere in the word and choose Edit, Thesaurus, Look Up. A window like this appears:

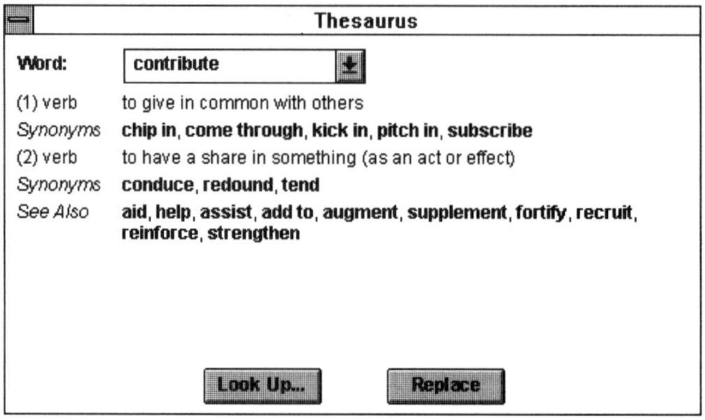


Definitions are displayed with synonyms listed in bold. To replace the current word with a synonym, select the synonym by clicking it and then click the Replace button. To look up a different word, click the Look Up button, type the desired word, and click Look Up again. When you are finished with the Thesaurus, close the window.

| Option | Description |
|---|---|
| Repeated Words | Finds two words in a row, as in "the the client's file." |
| Unusual Hyphenation | If this option is off, hyphenated words are considered and checked as two words. The word "non-Windows" would then be considered two words—"non" and "Windows." "Non" would be considered misspelled. |
| Unusual Capitalization | Finds words with unusual capitalization such "wIndows" or "WIndows." |
| Two in a Row | Finds double punctuation as specified in the text box. This option ignores three or more repeated punctuation marks. |
| Straight Quotes | Finds straight single and double quotation marks and suggests the curved marks as corrections. |
| Extra Spaces | Finds two spaces in a row and suggests a single space. This option ignores three or more spaces in a row as well as fixed spaces. |
| Space Before | Finds spaces before the punctuation mark specified. |
| Space After | Finds spaces after the punctuation mark specified. |
| Single-Character Words | Ignores single-character words. |
| Words That Are All Uppercase | Ignores words in all caps. |
| Words Containing | Ignores words containing the specified character. |
| Roman Numerals | Ignores uppercase and lowercase Roman numerals. |
| Words with Digits | Ignores words containing digits. |
| Get Defaults | Restores the settings to the original settings. |

**TABLE 5-1** *Spelling Options* ■

## PRACTICING

The following exercise takes you through most of the features discussed in this chapter.

1. Open a new file with portrait orientation.
2. Choose View from the menu and be sure that the following options have check marks: QuickAccess Bar, Formatting Bar, Borders, Text Symbols, and Rulers.
3. Choose Format, Document. Be sure that Smart Quotes and Smart Spaces are selected.
4. Type the following (including all errors) and try to enter two spaces after each sentence: **The new Musitech mouse is now available for distribution. Features include three button controls, ergonomic shape and design, glow-in-the-dark panel, musical on/off switch, and wake-up alarm. No computer should be without one.**
5. Press the ENTER key twice and type this line: **For a color brochure on the Musitech mouse, call 1-800-752-6083.**
6. Press the ENTER key until a new page is created.
7. Press the BACKSPACE key repeatedly to delete all the returns until you return to the end of the text typed in step 6.
8. Add the words "**and sale**" after the word "distribution."
9. Add the word "**user**" after the word "computer."
10. Choose Edit, Undo.
11. Use the Find/Change option to find the words "and design."
12. Close the Find/Change window.
13. Delete the highlighted text with the DEL key.
14. Undo the deletion by clicking the Undo icon.
15. Highlight the last sentence ("For a color brochure. . .") and cut it.
16. Click the text cursor in front of the word "No" (in "No computer should. . .").
17. Choose Edit, Paste.

18. Use the Find/Change command to change "Musitech" to "Musitech3." for all occurrences in the document.
19. Choose Edit, Spelling Checker, Options. Be sure the following options are selected and then choose Set: Find Repeated Words and Unusual Capitalization; Do not ignore Words with Digits.
20. Choose Start Checking. Correct the misspelled words and other errors. Select Allow in Document for Musitech3. When finished, close the window.
21. Click the text cursor in the word "shape." Choose Edit, Thesaurus, Look Up. Choose a synonym (such as configuration) and click the Replace button. Close the Thesaurus window.
22. Click the text cursor in front of the word "three" (in "Features include three. . ."). Press SHIFT+ENTER.
23. Type two em spaces, a bullet, and another em space.
24. Delete the comma and the space after "controls" and press SHIFT+ENTER.
25. Repeat step 23.
26. Delete the comma and the space after "design."
27. Repeat step 23 and continue the exercise until the five features are listed with bullets.
28. Insert two returns after the word "Alarm."
29. Close the file without saving.

# III

# Shaping text into Design

# 6

# Page Setup

By the time you get ready to use FrameMaker 4 to produce a printed piece, you should have a good idea of the paper size, the margins, the folds, and so on. All this information is necessary in order to set up a document properly.

Page setup can be done at two levels—either in FrameMaker 4 itself or in a word processing document (or Ventura Publisher document) that is opened by FrameMaker. If you open a document that has been created by another program, you will probably have to do additional formatting and "touch up" in FrameMaker 4.

In this chapter, FrameMaker 4's page setup commands are discussed first. This will give you a basis to understand how FrameMaker 4 uses page setup settings from word processing programs. In Chapter 7 you will learn how to use paragraph and text formatting.

## PAGE LAYOUT OPTIONS

When creating a new FrameMaker 4 document, you are presented with three blank paper options: Portrait, Landscape, and Custom. The portrait and landscape options use default settings for paper size, margins, columns, and pagination. If you select Custom, the following dialog box is displayed, and you can specify your own choices for the four options. Additionally, you can specify the unit of measure that you want to use.

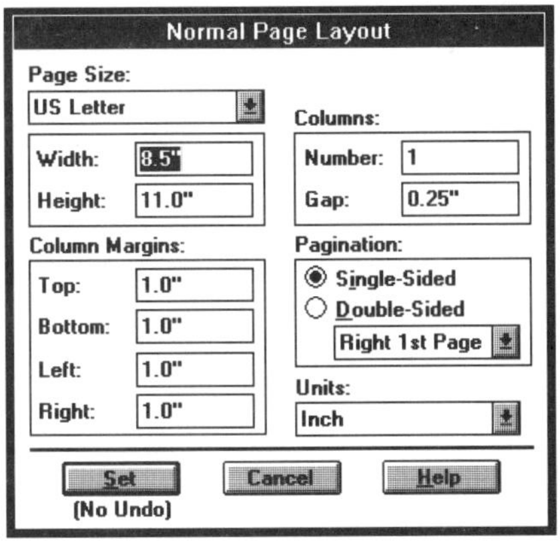


## Paper Size

FrameMaker 4 offers the following paper sizes:

US Letter (8.5×11 inches)
US Legal (8.5×14 inches)
Tabloid (11×17 inches)
A3 Tabloid (29.7×42 centimeters)
A4 Letter (21×29.7 centimeters)
A5 Letter (14.8×21 centimeters)
B5 Letter (17.6×25 centimeters)

The default paper size is 8.5×11 inches. In addition to the seven standard sizes, the Custom size lets you specify any width and height desired. Naturally the size of the paper needs to be a size that your printer can print. The largest page size that can be used is 216×216 inches.

If you are using a letter size paper (8.5×11 inches) to print on, but producing a smaller size, such as 5×7 inches, be sure to use the custom size of 5×7 inches rather than 8.5×11 inches. When you print, select Registration Marks, and FrameMaker 4 will center the 5×7-inch size in the middle of the paper and print "crop marks" so the commercial printer knows where to trim the paper.

Figure 6-1 shows a blank 5×7-inch page printed on an 8.5×11-inch piece of paper. The crop marks are the two perpendicular marks at each corner. The circle with the intersecting lines is a registration mark used for printing color.

**FIGURE 6-1**
*Crops marks printed on a 5×7-inch final size*

NoName3 Page 1 Monday, December 12, 1994 10:51 PM

This is a 5x7 document.

### Column Margins

Column margins default to one inch. If you are printing on only one side of the paper, the margins are Top, Bottom, Left, and Right. If you are printing on both sides of the paper, the margins are Top, Bottom, Inside, and Outside. If your printed piece will be bound, be certain to make the left or inside margin wide enough to accommodate the binding.

### Columns

The default number of columns is one. The maximum number of columns per page is determined by FrameMaker 4 based on the size of the page, the margins, and the gap set between columns.

The gap (or space between columns), also called the gutter, is .25 inches by default. If there is only one column, the gap measurement has no significance.

### Pagination

The default pagination is single-sided. If you select double-sided, you can also specify whether the document should start on a left-hand page or a right-hand page. Almost all printed media starts with a right-hand page.

### Units

The default unit of measurement is inches. Other choices include centimeters, millimeters, picas, points, didots, and ciceros. The unit chosen here is used for all menu options, but it does not change the display of the rulers. To set the ruler in accordance with the desired units, select View, Options.

### Changing Options

Once custom options have been set, they can be changed by choosing Format, Pages, Normal Page Layout. This menu sequence displays the same dialog box that you see if you choose Custom when creating a new document. Another way to display this dialog box is to choose Format, Pages, Layout Commands, Basic, Normal Page Layout.

## MASTER PAGES

Master pages are created automatically when the pagination option, discussed earlier, is selected. Selecting single-sided creates one right-hand master page for the document. Selecting double-sided creates a left-hand and a right-hand master page. The page size, number of columns, and column margins selected are the settings used for the master pages. As pages are added to the document, FrameMaker 4 automatically uses the page layout from the correct master page. For example, if a right-hand page is created, the right-hand master page is used for the page layout.

In addition to the automatically generated master pages, user-defined master pages can be created. These master pages can be applied to any page as desired. A document can have as many as 100 master pages.

All columns created on a master page are referred to as template columns, and they have a default text flow tag of "A", meaning that text will automatically flow from column to column. Different flow tags can be set on the master pages or on body pages. Flow is discussed in more detail later in this chapter.

### Changing Master Pages

Once the standard master pages are created by making selections in the Normal Page Layout dialog box, enhancements can be added. To go to a master page, choose View, Master Pages. Figure 6-2 shows a 25-percent view of a standard master page for a single-sided document with default settings. The dotted lines outline three text columns—the header, the footer, and the body text column. Notice that the status line indicates that master pages is a right page and there is only one master page. Figure 6-3 shows standard master pages for a double-sided document. Notice that the status line indicates that the right page is the current page, but there are two pages.

Text and graphics can be added to a master page so they will appear on every page that corresponds to that master page. For example, if you want a 24-point rule in the upper-left and upper-right corners of left and right pages, you can add these lines on the master pages instead of drawing them on each page. Figure 6-4 shows the master pages with the rules added.

For text that is placed on a master page to display on a body page, the text must be placed in a background column. Background columns are created by activating the Graphics Tools palette and drawing a column with the column tool. This tool is indicated in Figure 6-5.

**FIGURE 6-2**

*A standard master page for a single-sided document*

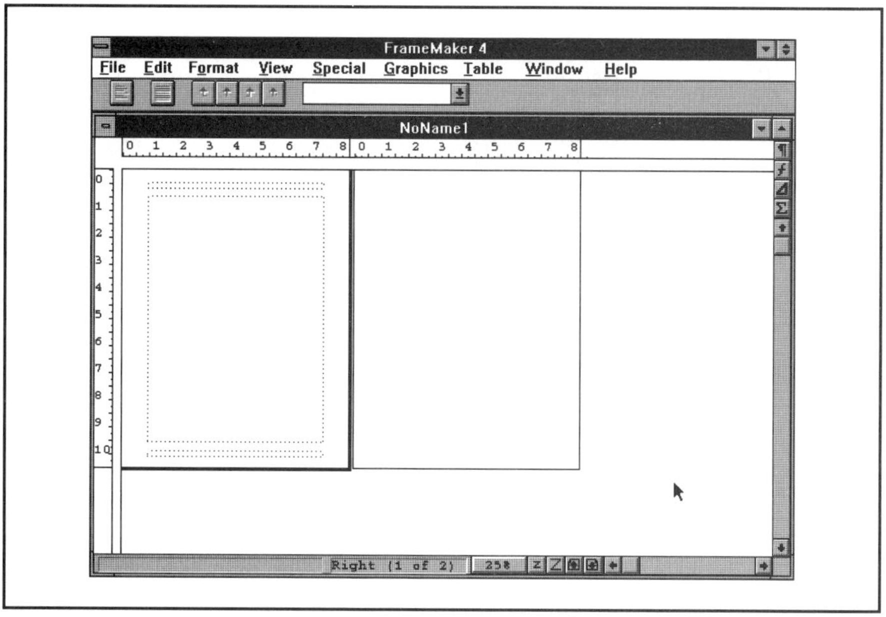


**FIGURE 6-3**

*Standard master pages for a double-sided document*

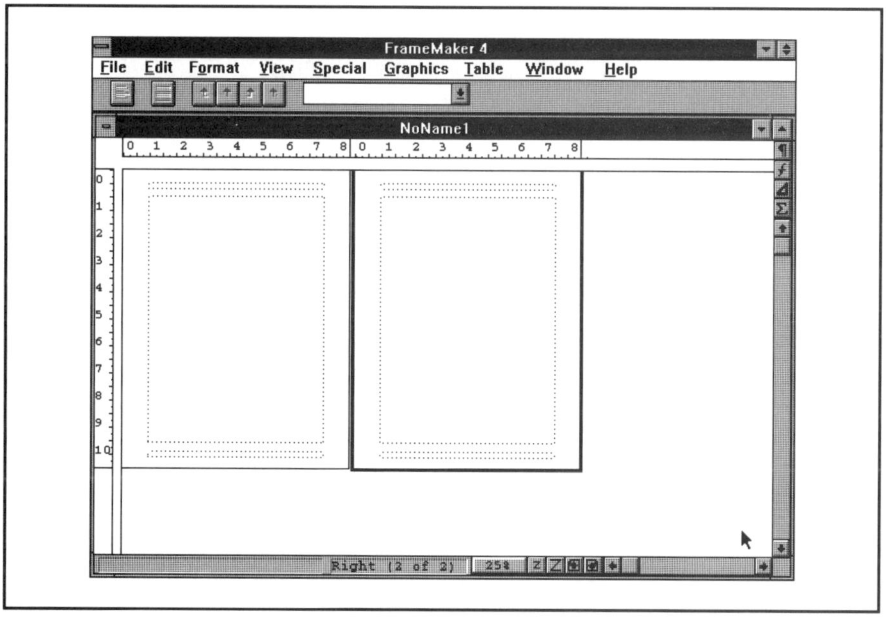

**FIGURE 6-4**

*Master pages with rules added*

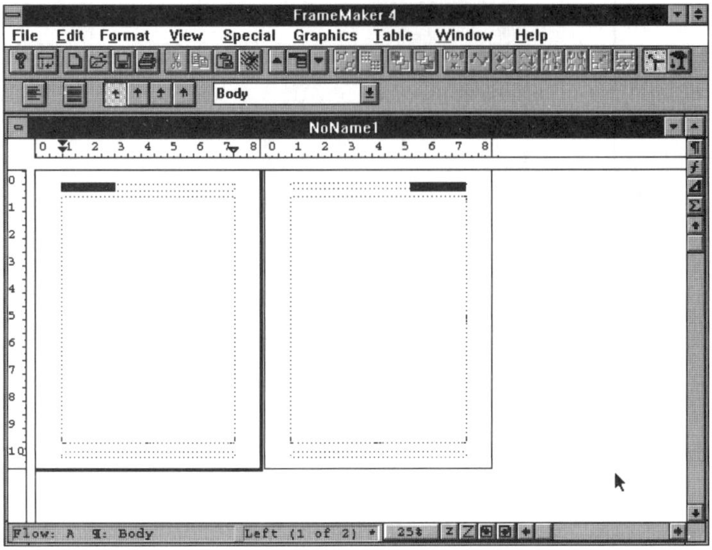


**TIP:** *Text in a background column should usually not be placed in a body column. The text in the actual body column will overwrite the text from the master page. The same is true of graphics that are placed in a body column, but sometimes a graphic is placed behind text for a watermark effect (see Figure 6-5).*

**FIGURE 6-5**

*The effect of text placed on a text column in a master page—in this case, a watermark*

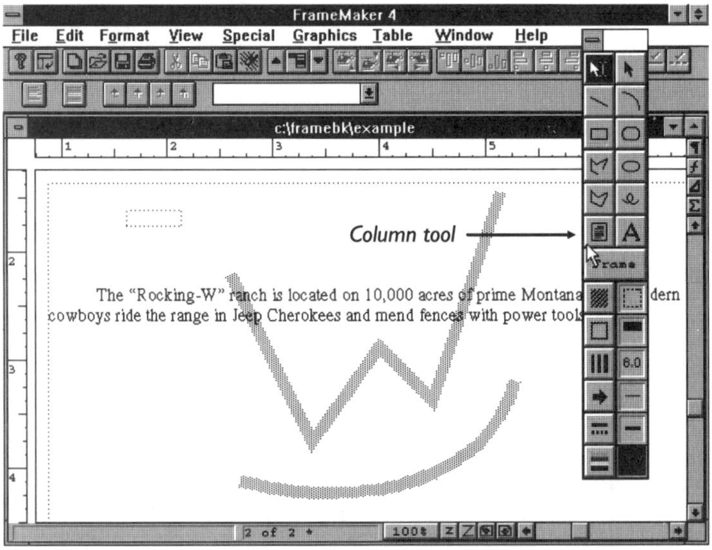

## Creating a Master Page

Some documents, like a newsletter, for example, need more than one or two master pages. A newsletter might need a left and right master page and a master page for the first and last page. To create your own master page, follow these steps:

1. Choose View, Master Pages.
2. Choose Special, Add Master Page to display this dialog box:

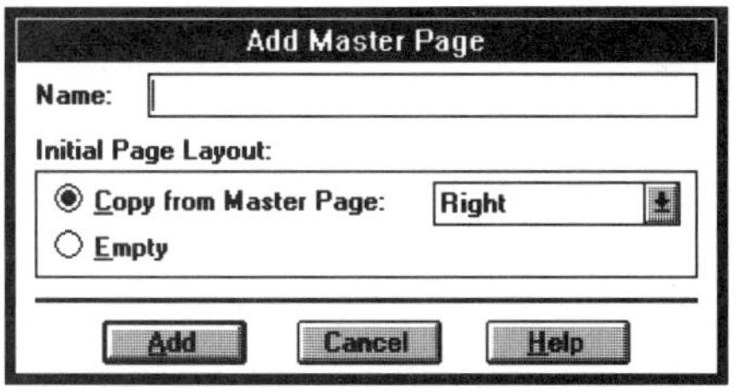


3. Type a name for the page.
4. Choose Copy from Master Page and then choose a page from the drop-down list—or choose Empty.
5. Choose Add.

After creating the page, make the desired modifications.
To assign a specific master page to a body page, follow these steps:

1. Display the body page.
2. Choose Format, Pages, Master Page Usage to display this dialog box:

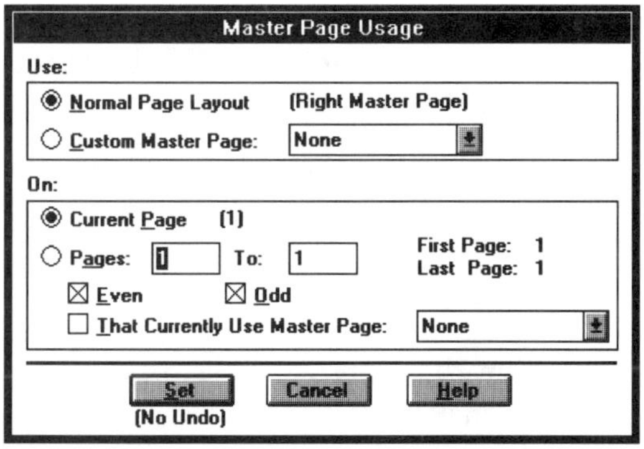

3. Choose Normal Page Layout or Custom Master Page and then select a custom master page from the drop-down list.
4. Choose the page or pages to which the master page should be applied.
5. Choose Set.

## CREATING HEADERS AND FOOTERS

Header and footer spaces are created on master pages automatically, as you have already seen. They have tab settings for centering text and for right-justifying text. To use a header or footer, simply go to the desired master page, click the cursor in the header or footer space, and type the desired text. In addition to text, headers and footers can contain variables such as page numbers, the date, the time, the document name, and so on. Headers and footers can also duplicate text that appears in the text column on a specific page. For example, the header can include the name of a topic that appears on the page. These are called "running" headers or footers, and this topic is discussed in more detail in Chapter 11.

### Sizing and Positioning Headers and Footers

By default, headers and footers contain one line and are positioned in the middle of the margin space. For example, if the top margin is one inch, the header will be positioned at half an inch. If the top margin is two inches, the header will be positioned at one inch.

To increase the size of the header or footer column, go to the master page and press CTRL while you click the header or footer space. Handles will appear like this:

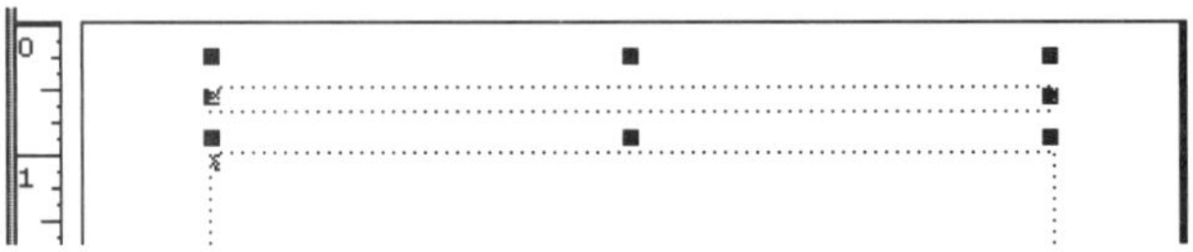

Position the mouse pointer on one of the corner handles and drag the handle to increase the size of the column. Figure 6-6 shows a header that has been enlarged. (Additionally, the height of the text column has been decreased.)

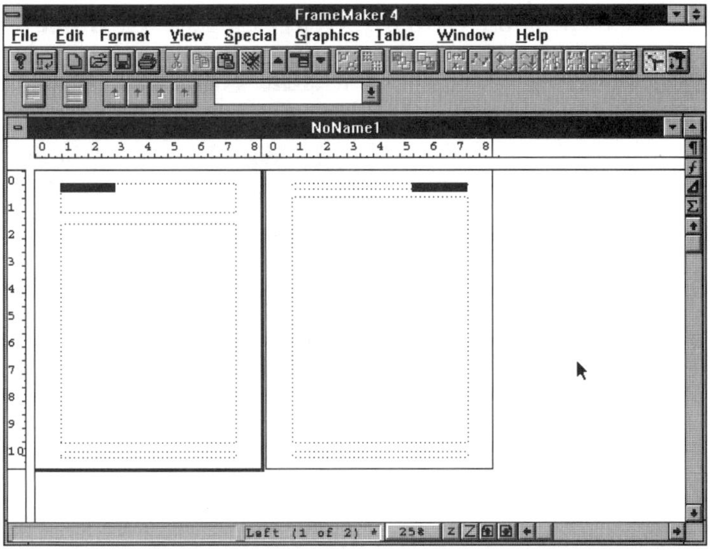


**FIGURE 6-6** *Master pages with an enlarged header column on the left page*

When a header or footer column has been enlarged, it usually must be moved to keep it in the middle of the margin space. To move the frame, select it with CTRL+click and then drag it with the mouse cursor to the desired location. (Do not drag a handle; this will change the size, not the position.)

**NOTE:** *The same mouse techniques used for sizing and moving a header and a footer can be used to resize and move text columns.*

Sizing and moving headers and footers with a mouse is easy, but imprecise. To size and position text columns with exact precision (whether they are headers, footers, or body text columns), you must treat the text columns as graphic objects. To set the exact size of a header, for example, select the header column with CTRL+click. Then select Graphics, Scale to display this dialog box:

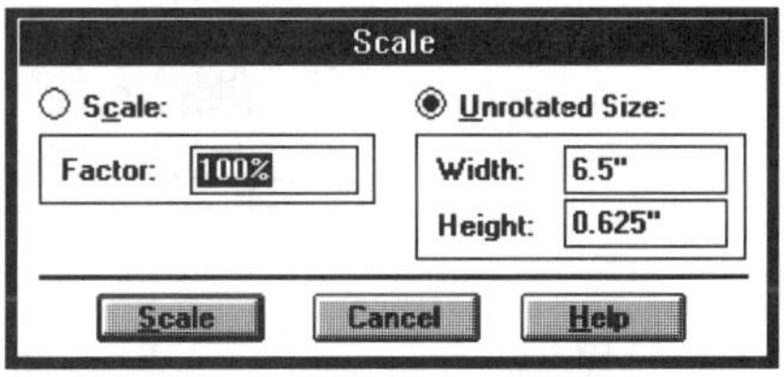


Set the desired width and height and select Scale.

To specify the exact location of a text column, select the text column and then choose Graphics, Object Properties to display this dialog box:

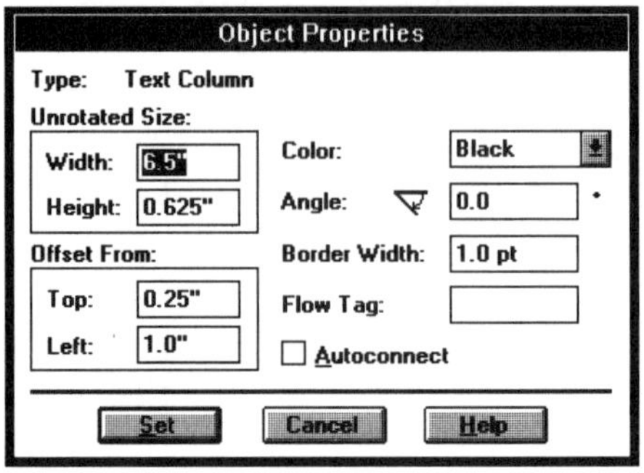


Set the desired offset from the top and left and choose Set.

## Numbering Pages in Headers and Footers

Page numbers are included in headers or footers by inserting a system variable, that is, a special code that produces the correct page number. To insert a numbering code, follow these steps:

1. Position the insertion cursor in the header or footer column where the number should display.
2. Choose Special, Variable. The dialog box shown here is displayed:

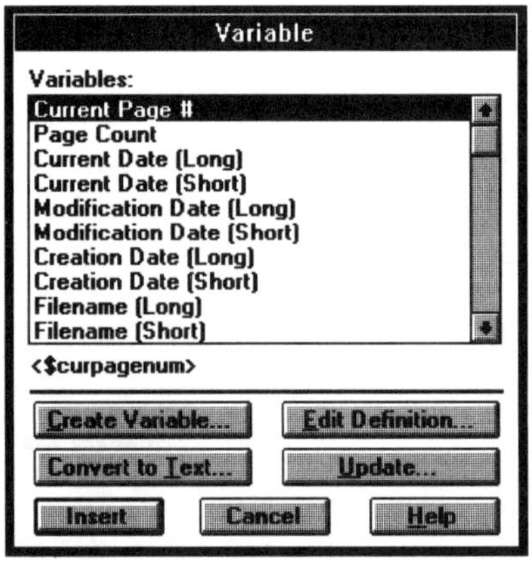


Notice that the variable selected in the scroll list, Current Page #, displays the code <$curpagenum> below the scroll list.

3. Select Current Page # from the scroll list.
4. Click the Insert button.

FrameMaker 4 uses Arabic numbers by default and numbers the first page as number one. To change either default, choose Format, Document to display this dialog box:

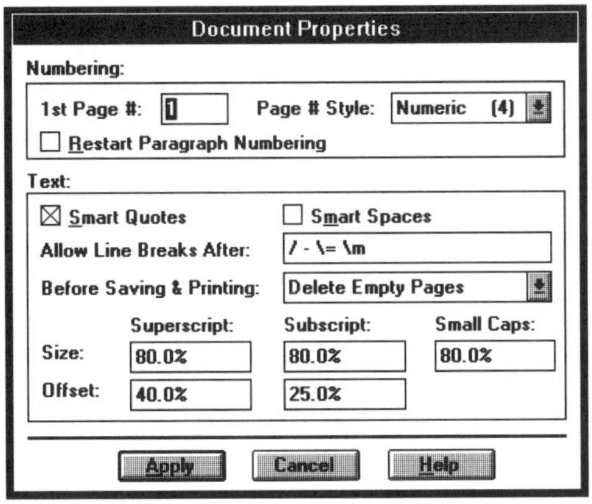


Enter the number for page one, if a number other than one is desired, and select a number style from these options:

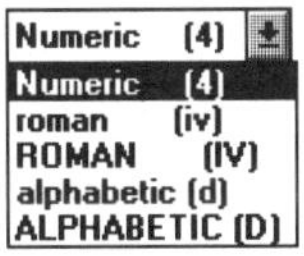


Then select Apply.

**NOTE:** *All body pages in a document use the same style of numbering; therefore, it is not possible to begin with pages i, ii, iii and then switch to 1, 2, 3, 4, and so on. Pages that must use different numbering styles must be contained in separate documents.*

## USING OTHER VARIABLES

You have already seen how the Current Page # variable is inserted in headers and footers, and you probably noticed that FrameMaker 4 also provides several other variables in the scroll list. What is not apparent from the list of variables is that two types of variables can be used—system variables and user-defined variables. User variables can be defined for any kind of variable information such as a product name, a price, or the name of a campaign or promotion.

## User-Defined Variables

User-defined variables are good for text that may change. For example, you may be producing a document about a testing method that has not been given an official name. You can create a variable for the name of the test, and then when the official name of the test is known, you can change the variable. FrameMaker 4 will then change the text of the variable in all locations. Of course, you could use the Find/Change command to accomplish the same thing, but inserting a variable involves less work.

To create a user-defined variable, follow these steps:

1. Click the cursor in a text column.
2. Choose Special, Variable.
3. Choose Create Variable.
4. Type the name of the variable (such as **test**, for example).
5. Enter the definition including any character formats (such as **<Emphasis>The Ticondaroga Testing Method**).
6. Choose Add.
7. Choose Done to close the first dialog box, and choose Done again to close the second dialog box.

The next time you want to insert a variable, the variable you have defined will be in the list with the system variables. When you insert the variable it will look like this: *The Ticondaroga Testing Method* because emphasis (italic) was included.

## System Variables

System variables include page numbers, page count, current date, modification date, creation date, filenames, running headers, and so on. Table 6-1 lists the system variable names and their codes, and Figure 6-7 shows how some of the most commonly used variables appear in a document.

| **Variable** | **Code** |
|---|---|
| Current Page # | <$curpagenum> |
| Page Count | <$lastpagenum> |
| Current Date (Long) | <$monthname> <$daynum> <$year> |
| Current Date (Short) | <$monthnum>/<$daynum>/<$shortyear> |
| Modification Date (Long) | <$monthname> <$daynum> <$year>, <$hour>:<$minute00> <$ampm> |
| Modification Date (Short) | <$monthnum>/<$daynum>/<$shortyear> |
| Creation Date (Long) | <$monthname> <$daynum> <$year> |
| Creation Date (Short) | <$monthnum>/<$daynum>/<$shortyear> |
| Filename (Long) | <$fullfilename> |
| Filename (Short) | <$filename> |
| Running H/F 1 | <$paratext {Title}> |
| Running H/F 2 | <$paratext {Heading]> |
| Running H/F 3 | <$marker1> |
| Running H/F 4 | <$marker2> |
| Table Continuation | (Continued) |
| Table Sheet | (Sheet <$tblsheetnum> of <$tblsheetcount>) |

**TABLE 6-1** *System Variables* ■

**FIGURE 6-7** *Commonly used system variables* ■

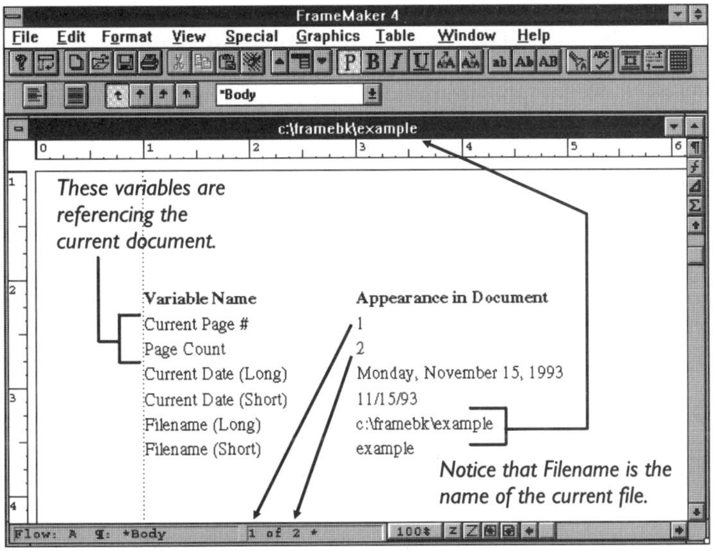

If you know the variable name, you can insert the variable using the keyboard shortcut outlined in these steps:

1. Position the insertion cursor in the desired text column.
2. Press CTRL+0 (zero). The status line displays **V:** to indicate that a variable name can be typed.
3. Begin typing the name of the variable. (You may have to type only a few letters before the complete name of the variable is displayed.)

   When a variable name is displayed, you can press the UP or DOWN ARROW keys to scroll the names on the status line.
4. Press ENTER.

## Changing Variables

Variables can be deleted, cut, copied, and pasted just like any other text. The only difference in the procedures is the way a variable is selected. Instead of dragging the cursor through the text of the variable, you can simply click the cursor anywhere in the variable and the complete variable will be highlighted.

Variables can also be modified. For example, you might want to change the Creation Date variable so it includes the text "Creation date:". To modify a variable, follow these steps:

1. Choose Special, Variable.
2. Select the variable you want to modify.
3. Choose Edit Definition.
4. Add the desired text in the definition box as shown here:

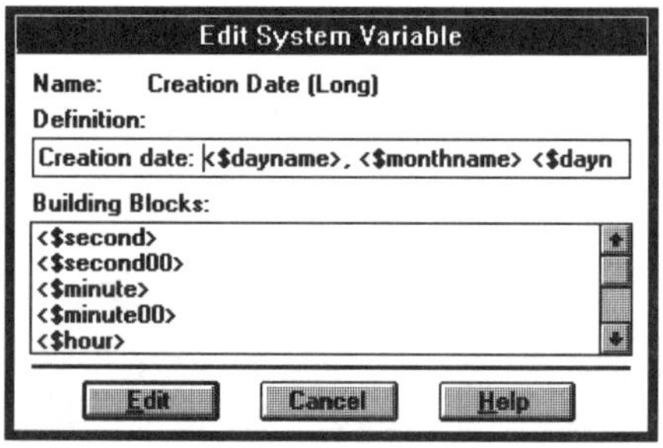

5. Add other variables from the Building Blocks list if desired.
6. Choose Edit when finished.
7. Click the Replace button.

When a variable is modified, all occurrences of the variable are updated in a document.

**NOTE:** *Some variables, like Current Page #, can only be placed in background columns if placed on master pages. Background columns are discussed in more detail in Chapter 8.*

### Converting Variables to Text

A variable that has been inserted in a document can be converted to regular text. You might want to do this if the variable should not act as a variable any longer. For example, if you have inserted the current date variable, you might want it to change to text so that the date stays the same each time you use the file instead of changing to the current date. By changing a variable to text, the text can be copied, deleted, and edited. Of course, the converted text will no longer be updated if the variable is modified.

To convert all variables or a specific variable to text, follow these steps:

1. Click the cursor in a text column or select a portion of text.
2. Choose Special, Variable.
3. Choose Convert to Text to display this dialog box:

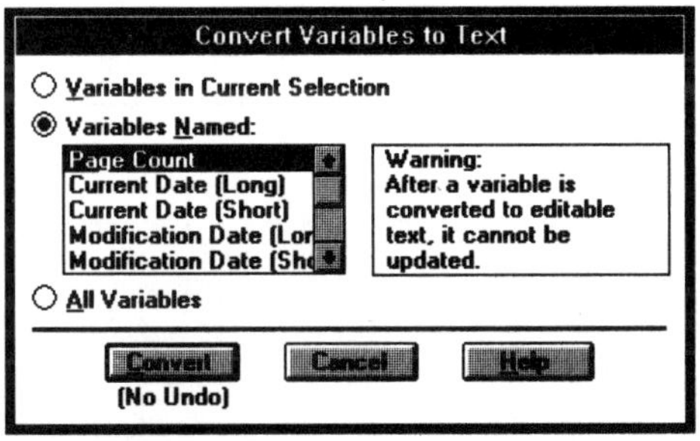


4. Choose Variables in Current Selection to convert all variables in the highlighted section—or—choose Variables Named and select a variable from the scroll list—or—choose All Variables.
5. Choose Convert.
6. Choose Done.

FLOW

When columns are defined in the Normal Page Layout dialog box, FrameMaker 4 assigns all the columns a flow tag of "A" and connects all columns so that data flows from the bottom of one column to the top of the next as shown in Figure 6-8. Different flows can be assigned to columns by first disconnecting the columns and then assigning new flow tags. Flow tags are usually assigned on master pages, but they can also be assigned on body pages.

### Disconnecting Flow and Assigning New Flow Tags

To disconnect a flow tag, follow these steps:

1. Select the column you want to disconnect by pressing CTRL while clicking on the column.
2. Select Format, Pages, Layout Commands.
3. Select Disconnect Current Column.
4. Select From Previous, From Next, or From Both. If the column is the last column in the flow, From Next and From Both are not valid selections. If the column is the first column in a flow, From Previous and From Both are not valid selections. Depending on your selections, you may get screen messages asking you to validate your choices.

**FIGURE 6-8** *Connected columns for flow tag A*

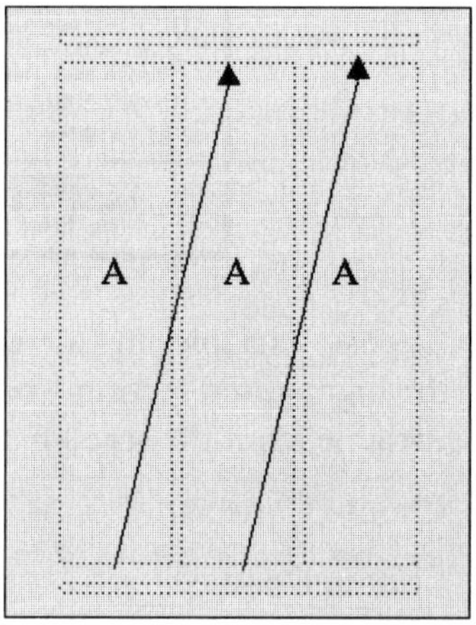

After disconnecting flow, new flow tags must be assigned to the disconnected columns. This can be accomplished with these steps:

1. Select the desired column with CTRL+click.
2. Choose Format, Flow, and the following dialog box is displayed:

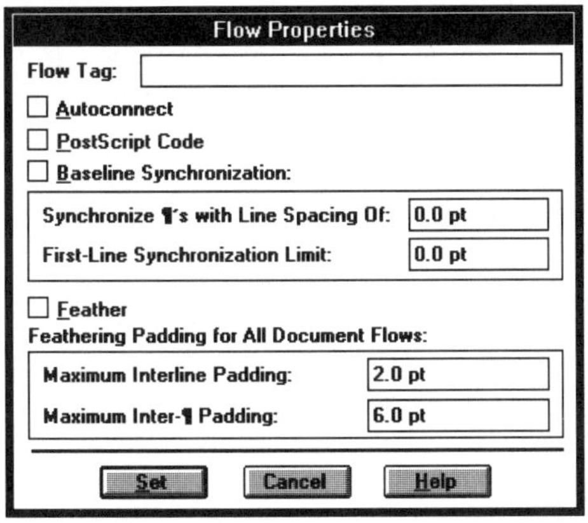


3. Type a flow tag, such as **B** or **C**.
4. Choose Set.

**NOTE:** *Disable the Autoconnect option if you do not want FrameMaker 4 to add a new page when a column overflows with text. This allows you to insert disconnected pages and determine the flow yourself.*

### Connecting Flow

Flow can be connected from one column to another column on the same master page and from any column on a body page to any column on a different body page. To connect flow, follow these steps:

1. Press CTRL+click to select the first column in the flow.
2. Press CTRL+SHIFT+click to select the second column in the flow.
3. Select Format, Pages, Layout Commands.
4. Choose Basic and then Connect Columns.

### Tracking Flow

If a flow becomes very complicated, you can see the flow by zooming out to 25 percent so you can see as many pages as possible. Then you can click in the desired flow and choose Edit, Select All in Flow.

Alternately you can move through the flow by clicking in the last line of the column and then pressing DOWN ARROW to move to the next column that is connected. Or you can click in the first line of a column and press the UP ARROW to go to the last line of the previous, connected column.

### Practicing with Flow

The subject of flow will become clear if you try this simple exercise using the training document called FOREST6 (located in maker4\training\maker):

1. Adjust the zoom to 80 percent.
2. Got to page two and then scroll down so you can see the top of page three as well as the bottom of page two.
3. Disconnect the left column on page three from both columns (before and after).
4. Give the left column on page three a flow tag of B.
5. Give the right column on page three a flow tag of A.
6. Give the left column on page two a flow tag of A.
7. Connect the right column on page two to the right column on page three.
8. Place the cursor at the bottom of the right column on page two and begin typing. You should see text flow to the right column of page three.

## CREATING TEMPLATES

A template is a file that is used to create another file. The template's page settings, paragraph settings, graphics, text, and so on, are used as a model for the new file. FrameMaker 4 provides many predefined templates for you in the maker4\template directory, which has five subdirectories—book, business, outlines, reports, and special. Each subdirectory has related types of templates. For example, the book subdirectory has templates called chapter, frontmat (front matter), index, and toc (table of contents). The business subdirectory has these templates: buscard, envelope, fax, letter, memo, viewtall, and viewwide.

**TIP:** *To see what the standard templates are, click the Explore Standard Templates button in the New dialog box.*

You are not limited to using the templates supplied by FrameMaker 4; you can create your own templates. In fact, you can use any file already in existence as a template. Just remember that everything in the file will be used in a new file, including all text. (Most templates do not have an abundance of text in them.)

To create a template from scratch, simply create a new file and make all the desired settings in the Normal Page Layout dialog box. Then create the master pages, including headers and footers and any repetitive graphics and text desired. Create paragraph formats, table formats, equations, and so on. When all the settings have been made, save the file just like any other file. It is not necessary to give the file a special name, but it may be helpful to store the file in one of the subdirectories in the template directory.

**HINT:** *Instead of creating a template from scratch, start with an existing template and modify it.*

## Using a Template to Create a Document

When you choose File, New, you will notice that one of the list boxes in the New dialog box, pictured in Figure 6-9, lists templates. When you choose a template file instead of Portrait, Landscape, or Custom, the new document will be based on the template. Of course you are not restricted to the settings in the template—you can modify the new document in any way you choose.

## Examples

A periodic newsletter is a perfect type of document with which to use a template. A newsletter typically has the same masthead every time, the same number of pages, the same mailing address panel, the same type and size of headlines, the same number of columns, and so on.

**FIGURE 6-9**

*The New dialog box*

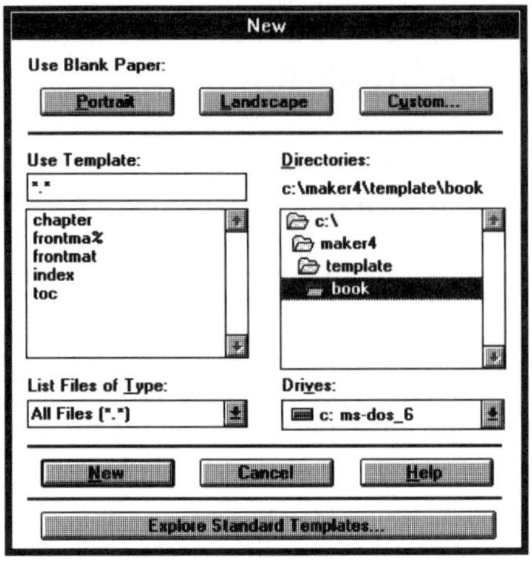


Something as simple as a letter printed on letterhead benefits from the use of a template. Such a template would have the necessary margins for the first page and the second page and would probably have the system variable Creation Date for the date of the letter.

## USING THE PAGE SETUP OF OTHER DOCUMENTS

At the beginning of this chapter you were told that page setup can be accomplished in FrameMaker 4 itself or in a word processing document that is opened in FrameMaker 4. In this chapter you have learned how to set up a page in FrameMaker 4 and you should be familiar with the settings involved in page setup. When you open a document that has been created in a word processing program or another program, such as Ventura Publisher, FrameMaker 4 accepts the page setup settings that have been set in the document. For example, if the document has a top and bottom margin of two inches, then those are the margins used in the FrameMaker 4 document. FrameMaker 4 also uses the paper size, the number of columns set up on the first page, and the headers and footers. Master pages are created automatically based on the page settings.

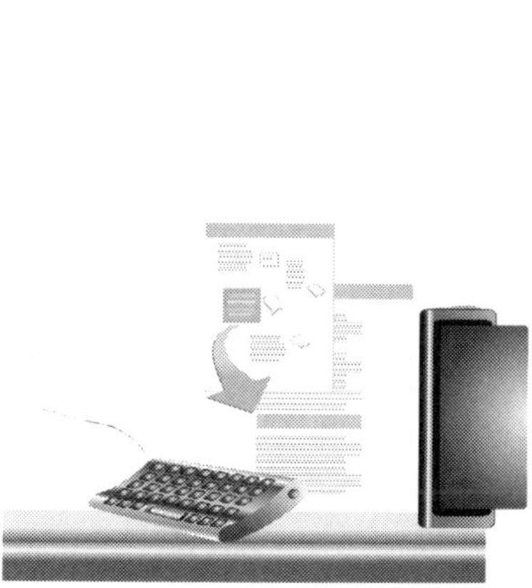

# 7

# Text Formatting

FORMATTING text may actually be the most time consuming part of desktop publishing. It involves all of the following:

- selection of a typeface
- selection of font sizes
- use of font styles
- alignment
- spacing
- tabs and indents
- column and page breaks
- hyphenation
- numbering and bulleting

In this chapter you will learn not only how to format text, but why specific format choices should be made.

As with page setup (discussed in Chapter 6), text formatting can be done in a FrameMaker 4 document or in a document that is created by another program and then opened in FrameMaker 4. Text that is formatted by another program generally needs some touch up when the document is opened in FrameMaker 4, but not as much touch up is needed for text formatting as for page setup. In this chapter, FrameMaker's paragraph and character formatting commands are discussed first so you can better understand the kind of formatting you can do in a document created by another program and opened in FrameMaker 4.

CHARACTER FORMATTING

The character formats include font, size, and style. Each feature is listed as an option on the Format menu. You can select the desired font, size, and style before you begin to type, or you can apply any of the three to text that is selected. FrameMaker 4 offers several methods of applying formatting to selected characters—you can use the menus, the Character Designer window, or the text editing icons on the QuickAccess bar.

## Choosing a Font from the Menu

When you select Format, Font, the list of available fonts is displayed like this:

The font that has a check mark beside it is the selected font.

**NOTE:** *If you have a large number of fonts installed, this menu may be too small to list them all. It is not a scrolling list. You would have to use the Paragraph Designer window, discussed later in this chapter, to access the desired font if it is not listed.*

When selecting a font, try not to loose sight of the fact that an effective document does two things—it attracts attention and conveys a message. Unwise font selections will accomplish the first purpose at the expense of the second.

In Chapter 3 two types of fonts were defined—body fonts, for use with long passages of text, and display fonts, for use with short passages and

*A study conducted on two sample layouts—one using sans serif type and one using serif type with the same point size body copy—showed that 2.5 times as many people comprehended the serif sample better. In the study 53 percent of the readers complained strongly that the sans serif type was hard to read.*

headlines. When selecting fonts, remember that body fonts are much easier to read than display fonts. Also remember that serif typefaces are preferred by readers and seem to be more legible than sans serif type. In fact 95.6 percent of all newspaper use serif type.

Try to select a font that conveys the right "feeling." This is not always easy for beginners. Selecting a font is like selecting an opera to attend. If you don't know anything about the music, the singers, the story, or the composer, you might select an opera to attend that doesn't conflict with Monday night football, or one that doesn't last too long, or one that has lavish costumes. Likewise, if you don't know anything about fonts, you might select the wrong one for the wrong reason.

*The following description of fonts is included to "educate" you on the subject.*

*Avant Garde Gothic is contemporary, crisp, and geometric.*

*Benguiat is more ornate than traditional styles, yet it is still highly readable. This font is often used when a distinctive capital letter is desired.*

*Bodoni was the first roman style typeface. Designed in the 18th century, it is still popular today. It's combination of thick stems and thin serifs makes it unique. Its weight makes it a little more difficult to read than Times Roman or Century Schoolbook.*

*Bombay is a script font that uses a heavier weight than most script fonts, making it an appropriate headline face.*

*Dorovar has a Middle East elegance.*

*Garamond is graceful and refined.*

*Goudy Old Style achieves a feeling of grace, elegance, and richness. It is very readable and is used equally well in large or small point sizes.*

*Helvetica is a good readable type used for a wide variety of printed material.*

*New Century Schoolbook is sturdy and easily legible—probably one of the perfect typefaces because it was extensively researched and systematically designed to be legible.*

*Optima is elegant, highly readable, and soothing to the eye.*

*Castle is often used to convey an Old English feeling. This font is the closest font to the one used by Gutenburg to produce the world's first printed document.*

*Palatino is considered elegant.*

*Ritz has a clean, art deco appearance.*

*Script fonts, including Zapf Chancery, Regency Script, Coventry Script, Brush Script, are designed to be continuous, that is, each lowercase letter flows into the next as if it were handwritten. Script fonts are formal and elegant and add flair to invitations, awards, and certificates, but are not legible when set in small sizes or all caps.*

*Souvenir is friendly, informal, and businesslike at the same time. Its rounded features soften the look without being overpowering and difficult to read.*

*Times Roman is as multifunctional as Helvetica.*

> ***Use the following guidelines for selecting font sizes:***
>
> ***Body copy*** *is usually 8 to 12 points, with 10 points being the most commonly used. Type that is set in 8 points is on the edge of being too small to read, especially by older readers.*
>
> ***Subheads*** *can be the same size as the body copy or several points larger than the body copy.*
>
> ***Main heads*** *are usually in the range of 14 to 20 points. Research tells us that larger heads attract more readers, but headlines above 36 points do not attract proportionally more readers. Research also shows that there is no difference in legibility in type sizes from 14 to 30 points.*
>
> ***Titles*** *(such as used on a cover page) are usually 24 to 48 points.*
>
> ***Captions, headers, and footers*** *are usually the same size as the body copy.*
>
> ***Page numbers*** *are usually 2 to 4 points larger than body copy.*

## Choosing a Font Size from the Menu

The font sizes are displayed by selecting Format, Size.

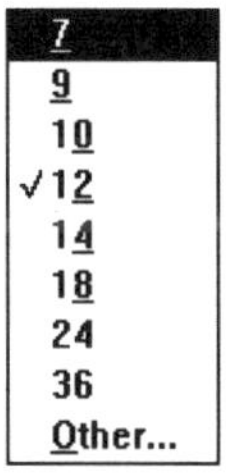


Again, the size with the check mark is the selected size. The list of font sizes displayed is not complete. Since fonts can be scaled from 2 points to 400 points by the Windows font program, it is not possible to list all the sizes. The Other option displays this dialog box so you can enter the desired point size. Notice that you can specify two decimal places.

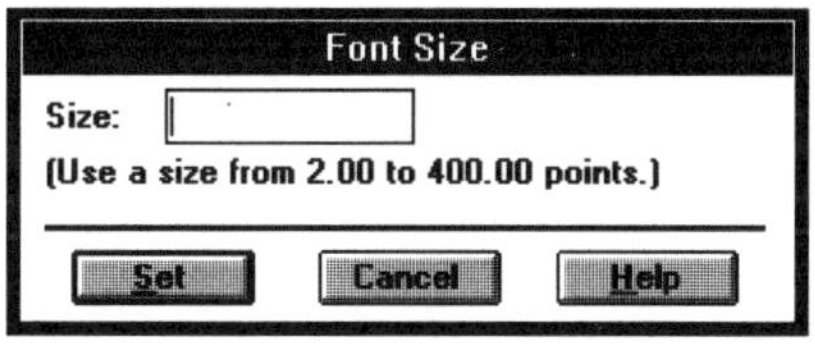


## Choosing a Style from the Menu

The Format, Style option displays this list of styles:

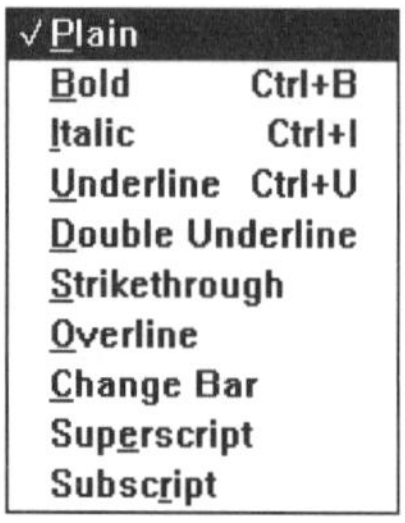


You may want to look back at the examples of styles given in Chapter 3 if you are unfamiliar with any of the styles in the list. The style that is checked is the current style.

## Using the Character Designer

It is more efficient to use the Character Designer window than the menus if you want to apply several formatting characteristics to text. To use the Character Designer window, first position the cursor or select the desired text. Then choose Format, Characters, Designer. The window looks like this:

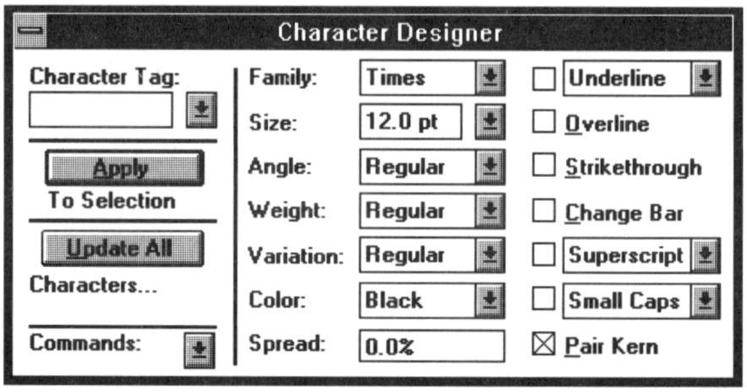


The Family option allows you to select a font; the Size option allows you to specify a size; the Angle option includes italic, regular, and as is; the Weight option includes Bold, Regular, and as is. All of these options have corresponding menu selections.

The Variation, Color, and Spread options do not have menu equivalents. The Variation option allows you to select a variation of a font if it has one. For example, you may have Helvetica as a font and Condensed or Narrow as a variation. The Color option allows you to specify a color for the character, and the Spread option increases or decreases the space between characters.

*Avoid using bold or italic in large blocks of text. Italic type is read up to 20 words per minute slower than regular type. Bold print set in 9 points or smaller begins to blur the letters because of the excess ink, especially if printed on newsprint or other porous paper.*

Except for Small Caps and Pair Kern, all the options in the third column of the window also have menu equivalents. The Small Caps option uses all uppercase letters in a smaller font so the letters do not stand out from the surrounding text so much. The Pair Kern option decreases the space between selected pairs of letters. It also turns on ligatures (letters that are connected if they occur together like "fl" and "fi" for example) if ligatures are defined in the selected font. (Not all font manufacturers create ligatures for fonts.)

After all options are set in the window, choose Apply and close the window. If you display the Character Designer window and decide that you do not want to make changes, simply close the window. If you change your mind about the settings you have made before you select Apply, you can select the previous settings again or click the Commands list box and select Reset Window from Selection. This will change all the options in the Character Designer window to the options of the selection.

## Using the QuickAccess Bar

To display the text editing icons on the QuickAccess Bar, click the up or down arrow icon in the middle of the bar until these icons are displayed on the right side of the bar:

The first four icons change the style of the text to plain, bold, italic, and underline. The next two icons increase or decrease the size of the font by 1 point increments. The next three icons change the capitalization to lowercase, initial capital, and uppercase.

When using the icons to format text, you generally select the text and then click the desired icons to apply the format. In the case of plain, bold, italic, and underline, however, you can click the desired icon, begin typing, and the text will have the desired style. You can choose any combination of bold, italic, and underline before you start typing.

## Character Tags

A character tag is a name that is given to a particular group of character formats for the purpose of applying to selected text. FrameMaker 4 supplies three character tags—Default ¶ font, Emphasis, and EquationVariables. You can modify these character tags or create your own.

Character tags are stored in a Character Catalog as shown here:

This catalog can be displayed by clicking the button in the right border that has a script "f."

### *Applying a Character Tag*

To apply a character tag, select the text and click the desired tag in the Character Catalog or choose Format, Characters, and select the tag from the list.

### *Creating a Character Tag*

To create your own character tag, choose Format, Characters, Designer. Make the desired settings and choose Commands, New Format. Type a name for the tag in the Tag box, choose Store In Catalog and Apply to Selection if desired. Choose Create. Close the Character Designer window if finished.

### *Deleting a Character Tag*

The easiest way to delete a character tag is to click the Delete button in the Character Catalog, select the tag, click Delete again and then click Done. Tags can also be deleted from the Character Designer window by choosing Commands, Delete Format. When the Delete Formats from Catalog dialog box displays, select the tag, click the Delete button and then click Done.

## FORMATTING PARAGRAPHS

In DTP programs, paragraphs are not defined in the "traditional" sense; that is, a paragraph is not a group of related sentences with a topic sentence and so on. A paragraph is created by pressing the Enter key; therefore, a paragraph can be a blank line, a heading, or a group of lines.

Paragraph formats include alignment, spacing, tabs, indents, fonts, column and page breaks, hyphenation, and numbering. Some or all of these characteristics can be applied from the menus, the Paragraph Designer window, or the formatting bar. Later in this chapter you will also learn how paragraph formats are defined and applied as a "tag."

## Alignment

FrameMaker 4 has four paragraph alignments—left aligned, right aligned, centered, and justified. As discussed in Chapter 3, left aligned text is the easiest to read.

To set the alignment of a single paragraph, simply click the cursor anywhere in the paragraph and click the Alignment icon in the formatting bar to display this pop-up menu:

To set the alignment of several paragraphs, select all the paragraphs first, and then click the Alignment icon and choose an alignment.

To set the alignment using the Paragraph Designer window, click in the desired paragraph or highlight several paragraphs, and choose Format, Paragraphs, Designer to display this window:

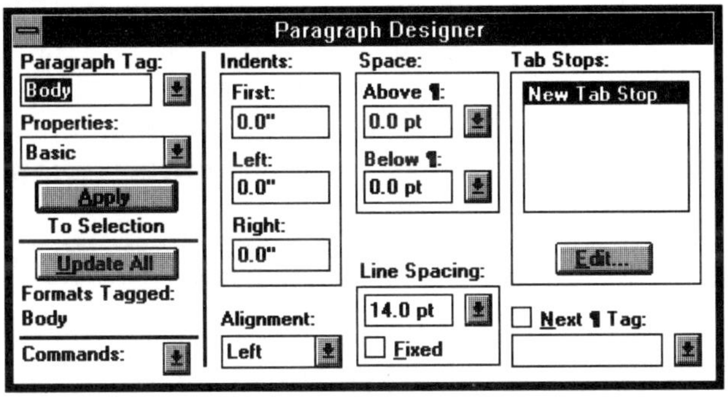


Click the list box arrow for Alignment, choose the desired alignment, and click the Apply button. When finished, close the window.

> *Research studies have found that when we read, our eyes move in "saccadic" jumps, focusing on a small group of words for about a quarter of a second, then moving to the next group. At the end of a line the eye must track to the beginning of the next line. Ragged left text is harder to read because there is no fixed point at the beginning of a line. There is also some argument that justified text (especially serif fonts) is more difficult to read than ragged right because the extra spacing in the line interrupts the eye's natural saccadic jumps.*

## Spacing

Paragraph spacing includes the space above and below a paragraph as well as the space between the lines in a paragraph. You can set the spacing between lines and between paragraphs with the Spacing icon in the formatting bar or with the Paragraph Designer window.

When you click the Spacing icon this menu pops up:

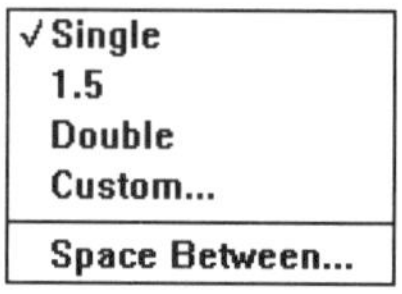


The first four options (Single, 1.5, Double, and Custom) set the spacing between lines. The last option, Space Between, sets the spacing between two selected paragraphs. In Chapter 3 line spacing is referred to as "leading." FrameMaker 4 has dropped this term, but the concept remains. When you choose single spacing or double spacing the leading amount is computed automatically by FrameMaker 4 based on the point size of the font being used. The amount of leading is displayed as "Line Spacing" in the Paragraph Designer window. If you are using a 10 point font with "single spacing," FrameMaker 4 uses a leading value of 12 points.

When you set a spacing increment between lines, FrameMaker 4 automatically adds this increment before and after the paragraph. This means that a paragraph which has one blank line between each line in the paragraph will also have one blank line after the paragraph as well. This space must be taken into consideration when adding additional space above or below the paragraph. For example, if two consecutive, double-spaced paragraphs are selected, and you then select Space Between, this dialog box is displayed with None selected:

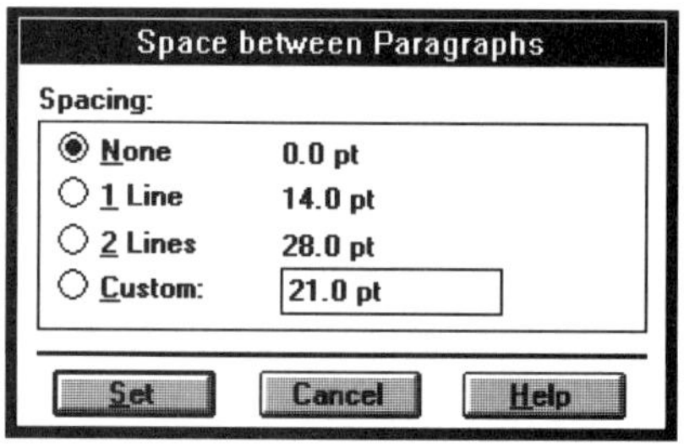


*The most commonly used leading for 10 point type is 11 and 12. Research shows that avid readers prefer 10 on 12 and less practiced readers prefer 10 on 13.*

This seems to indicate that there is no space between the paragraphs, when in reality there is one line between them due to the double space setting for the line spacing. If you want two lines of spacing between the paragraphs, you should choose 1 Line, not 2 Lines. If you want no space between paragraphs (in this example) you must choose Custom and indicate a negative value (equal to half the point size listed for 1 line) as shown here:

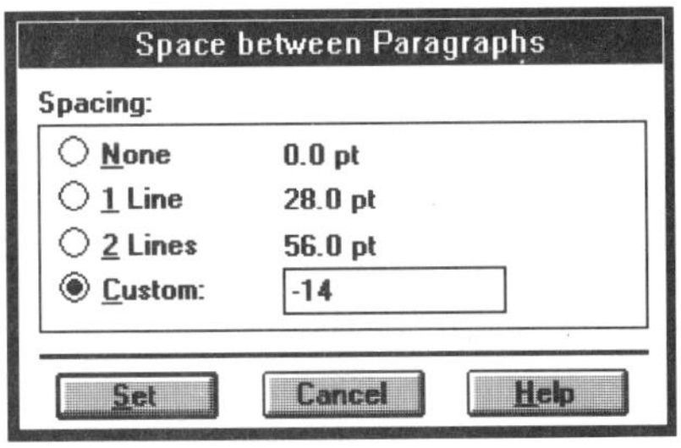


Of course, if the line spacing is set on single, there is no line added after the paragraph. Therefore, you would choose 1 Line to get one line between paragraphs and 2 Lines to get two lines between paragraphs.

To set line spacing in the Paragraph Designer window, choose Format, Paragraphs, Designer. This window is displayed:

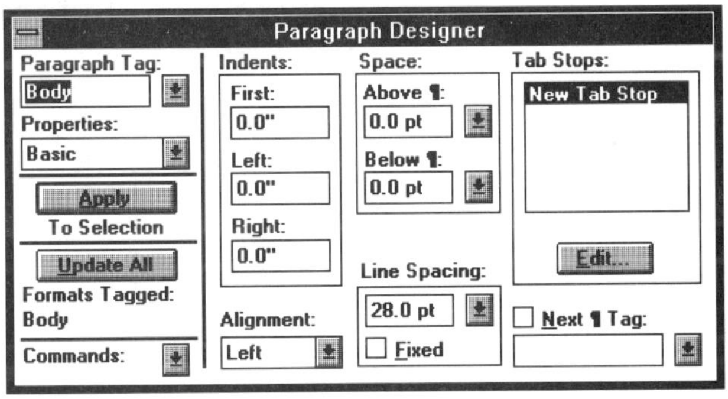


You can enter the Space Above, the Space Below, and the Line Spacing in this window. Select Apply and close the window.

## Setting Tabs

Tabs and indents can be set in the Paragraph Designer box or by using the formatting bar and the ruler itself. The formatting bar has four types of tab stops as shown here:

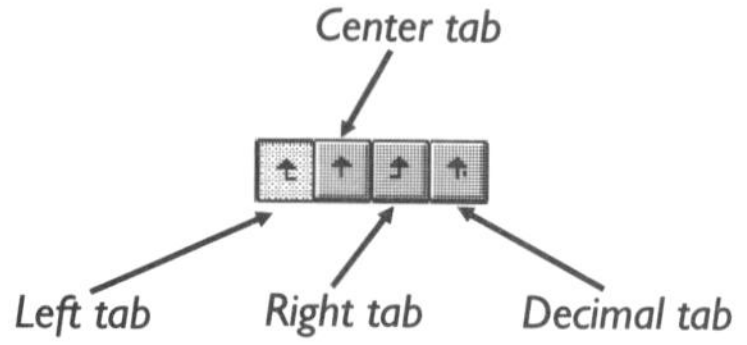


The left tab aligns text on the left; the center tab centers text on the tab stop, the right tab aligns text on the right, and the decimal tab aligns text on a decimal point.

Whether you are setting a tab with the ruler or with the Paragraph Designer window, you must click the cursor in the desired paragraph or select all the paragraphs to which you want the tabs to apply. To set a tab with the formatting bar, simply drag the desired tab to the desired location on the ruler.

**TIP:** *Tabs will snap to the ruler markings if you have Snap selected on the Graphics menu.*

To set tabs in the Paragraph Designer window, choose Format, Paragraphs, Designer, and choose Edit to display this dialog box:

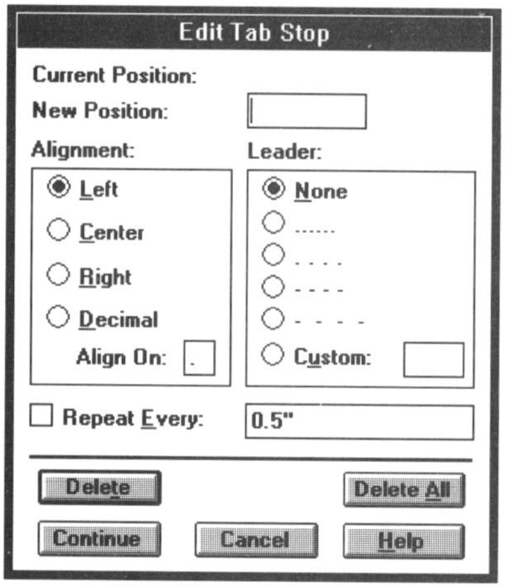


The cursor will be flashing in the New Position box where you can enter the desired position on the ruler. The number that you enter in this box will be added to the left margin, so if you have a left margin of one inch and you enter "2" in this box, the tab will be set on 3" on the ruler. Next select an alignment and a leader if desired. Leaders are dots or dashes (or any custom character that you want to use) displayed between the tab stop and the text like this:

Chapter 1. . . . . . . . . . . . .6
Chapter 2. . . . . . . . . . . . .7

Select Continue to set the tab. Add additional tabs by choosing Edit for each tab. When all tabs have been set, choose Apply and close the window if desired.

Tabs can be repositioned by dragging them to a new position on the ruler with the mouse. Tabs can also be deleted by dragging them off the ruler. To delete a tab with the Paragraph Designer window, select the tab in the Tab Stops list and choose Edit, then Delete.

## Setting Indents

FrameMaker 4 has three kinds of indents—a left indent, a first line indent, and a right indent. The indention locations are marked on the ruler with triangles like this:

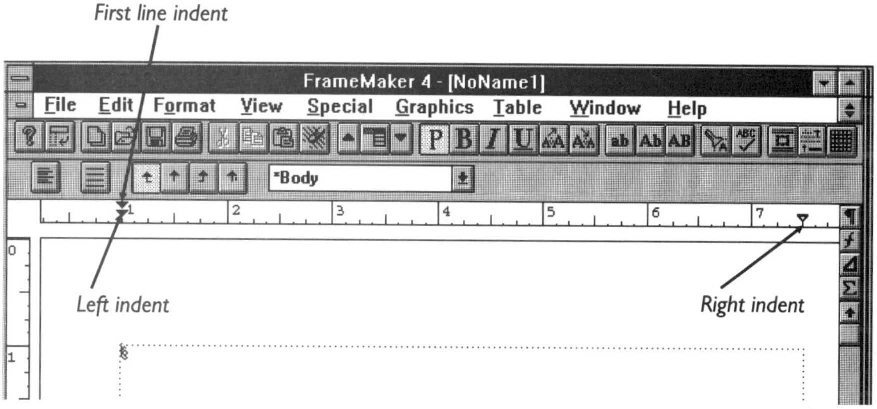


Notice that two triangles are set on the 1" mark where the left margin is set. The triangle on the top is the first line indent symbol and the triangle on the bottom is the left indent symbol. When these two symbols are lined up on the same mark, all lines in the paragraph are indented the same amount. The triangle on the 7.5" mark is the right indent mark. By default it is aligned with the right margin.

Like tab stops, indents can be moved in the ruler with the mouse or they can be set in the Paragraph Designer window. To change the location of indents in the Paragraph Designer window, choose Format, Paragraphs, Designer. Type the precise measurements in the First, Left, and Right boxes under Indents. The measurement entered in the First and Left boxes is the distance from the left margin to the indent. The measurement entered in the Right box is the distance from the right indent to the right margin. After entering the desired measurements, choose Apply and close the window if desired.

Study the text in the following illustrations to see how the indents work:

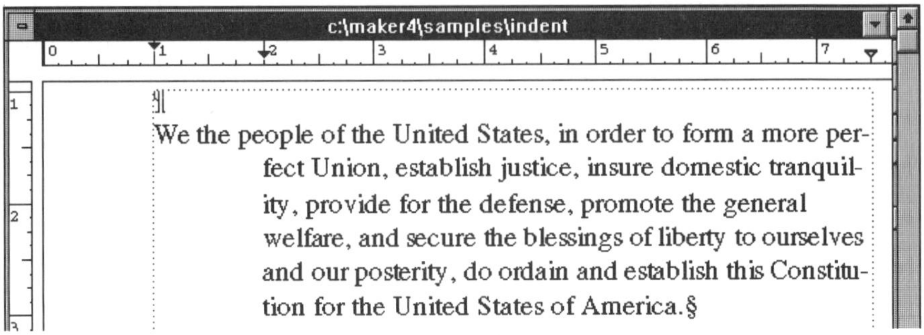


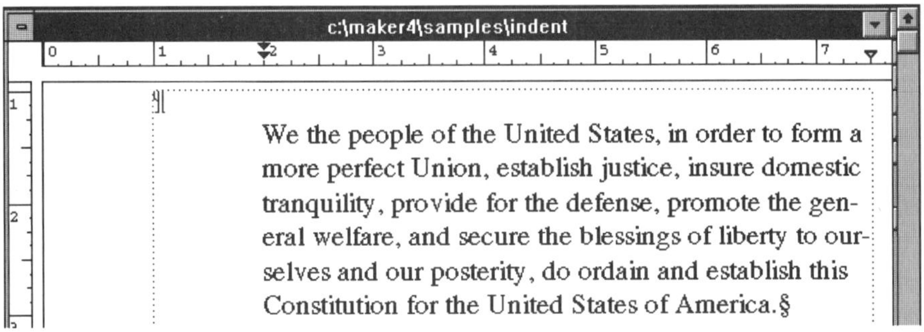


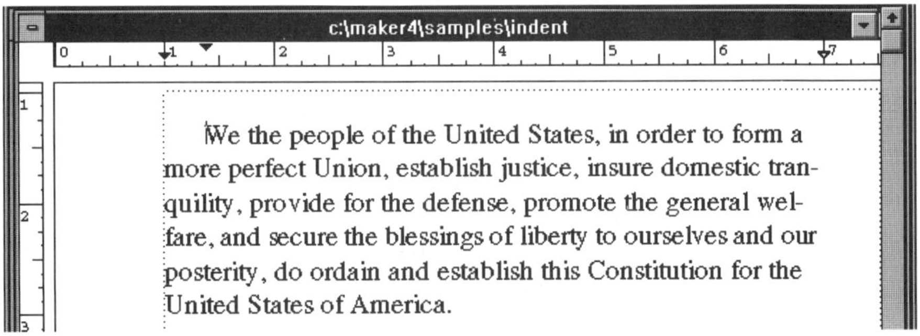

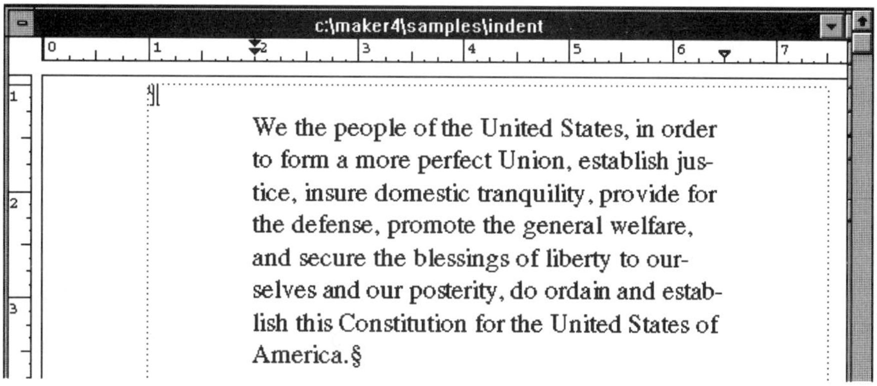


Paragraphs in body copy should be indented at least one pica, or for purists, one em space (the point size of the font). Flush paragraphs may look cleaner to a designer, but studies show that reading speed is increased 7 percent if paragraphs are indented.

## Setting a Hanging Indent

A hanging indent, shown here, is created by setting a tab at the same location as the left indent.

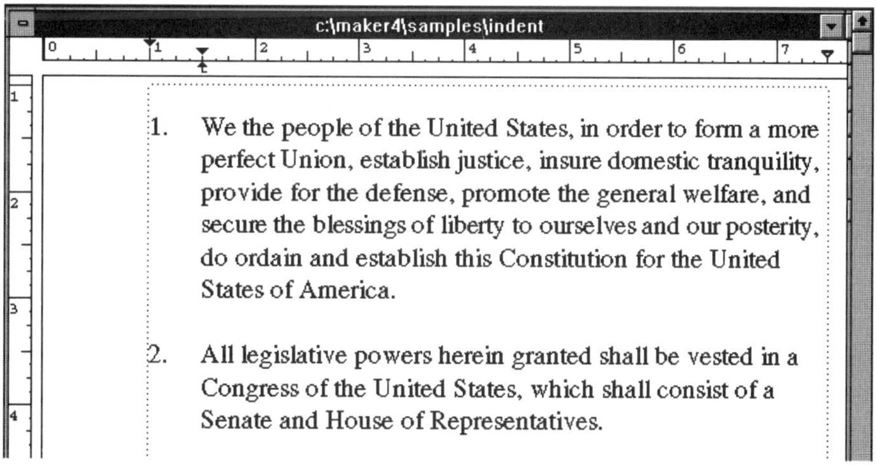


In this example, the numbers are typed on the left margin and a tab moves the text on the first line to the position where subsequent lines will be wrapped automatically by the left indent.

## Setting Fonts

The character formats for a paragraph can be set in the Paragraph Designer window. You may have noticed the Properties box in the Paragraph Designer window. The Basic properties (indents, alignment, space, line spacing, tab stops) are displayed by default. Other properties include Default Font, Pagination, Numbering, Advanced, and Table Cell. The Default font selections look like this:

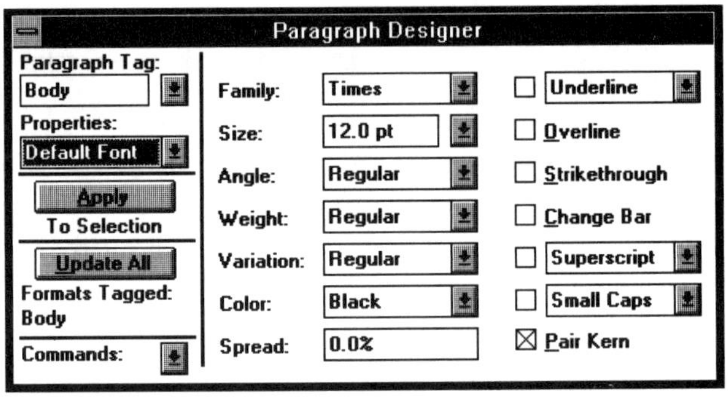


After setting all the font options, choose Apply.

## Setting Column and Page Breaks

To determine whether a paragraph will start anywhere, at the top of the next column, at the top of the next page, or at the top of the next left or right page, choose Format, Page Break to display this dialog box:

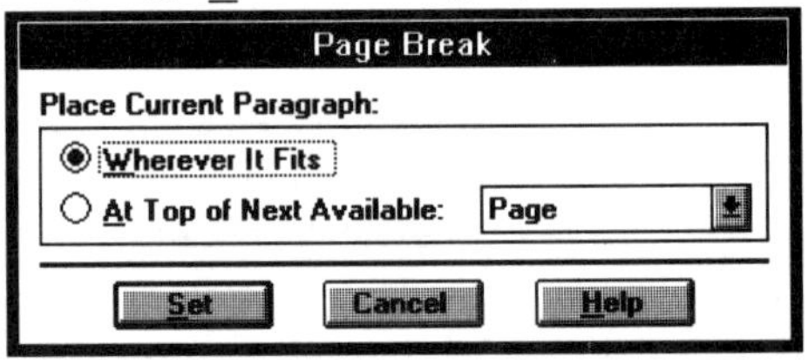


If you want the paragraph to make a column or page break, choose At Top of Next Available, and then click the list box arrow and choose Column, Page, Left Page, or Right Page. Then choose Set. You can also accomplish a break by choosing Format, Paragraphs, Designer, clicking the Properties list box arrow, and choosing Pagination. The settings look like this:

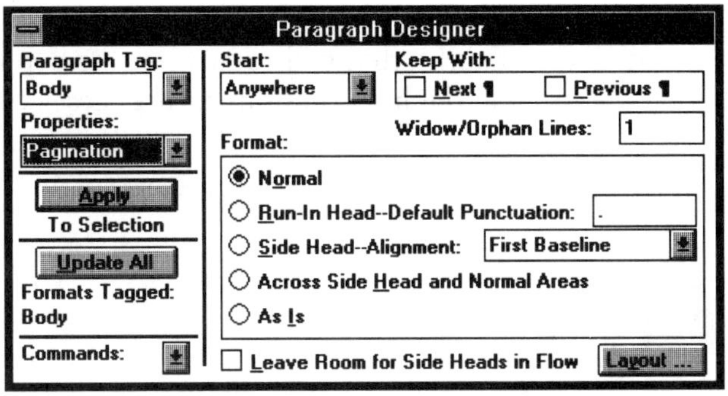

Choose an option from the Start list box as shown here and choose Apply.

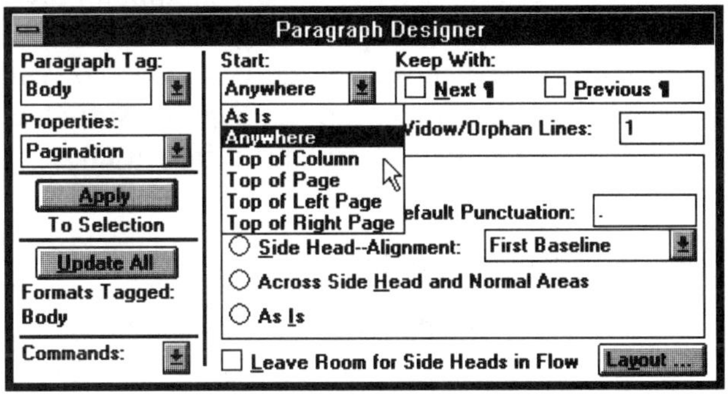

## Hyphenation

By default all FrameMaker 4 tags have hyphenation turned on and will hyphenate no more than two adjacent lines. To make hyphenation settings, display the Paragraph Designer window and choose the Advanced property in the Properties list box. The options look like this:

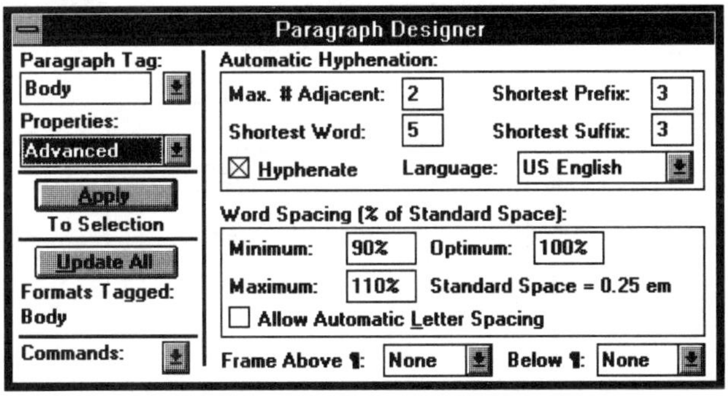

Notice that you can set the following options: the maximum number of adjacent hyphenated lines, the number of characters for the shortest word that will be hyphenated, the shortest prefix that can precede the hyphen, and the shortest suffix that will come after the hyphen.

To disable the hyphenation feature, deselect Hyphenate. When finished with settings, choose Apply and close the window if desired.

## PARAGRAPH TAGS

A group of settings can be assigned to a name, called a "tag." When a tag is assigned to a paragraph, all the settings of the tag take effect automatically, thus providing the easiest method of formatting. FrameMaker 4 provides several tags for you. You can modify these tags or create your own tags if you choose. Tags are stored with individual documents, so different documents can have different tags.

### Applying a Paragraph Tag

Tags can be applied to selected paragraphs by choosing a tag name from the Format-Paragraphs menu, from the tag list box in the formatting bar, or from a window called the ¶ Catalog. Figure 7-1 shows both the ¶ Catalog window and the list in the formatting bar.

**FIGURE 7-1**

*The Paragraph Catalog and the Tag List*

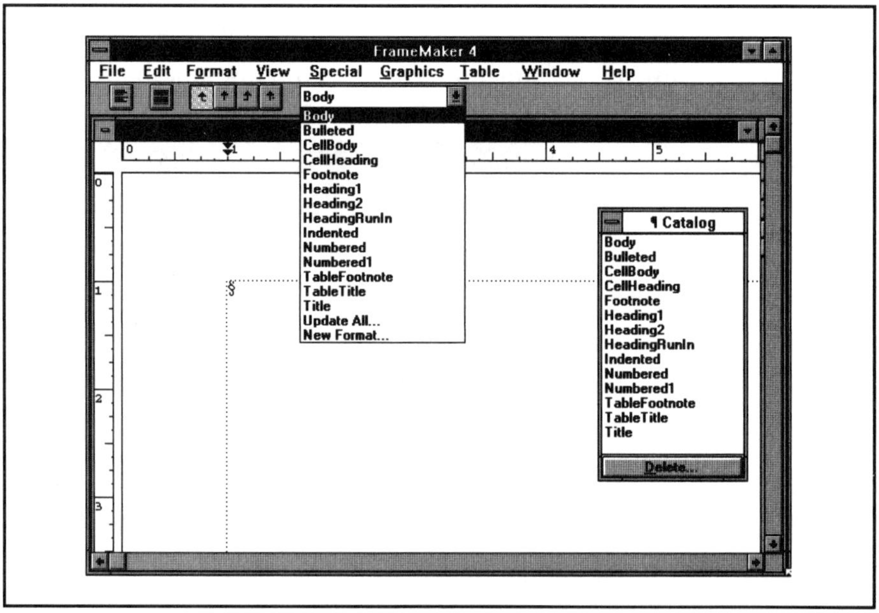

To display the ¶ Catalog window, choose Format, Paragraphs, Catalog or simply click the button with the paragraph symbol (¶) on the right border.

## Creating a Paragraph Tag

To create a new tag, choose Format, Paragraphs, Designer. Make changes to all properties as desired. Choose Commands, New Format to display this dialog box:

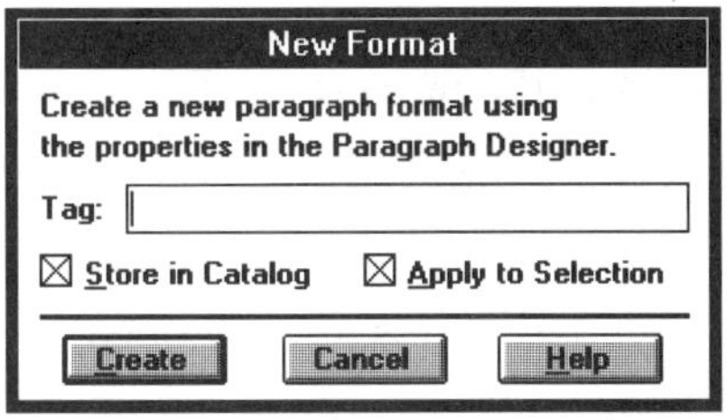


Enter the name of the tag, choose Store in Catalog and Apply to Selection if desired, and then select Create.

To create a tag that copies the attributes of an existing paragraph, select the paragraph then display the Paragraph Designer window. Make no changes to the properties and choose Commands, New Format. Enter the name of the tag, choose Store in Catalog and Apply to Selection if desired, and then select Create. Close the designer window if desired.

## Modifying a Paragraph Tag

To modify tags that already exist, choose Format, Paragraphs, Designer and then select the desired tag from the Paragraph Tag list. Make changes as desired and select Update All. FrameMaker 4 changes the characteristics of the tag and applies the new settings to all paragraphs that have the tag name.

**NOTE:** *Sometimes you may not want to apply the new settings to all paragraphs with the tag name. In this case you can choose Apply, and the changes will be made to the selected paragraphs only.*

## Deleting a Paragraph Tag

To delete a tag, click the Delete button in the Paragraph Catalog window. Choose the tag to delete and select Delete. Other tags may be deleted if desired. When finished, choose Done. When a tag is deleted, the paragraphs that were tagged with the deleted tag still reflect the name of the tag and its formats. Deleting a tag from the catalog does not change paragraphs that use the tag in any way.

### Copying Tags to Other Documents

Since all tags are stored with the documents where they were created or modified, you might want to copy a format from one document to another. To copy a format and add it to the paragraph catalog, follow these steps:

1. Select the paragraph that has the format you want to copy.
2. Choose Edit, Copy Special, Paragraph Format.
3. Open the document you want to copy the format to (or go to the window if it is already open).
4. Select a paragraph that should use the copied format.
5. Choose Edit, Paste.
6. With the same paragraph selected, display the Paragraph Designer window.
7. Choose Commands, New Format.
8. Choose Store in Catalog.
9. Choose Create.
10. Close the Paragraph Designer window, if desired.

### Tags that Are Not Stored

Tags that are created and not stored in the paragraph catalog can be copied to other paragraphs in the same or a different document. Because they are not stored in the paragraph catalog, though, they cannot be modified or updated.

**NOTE:** *Deleting a tag has the same effect as creating a tag without storing it in the catalog.*

### Format Overrides

When the formatting options of a paragraph have been changed, the paragraph is said to have a "format override." Paragraphs that have overrides are denoted with an asterisk in front of the tag name in the tag list box in the formatting line and on the status line.

## MORE ABOUT USING DESIGNER WINDOWS

You have seen two designer windows in this chapter, the Character Designer and the Paragraph Designer. One other designer window, the Table Designer, is discussed in Chapter 10, *Creating Tables*. By now you have undoubtedly seen that it is more efficient to use designer windows if you want to apply several formatting characteristics to selected text or paragraphs.

Additionally you should be aware of the fact that these windows can be moved just like any other window, but, unfortunately, they cannot be resized. By moving a window you may be able to see the setting that you have applied take effect in the text.

It is not necessary to close a window immediately when you are finished with it. In fact, all three designer windows can be open at once as shown in Figure 7-2. You might want to keep a designer window open for other tasks. When you click the cursor in the document window, the designer window becomes inactive. You can then select different text or paragraphs to format and return to the designer window to make the settings and apply them.

**FIGURE 7-2** *All designer windows open*

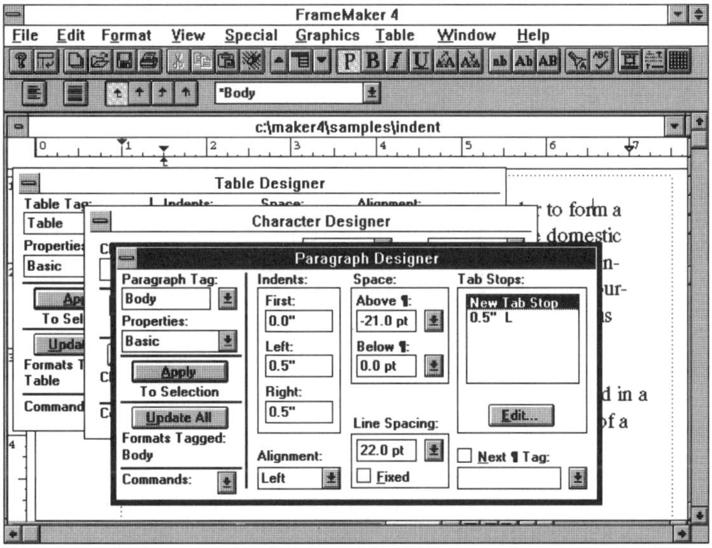

All designer windows have a Commands pop-up menu with these options:

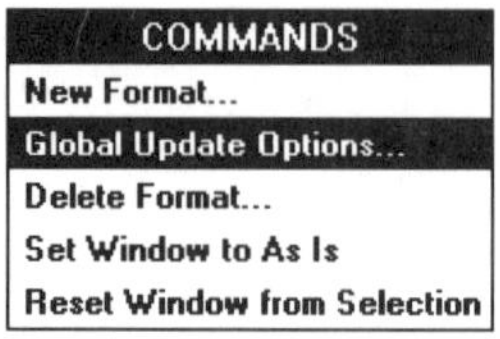


The New Format command is used to create a new character format or a new paragraph tag. The Global Update Options specify which properties you want to update if you are retagging paragraphs or changing character formats. The Delete Format deletes a character format or a paragraph tag. The Set Window to As Is command changes all properties to As Is. The Reset Window from Selection command changes all the properties so they match the selected text or paragraph.

## FORMATTING NUMBERED AND BULLETED LISTS

Automatic numbering or bulleting of paragraphs is set up as an option in the Paragraph Designer window, but FrameMaker provides standard paragraph tags for these features. (The tags are called Bulleted and Numbered.) You can create your own tags for numbering and bullets or modify the standard tags. The Paragraph Designer window for the Bulleted tag looks like this when the Numbering properties are displayed:

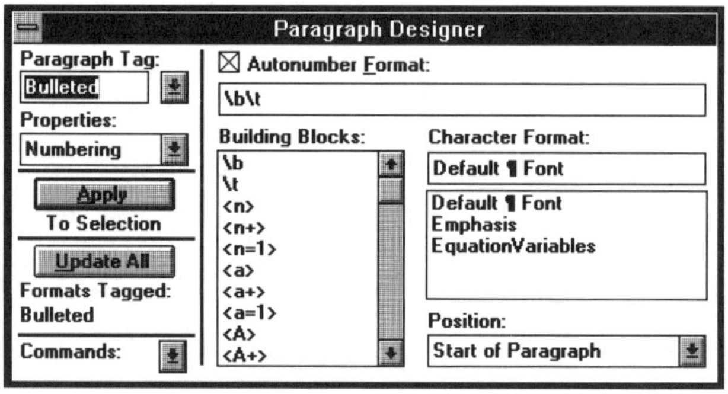


Notice that Autonumber Format is selected and codes are entered in the box below.

The codes \b\t stand for bullet and tab, meaning that the paragraph will begin with a bullet character followed by a tab. If you want the paragraph

*The Building Blocks for autonumbering include "n" for numbers, "a" and "A" for lowercase and uppercase letters, and "r" and "R" for lowercase and uppercase Roman numerals.*

to be indented, you can use the codes \t\b\t. Naturally you must set an appropriate number of tabs in the ruler and set the left indent even with the second tab as shown in Figure 7-3.

The Numbered tag has these codes in the Numbering properties:

<n+>.\t

The code <n+> starts numbering with the number 1 and adds 1 to each paragraph. The period is added as punctuation, followed by a tab.

## PREPARING TEXT IN ANOTHER PROGRAM

FrameMaker 4 can read the following types of files: Ami Pro, DCA/RFT, several versions of Displaywrite, MIF, MML, several versions of MS Word

**FIGURE 7-3** *A bulleted list indented with one tab stop*

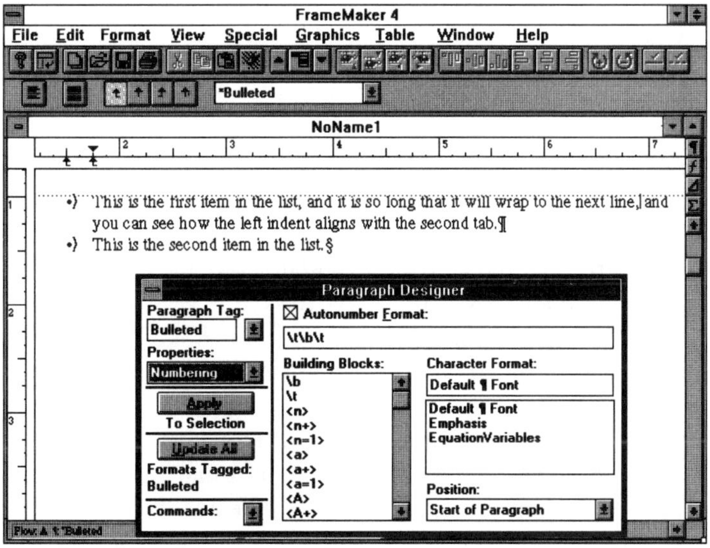

(for DOS, Windows, and Mac), MSI, RTF, Text, several versions of Ventura Publisher, and several versions of WordPerfect (DOS and Mac). Most users do not prepare a file in Ventura Publisher specifically for use with FrameMaker 4, so we will limit our discussion in this section to preparing a file in a word processing program.

When typing a document in a word processing program, you will have less touch up work to do in FrameMaker 4 if you follow these simple rules:

- Do not use an extra Return to skip lines between paragraphs. Use the Space Before and the Space After paragraph formats in FrameMaker 4 to add space between paragraphs.
- Do not use the SPACEBAR to indent paragraphs or line up columns of text. Set tab stops and use the TAB key.
- Do not type two spaces after a sentence.
- Use ANSI codes to enter non-keyboard characters like the Registered Trademark (™) or Copyright (©) symbols. To enter an ANSI code, press ALT and type the number with the number pad keys. For example, to enter the Copyright symbol, press ALT and type 0169. The ANSI codes are listed in the FrameMaker 4 *Quick Reference.*
- Do not substitute letters for numbers; that is, do not use a lowercase "L" for the number one or an uppercase "O" for a zero. Characters and numbers have different appearances and proportional widths.
- Do not choose a font that is incompatible with the fonts you will use in FrameMaker 4.
- Do not use asterisks or lowercase "o" for bullets. Add bullets in the document in FrameMaker 4.

## Using MML

If you are using a word processing program that FrameMaker 4 cannot read, and the program will not save files in another format that FrameMaker 4 can read, you may have to save all your files in ASCII format. (FrameMaker uses the "Text" filter to open an ASCII file.) Unfortunately, ASCII files do not have embedded formatting codes for bold, italic, font style, and so on. All of these formatting characteristics will have to added after the file is opened in FrameMaker 4. However, you can enter special codes that FrameMaker 4 will convert to formatting if you know how to use the Maker Markup Language (MML). The MML is a set of codes and rules for using the codes, i.e. the syntax.

**NOTE:** *Although the MML is part of the program, the documentation is shipped by request and is not included in the standard documentation.*

# IV

## Using Graphics and Color

# 8

# Using Graphic Tools

In this chapter you can learn to use the drawing tools by producing the robotic hand shown in Figure 8-1. Step-by-step instructions will lead you through a fairly complex drawing using all the drawing tools on the palette. This hands-on exercise will teach you to use the drawing tools in a way that reading about them never could.

## GETTING STARTED

Before starting the drawing exercise, however, you need some background information. The graphic tools, shown in Figure 8-2, are displayed

**FIGURE 8-1** *A technical drawing produced with FrameMaker 4*

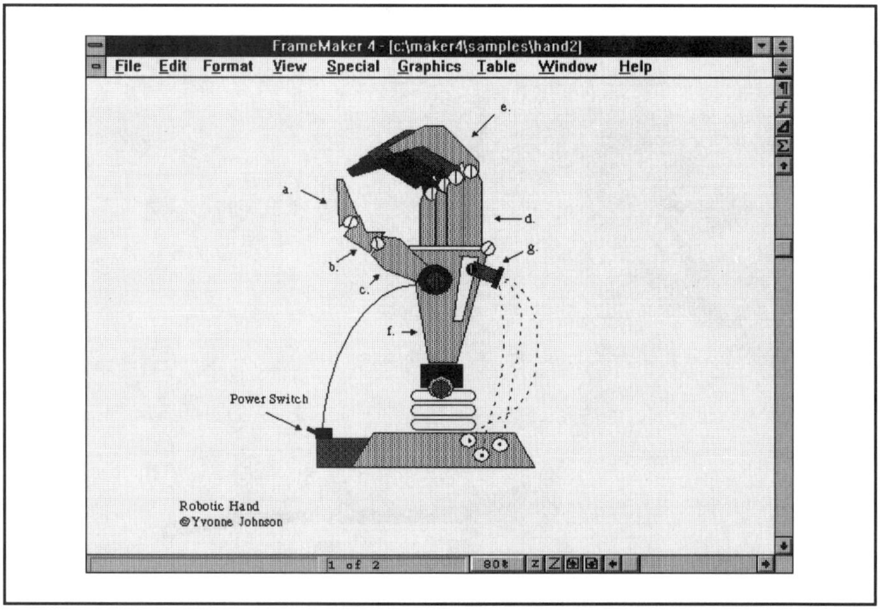

FIGURE 8-2

The Graphics Tools palette

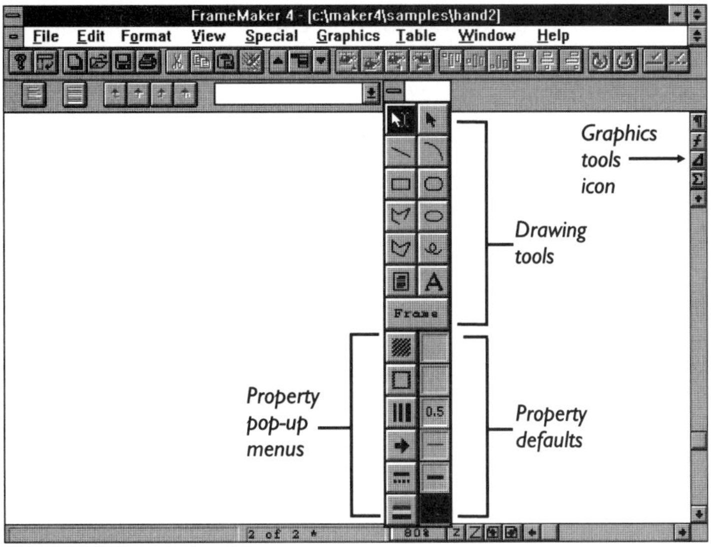


by selecting Graphics, Tools, or by clicking the icon (with the right angle) in the right border.

The tools in the upper-half of the palette (down to and including Frame) are drawing tools. The icons below the Frame icon are used to change or display object properties. The icons on the right show the current property, and the icons on the left display pop-up menus that allow you to change the properties.

These two icon palettes in the QuickAccess bar are also useful when drawing:

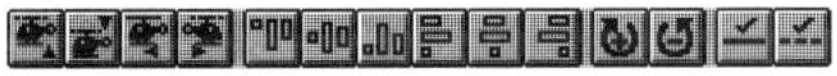

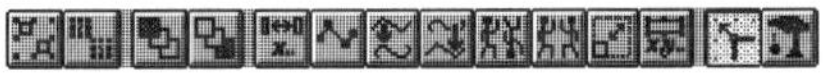

The icons on the left move objects up, down, left and right, align objects, rotate objects, and change lines to solid or dotted. The icons on the right, group and ungroup objects; send objects to the front or back; distribute objects, reshape, smooth, unsmooth, and flip objects; scale objects; display the Object Properties dialog box; and turn snap and gravity on or off.

## Drawing Tools and Property Icons

This section summarizes the purpose and/or the technique for using each drawing tool and property icon. If you feel you need more information about the use of a tool, refer to the FrameMaker 4 printed documentation. It explains each tool in detail. The tools above and including the Frame icon are used for drawing and entering text. The icons below the Frame icon are property icons; that is, they are used to change the characteristics of drawings.

SMART SELECTION This tool is usually selected by default. It changes its shape based on the object that it is pointing to. If it is pointing to a text object, it takes the shape of the I-beam (text cursor); otherwise, it takes the shape of a hollow arrow. When the tool has the I-beam shape, you can place the cursor in text or highlight text. After an object is drawn, the Smart Selection tool is automatically activated; therefore, to use a different tool, you must click the desired tool.

OBJECT SELECTION The Object Selection tool can select drawn objects or text that has been placed as an object with the Text Line tool. You cannot select "regular" text with this tool. To activate this tool automatically after drawing an object, press SHIFT while clicking the tool before drawing the object.

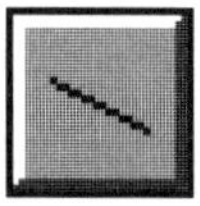

LINE To draw a line, click where the line should start and click where the line should end, or click the starting point and drag to the ending point. To draw a horizontal, vertical, or 45-degree angle, hold SHIFT when you click or drag.

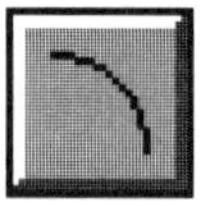

ARC This tool draws a 90-degree arc. Click the cursor where you want the arc to start and then drag along the path of the arc. For a circular arc, hold SHIFT as you drag.

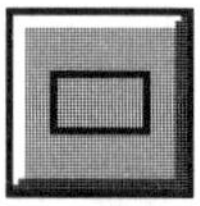

RECTANGLE To draw a rectangle, click the cursor at one corner and drag to a diagonal corner. To constrain the rectangle to a square, hold SHIFT while you click and drag.

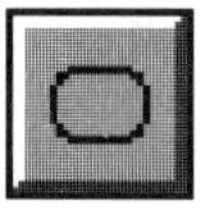

ROUNDED RECTANGLE To draw a rounded corner rectangle, click the cursor at one corner and drag to a diagonal corner. To constrain the rectangle to a square, hold SHIFT while you click and drag.

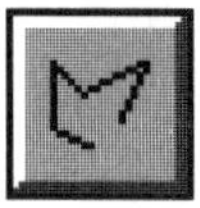

POLYLINE A polyline is a series of connected lines that can, but do not have to form a closed figure. To draw a series of connected lines, click at any staring point, move to a connecting point (called a vertex) and click again. Continue clicking at each vertex, and double-click on the end point. To create a vertical, horizontal or 45-degree line between vertexes, hold SHIFT while you move the cursor.

OVAL To draw an oval, click the cursor at one corner and drag to a diagonal corner. To constrain the oval to a circle, hold SHIFT while you click and drag.

POLYGON The Polygon tool can draw regular and irregular polygons. A regular polygon is a closed figure that has equal sides and equal angles. An irregular polygon has unequal sides and angles. To draw a regular polygon, first draw a circle or square that is just large enough to contain the polygon. While the circle or square is selected, choose Graphics, Set # Sides, and type the number of sides desired. If you want the object to be rotated, enter a starting angle. Then select Set. To draw an irregular polygon, click the cursor at the starting point and click the cursor at each vertex. Double-click on the last vertex.

FREEHAND This tool allows you draw as you would with a pen or pencil. Click the cursor at the starting position and drag the cursor along the desired path. You cannot constrain freehand curves to vertical, horizontal, or 45-degree lines. Also, if you have snap activated, only the starting point of the freehand drawing will snap to the grid. (Freehand curves are often referred to as Bezier curves.)

TEXT COLUMN This tool creates a column for text just like the default columns for headers, footers, and regular text. Use this tool to enter text that is several lines.

**NOTE:** *This tool must also be used to add text to master pages.*

TEXT LINE Use this tool to click anywhere on the page and type a line of text. While this tool is activated you can type as many lines of text as you want, but each line will be considered a separate object. This differs from typing text in a text column in which all the lines in the column are part of one object.

FRAME This tool creates a frame that is anchored to the page and will not move as you edit text. A frame can also be used to crop graphics.

**NOTE:** *A frame that is anchored to text is created by using the Special menu.*

FILL This icon displays a group of fill patterns that can be used to fill any object except lines and text lines. The selected pattern is displayed in the icon to the right of Fill.

PEN This icon displays a group of patterns that will be used when drawing the border of an object. The current pattern is displayed in the icon to the right of Pen.

LINE WIDTH This tool displays four line widths that can be selected for the width of an object's border. The current width is displayed in the icon to the right of Line Width. To set these four selections to different measurements, select Set, enter the desired measurements, and choose Set.

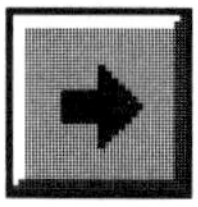

LINE END This icon displays four different line endings that will be used if you draw an arc, a line, a polyline, or a freehand curve. To choose a different line ending, select the desired line ending and then select Set. Choose an arrow style and an end style and choose Set. To design your own arrow, select the line, choose Set, and enter the angle for the base and the tip and the length of the side of the arrow (for a 1-point width). Select a style for the line of the arrow, and select a cap style. Then select Set.

LINE STYLE This icon displays two line styles—broken and unbroken. The current style in displayed in the icon to the right of the Line Style icon. The broken style line can be changed by selecting the broken style and then selecting Set. Eight different broken patterns are displayed. Select the desired pattern and choose Set.

COLOR This icon assigns a color to a selected object. The default color is black. After drawing an object with a different color, the color changes back to black when you choose a new tool. To draw several objects in the same color, press SHIFT when you select the color. To assign the same color to all objects, select any object, then press ALT+SHIFT while you select the color.

**NOTE:** *It is not possible to select one color for a border and a different color for the fill pattern.*

## TECHNIQUES OF DRAWING

Basically, objects are drawn by selecting a tool and clicking or dragging the tool. When an object is drawn it is automatically selected, meaning that it has selection handles as shown here:

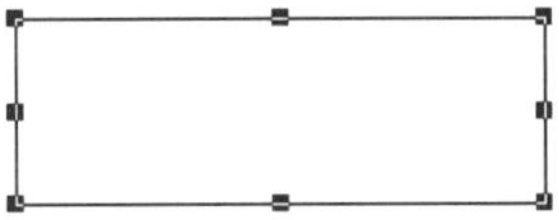

To move an object, first select the object, then drag the border of the object to the desired location. Be careful not to drag a handle. You can also move a selected object by clicking the "helicopter" icons which move left, right, up, or down in 1-point increments.

To resize an object, select the object and drag a handle. If you are resizing a square, circle, or line that has been constrained to horizontal, vertical, or 45 degrees, press SHIFT while you drag the handle to maintain the original shape.

To delete an object, select it and press DEL. To undelete the object, choose Edit, Undo immediately after deleting.

FrameMaker 4 provides several techniques that can help even the amateur artist create better drawings. The first techniques reviewed in this section concern setting up the drawing environment. These techniques include use of grids, snap and gravity, and zooming in and out. Other topics concern actual drawing techniques, like selecting objects, stacking objects, flipping, rotating, scaling, and so on.

### Using Grids

FrameMaker 4 has two grids to aid the user. The display of one grid can be turned on and off, and the increment of the grids can be controlled by the user. The other grid is invisible, but the increment of the grid can still be controlled by the user.

The visible grid is turned on by selecting View, Grid Lines. Figure 8-3 shows a grid based on half an inch. The invisible grid is activated by turning snap on, either by clicking the Snap icon in the QuickAccess bar or by choosing Graphics, Snap. It is deactivated in the same way. When the invisible grid is activated, a "magnetic force" causes objects to "snap" to the invisible grid when they are drawn, moved, resized or reshaped.

**NOTE:** *The visible grid does not print when you print your document.*

To set the increments for both grids, choose View, Options. This dialog box is displayed:

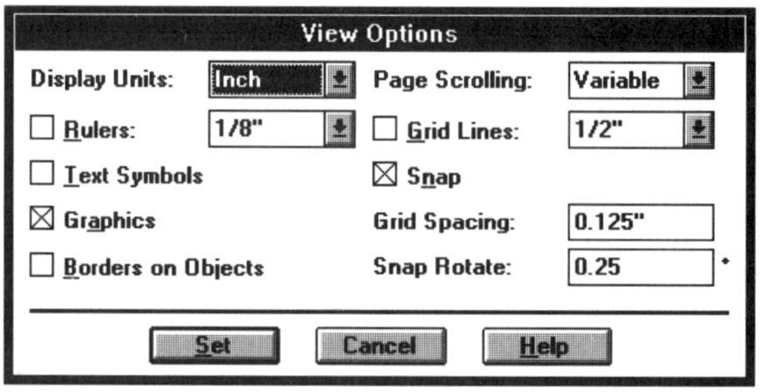


The Grid Lines option sets the increment for the visible grid. The choices in the list box are 2 cm, 1 cm, 1/2 cm, 1", 1/2", 1/3", and 1/4". The Grid Spacing

**FIGURE 8-3**

*Half-inch grids*

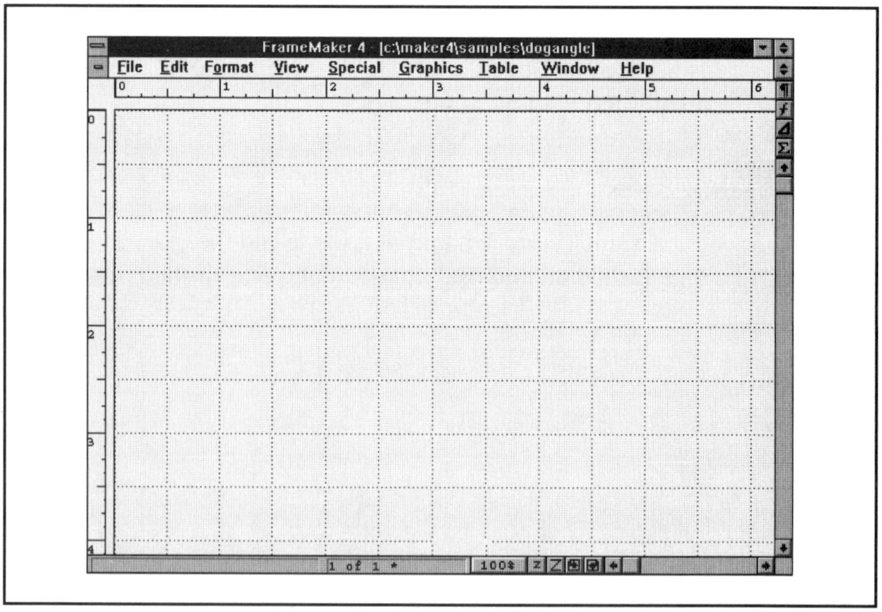

option sets the increment for the invisible grid. The value entered in the Grid Lines option should be a multiple of the value entered for Grid Spacing. For example, if Grid Spacing is .125", Grid Lines could be 1/4", 1/2", or 1".

**NOTE:** *When entering a value for Grid Spacing, decimals must be used instead of fractions.*

## Using Snap

The snap feature is very helpful when you are drawing items that should be aligned or should be the same size. To see how snap works, turn the feature on, set one inch grids for the visible grid and .125 inches (1/8 of an inch) for the invisible grid. Zoom in to 160%. Then begin drawing a one-inch square starting in the corner of a grid. Slowly drag the pointer down and notice how the size of the rectangle jumps eight times before you get to the next grid line. Now turn the snap off, and draw another one-inch square. Notice that the dragging motion is continuous and does not snap to the invisible grid. As you work, you will find it necessary to turn the snap feature on and off many times depending on what you are doing.

**TIP:** *To make objects a precise size or give them a precise location, turn off the snap feature.*

## Zooming In

The zoom feature is especially helpful when you are working with graphics. The two illustrations below point out the difference between a drawing's appearance at two different magnifications. The first illustration, shown at 35%, looks like two lines that meet at a corner. The second illustration, shown at 400%, reveals that the two lines do not really meet at all. When the graphic is printed, the gap between the two lines will be noticeable.

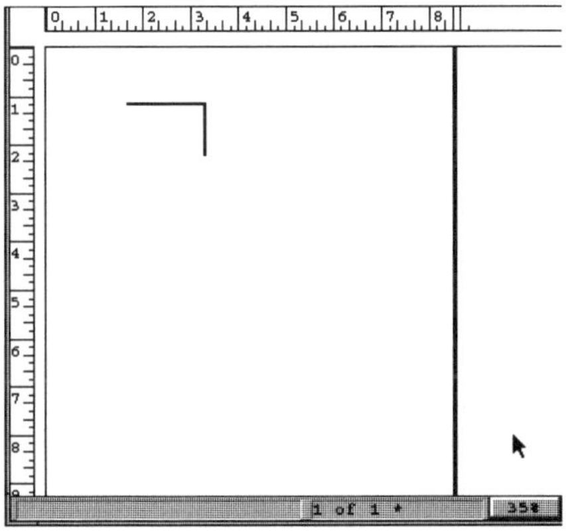

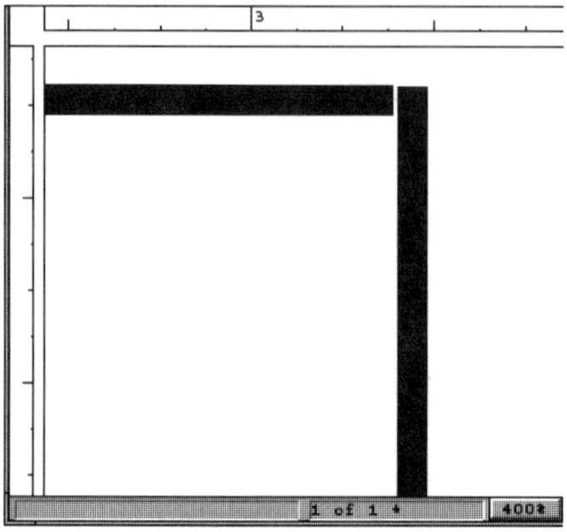

**NOTE:** *It is a bit difficult to continuously work in zoom modes above 100%, but as you work, you can zoom in and out to fine tune your drawing. Be sure to notice the coordinates of the object's location before zooming in to 400%. It may be difficult to locate an object at that high a zoom.*

## Using Gravity

Gravity is a feature that causes objects to be attracted to each other. This feature is helpful if you want to connect objects. If gravity is activated, when you draw an object (or drag the handle of an object) close to another object, the handle jumps to connect the two objects.

## Using Edit and Format Commands

When you are using the drawing tools, do not loose sight of the fact that you can still use some of the Edit and Format commands. You can cut, copy, and paste objects just like regular text, and the Undo command can be an invaluable tool. If you delete, move, or resize an object by mistake, you can undo it. The formatting commands for font, size, and style can be used to format text that is created by the text tools.

## Selecting and Deselecting Objects

When an object is drawn, it is automatically selected and it remains selected unless you deselect it, choose another drawing tool, or select another object. Objects are selected by clicking them with the Smart Selection tool or the Object Selection tool. To select several objects, click the first object and press SHIFT while clicking each of the other objects. When several objects are selected, they can be moved as a group, but cannot be resized as a group.

**NOTE:** *To select a text line or text column with the Smart Selection tool, you must press CTRL when you click the object.*

You can also select several objects by drawing a selection border around the objects. To draw a selection border simply drag a rectangle around the objects with either selection tool. Sometimes this method is risky, however, because you might be so close to an object, that you move or reshape the object instead of drawing a border. If this happens, select Edit, Undo immediately to move the object back into place. If there is a possibility that you might move or resize an object instead of drawing a border, hold down CTRL and drag the selection border with the right mouse button.

**TIP:** *To select all the objects on a page, press CTRL+A or choose Edit, Select All on Page.*

To deselect one or several objects, click outside the object or objects. If several objects are selected at once, you can deselect one of the objects by pressing SHIFT and clicking the object (not a handle). To deselect several objects but not all objects, draw a selection border around the objects that you want to deselect. (If any objects that were not previously selected fall within the selection border, they will be selected.)

## Stacking

Two commands on the Graphics menu can change the order in which objects are stacked if they are overlapping—Bring to Front and Send to Back. These commands are also available as icons on the QuickAccess bar.

When you start stacking objects with these commands, selecting objects may become tricky. One problem you may encounter is the inability to select an object again once it has been sent to the back. This can happen if the object is completely covered by another object. If this happens, you can send the larger object to the back to expose the object that was behind it.

It is also possible that you will not be able to select an object that has been sent to the back even though it is partially visible. In this case, it is likely that the object is covered by the text column. Since the text column has no fill, when an object is sent to the back it still "shows through," but the object actually is completely covered. To select an object that is behind a text column, select the text column, and send it to the back. Then you will be able to select the other object.

**NOTE:** *Every page has a text column for the flow of text, and that column is considered an object. So when you draw the first object on a page, you are actually adding the second object to the page and putting it on top of the text column.*

To avoid sending the text column to the back all the time, delete the text column altogether by selecting it and pressing DEL. If the column contains text that should not be deleted, resize the text column so that it takes up as little room as possible, and your drawings do not have to be positioned on top of the text column.

## Grouping and Ungrouping

When working with a complex drawing, it sometimes is helpful to work with a group of objects rather than individual objects. You can draw the individual objects, move them into position, stacking them if needed, and then group the objects into one element. This element can then be moved as a whole, and individual elements are protected from being accidentally selected, moved, resized, or restacked. If you need to work with one object in a group, you can ungroup the objects, revise the single object, and then group the objects again.

To group objects, first select each object or draw a selection border around them if possible, then click the Group icon in the QuickAccess bar or choose Graphics, Group. To ungroup, select the grouped object and click the Ungroup icon or choose Graphics, Ungroup.

## Rotating and Flipping

Rotating objects can create some special effects like the rotated letters shown here:

u p t h e h i l l

To rotate an object, select the object and click one of the Rotate icons, or choose Graphics, Rotate. If you click a Rotate icon, either the clockwise or counterclockwise icon, the object rotates 15 degrees each time you click the icon. If you select Graphics, Rotate, you see this dialog box:

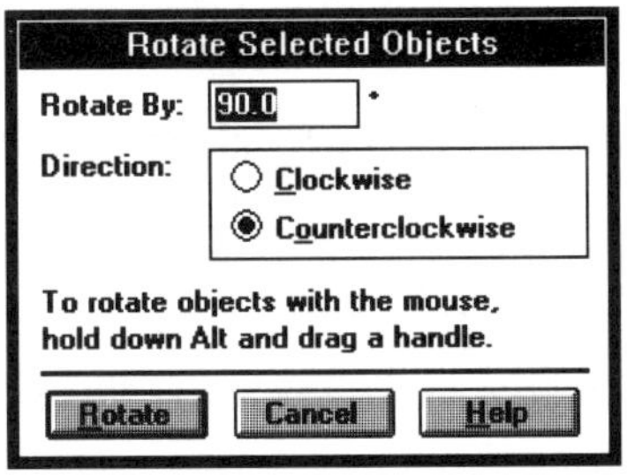


Enter a degree of rotation and a direction. Then select Rotate.

**NOTE:** *Frames can only be rotated in 90 degree increments.*

A third way to rotate objects is with the mouse. Select the object and then drag a handle while pressing the ALT key. When you use this method, the pointer shows a two headed arrow like this:

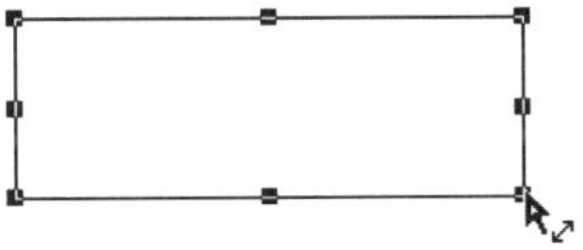

When rotating an object with the mouse, the object snaps to a preset degree determined by the user in the Snap Rotate box of the View Options dialog box as shown here:

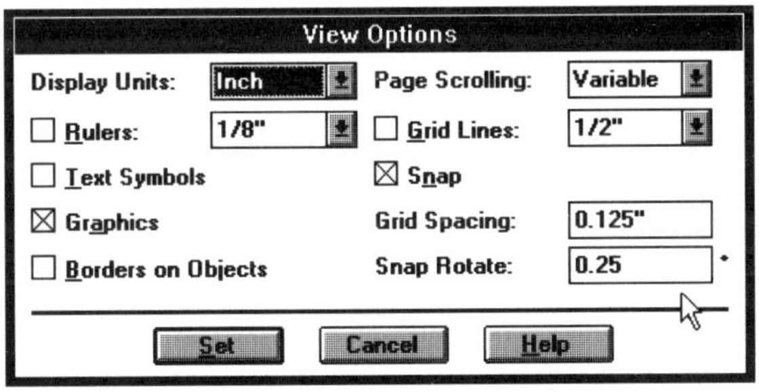


To unrotate an object, select the object and press ESC, g, 0 (zero). To return the object to its previous degree of rotation, select the object and press ESC, g, 1 (one).

**TIP:** *You can select several objects (as long as they are not grouped) and rotate them at the same time using the icons or the Rotate dialog box. If using the mouse, you can rotate only one object at a time.*

Objects can be flipped, left to right or top to bottom, by clicking an icon or by choosing Graphics, Flip Up/Down or Flip Left/Right. Flipping an object can be used in combination with the Copy/Paste commands to create an object with perfect symmetry. For example, to create the simple outline of a house, draw one side, copy it, flip the copy, and then move the two objects together.

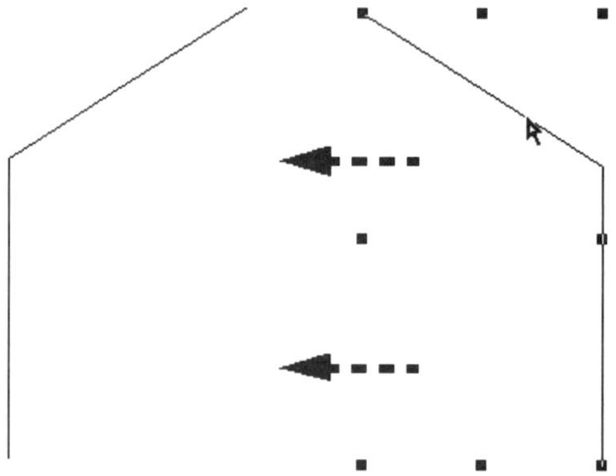

**NOTE:** *Line text and text columns that have not been rotated cannot be flipped. Frames cannot be flipped at all.*

## Aligning and Distributing Objects

Although the snap feature helps you align objects as you draw them, it is not a complete solution. The Graphics, Align command provides more alignment options available in the Align dialog box shown here:

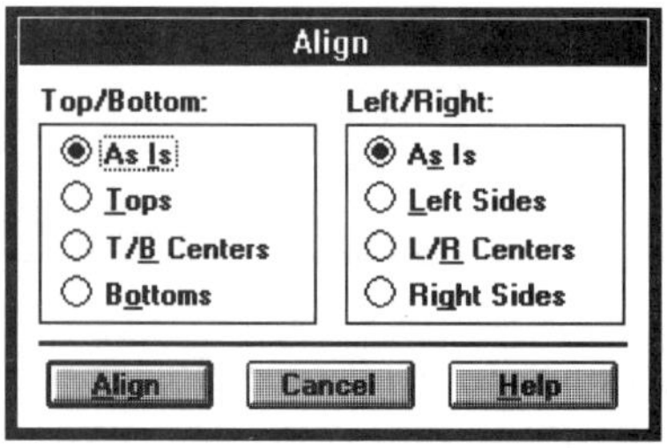

**NOTE:** *The same alignments can be achieved by using any of the six alignment icons on the QuickAccess bar.*

The Graphics, Distribution command displays this dialog box which allows you to position two or more objects based on a specified space between the edges, an equal distance between their centers, or an equal distance between the edges of the objects.

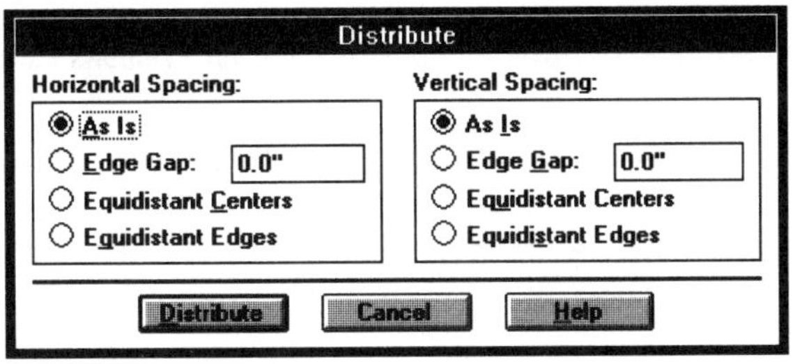


**TIP:** *The Distribution command can be used to place two objects right next to each other by specifying a zero gap between edges. For example, you could use the Distribution command to join a flipped copy of an object to form a symmetrical design.*

## Scaling, Reshaping, Smoothing, and Unsmoothing

Scaling an object increases or decrease the size of an object. FrameMaker 4 allows you to scale an object proportionally by a percentage or change the width and height by entering arbitrary amounts. To scale an object proportionally, select the object and click the Scale icon or choose Graphics, Scale. This dialog box is displayed:

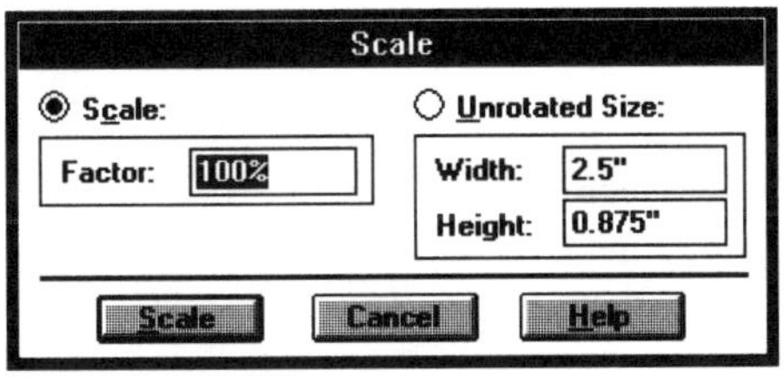


Enter a percent for the scaling factor, and select Scale. To change the size of an object without keeping the same proportions, display the Scale dialog box and change either or both of the measurements for width and height and choose Scale.

To reshape an object, select the object and choose Graphics, Reshape. Selection handles appear on the border of the object. Drag a handle to reshape. To add a vertex to a line, polyline, or polygon, select the object, choose Graphics, Reshape, and then press CTRL while you click where the handle should be added. Once the handle is added you can drag it to reshape the object.

**NOTE:** *Early releases of FrameMaker 4 for Windows did not support reshaping a line.*

To remove a vertex, select the object, choose Graphics, Reshape, and press CTRL while clicking the handle you want to remove. The shape of the object will automatically change. For example, when vertex B is removed in the following illustration, the shape changes to a straight line from points A to C.

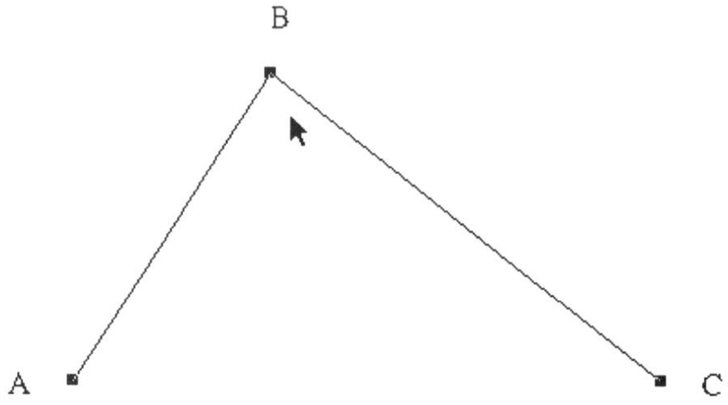


Smoothing polylines and unsmoothing freehand drawings (Bezier curves) is a special way to reshape objects. Unsmoothing freehand drawings turns them into polylines. Smoothing polylines turns them into freehand curves. The freehand drawing on the left looks like the drawing on the right when it is unsmoothed.

**NOTE:** *Smooth and Unsmooth cannot be used as "undo functions" of each other. For example, if you smooth the drawing on the right it may not look exactly like the drawing on the left again; however, the angles will become curves again.*

## Picking Up Object Properties

If you have objects that have different line widths, different fill patterns, different colors, and so on, you can transfer the properties of one object to another or other objects. To transfer properties, follow these steps:

1. Select the object whose properties you want to transfer.
2. Press SHIFT and click the Graphics option on the menu bar.
3. Choose Pick up Object Properties. The properties of the selected item are displayed in the Properties section of the Graphics Tools palette.
4. Select the object (or objects) you want to change.
5. Click each property in the Graphics Tools palette that you want to transfer.

**HINT:** *If you want to get a quick look at an object's properties, follow only Steps 1 through 3 above.*

## Object Properties

Drawing objects with a mouse lacks precision, but FrameMaker 4 gives you the precision that you need with the Graphics, Object Properties command, which displays a dialog box like this:

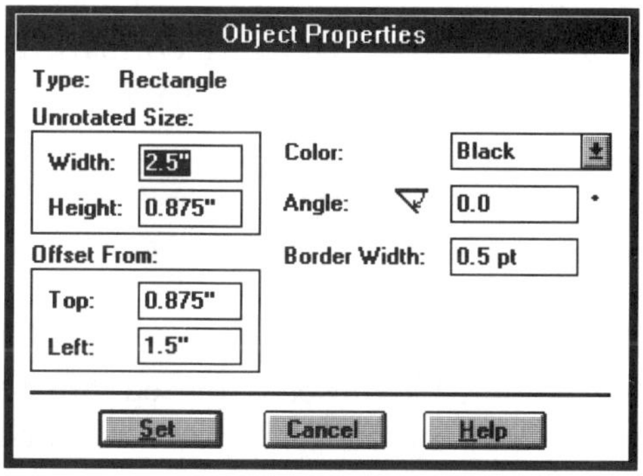

You can specify an exact size, location, rotation, and border width using this dialog box. Further you can specify a color and, if an arc is selected, you can specify the starting and ending angle as shown here:

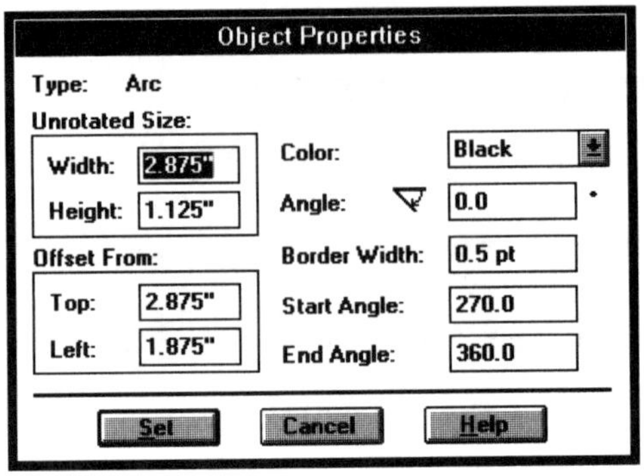


**TIP:** *If you want to get a quick measurement of an object, turn off snap, select the object, point to a handle, and hold down the mouse button. The measurements appear in the left side of the status line. The location of an object also appears in the status line when you move the object.*

## IMPORTING GRAPHICS

In addition to drawing your own graphics, you can also import drawings that have been created by other programs or digitized with a scanner. FrameMaker 4 can read the following graphic formats: MIF (Maker Interchange Format), CGM, CDR (CorelDraw), BMP (bitmapped images), DXF, EPS (Encapsulated PostScript), GEM, GIF, HGL, IGS, MPT (McPaint), DRW (Micrografx Drawing Format), PCX, PCT, RF, TIF, WMF, WPG (WordPerfect graphics), and XWD.

**TIP:** *If you buy clipart packages to use with FrameMaker 4, be sure the format is one that FrameMaker 4 can read. Most clip art comes in PCX, BMP, or EPS format—all of which are readable by FrameMaker 4.*

A graphic file can be imported into a frame, a rectangle, a text column, or simply on a page. To import a file, first indicate where you want to place the file by selecting a frame or rectangle, clicking in a text column, or clicking in the page margin (to place the graphic on the page). Then choose File, Import, File to display this dialog box:

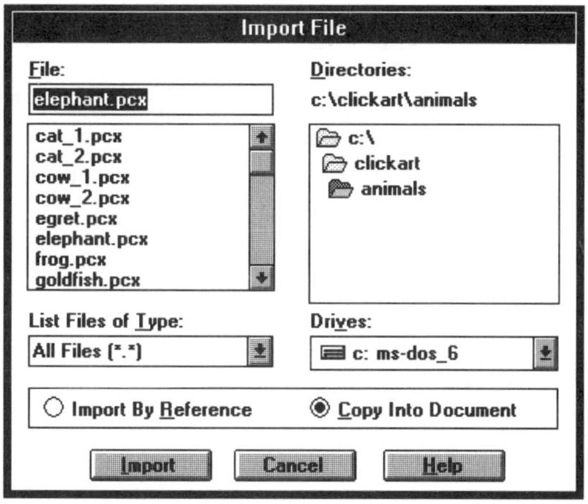


Choose the graphic file, and then choose either Import By Reference or Copy Into Document. (If you choose Import By Reference, FrameMaker 4 must find the graphic each time the document is opened. If you choose Copy Into Document, the graphic becomes part of the document.) Finally, choose Import.

If you are importing a bitmap, gray-scale, or color image, this dialog box is then displayed:

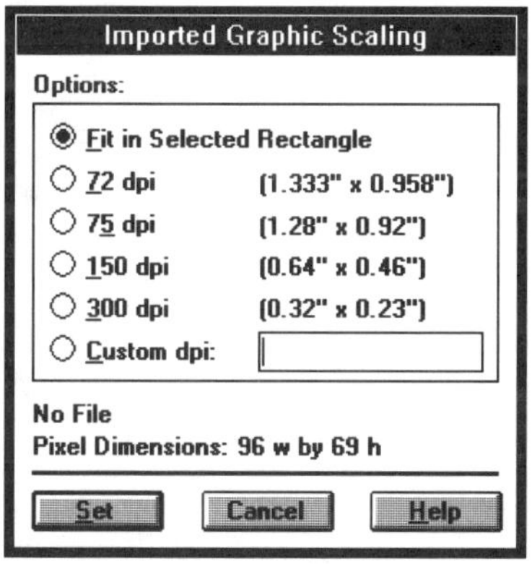


If you select Fit in Selected Rectangle, the graphic will be scaled so that the larger of its width or height fits in the rectangle. If you select a dpi setting, the graphic will have the dimensions displayed to the right of the settings. Select Set to complete the importing process.

A graphic that is imported is just like an object that you have drawn with the FrameMaker 4 drawing tools. It can be moved, resized, scaled, rotated, flipped, and so on.

### Cropping Imported Files

Imported images can be cropped in two ways—by placing them in a frame or by covering unwanted areas with a rectangle, polygon, circle, and so on. To crop an image with a frame, import the image in the frame or move the image into a frame, and then resize the frame around the image so that the unwanted part is no longer visible. To cover unwanted areas of an image, draw a rectangle, polygon, etc., and choose a white fill and a white border.

**EXERCISE**

To practice using the drawing tools and drawing techniques, follow the steps in this exercise to draw the robotic hand shown at the beginning of this chapter. (Figure 8-4 is the same figure you saw earlier in the chapter.)

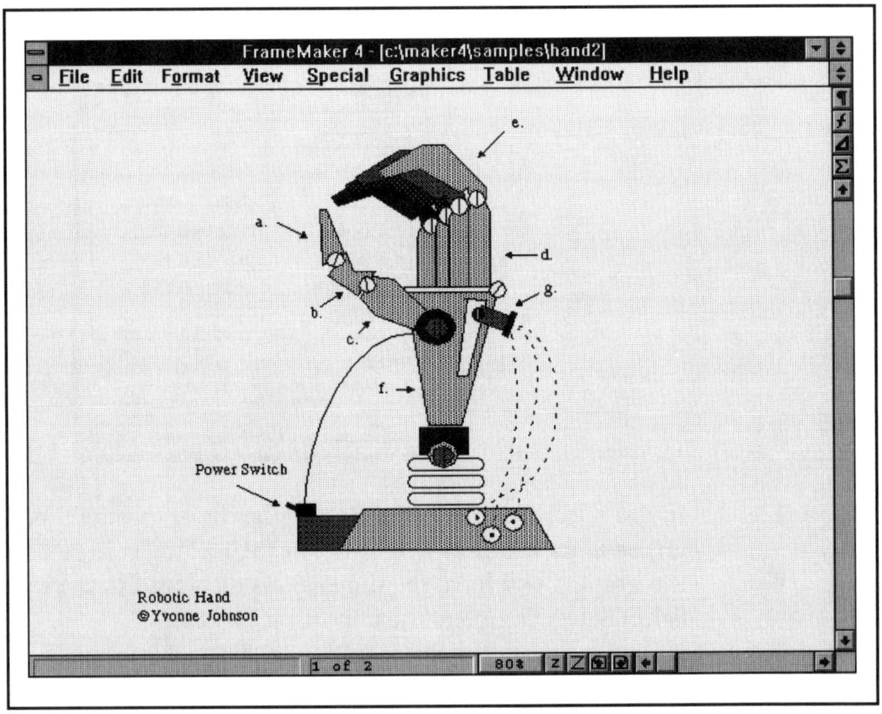


**FIGURE 8-4** *A technical drawing produced with FrameMaker 4*

You will find that the steps in this exercise are fairly specific but generally do not give you exact dimensions. You can experiment with size and practice resizing the elements of the drawing if you are not satisfied with the look.

1. First begin by opening a new document in portrait orientation. Turn on the view of the grids. (Grid lines should be 1/2".) Set the zoom on 100%. Display the Graphics Tools palette and check the default settings of all properties. The pen pattern should be solid black, the line width should be 0.5 wide with no arrow, and the line should be solid, not broken.
2. Click the border of the text column and delete it. If not deleted, the text column will cause a problem when selecting objects (as described earlier).
3. If Snap is on, turn it off.
4. Select the Rounded Rectangle tool and draw one vertical rectangle a little over an inch tall to form the bottom of the "finger" (part d).
5. While the rectangle is selected, choose the Fill icon and select the middle shade in the second row.
6. To draw part e, select the Polyline tool and draw the upper part of the finger. If you are not happy with the shape, choose Graphics, Reshape, and rework the shape. If the object is too large or too small, change the size with the Scale command.
7. Zoom to 200% and draw a circle between the upper and lower part of the finger.
8. Draw a line through the center of the circle.
9. Zoom back down to a comfortable working image. Draw a selection border around all four objects and group the objects.
10. Copy the group and paste it three times.
11. Move each group away from the other groups so they are not overlapping.
12. Ungroup the first group and select the upper part of the finger. Apply a solid black fill; then regroup the objects.
13. Repeat Step 12 for each group using a lighter fill pattern for each subsequent finger.

14. Move all four fingers together so they are overlapping and slightly staggered. Use Bring to Front and Send to Back to make the fingers overlap each other correctly.
15. When the four fingers are assembled to your satisfaction, group them.
16. Zoom to 25% and position the group in the middle of the page toward the top.
17. Zoom back to a comfortable working image.
18. In an area that is not close enough to overlap the fingers, draw the base of the hand (part f) by selecting the Polygon tool and drawing a four-sided figure like this:

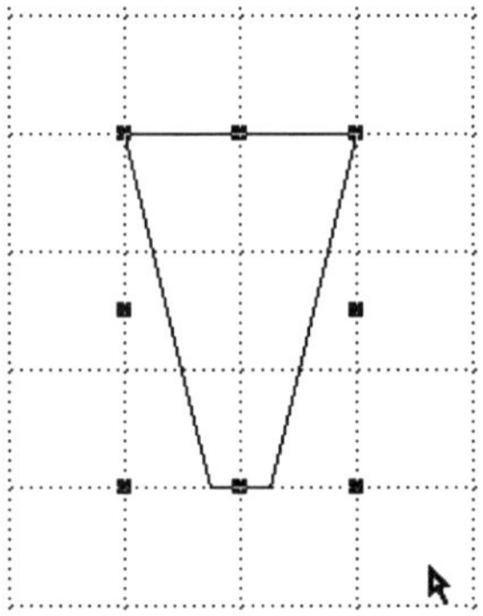

19. Fill this polygon with the middle fill pattern on the second row.
20. With the Rectangle tool, draw a narrow rectangle across the width of the top of the polygon. Fill this rectangle with white.
21. Draw a circle on the right end of the rectangle and draw a line through the center of the circle.
22. With the Polygon tool, draw a four-sided figure (with white fill) down the right side of the base like this:

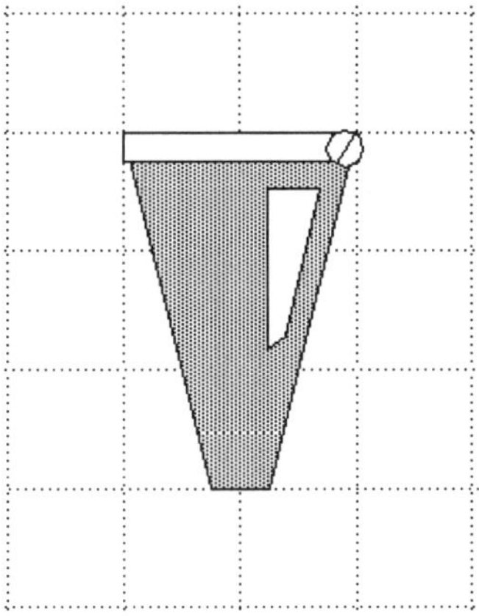

23. Draw a smaller rectangle (for part g) that overlaps the white polygon and fill it with a shaded pattern.
24. Rotate the rectangle using the mouse so it looks like this:

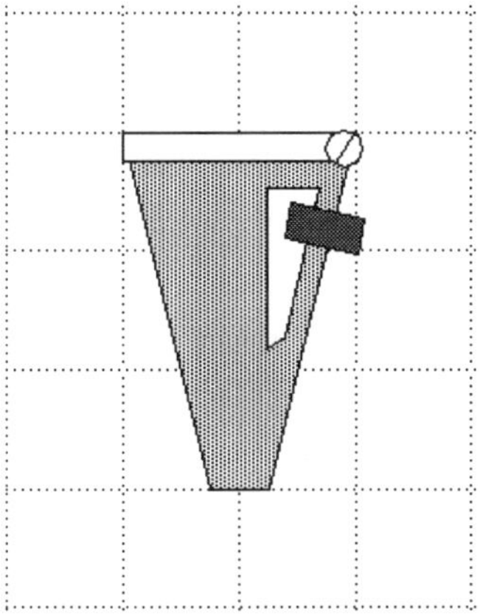

25. Draw the circle representing the screw that attaches the rotated rectangle to the white polygon. Fill the screw with solid black.
26. Draw a white line through the center of the circle.

27. Draw a smaller, vertical rectangle, fill it with solid black, rotate it, and move it to the end of the rectangle drawn in Step 23 (part g) so that it looks like this:

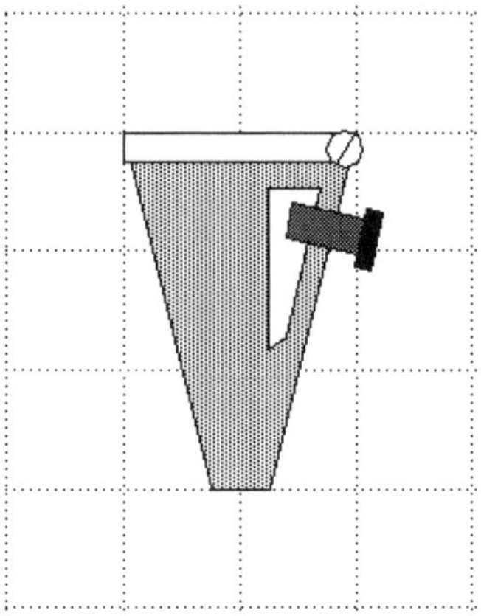

28. Draw a rectangle at the bottom of the base that is slightly wider than the base, and fill it with solid black.
29. Choose View, Options, and change the Grid Spacing to .063 and choose Snap.
30. Draw a rounded rectangle under the black rectangle and give it a white fill. Copy and paste it twice. Position the rectangles so they are evenly spaced under the black rectangle. Use the Align icon if necessary.
31. Using the Polygon tool, draw the polygon under the three rounded rectangles giving it a shaded fill.
32. Draw three white circles on the right side of the polygon.
33. Draw the rectangle that extends from the polygon on the left and give it a darker shade than the polygon. Send the rectangle to the back.
34. Draw the power switch with two rectangles filled with solid black. Rotate the smaller rectangle.
35. Draw an arc from the power switch to the base of the hand.
36. Group all objects drawn from Step 18 through Step 35.
37. Move the "base group" up to the fingers.
38. In another area of the page, draw the three pieces of the thumb (parts a, b, and c) using the Polygon tool. Add the screws with the

Ellipse tool and draw the lines through the centers of the circles. Group all objects in the thumb.

39. Move the thumb into position.
40. Draw the two large screws by drawing two circles with different shading.

**HINT:** *Draw the circles in a different place and move the smaller one into the larger one after the shading has been added to both.*

41. Add two lines to the screw that goes on the thumb and one line to the other screw.
42. Group each screw.
43. Move the screws into position.
44. Draw a text column below and to the left of the hand.
45. In the text column, type **Robotic Hand** and press ENTER. On the next line press and hold ALT while you type **0169** on the number pad. Then type **Yvonne Johnson.**
46. Click the Line End icon and choose the arrow that points to the right.
47. Draw lines (move the cursor from left to right only) pointing to each piece of the thumb, the base, and the power switch.
48. Click the Line End icon and choose the arrow that points to the left.
49. Draw lines (move the cursor from left to right only) pointing to the top of the finger and the base of the finger.
50. Choose the Line Text tool and add an appropriate letter to an arrow.
51. Repeat Step 50 for all arrows.
52. Using the Line Text tool, add the words **Power Switch** to the appropriate arrow.
53. Change the line style to a broken line that is 1.0 point wide.
54. Click the Line End icon and choose the line with no arrow.
55. Press SHIFT while you click the Freehand tool so you can draw three lines without choosing the tool each time.

56. Draw three curved lines from part g to the circles in the polygon at the bottom.

57. Save the file.

## COMBINING TEXT AND GRAPHICS

Thus far graphics have been dealt with as stand-alone objects, but graphics may be an integral part of text. For example, in this book, we might want to refer to an icon on the QuickAccess bar (the Help icon in this example) and show the icon right in the middle of the text like this:

The Help icon (  ) displays the Help menu.

Additionally, you might want a graphic to be placed in the middle of text and have the text wrap around as shown in Figure 8-5.

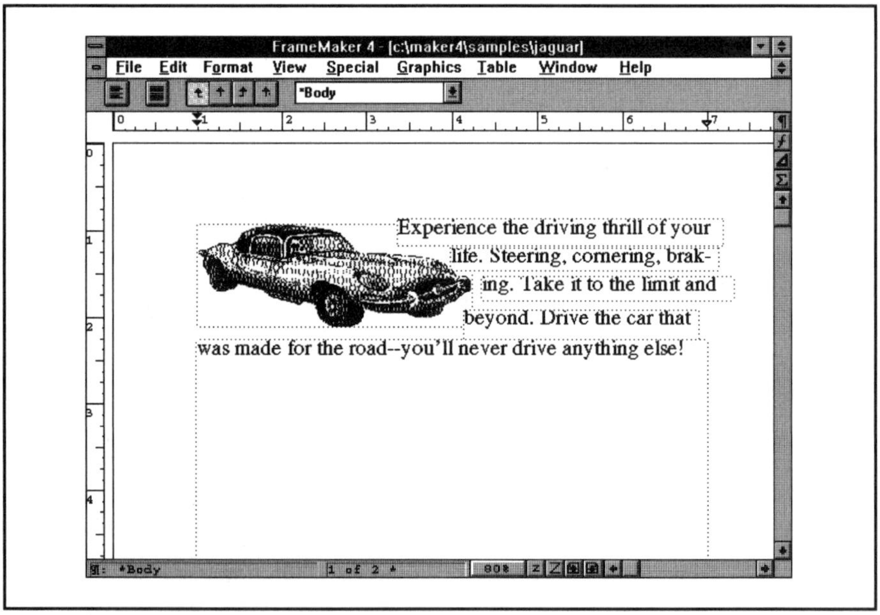


**FIGURE 8-5** *Text wrapped around a graphic*

## Anchoring Graphics in Text

A graphic is anchored to text by placing the graphic in an anchored frame which moves with the text. An anchored frame can be positioned in a text column at the insertion point, in the margin of the text column, just below the line that contains the insertion pointer, at the top of the column, or at the bottom of a column.

An anchored frame can be created manually or automatically. When you click the insertion pointer in text and then import a graphic, an anchored frame is created automatically. To manually create an anchored frame, follow these steps:

1. Click the insertion pointer in the text where you want to anchor the frame.
2. Choose Special, Anchored Frame. This dialog box displays:

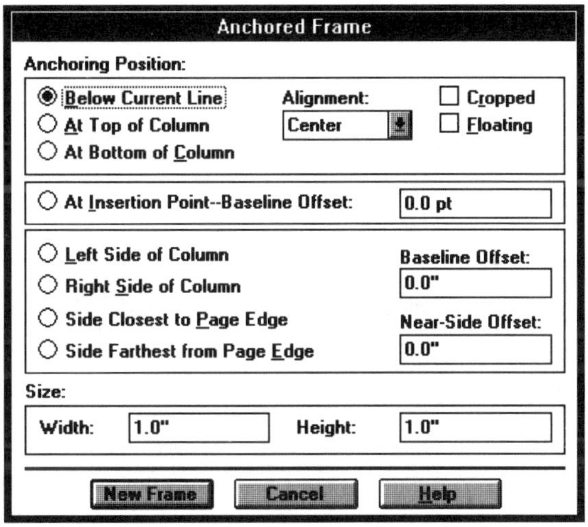


3. Choose the desired position options.
4. Specify the size.
5. Click New Frame.

An anchor mark (⊥) appears in the text to show the position of the frame. To complete the operation, import the desired graphic in the frame or create your own drawing in the frame.

**NOTE:** *The Alignment option in the Anchored Frame dialog box places the graphic horizontally in the center or on the left or right. If Cropped is selected, a wide frame will be cropped at the margin. If Floating is selected, a frame that is too large for its column will move to the next column.*

## WRAPPING TEXT AROUND GRAPHICS

A text column can be split horizontally so that a graphic can be placed between the text as shown in Figure 8-6. Also, a text column can be split into multiple columns to allow text to wrap around as seen earlier in Figure 8-5.

To split a text column into two columns, follow these steps:

1. Click the cursor where you want to split the column.
2. Choose Format, Pages, Layout Commands.

**FIGURE 8-6**

*Graphic inserted in a column that has been split*

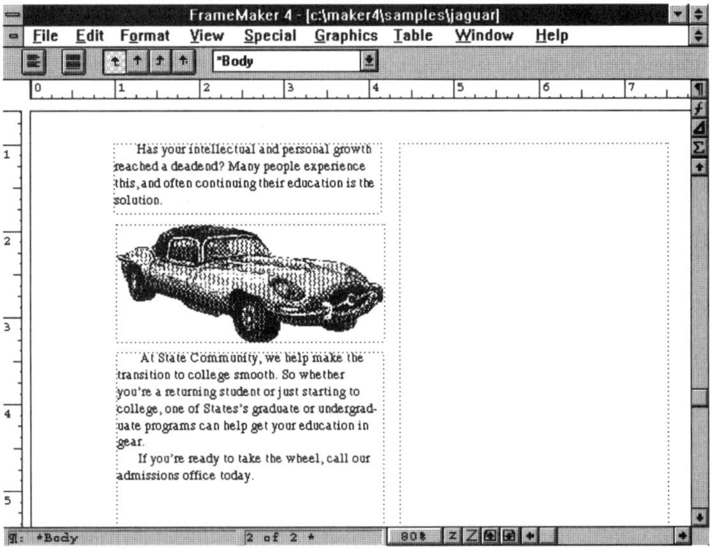

3. Choose Split Current Column, Below Selection.
4. Resize the columns to make room for the graphic and draw or import the graphic in the space that is opened.

To wrap text around an object, follow these steps:

1. Place the graphic on top of the text.
2. Position the cursor above the graphic and split the column as described above.
3. Position the cursor below the graphic and split the column again.
4. Select the text column that is under the graphic.
5. Choose Format, Pages, Layout Commands, Split Current Column, Into Lines.
6. Resize each line so it exposes the graphic.

**NOTE:** *Since the text flow has not be disconnected, the text will flow between the split columns.*

## EMBEDDING GRAPHICS

FrameMaker 4 uses the Windows technology called Object Linking and Embedding (OLE) which allows you to create an object in another application (that is an OLE "server") and embed the object in FrameMaker 4 (acting as "client"). When the object is embedded, it is still linked to the original file. If that file changes, the object in FrameMaker 4 reflects that change.

To embed an object in FrameMaker 4, follow these steps:

1. In the server application, create the file and copy it to the Clipboard.
2. In FrameMaker 4, position the arrow where you want to copy the object.
3. Choose Edit, Paste Special.
4. Choose OLE and click Paste.

# 9

# Using Color

THERE is a saying in the advertising industry—"Color sells." People seem to be naturally attracted to color, so printed media that uses color is more likely to be read. FrameMaker 4 lets you choose colors from several industry-standard color sets and assign them to almost anything.

## WHAT CAN YOU COLOR?

You can assign color to almost any element in FrameMaker 4 documents, including:

- Selected text
- Selected paragraphs
- Character tags
- Paragraph tags
- Background of a text column
- Graphic objects drawn with FrameMaker 4 tools
- Imported graphics
- Text in a table
- Cells in a table
- Change bars
- Equations or elements in an equation

When assigning color to documents, remember that—just as in overusing different fonts—too many colors can be distracting and actually discourage people from reading your document. Moderation is the key.

## WHAT COLORS SHOULD YOU USE?

The advertising industry has gone to great expense to study the effects of color on readers. Studies show that bright red catches the eye quickly, blue is the most favored color, and green is the least favored color followed by chocolate brown, murky tan, and burnt orange.

Certain color combinations are in style for a while, and then they go out of style. Using an out-of-style color combination makes your publication look dated. If you receive lots of advertising from big companies, you can probably see several trends in color styles. *Communications Arts*, a magazine published in Palo Alto, California, is also a good source of examples of contemporary design.

## WHY USE COLOR?

At this point you might be asking, "Why do I need to assign color to anything with FrameMaker 4? Why not just tell the printer what colors I want and where I want them?"

### Tips for Using Color

- Use loud, bright, or iridescent colors sparingly.
- Use light, pale colors in large areas.
- Use lots of white space with colors, especially bright colors. White space allows the eye to rest.
- Some color combinations are difficult to read. Avoid bright red text in a bright blue background (or vice versa). Also avoid using bright red with green. The eye has difficulty determining where one color stops and the other starts so the text seems to vibrate.
- Medium and light gray colors work with almost all other colors.

You could handle your color requirements just this way, and many people do, but the cost to you is greater. If you give the printer one sheet of paper (or piece of film) for each page, the printer will have to take several intermediate steps to create a plate for each color.

By assigning colors with FrameMaker 4, you can cut out some of those intermediate steps and better provide what the printer needs. The process is simple; you just follow these three easy steps:

1. Choose the colors you will use for the current document.
2. Assign the colors to all elements during the layout.
3. Print the document with Print Separations selected so that a separate page prints for each color. (The highest resolution possible should be used to print the separations. Many times this step is done by a service bureau, and the output is film, not paper.)

## CHOOSING COLORS

When choosing colors, you must first select the color model that you will use. FrameMaker 4 uses three color models to describe color—RGB (red, blue, and green), CMYK (cyan, magenta, yellow, and black), and HLS (hue, lightness, and saturation). The RGB model describes colors seen on the monitor, the CMYK describes process color, and HLS describes traditional colors used by artists.

**NOTE:** *The "K" in CMYK refers to the printer's word for black, "key."*

FrameMaker 4 also provides two aids for selecting color—the color picker and the Pantone Matching System. The color picker allows you to select a color from a region of colors and specify the luminosity of the color. The PANTONE MATCHING SYSTEM ® displays the hundreds of colors developed by Pantone, Inc.

### The RGB Model

The RGB colors on a monitor's screen are created by adding different color light to change the otherwise black screen. Three color guns (red, blue,

## The Color Process at the Print Shop

*Understanding the process your mechanicals go through at the print shop may help you understand why you need to provide the printer with a mechanical for each color you use. Here is the process:*

- The printer takes your mechanicals and turns them into film, unless you provide the film yourself by using a service bureau. One negative is created for each process color and for each spot color; therefore, you should supply one page (or film) for each.
- Halftones and color separations are *stripped into* the negatives where photographs or scanned images are positioned. In the case of a four-color separation, the cyan separation is stripped into the cyan film; the yellow separation is stripped into the yellow film; and so on. When a halftone or color film is stripped in, a hole is cut in the film at the desired position and the film for the halftone or the color film is taped in place.
- The films are assembled into *flats*. A flat contains all the pages that will print on a single piece of paper.
- A plate used on the printing press is *burned* for each flat. In the case of a four-color job, four plates are burned for each flat.
- The plates are mounted on the press for printing.

and green) light the phosphor on the inside of the screen to make it glow. If the three color guns are all fired at the same strength, the resulting color is white. If no guns are lighting an area, the resulting color is black. By mixing varying degrees of light intensity, different colors are created.

The RGB color model is used primarily for color presentations that will be viewed on the screen. Generally speaking, some of the very strong colors that can be created on the screen cannot be reproduced in print, mainly because the white on the screen is much brighter than a piece of white paper. So that colors seen on the screen will more closely match the actual printed color, FrameMaker 4 provides the CMYK and the PANTONE color models.

**NOTE:** *Because of differences in manufacturing, monitors do not display the same RGB values and so the same color looks different on a different monitor. You have probably experienced this if you have ever walked through the color TV section of a department store. For true color matching, the monitor must be calibrated. Calibration can be done through a software program or a hardware device.*

## The CMYK Model

The CMYK model is used to describe the colors seen in four-color process printing. This process separates a continuous color image (like a photograph) into four color negatives (cyan, magenta, yellow, and black), called a color separation, and each negative is used to create a plate for the press. Each plate is run with its color of ink to produce the final full-color print. See Color Plate 2.

## The HLS Model

The HLS model mixes colors by controlling the hue (like red, pink, or peach), the lightness (from dull to bright), and the saturation (intense color to pale color). Choosing colors with this color model is more like mixing paints and produces more colors that are perceptibly different than the RGB color model produces.

## The Common Color Picker

The common color picker has two color selection areas. One square area has the hue and saturation of all color, the rectangle has the brightness or dullness as shown here:

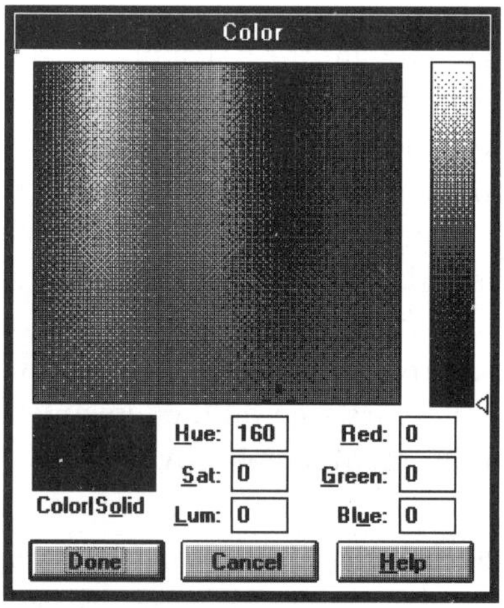


See Color Plate 3 for a better idea of what the Common Color Picker looks like.

### The Pantone Matching System

The PANTONE MATCHING SYSTEM (PMS), introduced in the early 1960s, is a precise color system with hundreds of colors. Each color has a number that identifies it and a specific mixture of ink colors that creates it. Printers everywhere can mix the colors according to the formula to produce the exact PMS color.

**NOTE:** *The PMS colors are often referred to as spot colors.*

## DEFINING AND SELECTING COLORS

By default, FrameMaker 4 includes these colors in the color menus: black, white, red, green, blue, cyan, magenta, and yellow. These represent all the colors in the RGB and the CMYK models plus white. By selecting or defining different colors and deleting existing colors, you can create a color palette that has just the colors needed for the current document. The colors you select will be saved with the document.

### Defining CMYK, RGB, and HLS Colors

If you are using the CMYK, RGB, or HLS color model, you can define a color with the Color Definitions dialog box by following these steps:

1. Choose View, Color, Definitions to display this dialog box:

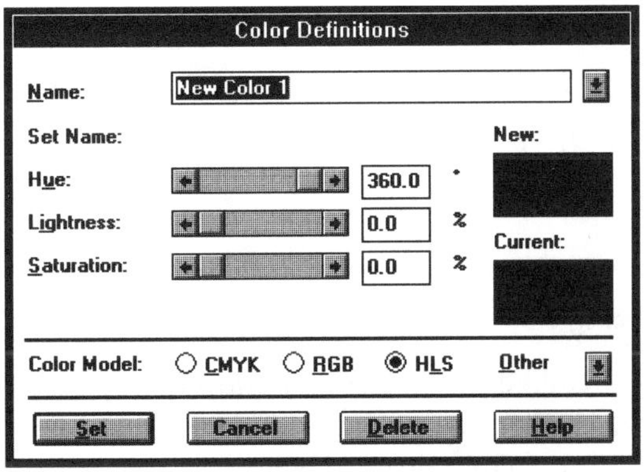

2. Choose the desired color model.
3. Use the elevator box to select a setting or enter a number in the setting box for each setting.
4. Type a name in the Name box and choose Set.

The new color name will appear in all color menus.

## Using the Common Color Picker

To define a new color using the common color picker, follow these steps:

1. Choose View, Color, Definitions.
2. Choose Other, Common Color Picker to display this dialog box:

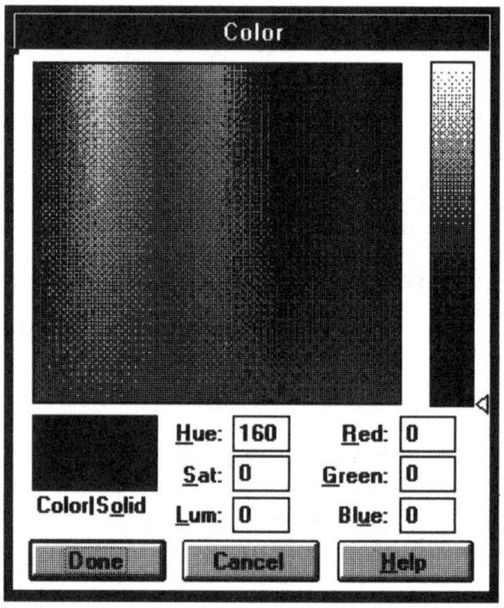


3. Click the mouse pointer on the color desired in the large square.
4. Slide the arrow to the desired brightness in the luminescence bar.
5. Choose Done.
6. Type a name in the Name box.
7. Choose Set.

## Selecting Pantone Colors

Unlike process colors and HLS colors, you cannot define a PANTONE color, because these colors have already been defined. To select a PANTONE color, follow these steps:

1. Choose View, Color, Definitions.
2. Choose Other, PANTONE. The following dialog box is displayed:

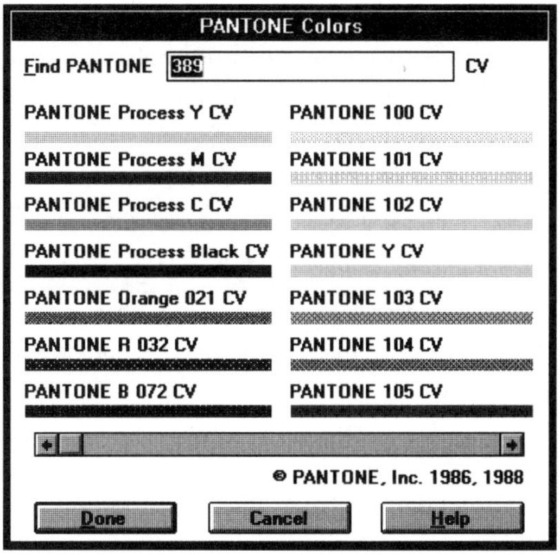


3. Enter the desired PANTONE number or choose one from the display.

**NOTE:** *You can use the scroll bar to scroll the display of PANTONE colors.*

4. Choose Done.
5. Enter a name for the color or leave the PANTONE name as is.

**TIP:** *Give PANTONE colors a name, but include the number. For example, change the name Pantone 512 to Blue 512.*

6. Choose Set.

**NOTE:** *A PANTONE MATCHING SYSTEM swatch book will give you a better idea of what the PANTONE color looks like than the representations on the screen.*

### Changing a Color

Any color that you have defined with the color picker or the CMYK, RGB, or HLS models can be modified. Once a color is modified, any objects that use that color will automatically be updated.

To change a color, follow these steps:

1. Choose View, Color, Definitions.
2. Click the arrow beside the color name to display the list of names and choose the desired color.
3. Make changes as desired.
4. Choose Set.
5. Choose Done.

**NOTE:** *FrameMaker 4 will not allow you to change the colors in any way for white, the process colors, cyan, yellow, magenta, and black or for the RGB colors, red, green, and blue.*

### Deleting a Color

To delete a color, follow these steps:

1. Choose View, Color, Definitions.
2. Click the arrow beside the color name to display the list of names and choose the desired color.
3. Choose Delete.
4. Choose Done.

## ASSIGNING COLORS

As mentioned previously, any new colors that you create are added to color menus. The color menus can be found in six places: the Character Designer window, the Paragraph Designer window, the Object Properties dialog box, the Graphics Tools palette, the Change Bar Properties dialog box, and the Custom Ruling and Shading window. These color menus are used in various ways to assign color to text and objects as explained here:

- To assign color to selected text or paragraphs, select a color from the color pop-up menu in either the Character Designer window or the Paragraph Designer window and choose Apply.

**Color Plate #1**
Specialty paper available from Paper Direct.

Yellow

Cyan

Magenta

Black

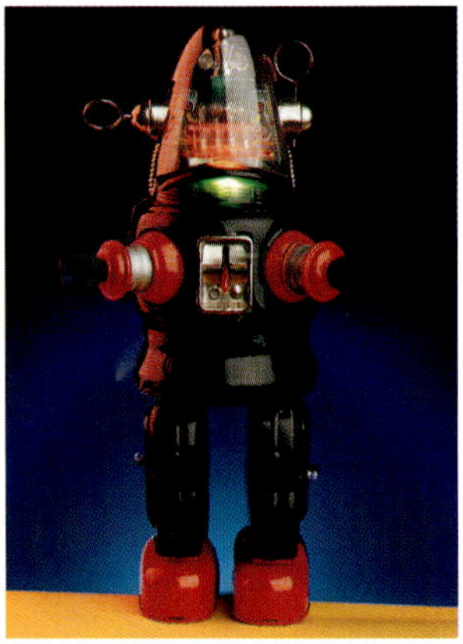

Photograph courtesy of
Geoffrey Carr Photography, Inc.

**Color Plate #2**

The four-color process. The photograph is separated into the individual color components, and a plate is created for each color. On the press, the four colors are combined to create the full-color image.

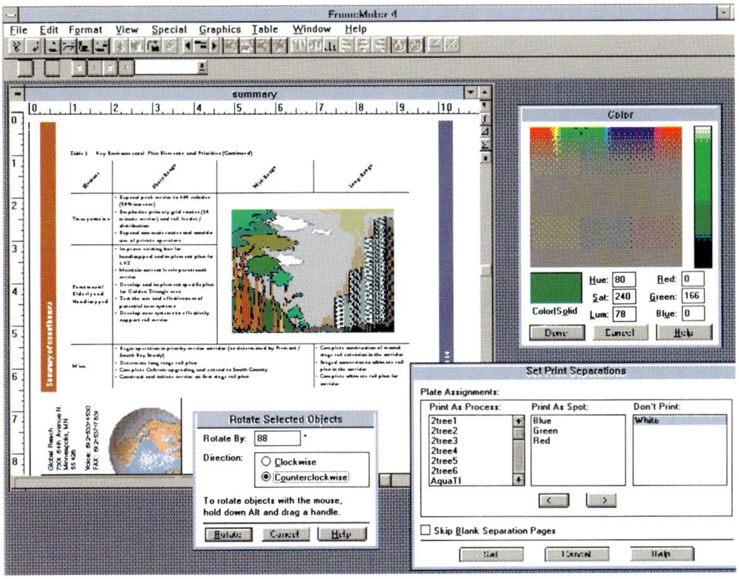


**Color Plate #3**
This window displays a complex layout as well as the Common Color Picker.

Photograph courtesy of Geoffrey Carr Photography, Inc.

**Color Plate #4**
A Moire pattern is created by improper line screen angles.

Yellow

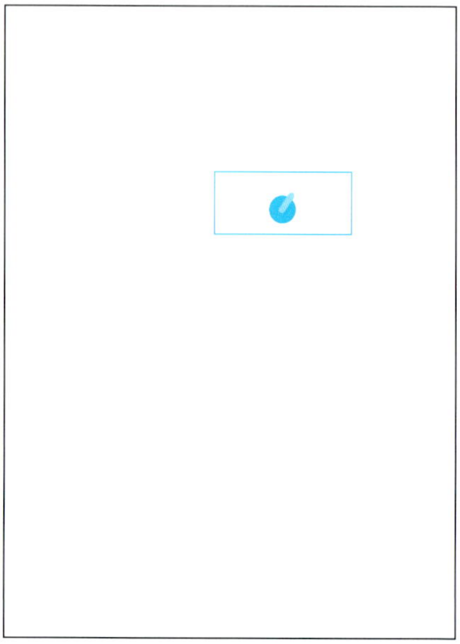

Cyan

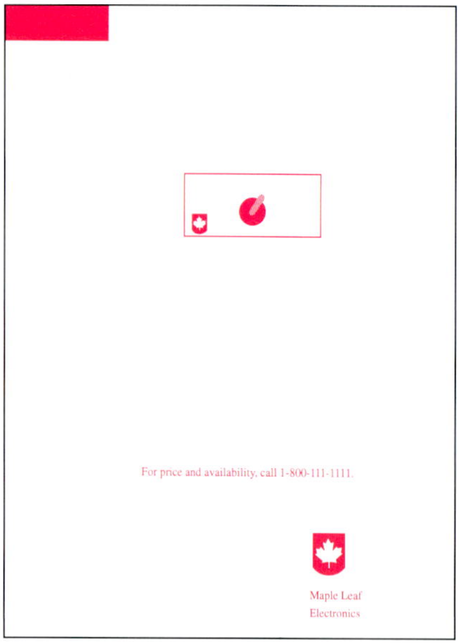


Magenta

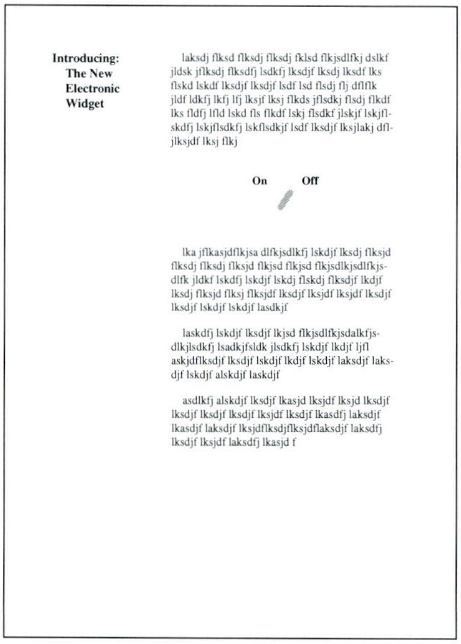


Black

**Color Plate #5**
An example of the four-color separation that is printed by Frame. Separations are printed in the correct colors if you are using a color printer, or printed in black and white and shades of gray if you are using a non-color printer.

Photograph courtesy of Geoffrey Carr Photography, Inc.

Photograph courtesy of Geoffrey Carr Photography, Inc.

**Color Plate #6**

Creating a duotone is similar to the four-color process, but only two colors are used.

**Color Plate #7**
The process of using color foil with a laser printer.

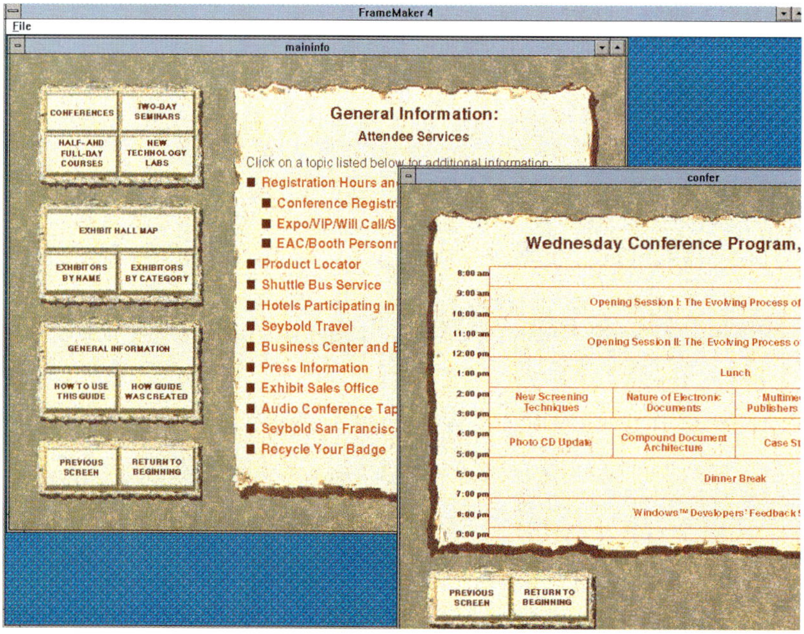


**Color Plate #8**
Sample screen of the Seybold Kiosk (a hypertext document).

- To include color as an attribute of a character or paragraph tag, choose the color from the pop-up menu in the Designer window when creating the tag.
- To assign a color to an object drawn with the drawing tools, select the object and choose a color from the Graphics Tools palette or use the Object Properties dialog box. (Be sure the object has a fill pattern. If the fill pattern is None, no color will be displayed.)
- To assign a color to an imported graphic, select the object and choose a color from the Graphics Tools color pop-up menu or assign a color in the Object Properties dialog box. If the graphic is not a color graphic, it will not change color on the screen, but it will print in color.
- To color the background of a text column, select the text column as an object, change the fill pattern from None to a visible fill pattern (solid is usually best), and then select a color from the Graphics Tools color pop-up menu or select a color from the Object Properties dialog box.
- To use color in equations and the text in tables, select the text or equation element, and then select a color from the color pop-up menu in either the Character Designer window or the Paragraph Designer window and choose Apply.
- To select a color for a change bar, choose Format, Change Bars, and choose a color from the color pop-up menu. Then choose Set.
- To add color to the background of a cell in a table, choose Table and Custom Ruling & Shading. Select a Fill percentage and then select a color from the color pop-up menu. Finally, select Apply. For more information about tables, see Chapter 10.

## PRINTING ON THE DESKTOP

Undoubtedly you will print out your document many times while you are creating it. No matter how good a document looks on screen, it always looks different in hard copy.

When you are printing a color document as a proof copy, you will probably print a composite page. A composite page prints all the colors on the page if you have a color printer. If you have a black-and-white printer, all the colors on a composite page are printed in black and white or black and shades of gray.

When you are ready to print the final copy, you will probably want to print color separations. Printing a color separation results in printing one page per color used (process color and/or spot colors).

To display the Print Document dialog box shown here, choose File, Print:

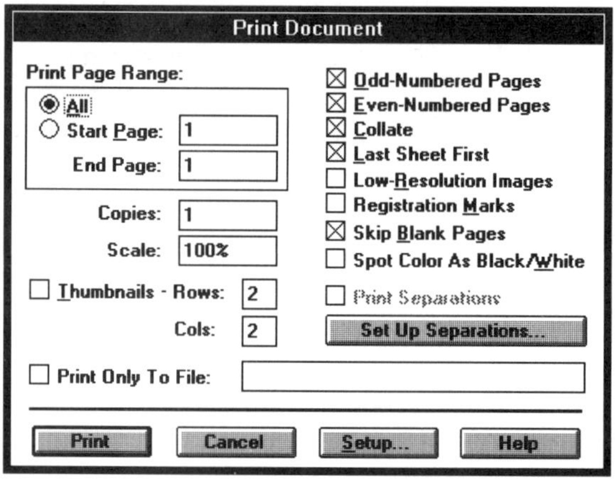


A composite page is printed by simply not selecting Print Separations. If you want to print color separations, you must first choose Set Up Separations to display this dialog box:

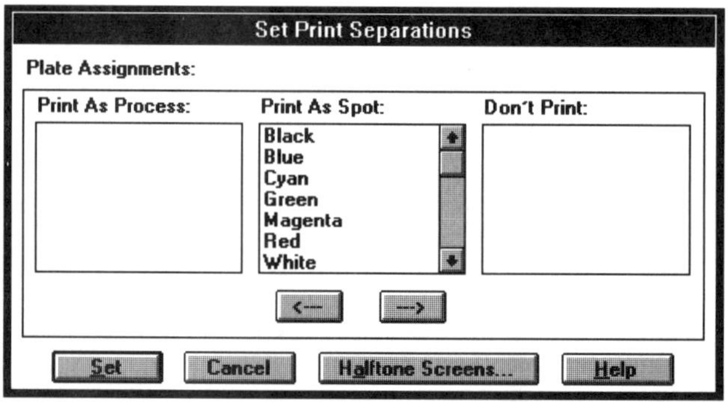


When setting up a separation, you list all the colors that you want to print as process colors (cyan, yellow, magenta, and black) and all the colors that you want to print as spot colors.

Additionally, you must choose Halftone Screens, which displays this dialog box:

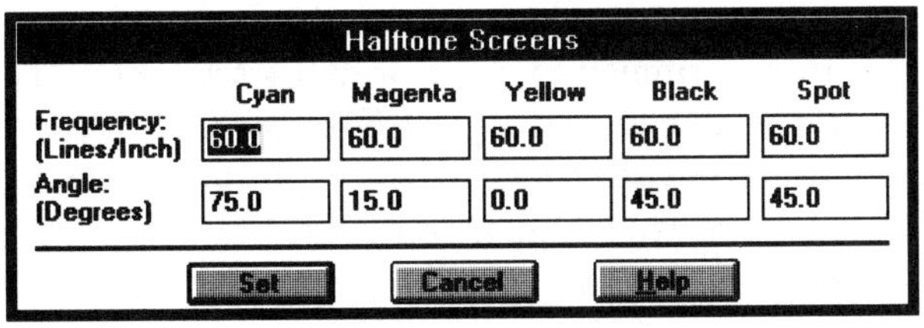


In the Halftone Screens dialog box, you must select the screen frequency and the screen angle for each process color. Regardless of the number of different spot colors used, only one setting is made for the spot color frequency and angle.

A halftone screen breaks images down into printable dots. The frequency refers to the resolution (or how close together the dots are) measured in lines per inch (lpi). The angle refers to the rotation of the screen.

In the case of black-and-white images, a 45 degree rotation from horizontal is the least noticeable. When a screen for each color is involved, each screen must be rotated so its dots do not print over the dots of another screen. Figure 9-1 shows two boxes printed with the same angle and different frequencies.

**NOTE:** *If screens are placed at incorrect angles, an undesirable effect is produced called a moire pattern. See Color Plate 4.*

**FIGURE 9-1**

*Different screen frequencies*

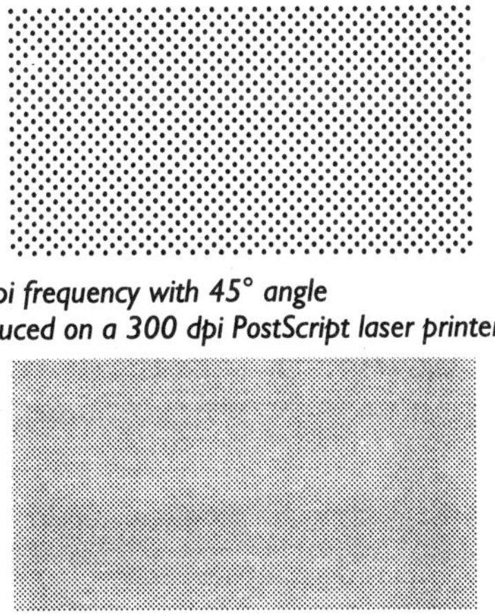

*20 lpi frequency with 45° angle*
*Produced on a 300 dpi PostScript laser printer*

*60 lpi frequency with 45% angle*
*Produced on a 300 dpi PostScript laser printer*

The settings that are initially displayed in the Halftone Screens dialog box are determined by your printer's resolution. For example, the initial setting for frequency on a 300 dots-per-inch (dpi) laser printer is 60 lpi. Laser printers with 300 dpi can reproduce only 32 shades of gray at a screen frequency of 60 lpi. If you set the resolution higher, the image will be sharper, but fewer shades of gray can be reproduced. Imagesetters with resolutions starting at 1200 dpi can reproduce 256 shades of gray.

**NOTE:** *If you have a 300 dpi laser printer, which is a common printer for desktop publishers, you can use your printer to print camera-ready copy for text documents and some color documents. But for documents that require high-quality printing, you will probably want to use an imagesetter or other high-resolution (600+ dpi) output devices. When creating high-quality print jobs, you will probably use the 300 dpi laser printer for proofs only.*

## PUTTING IT ALL TOGETHER

Now, perhaps you are saying to yourself, "All this information about color is good, but where do I start and what do I do?" The following exercise should help you put it all together. In the exercise you will use the CMYK color model and create a new color. When the layout is finished, you will print the four color separations.

Follow these steps to create the information sheet for Maple Leaf Electronics as shown in Figure 9-2.

1. Create a new document with one column, using these custom measurements:

   Width: 6"
   Height: 9"
   Left margin: 2"
   Top, bottom, and right margin: .75"

2. Create a new paragraph tag called Red12 based on the same attributes as the Body tag. Choose Default Font Properties, and select red from the color pop-up menu.

3. Modify the Body paragraph tag so that it has a first-line indent of 12.0 points and 12.0 points of space below.

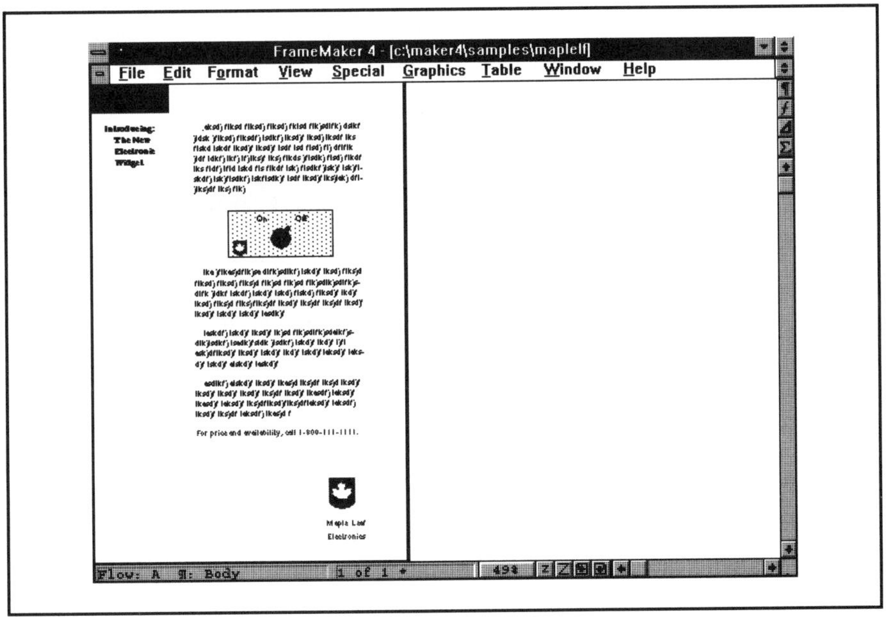


**FIGURE 9-2** *Information sheet for Maple Leaf Electronics*

4. Begin typing gibberish (using the Body tag) until you have about seven or eight lines. (There is an art to typing gibberish. You must press the SPACEBAR between characters every once in a while to make the gibberish look like words and to allow the line to wrap properly.)
5. Press ENTER and type another paragraph of gibberish.
6. Type two more paragraphs of gibberish.
7. Press ENTER.
8. Using the Red12 tag, type the following:

   **For price and availability, call 1-800-111-1111.**

9. Save the file with the name **maple**.
10. Split the text column (Format, Pages, Layout Commands, Split Current Column).
11. Move the lower portion of the text column down so there is about 1.5 inches between the columns.
12. Draw a rectangle in the middle of the blank space (created by splitting the column). Make the rectangle 2 inches wide and .875

inches tall. (Use the Object Properties dialog box to make the measurements precise.)

13. Fill the rectangle with the fill pattern indicated here by the cursor:

14. Select the color blue for the rectangle.
15. Draw a circle in the center of the rectangle and make the circle blue with a solid fill.
16. Draw a small rounded rectangle in the circle and rotate it as shown here:

17. Create a new CMYK color (View, Color, Definitions), called New Blue that is 48 percent cyan, 48 percent magenta, and 30 percent black.
18. Apply the color New Blue to the rounded rectangle drawn in Step 16.
19. Using the Text Line tool, type **Off** and **On**. Then select the text and make it bold as shown here:

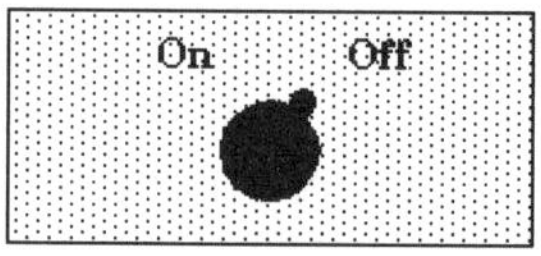


20. Draw a rectangle that is 1.75 inches wide and .75 inches tall.

21. Give the rectangle a solid fill and make it red.
22. Move the rectangle to the upper-left corner of the page.
23. This rectangle will bleed off the page at the top and the left edge, so move it .25 inch above the top edge and .25 inch to the left of the left edge. (Hint: Set the Object Properties settings for top and left to –0.25".)
24. Using the Text Line tool, type:

    **Introducing:**
    **The New**
    **Electronic**
    **Widget.**

25. Make the text bold and use the Align and Distribute tools as necessary.
26. Open the file maker4\clipart\maps.
27. Page through the file until you see the maple leaf symbol. Select the symbol and copy it to the clipboard. Then close the file.
28. In the MAPLE document, click the cursor anywhere in the margin and then choose Edit, Paste to bring in the maple leaf symbol.
29. Shrink the symbol proportionally (hold SHIFT as you drag a corner) and move it to the bottom-left corner of the rectangle drawn in Step 12.
30. Choose Edit, Paste again. This time enlarge the icon proportionally and move it to the bottom-right corner of the page.
31. Change the color of both maple leaf images to red.
32. Just below the maple leaf in the bottom-right corner of the page, type the following with the Text Line tool:

    **Maple Leaf**
    **Electronics**

33. Use the Align and Distribute tools as needed to align the text properly.
34. Select the text (typed in Step 32) and change it to red by applying red from the Character Designer window.
35. Save the file.
36. Choose File, Print.

37. Choose Set Up Separation.
38. Move all the colors into the Print As Process box.
39. Choose Set.
40. Choose Print Separations and Registration Marks.
41. Choose Print.

Four pages should print—one for the cyan process plate, one for the yellow process plate, one for the magenta process plate, and one for the black process plate. Each page will indicate somewhere along the bottom of the page the name of the color plate. These four pages can be taken to the printer and used to create the films that will be stripped into flats.

You will notice that each page is different. The black process plate has all the text on it except the text that is red. All red text and red images are printed on the magenta and yellow plates because these two colors are mixed to create red.

The magenta and cyan plates have cut-out areas. The shape of the logo is cut out of the rectangle in the cyan plate, and the words On and Off are cut out in both plates. Printers call this cut out a *knock out*. You could have used overprint for these items as described later in this chapter.

Some areas on the black, magenta, and cyan plates are made up of individual dots that you can see. This is how a percentage of a color is represented. If the percentage of the color is 100 percent, the object is solid.

**NOTE:** *When printing separations on a 300 dpi laser printer, your output will probably not be good enough to use for making negatives if you have mixed colors that use less than 100 percent of a process color.*

## VIEWING COLORS

If you are using several colors in a document, you may want to set up a view that includes or excludes certain colors. If you are using four-color process and one PMS spot color, you might want to set up five views showing each color. This would show you what is going to print on each color separation. Color Plate 5 shows the four views of the MAPLE document created in this chapter.

Another reason you might want to set up a view is to check the coloring of elements. For example, if you want to see if the line at the top of all pages is blue, you can set up a view that only shows the color blue.

The View feature is a necessity for users who have monochrome monitors. Instead of checking each object's color to be sure the colors have been set correctly, the view can show all the objects of one color at once.

## Setting Up a View

Setting up a view involves specifying which colors are visible, which colors are cut out, and which colors are invisible. You can create a maximum of six views, but you can change the views at any time.

To create a view, follow these steps:

1. Choose View, Color, Views to display this dialog box:

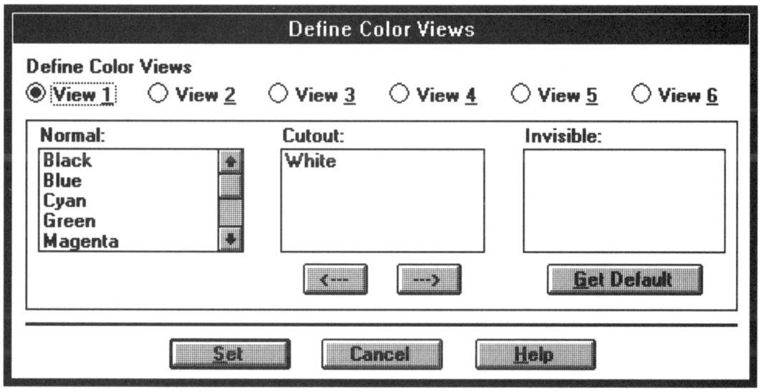


2. Select a view number.
3. Select a color that is not in the desired area (Normal, Cutout, or Invisible) and move it to the desired area by clicking the left or right arrow (below the Cutout list box).

   Colors in the Normal category are all visible. Colors in the Cutout category appear as white if they overlap another color. Colors in the Invisible category do not display at all.

**TIP:** *If you want to move all the colors in one category to another, select one color and then SHIFT-click the arrow button.*

4. Continue moving colors to the correct areas.

5. When all colors are in the correct categories, select a different view number and create another view if desired.
6. When all views have been created, select the view that you want to be the current view and choose Set.

**TIP:** *Use the defaults for View 1 so you have a view that shows all the colors. (You can change a view to the defaults by clicking the Get Defaults button.)*

### Displaying a View

Only one view can be activated at a time. To display a view, follow these steps:

1. Choose View, Color, Views.
2. Select the desired view.
3. Select Set.

## COUNTING THE COST

There is no way to get around it—printing more than one color of ink is more expensive. The question is, "Is the added expense worth it?" If you are printing an advertising brochure, the answer is unquestionably "yes." If you are printing a five-page instruction manual that comes with a fluorescent desk lamp, the answer is probably "no."

You must decide on a case-by-case basis whether color printing is desirable. Of course there are other costs involved in color printing besides the additional ink. The printer must make a plate for each color; time on color presses is more expensive than time on one-color presses; more experienced pressmen must be used, at a higher wage; color separations will be needed if you use continuous color images or photographs; a better grade of paper might be required, and so on. There are many things to be considered, so if you are planning to print in color, talk to your printer early in the process to see what will be involved.

## Watching Your Budget

Although color can be expensive, there are ways to trim the budget when using color. The following suggestions may give you some ideas:

- Print two colors, like black and PANTONE 221, and create additional colors without extra expense by using screens of the two colors. Screens are created in FrameMaker 4 by using fill patterns.
- Instead of printing full-color photos, print duotones. A duotone uses two colors of ink and two separations. See Color Plate 6.
- If you are going to print three colors, you might as well print four, but avoid using more than the four process colors. If you want to use a PANTONE color as a spot color, ask the printer to come as close as possible to the color with a mix of process colors instead of using a fifth color of ink.
- If you must use color separations for photographs, have the photos *gang separated* if possible. A gang separation is a four-color separation of many photographs on the same film. Gang separations can only be used with good results if all the photographs have a similar contrast.
- Consider printing more than one color job at a time.
- For periodic print runs, like monthly newsletters, print a large quantity of the color sheets and use them each month for printing the text in one color.

# PRINTING SPOT COLOR WITH A LASER PRINTER

Even if you do not have a color laser printer, you can use your laser to print color. A new process using colored foil allows you to fuse the foil to the paper by running it through the laser. Color foils are available from several specialty paper vendors such as Paper Direct and Paper Access. See Color Plate 7.

Using colored foils is work intensive, so it is not recommended for large print runs. However, it may be very impressive, effective, and economical to use for small print jobs—creating 15 report covers for a board meeting, for example.

## COLOR PRINTING IS NOT AS EASY AS IT MAY SEEM

This book intends to make all topics as easy to understand as possible. If that goal is reached in this chapter, the danger is that you will think that working with color is easier than it actually is.

Color printing is a complicated subject, and this chapter has not touched on all the issues involved. One reason is because FrameMaker 4 does not address all the issues. No desktop publishing package does. That is why there are so many other programs available that must be used in tandem with a desktop publishing program. These programs are used for making color corrections, creating color separations, enhancing color, and so on.

One of the complicated issues involved in color printing arises when one color object prints on top of another color object or when one color prints next to another color. Knockouts are commonly used when one color will print over the top of another color. Instead of printing the second color over the first (called *overprinting*), the first color is knocked out (left blank), letting the second color print directly on the paper, maintaining the integrity of the color. FrameMaker 4 uses the knockout feature automatically.

If you want an object to overprint another one, you must select the object and choose Graphics, Overprint. This dialog box is displayed:

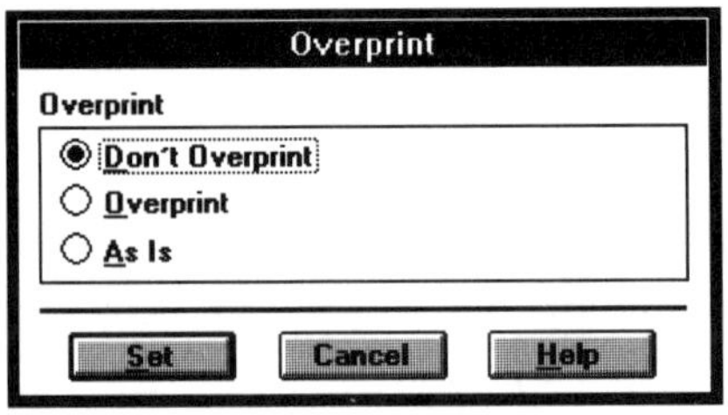


Choose Overprint and Set.

Overprinting is only recommended for printing dark colors, such as black, over light colors. In other cases, the overprinted object's color will be degraded. While knockout is recommended in these other cases, using knockouts carries its own set of problems. If the registration of the two objects is not correct or if the paper stretches on the press, the knockout may show, causing an outline around the object. See Color Plate 8. This is corrected with a process called trapping—a process not supported by FrameMaker 4.

*Trapping* is the process of overprinting only the edges of an object so that a paper gap does not show even if the registration is slightly off. Usually the lighter color object overlaps the darker color object. Where the edges overlap, a new color of ink is created but it is barely noticeable if light ink overprints dark ink. It is very noticeable if dark ink overprints light ink.

If your document involves complicated color issues, you will be forced to use other programs to rectify these issues or turn them over to the printer. Another option is to take your file to a prepress system that can scan color images, handle complex color correction, and create quality color separations. Prepress systems called CEPS (Color Electronic Prepress System) are very expensive and are usually found in color separation houses or in magazine and newspaper publishing companies.

# V

# High-Powered Features

# 10

## Creating Tables

TABLES are a useful and multifunctional feature of FrameMaker 4 that can be formatted with great detail. Of all the table features this author has personally used in other DTP programs, FrameMaker's is the best and most versatile.

## CREATING AND POSITIONING TABLES

Tables consist of rows and columns. Special rows are designated as title rows, heading rows, and footing rows. (The rows that contain the basic data can be considered "body rows" although they are not referred to as such in any menus.) To create a table, follow these steps:

1. Click the cursor in the line of text that should precede the table.
2. Choose Table, Insert Table. This dialog box is displayed:

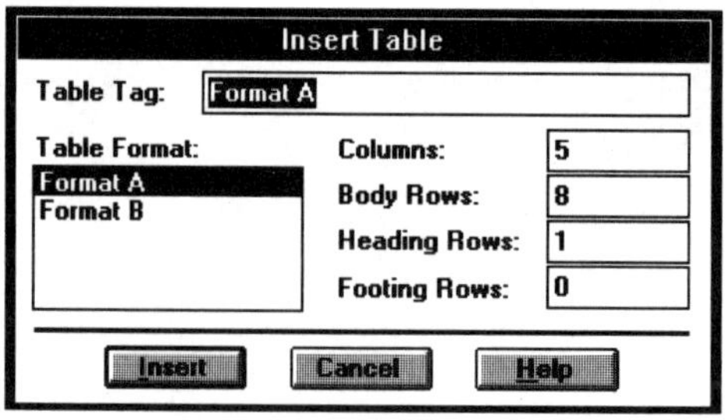


3. Choose a table format from the list box. The default formats are Format A and Format B, but other formats may be listed if

they have been created. (Creating formats is discussed later in this chapter.)

4. Enter a number for the desired columns, body rows, heading rows, and footing rows if the default numbers are not exactly what you want.
5. Choose Insert.

Figure 10-1 shows two tables on a page. The table at the top uses Format A and the table at the bottom uses Format B. As you can see, Format A and Format B use the same number of rows and columns, both have a title row and a heading row, and neither has a footing row. Format A positions the table on the left margin, while Format B centers the table between the margins.

The attributes of a table are defined in the Table Designer window displayed by choosing Table, Table Designer. After using the Character and Paragraph Designer windows, this window should look very familiar.

Shown here is the Table Designer window with the attributes of Format A. Notice that Format A has no indents on the left or right and the alignment is left.

**FIGURE 10-1**

*Two table formats*

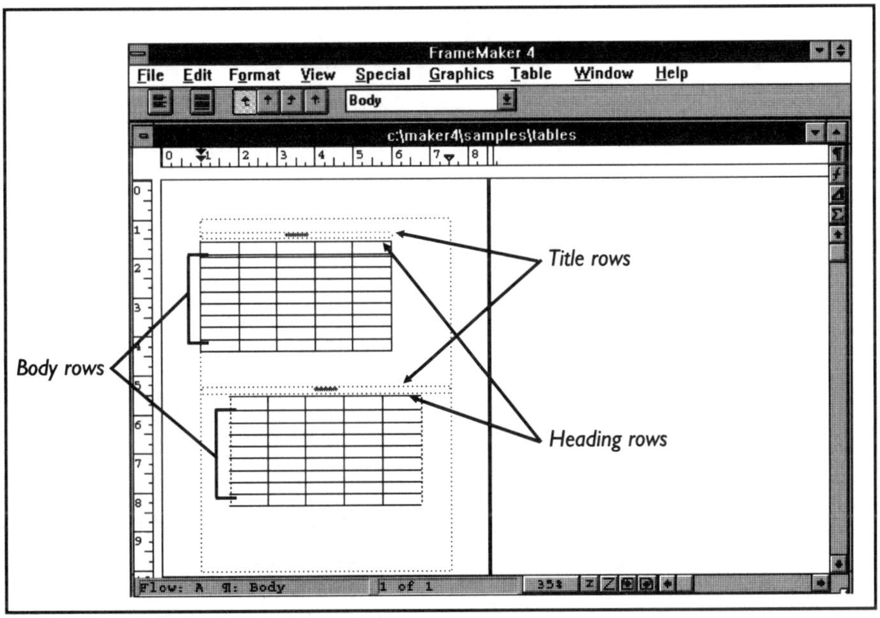

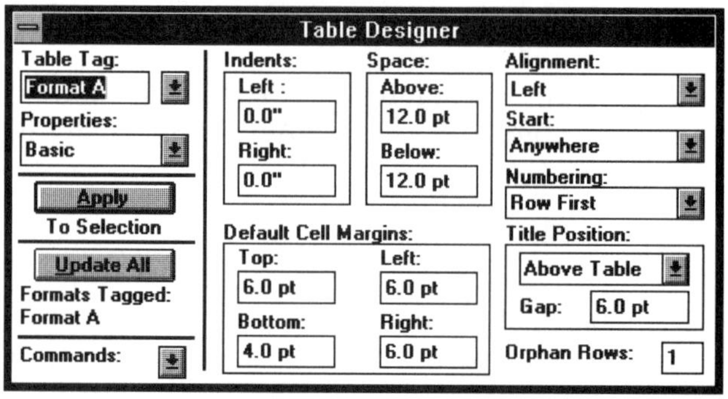


Format B, as shown here, has no indents, but the alignment is centered. By specifying indent values and alignment (left, right, or centered) you can position a table horizontally anywhere you want.

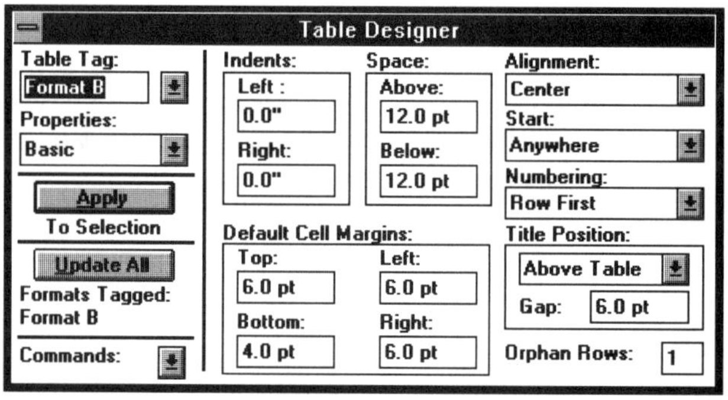


The vertical positioning of a table can be accomplished with the Start option and the Space Above and Space Below options. The Start options and their descriptions are listed below.

| Option | Function |
|---|---|
| As Is | maintains the current start value |
| Anywhere | positions the table in the next place it will fit |
| Top of Column | starts the table at the top of the next column |
| Top of Page | starts the table at the top of the next page |
| Top of Left Page | starts the table at the top of the next left page |
| Top of Right Page | starts the table at the top of the next right page |
| Float | allows a table to move to the first column in which it fits if it will not fit in the column where the line to which it is anchored is located |

**NOTE:** *A table will float only if the minimum number of orphan rows specified in the Table Designer window will not fit at the bottom of the current column.*

The Space Above and Space Below options add white space (vertical padding) between a table and the adjacent text. These options are similar to adding space above and below a paragraph. In fact, if the space above or below an adjacent paragraph is greater than the table's space values, the paragraph spacing will be used. FrameMaker 4 always uses the greater amount of space.

## ENTERING TEXT

To enter text in a table, click the text cursor in the desired cell (intersection of a column and row) and begin typing. Text will wrap in the cell and the row height will increase automatically to accommodate the text. Notice, we said the *row* height will increase, not just the height of the cell. All cells in the same row have the same height. If you press ENTER in a cell, a new line will be created in the cell.

To move to the next cell, press TAB. To move to the previous cell, press SHIFT+TAB. To move to the cell below the current cell, press ALT+CTRL+TAB. To move to the cell immediately above the current cell, press ALT+CTRL+SHIFT+TAB—oh, heck, just click in the cell, it's easier.

**NOTE:** *To actually include a Tab in a cell you must press ESC+TAB.*

When text is typed in a cell, it is actually entered in a text column. The text column is positioned inside the cell ruling lines by the cell margins defined in the Table Designer window as shown here:

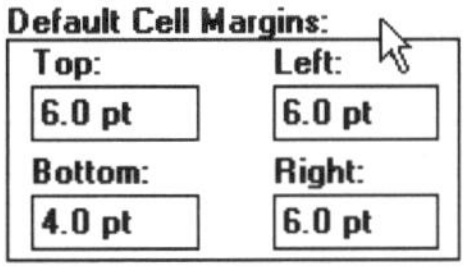


The attributes of text that you are to enter are determined by several paragraph tags created for use in tables—TableTitle, CellHeading, CellBody, and TableFootnote. The first three tags are automatically assigned in Format A and Format B. You can use these paragraph tags, modify them, or create your own as you learned in Chapter 6. You can also apply any of the character tags available or create your own for tables.

You can copy and delete text in a table just as you do any other text, but you can also copy and delete text in a cell in a different way. If you select the cell instead of the text, you can copy or delete all of the text in a cell. To copy text in a selected cell or cells, choose Edit, Copy and then paste the text in another cell. When text is copied in this way, the format is also copied. To delete text in a selected cell or cells, press DEL. If you select an entire row or column of cells to delete, FrameMaker 4 displays this message:

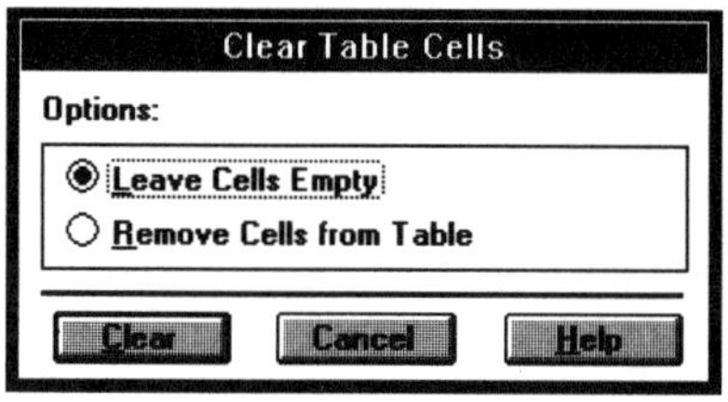


If you do not want to delete the row or column, select Leave Cells Empty and choose Clear.

## MANIPULATING TABLES

As mentioned earlier in the chapter, the table feature in FrameMaker 4 is very versatile and there are a multitude of commands that can be used to manipulate tables. The basic commands are listed in alphabetical order and explained in this section. Many of the commands involve selecting cells or the table itself. To select a cell, group of cells, a row, or a column, simply drag the mouse pointer across the desired area. A handle appears on the right border when you let go of the mouse button.

**TIP:** *To select a large table, select any cell and choose Edit, Select All of Table.*

ADD ROWS OR COLUMNS Click in a cell that will be adjacent to the row or column you want to add. Choose Table, Add Rows or Columns. A dialog box is displayed. Type the number of row or columns to add and select a location (above, below, left, right, or to heading or footing). Choose Add.

COMBINE CELLS (See Straddle Cells below.)

COMBINE TABLES Select all the columns and rows of a table and choose Edit, Cut to store the table in the clipboard. Paste the table in the clipboard into an existing table.

COPY AN ENTIRE TABLE Select the table. Choose Edit, Copy. Click the text cursor in the line below which the table should appear. Choose Edit, Paste.

COPY COLUMN WIDTH Select a cell in the column whose width you want to copy. Choose Edit, Copy Special, Table Column Width. Click in a cell in the column to which you want to copy the width. Choose Edit, Copy.

COPY ROWS OR COLUMNS Select the rows or columns to be copied. Choose Edit, Copy. Click the cursor in the row or column that will be adjacent to the copied row or column. Choose Edit, Paste. A dialog box is displayed. Specify the location and choose Paste.

DELETE A TABLE Select the table. Press DEL. Select Remove from Table and click Clear.

DELETE ROWS OR COLUMNS Select the rows or columns. Press DEL or choose Edit, Cut. Choose Remove Cells from Table and click Clear.

INCREASE ALL ROW HEIGHTS Select all rows in the table and choose Table, Row Format. A dialog box is displayed. Type a minimum height and choose Set.

INCREASE A ROW'S HEIGHT Click in the row to be increased and choose Table, Row Format. A dialog box is displayed. Type a minimum height and choose Set.

MOVE A TABLE Select the table, then choose Edit, Cut. Choose Remove Cells from Table and click Cut. Click the text cursor in the line of text below which the table should appear. Choose Edit, Paste.

MOVE ROWS OR COLUMNS Select the rows or columns to be moved. Choose Edit, Cut. Choose Remove Cells from Table and click Cut. Click the cursor in the row or column that will be adjacent to the moved row or column. Choose Edit, Paste. A dialog box is displayed. Specify a location and choose Paste.

RESIZE ALL COLUMNS Select all the columns in the table and choose Table, Resize Columns. Choose To Equal Widths Totalling and leave the value in the text box unchanged. Choose Resize.

RESIZE A COLUMN A Column can be sized with the mouse or with menu selections. To resize a column with the mouse, select the entire column and drag a handle. The width of the entire table will be increased or decreased.

To change the width of a column without changing the overall width of the table, select only one cell in the desired column and press ALT as you drag it to a new width. To change the width of a column with the menus, select cells in the columns to be resized and choose Table, Resize Columns. Choose an option from this dialog box:

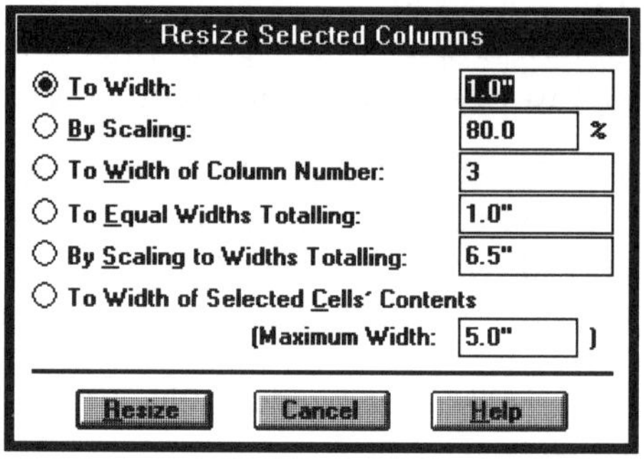


Then choose Resize.

ROTATE A TABLE To rotate a table on a page by itself, create a rotated master page if you do not have one and apply it to the page where the rotated table will be positioned. To include a rotated table on a portrait-oriented page, create an anchored frame and draw a text column inside the frame. Insert the table in the text column and rotate the text column.

ROTATE A CELL OR CELLS Select the cells to be rotated (usually the heading cells). Choose Graphics, Rotate. A dialog box is displayed with four possible rotations. Choose the rotation desired and click Rotate.

SPLIT A TABLE Select the rows and columns that include the cells you want to include in the new table. Choose Edit, Cut. Click the cursor in a text column and choose Edit, Paste. The new table will have the format of the table from which it was split.

STRADDLE CELLS Select the cells you want to combine. Choose Table, Straddle.

UNSTRADDLE CELLS Select the cells you want to divide into individual cells. Choose Table, Unstraddle.

## PLACING A GRAPH IN A TABLE

The quick way to import a graphic is to click the cursor in the cell that will contain the graphic; choose File, Import, File; select the file; and choose Import. Then choose Fit in Selected Rectangle. The graphic will be inserted in the cell inside an anchored frame. The graphic may have to be resized slightly to fit in the cell. The frame can also be resized. (Remember, if the frame is made smaller it has the effect of cropping the graphic.)

Another way to place a graphic in a cell is to import an unanchored graphic and move it into the cell. This method only stacks the graphic object over the table object, it does not actually anchor the graphic in the cell. If the cell is cut or the table is moved, the graphic will remain.

If you want to place a graphic in the exact center of a cell, follow these steps:

1. Click the cursor in the desired cell on a blank line.
2. Choose Format, Paragraphs, Designer.
3. Choose Center Alignment and be sure Fixed is not selected.
4. Click the Apply button.
5. Choose Table Cells in the Properties list.
6. Choose Middle in the Cell Vertical Alignment list.
7. Click the Apply button.
8. Close the Paragraph Designer window.
9. Choose Special, Anchored Frame.
10. Choose At Insertion Point.
11. Enter a width and height that will fit in the table cell and click New Frame.
12. If the frame size is not quite right, resize the frame or the cell.
13. Import the graphic in the frame, selecting Fit in Selected Rectangle.

## PLACING A TABLE WITHIN A TABLE

To place a table within a table cell, first create an anchored frame in the cell that will hold the table. Then draw a text column in the frame and insert the table in the text column. You can continue the process of inserting tables within tables. There is no limit set by FrameMaker 4 to the number of tables that can be embedded, but practically speaking the number of tables that can be embedded will be limited by the size.

## PUTTING IT ALL TOGETHER

To understand the table feature better, try the following exercise which creates the calendar of July 1994 shown in Figure 10-2. To create the calendar, follow these steps:

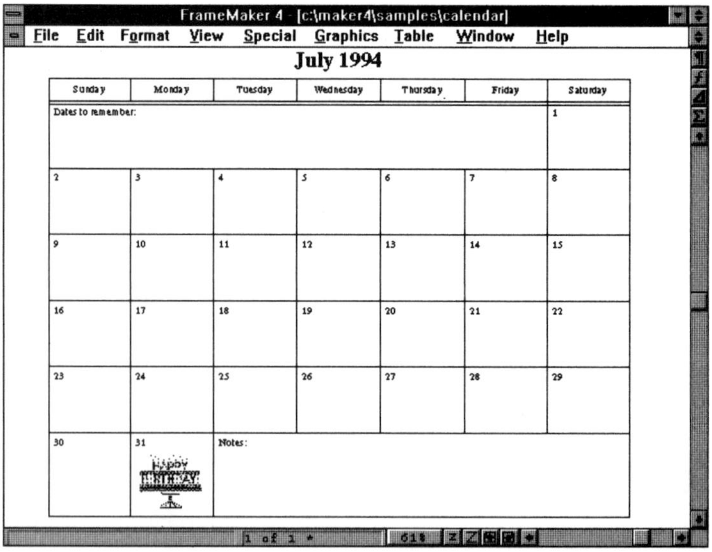


**FIGURE 10-2** *A calendar created with the table feature*

1. Create a new document with a landscape orientation using a top margin of .25" and all other margins of 1".
2. Insert a table with seven columns, five body rows, and one heading row. Use Format A.
3. Select all the columns in the table and increase the widths of the columns equally so that the width of the entire table totals 9".
4. Select all the body rows and increase the height to a minimum of 1".
5. Type the days of the week (starting with Sunday) in the heading row.
6. Apply the Body tag to the title in the title row. Type **July 1994** in 24 point bold and center the paragraph.
7. Apply the Body tag to the first six cells in the first body row.
8. Straddle the first six cells in the first body row.
9. Click the cursor in the last cell on the first body row and display the Paragraph Designer window.
10. Choose Numbering in the Properties list.
11. Turn on Autonumber Format.
12. Select the <n+> building block.
13. Choose Update All and close the window.
14. Add a row to the bottom of the calendar.
15. Apply the Body tag to the last five cells in the new row.
16. Straddle the last five cells in the new row.
17. In the first cell, type **Dates to remember:**
18. In the last cell, type **Notes:**
19. Click in the cell for July 31 and import a graphic of a birthday cake if you have one. (This will remind you to send the author a nice check on her birthday.) If you do not have any clip art to use, open the file called \maker4\clipart\symbols and go to page 9. Select the wrapped package and copy it to the clipboard. Close the file and paste the graphic in the cell for July 31.
20. Save the file.

This file could be used as a template. To create calendars for each month, you would change the name of the title and change the paragraph tags in the first row of cells so that the first day of the month and the cells that follow use the CellBody tag. The cells before the first day of the month would use the Body tag.

## MULTIPAGE TABLES

Tables that span several pages need some special consideration. Titles and headings need to be repeated on each page, and page breaks must be placed at logical breaking points.

FrameMaker automatically repeats the title and heading/footing rows on every page for you, but you may want the title to include the word "continued" or to display numbers. Two special variables, Table Continuation and Table Sheet, are provided for continuation text and for numbering. Other variables can be used as well.

To insert a variable, follow these steps:

1. Click the cursor in the heading row on the first page of the table where you want a variable.
2. Choose Special, Variable, and select the variable.
3. Edit the variable if you want to change the wording or add emphasis.
4. Click the Insert button.

Figure 10-3 shows the headings on the first and second pages of a multipage table document. Notice that the word "(Continued)" does not appear until the second page even though it is inserted on the first page.

**NOTE:** *You cannot edit a title, heading, or footing row on any page except the first page of the table.*

FrameMaker 4 automatically breaks a table and places it on another page or in another column based on the number of orphan rows specified in the Table Designer window as shown here:

**FIGURE 10-3**

*Headings with variables*

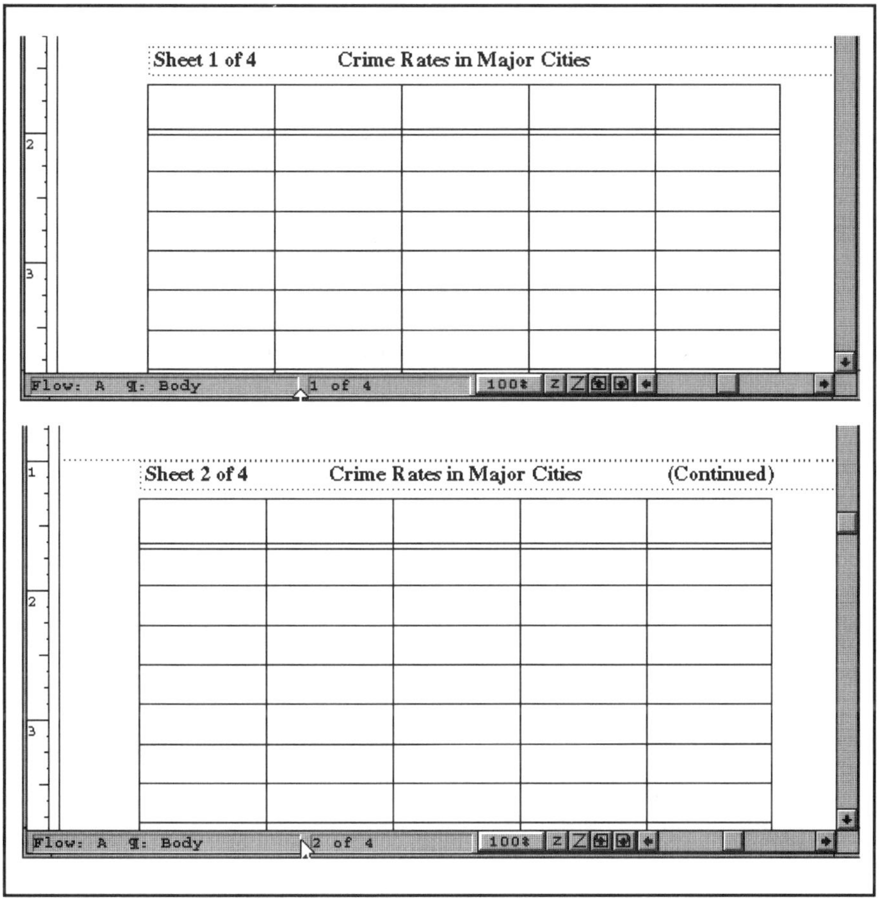


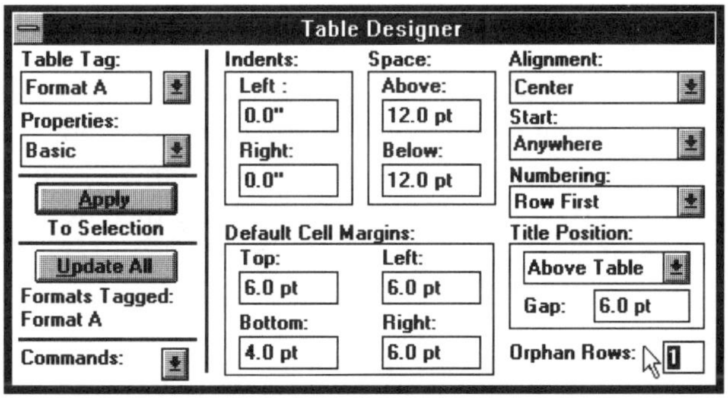


The number of orphan rows specified is the minimum number of body rows that FrameMaker 4 must keep together on a page or in a column.

If you want to keep specific rows together, you can click in the row and then choose Table, Row Format to display this dialog box. Choose Keep With Next Row or Previous Row.

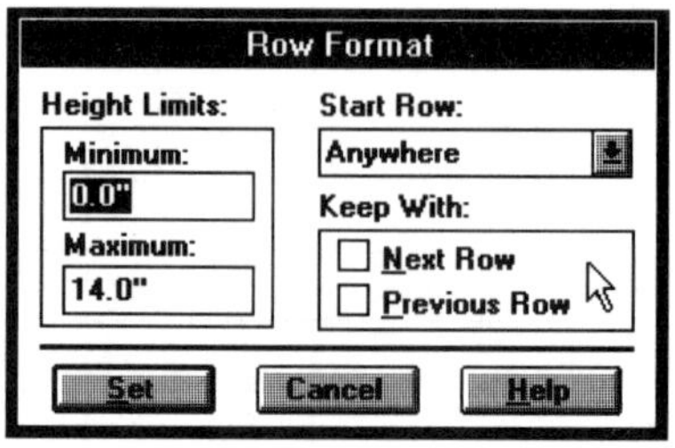


To insert a page break manually, choose the row that should go to the next column or page and display the Row Format dialog box. Choose the desired location for the Start Row option as shown here:

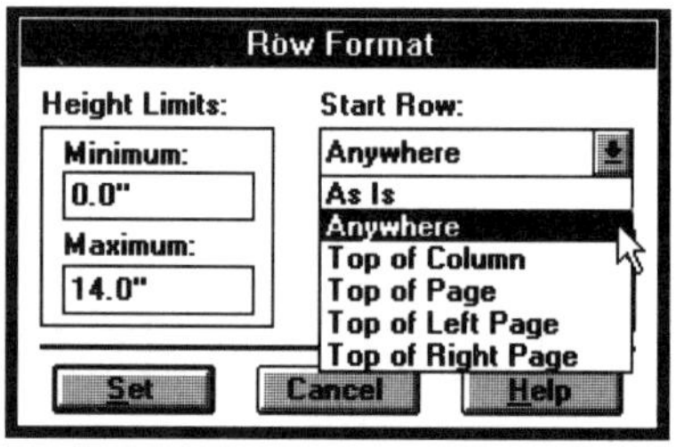


To remove the break, select the row, choose Table, Row Format, and select Anywhere for Start Row.

## REFORMATTING TABLES

FrameMaker 4 gives you even more flexibility with the table feature by allowing you to convert text to a table and convert a table to text. You can see how this capability gives you more layout options and saves you time. If you start a layout with a table and then decide that text would look better, you do not have to scrap everything and start again.

### Converting Text to a Table

Existing text or text that is imported can be converted to a table. If the text is already present in a document, it can be converted to a table by following these steps:

1. Select the text to be converted.
2. Choose Table, Convert to Table. This dialog box is displayed:

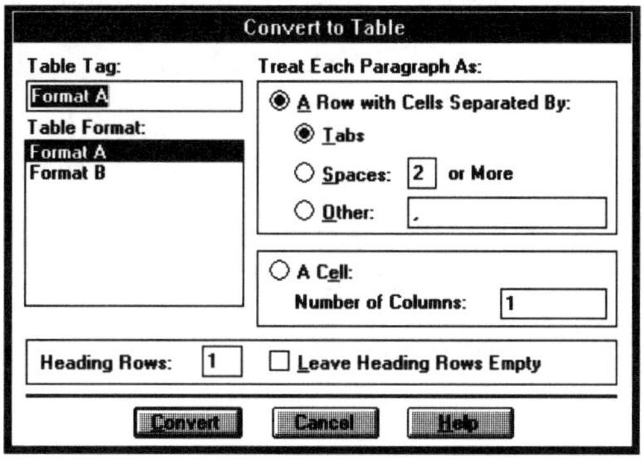


3. Choose a Table Format. (The format you choose will appear in the Table Tag area.)
4. Make a selection in one of the Treat Each Paragraph As boxes. (See Table 10-1.)
5. Enter a number for the Heading Rows (if 1 is not what you want) and turn on Leave Heading Rows Empty if you do not want the first paragraph(s) copied to the heading row(s).
6. Choose Convert.

| **Treat Each Paragraph As:** | **Description of Text** |
|---|---|
| A Row with Cells Separated By Tabs | The text is typed in a columnar format with tabs separating each column. |
| A Row with Cells Separated By Spaces | The text is typed in a columnar format with spaces separating each column. If this option is selected, you must also specify the number of spaces below which FrameMaker 4 should not separate as a cell. |
| A Row with Cells Separated By Other | The text is not columnar, but each portion of text that should occupy a single cell is separated by some other symbol like a comma. |
| A Cell | Each paragraph should be placed in a separate cell. If you select this option, you must also designate the number of columns. |

**TABLE 10-1** *Options in the Convert to Text Dialog Box* ■

To convert text that is imported, follow these steps:

1. Click the cursor in the document where text should appear.
2. Choose File, Import, File.
3. Specify the filename and select Import. If the Unknown File Type dialog box is displayed, select the file type and click Convert.
4. When the Reading Text File dialog box is displayed, select Convert to Table and click Read. The Convert to Table dialog box displays.
5. Make selections in Convert to Table dialog box and choose Convert.

## Converting a Table to Text

To convert a table to text, select the table and choose Table, Convert to Paragraphs. Select either Row by Row or Column by Column and click Convert. If you select Row by Row, FrameMaker will create a paragraph for each cell in a row, progressing by rows. If you choose Column by Column, FrameMaker 4 will create a paragraph for each cell in a column, progressing by columns.

Text that has been converted from a table does not retain a columnar format. Each cell is converted into a paragraph as shown in Figure 10-4. If you convert a table to text, you will have to do some editing to get the data back into a form that is acceptable.

**FIGURE 10-4**

*A table converted to text*

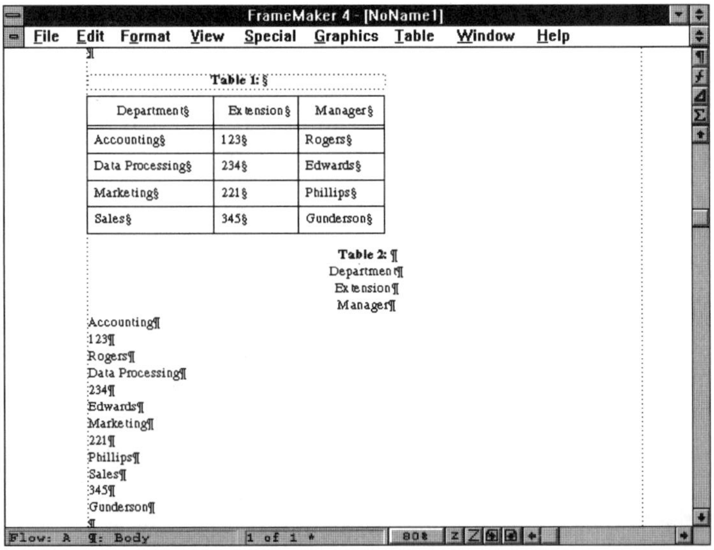

# CREATING TABLE FORMATS

As you have already seen, FrameMaker 4 has two default table formats called Format A and Format B. These formats have only slight differences. You can modify these formats for the particular needs of a table or create a new format.

The format of a table is specified in the Table Designer window. You have already seen how this window is used to set the indentation of a table, the space above and below a table, the alignment, where the table starts, and the number of orphan rows. These settings are part of the Basic properties. In addition to Basic properties, the Table Designer window also has Ruling properties and Shading properties.

## Basic Properties

In addition to the Basic properties that you have already learned, other Basic properties include the cell margins, where the table starts, how numbering should be ordered (by row or by column) if autonumbering is used, and the position and spacing under the title.

### *Cell Margins*

Cell margins function exactly like page margins. The border of the cell is comparable to the edge of the paper. The margins keep the text in the cell from printing too close to the borders. The default cell margins for Format A are 6 points for Top, Left, and Right and 4 points for the Bottom margin as you can see here:

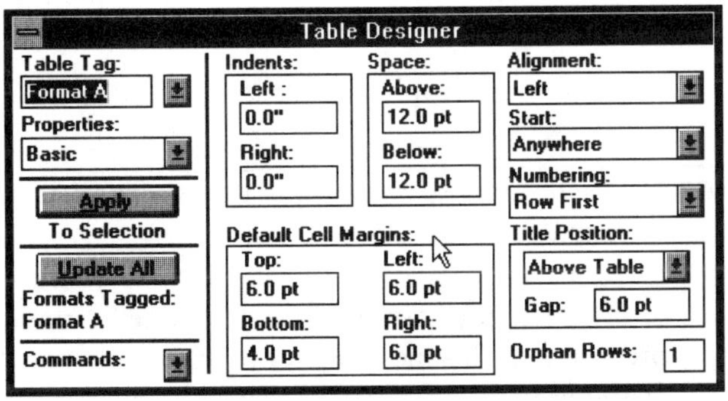

Remember that there are 12 points in a pica and 6 picas in an inch, so 6 points is 1/12 of an inch.

**NOTE:** *To make text look vertically centered in a cell, use a larger Top margin or set vertical alignment to Middle in the Table Cell properties of the Paragraph Designer window.*

The margins specified in the Table Designer window are used for all cells in the table, but you can set margins for cells individually. To set a custom margin for an individual cell, follow these steps:

1. Click the cursor in the desired cell.
2. Choose Format, Paragraphs, Designer.
3. Choose Table Cell in the Properties list. This dialog box is displayed:

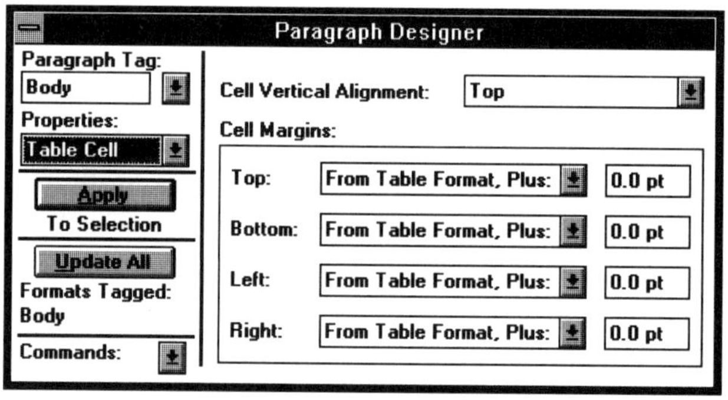


4. Make the desired selections and enter the measurements for Top, Bottom, Left, and Right. If you select From Table Format, Plus, the number of points you specify will be added to the margin value set in the Table Designer window. If you do not want the margin measurement to be dependent on the default settings, choose Custom and specify a measurement.
5. Choose Apply and close the window.

**NOTE:** *You can also apply the margins to all paragraph tags with the same name by choosing Update All.*

If you apply custom formats to cells, these formats will always take precedence. This means that even if you change the cell margins in the Table Designer window, the cells that have custom margins will not change.

### Numbering

The options for Numbering are Row First and Column First. This option comes into play if you have specified paragraph numbering in the tag that is used in the cells. You have seen an example of this in the exercise that created the calendar. Figure 10-5 shows two tables that use paragraph numbering. Table 1 numbers rows first, and Table 2 numbers columns first.

### Title Position

The Title Position options shown below include No Title, Above Table, and Below Table. The Gap is the space between the title and the adjacent body row.

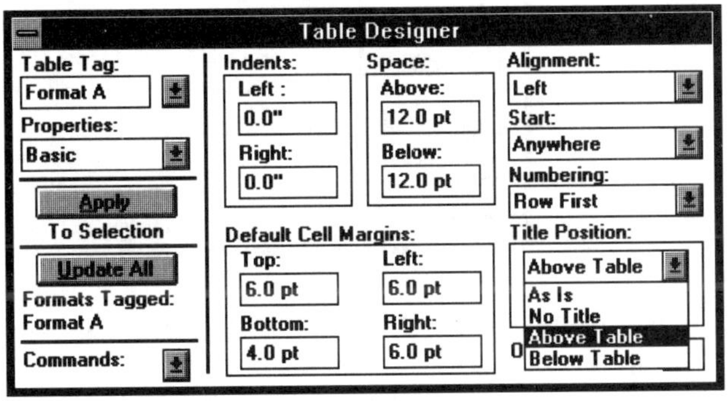


**FIGURE 10-5** Numbering by row and by column

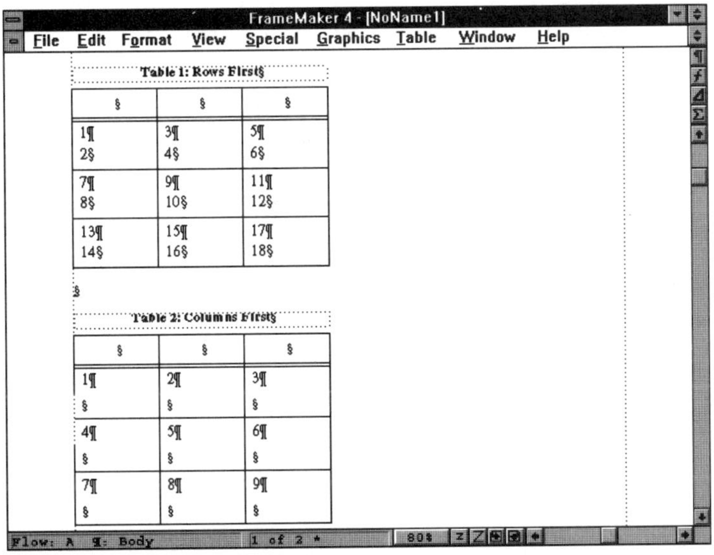

**NOTE:** *It is not possible to display a table title on just the first page of a multipage table. To work around this, you can create the table with no title and then add a title as regular text above the table.*

## Ruling Properties

When Ruling properties is selected, the Table Designer window displays new options. Format A looks like this when the Ruling properties are displayed:

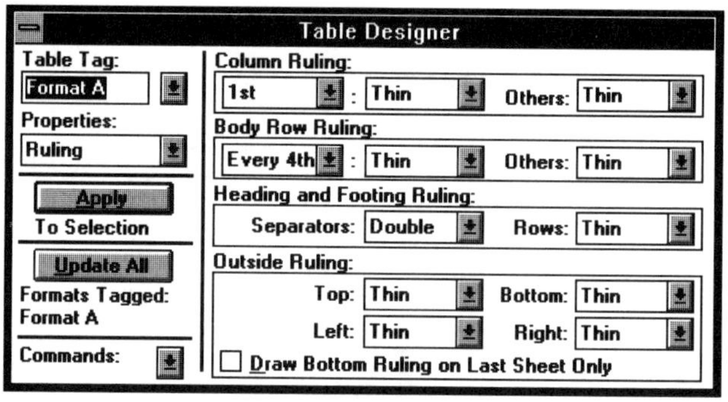


Notice that you can specify ruling lines for columns, rows, heading and footing rows, and the outside borders of a table.

The options for ruling lines are None, Double, Medium, Thick, Thin, and Very Thin. For columns, you can set something different for the first column, but all other columns must be the same. For rows, you can set up something different for every 4th row, but the other rows must be the same. (Tables with many rows will be easier to read if the ruling line is a little thicker on every 4th row.) The Heading and Footing rows can have a different rule for the rule that separates the Heading/Footing row(s) from the adjacent body row. Different rules can be specified for each of the outside borders (Top, Bottom, Left, and Right). In addition, for multipage tables, you can specify that the bottom border is drawn only on the last sheet.

## Shading Properties

The Shading properties include options for shading the Heading/Footing rows and the body rows. Shading includes fill and color. Format A shading properties look like this:

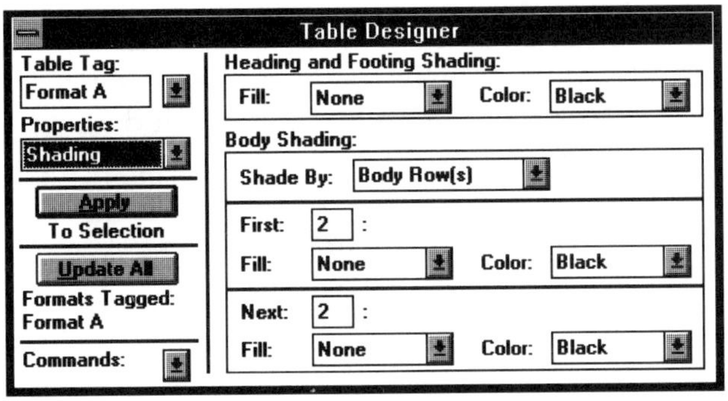


The fill options are None, 100%, 90%, 70%, 50%, 30%, 10%, 3%, and White. The colors include all the standard colors and any colors that you have created or selected from the Pantone palette.

Notice that you can specify alternating fills for body rows. For example, you could apply a fill to the first row and not to the next row, or you could apply a fill to the first two rows and not to the next two rows. Alternating fills makes a table easier to read if there are many rows.

## Custom Ruling and Shading

The ruling and shading options selected in the Table Designer window apply to the whole table. To apply ruling and shading attributes to individual cells, select the cells, and choose Table, Custom Ruling & Shading. This dialog box is displayed:

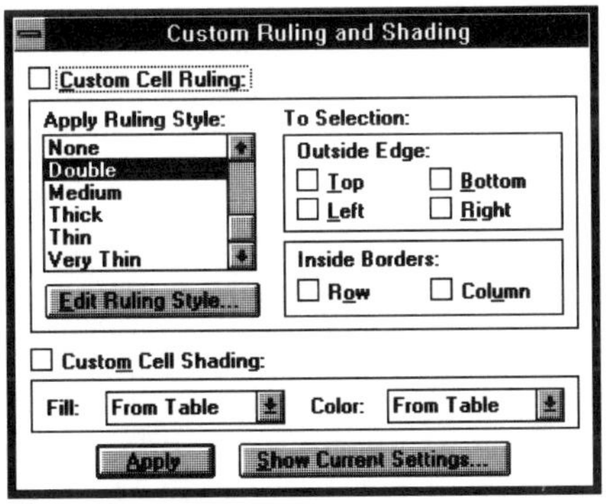


To change the rules and shading at the same time, select Custom Cell Ruling, select the edges or borders that you want to change, and select the ruling style. Select Custom Cell Shading, select the desired Fill and Color and choose Apply. To change the ruling and shading independently, select only Custom Cell Ruling or Custom Cell Shading before applying.

Figure 10-6 shows the calendar you created earlier, with a thick border around the author's birthday, and a double border and a 30% shade on the July 4th legal holiday. The ruling lines above and below the days of the month were changed by selecting all the cells in the row and making the following selections:

- Left and Right Outside Edge: None
- Column Inside Borders: None
- Top Outside Edge: Thick

## *Adding Color to Rules*

To make the ruling lines a different color or width, follow these steps:

1. Select the desired cell or cells.
2. Choose Table, Custom Ruling and Shading.
3. Select Custom Cell Ruling.
4. Select the desired rules (Top, Bottom, Left, Right, Row Border, Column Border).

**FIGURE 10-6**

*A calendar with border and shading changes*

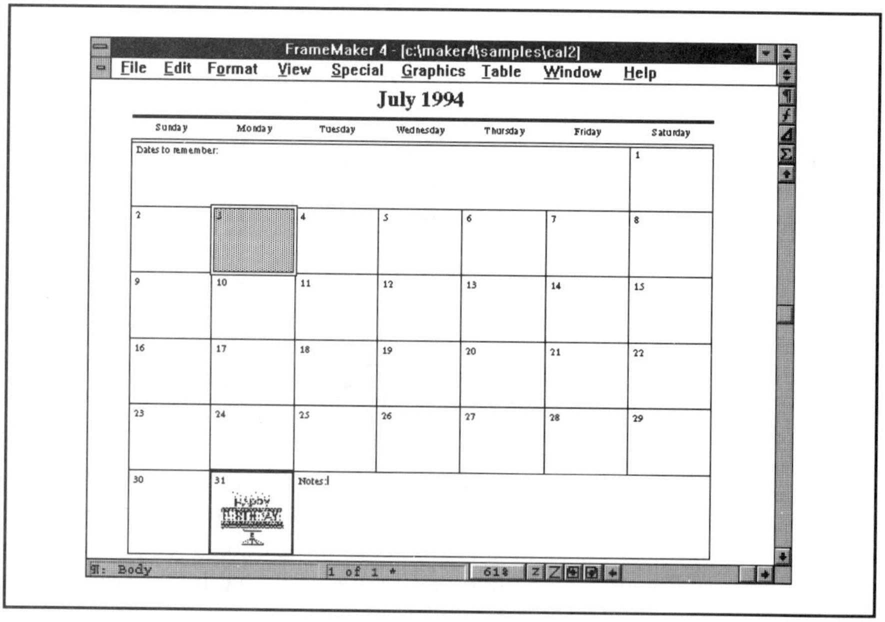

5. Click the Edit Ruling Style button. This dialog box displays:

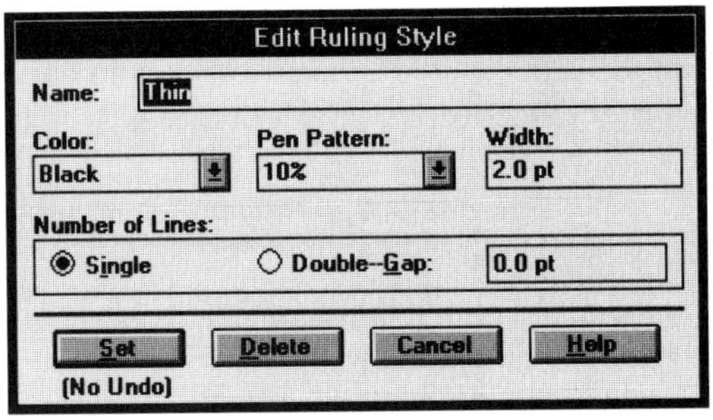


6. Choose a color from the Color list.
7. Choose a pen pattern if desired. (Pen Pattern lightens the color that you select by percentages.)
8. Change the width if desired.

**NOTE:** *If you have selected a double-line style, Double–Gap will be selected instead of Single in the Number of Lines section of the dialog box. You can change the space between the lines by entering a value in the text box.*

9. Select Set.
10. Select Apply.

### *Creating Your Own Ruling Style*

You can create your own ruling style to be used in tables by following these steps:

1. Choose Table, Custom Ruling And Shading.
2. Choose Edit Ruling Style.
3. Enter a new name for the style.
4. Choose a color, pen pattern, and width.
5. Choose Single for a single line or Double--Gap for a double line. If you select Double--Gap, enter an amount for the width between the lines.
6. Choose Set.

7. Close the window.

To delete a ruling style, display the Edit Ruling Style dialog box, select the style to be deleted in the list box, and choose Delete. If the style has been used in the document, FrameMaker 4 displays this message

Choose OK to delete or Cancel to reconsider.

## CREATING AND MAINTAINING TABLE FORMATS

As you know, formats are stored in the Table Designer window. They can be created, modified, renamed, and deleted.

### Creating a Format

To create a new table format, display the Table Designer window, set all the desired properties, and choose Commands, New Format. Give the format a name, select or deselect Store in Catalog and Apply to Selection, and choose Create.

### Modifying a Format

You can modify the format of a particular table or modify a table format tag so that it applies to all tables that use the format tag. To modify a table format, follow these steps:

1. Select the table that has the format you want to change.
2. Choose Table, Table Designer.

3. Choose the table tag from the pop-up menu (even though it is already displayed).
4. Make the desired changes to the properties.
5. If you want to change only the selected table, choose Apply. The change will be applied to only the selected table and the table format will have an *override*. To change all tables that use the tag, choose Update All.

**NOTE:** *When you have selected a table and displayed the Table Designer window, you cannot tell whether the properties displayed have overrides or not. To see the default values of a format tag, display the Table Designer window when the cursor is not clicked in a table.*

## Renaming a Format

To rename a format, follow these steps:

1. Click the cursor in a table that has the format you want to rename.
2. Choose Table, Table Designer.
3. Choose the format from the Table Tag list. (This step seems repetitive, since the name is already displayed, but it is necessary to insure that all the table properties are displayed.)
4. Type a different, unique name in the Table Tag box.
5. Choose Update All.
6. Click OK to rename.

## Deleting a Format

To delete a table format, display the Table Designer window and choose Commands, Delete Format. Select the format you want to delete and choose Delete. Then choose Done.

# 11

## Creating Complex Documents

If any capability of the FrameMaker 4 program can be considered its forte, it is creating complex documents such as multichapter books, documents that use text based on certain conditions, and scientific/mathematical documents that require complicated equations. FrameMaker can create many features of a complex document automatically, including a table of contents, an index, a list of footnotes, a list of cross-references, a list of figures, a list of tables, and a list of any element you have marked consistently in a document. It can build multiple versions of a document with conditional text, and its equation feature not only builds equations with the proper format, it can calculate the equations as well.

Reading a straightforward treatment of the topics in this chapter could be declared a new cure for insomnia, so instead the features are explained in the context of an exercise. It's always more fun to actually *do* something than to read about it. In this exercise you will create an employee manual. The manual will be a multichapter book with cross-references, footnotes, a table of contents, an index, and a generated list.

## SETTING UP THE EXERCISE

Before plunging into the topics in this chapter, follow these steps to create a template to use in the exercise:

1. Create a new document with a width of 5.5 inches and a height of 8.5 inches.
2. Press ENTER on the first line.
3. Move the cursor back up to the first line and assign the Title tag to the paragraph.

**NOTE:** *This tag may have been changed or deleted in your list of paragraph tags. If so, use another tag that is appropriate for the title of a page.*

4. Go to the Master page and add a page number in the middle of the footer. (Remember, this is done by inserting a variable.)
5. Save the file as a template called empnam.
6. Close the file.

## CREATING CROSS-REFERENCES

The FrameMaker 4 documentation refers to two types of cross-references—paragraph references and spot references. The difference between these two references is very mystical—defying definition. In fact, it is very likely that the spot reference feature will be eliminated in revised editions of the program; therefore, only the paragraph cross-reference is covered in this book. If the spot reference is not eliminated, it will be changed so that it can pull a word or a phrase from a paragraph.

Paragraph cross-references can be made within the current document or to another open document. To insert a paragraph cross-reference, follow these steps:

1. If the reference will be made to another document, open the document.
2. Click the cursor where the reference should be inserted.
3. Choose Special, Cross-Reference. This dialog box displays:

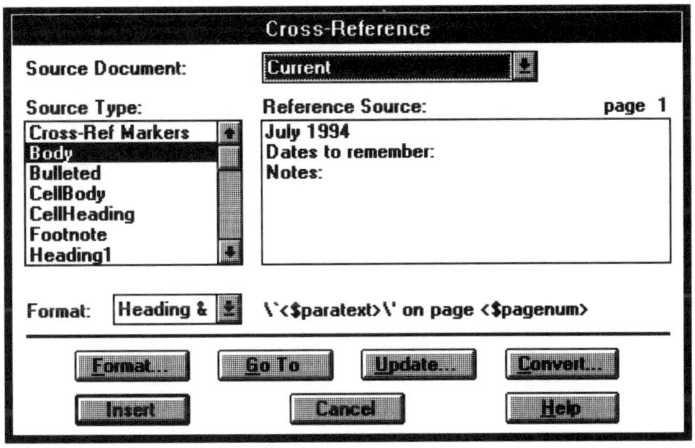

4. Select the Source Document. (If cross-referencing to the current document, choose Current. If cross-referencing to another open document, select the desired document from the pop-up list.)
5. Select a Source Type (a paragraph tag) from the list box.
6. Select a Reference Source (the actual paragraph) from the list box.
7. Select the desired format and click Insert. (If the desired format has not been created, choose Format before clicking Insert and design a format. Details for creating a format are given next.)

When a cross-reference is created, FrameMaker 4 inserts the cross-reference in the current document and inserts a marker at the beginning of the paragraph that is referenced in the current or other document as shown here:

> **The Secret to Success¶**
>
> TWe have been asked many times, "What makes XYZ Industries so successful?" Our reply is, "There are no secrets to success. It is the result of preparation, hard work, learning from failure."[1]¶

**NOTE:** *A marker is not visible if Text Symbols are turned off in the View menu.*

### Creating a Cross-Reference Style

The style of a cross-reference is created with any desired combination of variables, also called building blocks, and text. To create a format, follow these steps:

1. Choose Special, Cross-Reference.
2. Click the Format button. This dialog box displays:

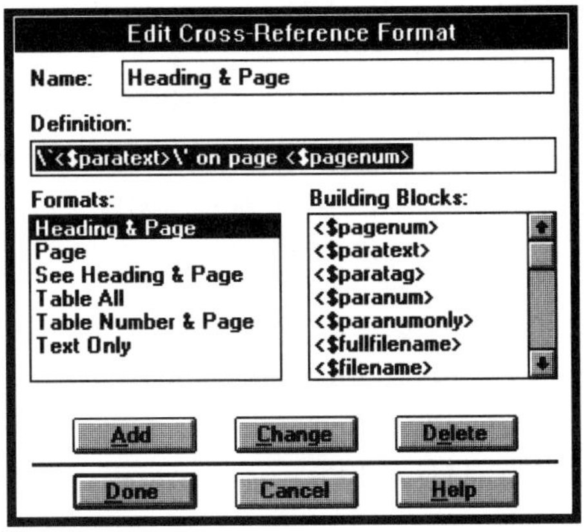


3. Type a name for the format in the Name text box.
4. Create the Definition by typing the desired text and using any of the desired variables. (The variables are explained in Table 11-1, and an example is shown in the sidebar.)
5. Click the Add button.
6. Click the Done button in the Edit Cross-Reference Format dialog box.
7. Click the Done button in the Cross-Reference dialog box.

**NOTE:** *The Building Blocks scroll list also includes the character formats listed in the document's Character Catalog. These codes can be used in the definition to add emphasis.*

*This definition:*

*<Emphasis>See <$paratext> on page <$pagenum>.<Default ¶ Font>*
*looks like this in text:*

*See Benefits and Deductions on page 10.*

*Note that the code <Default ¶ Font> is necessary to return the font back to normal.*

| Variable | Description |
|---|---|
| <$pagenum> | Displays the page number. |
| <$paratext> | Displays the complete text of the paragraph. |
| <$paratag> | Displays the paragraph tag name. |
| <$paranum> | Displays the paragraph number if the format of the paragraph contains autonumbering and the text (if any) in the numbering format. |
| <$paranumonly> | Displays only the number of a paragraph if the paragraph has autonumbering. |
| <$fullfilename> | Displays the filename and path of the referenced file. |
| <$filename> | Displays only the filename of the referenced file. |
| <$pagenum[paratag]> | Displays the page number of the of the preceding paragraph with the specified tag.* |
| <$paratext[paratag]> | Displays the paragraph text of the preceding paragraph with the specified tag.* |
| <$paranum[paratag]> | Displays the paragraph number of the preceding paragraph in the specified tag including any text in the number format.* |
| <$paranumonly[paratag]> | Displays the paragraph number of the preceding paragraph in the specified tag.* |

*(Replace "paratag" in square brackets with the desired tag name. Do not remove the square brackets.) "Preceding" in this case means the reference before the marker.

**TABLE 11-1** *Format Variables* ■

### Exercise

Follow these steps to create the first two documents in the employee manual. The second document will have a cross-reference to the first.

1. Create a new file using the empnam template.
2. Type **Welcome** on the first line.
3. Type this text as the first paragraph:

   **Welcome to XYZ Industries. You have become a part of a unique team and family.**

4. Type the next three sentences as separate paragraphs and apply the Bulleted tag to each:

   **As a team, we are well trained and ready to meet any competition.**
   **As a family, we care about each other.**
   **You are now a valuable member of both.**

5. Save the file, calling it welcome, but do not close the file.
6. Create a new document using the empman template.
7. For the title type **History of XYZ Industries.**
8. Type this text for the first paragraph:

   **XYZ Industries was established in 1947 and has shown a steady increase in growth every year since 1950. With over 400 locations in the US and Canada, we are the largest distributor in the world.**

9. Type this text for the second paragraph:

   **We have been asked many times, "What makes XYZ Industries so successful?" Our reply is "There are no secrets to success. It is the result of preparation, hard work, learning from failure."**

10. Type this sentence as the third paragraph:

    **We subscribe to the team concept.**

11. With the cursor at the end of the third paragraph, choose Special, Cross-Reference.

**NOTE:** *If the document has not been saved, you will be prompted to do so before a cross-reference can be created.*

12. Choose welcome as the Source Document.
13. Choose Bulleted as the Source Type.
14. Choose the first paragraph listed in the Reference Source. (It should be **\b As a team, we are well trained and ready to ...**)
15. Click the Format button.
16. Type **Text Only** in the Name text box.
17. Type **<$paratext>** in the Definition text box.
18. Click the Add button.
19. Click the Done button.
20. Click Insert.
21. Save the file and call it history.

## Updating Cross-References

Sometimes cross-references become inaccurate due to changes in pagination or revisions in the text. If a cross-reference does become inaccurate, FrameMaker 4 does not notify you; therefore, it is a good idea to update cross-references periodically.

To update cross-references, follow these steps:

1. Choose Special, Cross-Reference.
2. Choose Update. This dialog box displays:

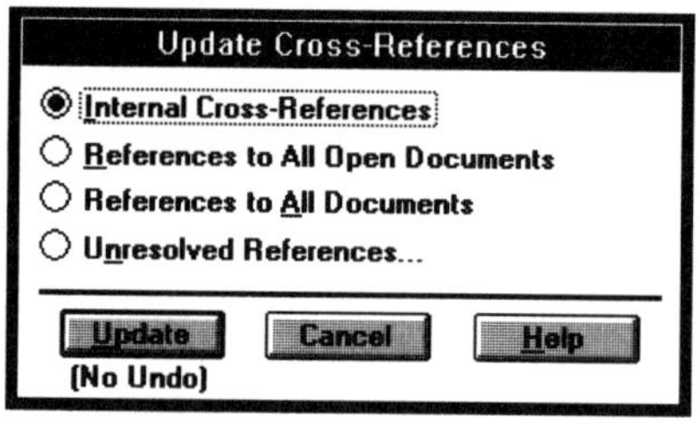


3. Choose an appropriate option for your document.
4. Choose Update.
5. Click the Done button.

If a cross-reference cannot be updated, this dialog box is displayed:

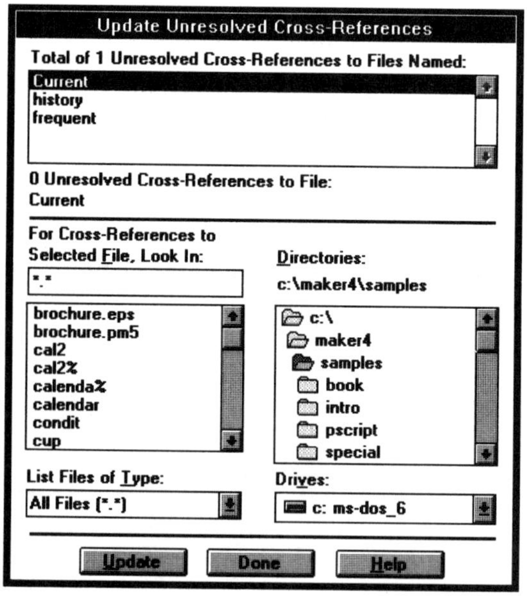

An unresolved cross-reference results if a source document name changes, if the document is deleted or moved to a different directory, or if the text of the reference is deleted. If the document name has changed or been moved to a new location, you can specify the correct document in the dialog box and then choose Update. If the text of the reference or the marker has been deleted, you must reenter it or delete the cross-reference.

If you want to reinsert a marker that has been deleted, follow these steps:

1. In the document that contains the cross-references, update the references so that the unresolved references will be identified.
2. Close the Cross-Reference dialog boxes.
3. Choose Edit, Find/Change.
4. Choose Unresolved Cross-Reference in the Find scroll list.
5. Click the Find button.
6. When the unresolved reference is highlighted, double-click it. The Cross-Reference dialog box will display.
7. Specify the Source Type and Reference Source.
8. Click Replace.
9. Continue the search if other unresolved cross-references exist.

## CREATING FOOTNOTES

FrameMaker 4 can create footnotes (numbered notes at the bottom of a page), automatically number them, and maintain their position and numbering through successive revisions. When you insert a footnote reference, the footnote is placed in the same text column as the reference. If the reference moves, the footnote moves with it. It can also create endnotes (numbered notes at the end of a document).

To insert a footnote, follow these steps:

1. Click the cursor in the text where you want the reference number to appear.
2. Choose Special, Footnote. Although you may not see it as it happens, FrameMaker 4 inserts the reference number in the text and jumps to the bottom of the text column where it inserts the

reference number again below a dividing line. The cursor is positioned after the number, waiting for you to type the text of the footnote. (See Figure 11-1.)

3. Type the text of the footnote. Add formatting as desired.

## Deleting a Footnote

To delete a footnote, simply highlight the footnote reference number in the text and press DEL. (When you highlight the number, the footnote at the bottom of the page is also highlighted.)

## Inserting Two Footnotes Together

Two footnotes can be inserted side by side if they are separated by a comma or a space as shown here:

> We subscribe to the team concept. As a team, we are well trained and ready to meet any competition.[1,2]§

In this example, it was necessary to apply superscript to the comma so the references would not look like this:

> We subscribe to the team concept. As a team, we are well trained and ready to meet any competition.[1],[2]§

## Formatting a Footnote

The footnote tag has its own dialog box that is used to set up the format. To access this dialog box, choose Format, Footnote Properties. The dialog box looks like this with the default settings:

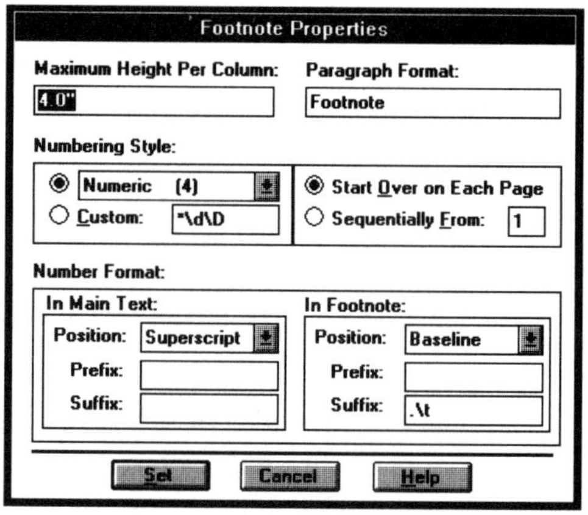

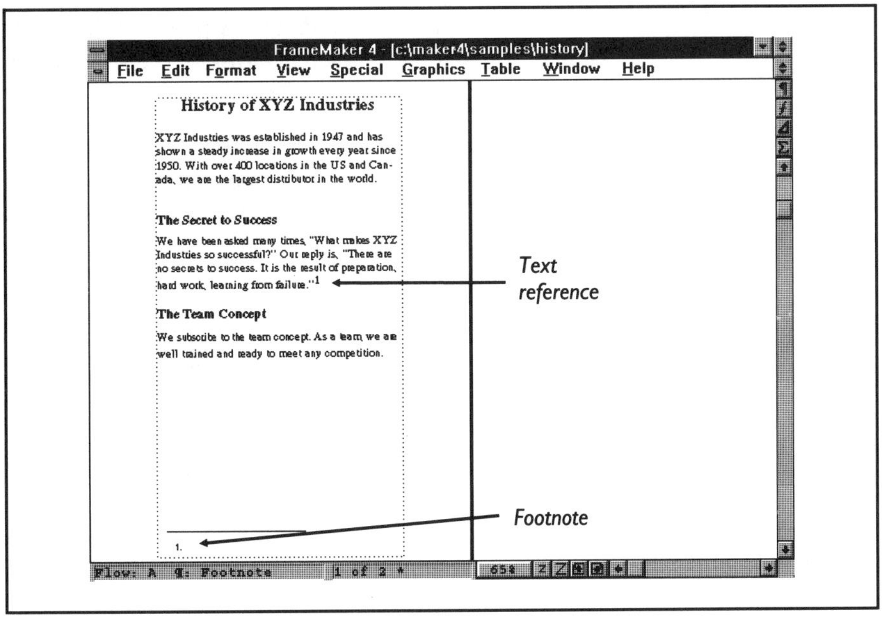


**FIGURE 11-1**

*Frame inserts a reference in the text and at the bottom of the page.*

Notice that the space allowed for footnotes per column is 4 inches. This number may have to be increased if a footnote will not fit on the proper page. Footnotes that will not fit move to the bottom of the next text column.

The Paragraph Format (the tag) is the default name for the tag supplied by FrameMaker 4. You can, of course, define your own paragraph tag for a footnote and adjust its properties in this box.

The number style is set for Numeric (4), but the other choices include upper and lowercase Roman numerals and upper and lowercase alphabetic characters. A custom numbering style, which could include special characters, can be defined instead of using the standard choices. The reference numbering can start over on each page or continue numbering sequentially throughout the document.

The position of the reference in the main text and in the footnote can be baseline, superscript, or subscript. Prefixes and suffixes such as parentheses or square brackets can be included. In the illustration, a period followed by a tab (.\t) is defined as the suffix for the number in the footnote.

When the footnote properties have been defined, choose Set. Changes to the footnote properties are applied automatically to any existing footnotes.

The line that separates the main text from the footnotes at the bottom of the text column is inserted automatically by FrameMaker 4. To change this separator, follow these steps:

1. Choose View, Reference Pages. A page similar to the one shown in Figure 11-2 displays. As you can see, the separating line is drawn in a frame.
2. Use the Graphics Tools palette and/or the Object Properties dialog box to change the line's style, thickness, color, length, and so on. You can also delete the line and create a custom separator, such as a row of asterisks. To type in the frame you must use the text tool from the Graphics Tools palette.
3. Increase or decrease the size of the frame to change the spacing between the main text and the footnotes.
4. Choose View, Body Pages.

## Continuing the Exercise

Follow these steps to add two footnotes to the history document:

1. Click the cursor at the end of the second paragraph of text (just after the quote).
2. Choose Special, Footnote.
3. Type **General Colin Powell in The Black Collegian.**
4. Apply italic to the title of the book just typed in step 3.
5. Click the cursor at the end of the third paragraph of text.
6. Choose Special, Footnote.
7. Type **This is the company motto for 1994.**
8. Choose Format, Footnote Properties.
9. Change the numbering style to alphabetic (d).
10. Change the position of the footnote to superscript.
11. Click Set and note the changes in the document.
12. Save the document.

## Creating Additional References to the Same Footnote

Although *The Chicago Manual of Style* says that "one footnote reference should never apply to material in more than one paragraph," it is possible

**FIGURE 11-2**

*A Reference page*

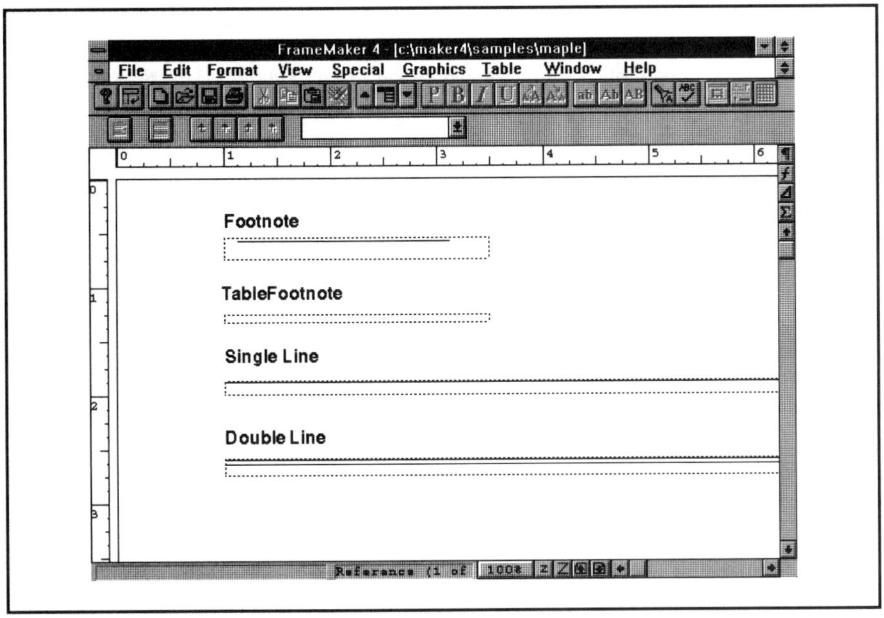


to do so with FrameMaker 4. Given *The Chicago Manual of Style's* recommendation, we'll let you decide whether you should use this feature or not.

To create an additional reference to the same footnote, you must use a cross-reference. The technique involves these steps:

1. Insert the first reference as you normally would.
2. Click the cursor in the text where the additional reference should appear.
3. Choose Special, Cross-Reference.
4. Select the footnote tag as the Source Type.
5. Select the desired footnote as the Reference Source.
6. Use (or create) the format <$paranumonly> so the cross-reference will pick up the footnote number without the prefix or suffix text that might be defined.
7. Click Insert.
8. Apply a character style to make the cross-reference look like the regular footnote. For example, if the footnote reference is superscripted, apply superscript to the cross-reference.

**TIP:** *A page that has more footnotes than text is uninviting to the eye. The number and length of footnotes should be kept to a minimum if possible.*

### Creating Endnotes

When two or more footnotes fall in the last line of text on a page, it is difficult to format the page. The same is true when several long footnotes have references near the end of the page. This problem can be solved by using endnotes. The length and number of endnotes used is not a problem. In addition, endnotes can contain tables and lists.

To create endnotes, type all the notes at the end of the document and use a paragraph tag with autonumbering. In the main body of text insert cross-references (with the <$paranumonly> format) that refer to the numbered notes.

**NOTE:** *Remember that cross-references must be maintained for accuracy.*

## GENERATING LISTS

A table of contents, a list of figures, or a glossary are all lists that FrameMaker 4 can generate automatically, but FrameMaker 4 is not limited to these lists. It can generate a list of any paragraph tags or markers.

### Generating a Table of Contents

A table of contents (TOC) is a list of paragraph tags. Depending on the degree of detail desired, a TOC may contain one to three (or more) levels of headings. Most people create paragraph tag names that indicate the hierarchy of the headings. For example, Heading1 and Heading2 would be used for a main topic and a subtopic respectively. Using this naming scheme, if a heading is needed for a subtopic of Heading2, the tag would be called Heading3.

If all headings use the proper tags, it is a simple matter to generate a TOC in the current document by following these steps:

1. Choose File, Generate/Book.
2. Choose Table of Contents in the List pop-up menu.

3. Click the Generate button.
4. Move the desired paragraph tags into the list box on the left (Include Paragraphs Tagged). The order of the tags in this box is not important.
5. Choose Create Hypertext Links if you want the entries in the table of contents document to be linked to the source document. (This is strongly recommended because it makes editing the TOC easier.)
6. Click Generate.

FrameMaker 4 creates and displays a file with the same name as the document and an extension of TOC. This document lists the text of the paragraph tags in the order in which they appear and the page numbers on which they appear. You can correct entries, if necessary, format the file, and then save it.

**NOTE:** *If you add or delete headings in the source document, you must generate the TOC again.*

## *Correcting the TOC*

A variety of problems can arise when creating a TOC including the following:

- Headings are missing.
- A blank heading with a page number is included.
- Headings are tagged incorrectly.
- Heading that are longer than one line appear as separate headings instead of one heading.

All of these problems can be easily corrected if you have generated the list with hypertext links. You simply double-click the heading that is incorrect, FrameMaker 4 takes you to the heading in the source document, and you make the correction in the source document. If you have problems in the TOC document, but you did not generate the list with links to hypertext, generate the list again. This time turn on the hypertext option.

Headings that are missing cannot be traced with the hypertext link because they do not appear in the TOC document. Two mistakes can cause missing heads—the head is tagged incorrectly or you did not include the tag in the list of paragraph tags to be included in the TOC. To correct this problem, check the headings in the source document to be sure they have the correct tags or generate the list again and be sure the tag is included.

A blank heading with a page number is a blank line with the incorrect tag. Change the paragraph tag to an appropriate tag. Headings that have the wrong tags also need to be tagged with the appropriate tag.

Multiline headings that appear as separate headings have been typed with a return or a forced return (SHIFT+ENTER) at the end of each line. To correct this problem, make the heading wrap by changing the right indent.

**NOTE:** *Do not make revisions in the TOC document itself. The changes you make will be overwritten the next time the TOC is generated. After all corrections have been made in the source document, generate the TOC again.*

## *Formatting a TOC*

When a TOC document is generated the first time, the format of the file is copied from the source document. When you format this file and save it with the same name, the new format becomes a template for subsequent generations of the TOC.

Each heading in the TOC document has a paragraph tag generated for it automatically. The tag name is the same as the original tag name with TOC added. For example, if the original tag is Heading1, the new heading in the TOC document is Heading1TOC.

To change the format of these tags, you can edit the special codes for these headings on the Reference page or use the Paragraph Designer window. (Some changes must be made on the Reference page and some changes must be made in the Paragraph Designer window.)

To display the Reference page that contains the TOC formatting information, choose View, Reference Pages, and then click the Next Page button until a page like Figure 11-3 is displayed.

Figure 11-3 shows the Reference page for a TOC that includes three levels of heads and has hypertext links active. The three lines that are the same correspond to the three headings. The building blocks in these lines cause the table of contents to display the text of a heading followed by the page number. If you want the page number to come before the text, you can rearrange the building blocks like this:

<$pagenum><$paratext>

**FIGURE 11-3** *Table of contents codes on the Reference page*

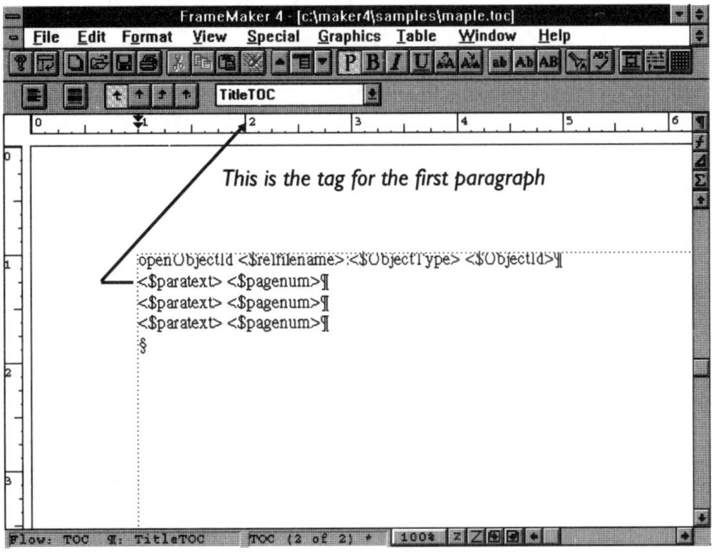


To add character formats, include the name of a character format in angle brackets like the following example, and be sure to return the font to the default style with the code shown:

<$paratext><bold><$pagenum><default para font>

After changing the format, be sure to save the file with the same name.

To add a tab between the text of the heading and the page number, simply press the TAB key between the two building blocks on the Reference page. Then add a tab stop (using leaders if desired) to the paragraph tag, update all tags, and save the file with the same name. If you do not update all tags, the new format will not be retained when the TOC is regenerated.

## Exercise

Before creating a table of contents for the history document, you will add another page of text. Follow these steps:

1. Click the cursor after the last character in the document.
2. Press ENTER.

3. Choose Format, Paragraphs, Designer.
4. Choose the Title tag.
5. Choose Pagination from the properties pop-up menu.
6. Choose Top of Page in the Start pop-up menu.
7. Choose Apply.
8. Close the window.
9. Type **Future of XYZ Industries.**
10. Press ENTER.
11. Type this paragraph:

    **Our plans for the future include opening 20 new locations each year. That represents a yearly gain of 20,000 employees.**

12. Press ENTER.
13. Type **Product Development** and assign the Heading1 tag to it.

**NOTE:** *If you do not have a Heading1 tag, use a tag that is appropriate for a level one heading in the body of text.*

14. Press ENTER.
15. Type this paragraph:

    **Our research and development department is constantly working on improving our products and developing new products. It is our goal to introduce a new product or an improvement to an existing product once a quarter.**

16. Press ENTER.
17. Type **Facility Expansion** and assign the Heading1 tag to it.
18. Press ENTER.
19. Type this paragraph:

    **Our plant facilities are scheduled for yearly maintenance and expansion if needed. This makes your working environment pleasant and safe.**

20. Save the document.

Now follow these steps to create a table of contents for the document and format it:

1. Choose File, Generate/Book.
2. Choose Table of Contents in the List pop-up menu.
3. Click the Generate button.
4. Move the tags Title and Heading1 into the list box on the left (Include Paragraphs Tagged).
5. Select Create Hypertext Links.
6. Click Generate.
7. Go to the Reference page that has the table of contents building blocks.
8. Click the cursor after the <$paratext> code.
9. Press TAB.
10. Repeat steps 8 and 9 for the other <$paratext> code.
11. Click the cursor before the <$paratext> code in the Heading1TOC paragraph.
12. Press TAB.
13. Choose Format, Paragraphs, Designer.
14. Select the TitleTOC tag and add a right tab with leaders at position 3.5.
15. Click Update All.
16. Choose the Heading1TOC tag and add a left tab at position .5 and a right tab with leaders at position 3.5.
17. Click Update All.
18. Close the Designer window.
19. Return to the Body page.
20. Save the file and close it.
21. Generate the table of contents again.
22. Save and close the file.

## Creating Other Types of Lists

As you have seen, generating a TOC creates a list of paragraphs. Generating a list of figures or a list of tables works the same way. When you choose File, Generate/Book, you then select List of Figures or List of Table as the list type. When you click the Generate button, you select the paragraph tags that you have used for figures or table and generate the list.

A different way to generate a list involves setting markers. After setting markers, you can generate a list of markers either in the order that they occur in the document or in alphabetic order. FrameMaker 4 has special markers called Comment, Glossary, Author, Cross-Ref and so on. Most of these markers are intended for specified purposes, like the Cross-Ref marker, but many of the markers can really be used for any purpose. In addition to these named markers, FrameMaker 4 lists markers called Type 11 through Type 25. These are markers that you can use for your own purposes. For example, you might place markers Type 11, Type 12, and Type 13 before particular key words. Then you could get a list of the key words and every place they occurred.

To understand how this works, follow the steps in this exercise, which will guide you through inserting markers and generating the list:

1. Go to the welcome document (it should still be open).
2. Click the cursor in the text before the first word (Welcome).
3. Choose Special, Marker.
4. In the Marker Type pop-up menu, choose Glossary.
5. Move the Marker window so that it does not obscure any text in the document. This window will stay open as you continue the steps in this exercise.
6. Click New Marker. (A marker is inserted in the text, but it is not visible unless you have Text Symbols turned on in the View menu.)
7. Click the cursor before the word "A" and click New Marker.
8. Click the cursor before the word "competition" and click the New Marker button.
9. Click the cursor before the word "valuable" and click the New Marker button.

10. Mark as many other words as you want and close the Marker window.
11. Choose File, Generate/Book.
12. From the List pop-up menu, choose List of Markers.
13. Click the Generate button.
14. Move Glossary to the Include Markers of Type list.
15. Click Generate. FrameMaker 4 displays a document called welcome.lom. Notice that the markers are listed as they occur in the document with page numbers following.
16. Close the file (welcome.lom) without saving.

Generally, the purpose of a glossary is to define words that are listed in alphabetic order. In such a list, the page number on which the word appears is not usually listed. To create a glossary document like this, follow these steps:

1. In the welcome document, choose File, Generate/Book.
2. In the List pop-up menu, choose Alphabetical Marker List.
3. Click Generate.
4. The Glossary marker type should still be displayed in the list on the left. If it is not, move it over to the box.
5. Click Generate. FrameMaker 4 displays a file called welcome.aml. Notice that the markers are alphabetized with no regard to capitalization.
6. Go to the Reference page that contains the building blocks for the generated list.
7. Delete the block <$pagenum>.
8. Save and close the file.
9. Generate the list again. Notice that the page numbers do not appear this time.
10. Now you can proceed to type the definitions of the words to finish the glossary file.
11. Save the file with a different name.
12. Close the file.

## Creating an Index

To create an index, first insert an index marker in the text for each word that should be in the index. By this time, you know how to insert a marker, but the type of marker you can insert for an index is not limited to Index. You could also choose Author, Subject, Type 11, and so on. You cannot, however, choose Conditional Text, Header/Footer $1, Header/Footer $2, Hypertext, or Cross-Ref. These markers are reserved for specified purposes.

When inserting a marker, you can leave the Marker Text box blank if you want the word that follows the marker to be the index entry. If you want a phrase to be the index entry, highlight the phrase before inserting the marker, and the phrase will be placed in the Marker Text box automatically. You can also use building blocks in the Marker Text box to control the index entry. See Table 11-2 for a list of the building blocks you can use.

### *Denoting a Level*

If the index entry should be listed as a subtopic of another entry, enter something like this in the Marker Text box:

**benefits: health**

The index will look like this:

benefits
  dental 13
  health 14
  vacation 15

| Building Block | Purpose |
|---|---|
| : (colon) | Denotes a level in an entry. |
| ; (semicolon) | Separates multiple entries in a marker. |
| [ ] | Specifies a special sort order. |
| <$startrange> | Specifies the beginning of a page range. |
| <$endrange> | Specifies the end of a page range. |
| <$nopage> | Suppresses the page number. |
| <$singlepage> | In a marker with multiple entries, activates pagenumber if it has been suppressed by <$nopage>. |
| <*format*> | A character format, where *format* is the name of a character format. |
| <Default Para Font> | Restores the default paragraph format after the use of a <*format*> code. |

**TABLE 11-2** *Building Blocks for Index Markers* ■

### *Separating Entries in a Marker*

To create multiple entries for the same marker, use the semicolon to separate the entries in the Marker Text box like this:

benefits; dental; health; vacation

This produces four entries in the index. Each entry is listed with the same page number.

### *Specifying a Special Sort Order*

If the word that you want to reference should be placed in a different sort order, use square brackets in the Marker Text box like this:

401K [four o one k]

The entry will be indexed with the words that start with "f" like this:

family benefits 16
first review 22
401K 15
funeral leave 14

### *Marking Entries with Page Ranges*

To mark an entry that spans several pages, mark the entry on the first page like this:

<$startrange>benefits

Mark the entry on the last page of the range like this:

<$endrange>benefits

In the index, the entry will look like this:

benefits 13-15

### *Suppressing a Page Number*

You might want to suppress a page number for an item that has a reference to another word. For example, you may have used the term "investment plan" instead of "savings plan," but you can have a marker for "savings plan" on the page that has the phrase "investment plan." The index entry for "savings plan" should not have a page number since the phrase does not actually appear on the page. Instead the index entry should look like this:

savings plan. See investment plan

To accomplish this, the Marker Text would look like this:

<$nopage>savings plan. See investment
plan;<$singlepage>investment plan

### *Using Character Formats*

To use a character format in Marker Text, enclose the name of the character format in angle brackets like this:

<$nopage>savings plan. <Emphasis>See<Default Para Font>
investment plan;<$singlepage>investment plan

Notice that the code <Default Para Font> is used to restore the character format to the default setting.

## Generating the Index

The steps to generate an index are very similar to the steps you have already learned for generating other lists. They are as follows:

1. In the document that contains the index markers, choose File, Generate/Book.
2. Choose Index.
3. Choose the kind of index you want to generate. This depends on the kind of markers you have inserted. If you have inserted index markers, select Standard Index. If you have inserted author markers, choose Author Index, and so on.

4. Move the type of markers you have used into the list on the left (Include Markers of Type).
5. Select Create Hypertext Links. (This is optional but highly recommended.)
6. Click the Generate button.

FrameMaker 4 displays a document with the same name as the source document and an extension of IX. Each letter of the alphabet for which there are entries is displayed above the list of words for that letter. The words are listed in alphabetic order followed by a marker and a page number.

### Correcting the Index

Several problems can arise when creating an index. These can include question marks in page ranges and items that seem to be out of order or grouped incorrectly. If a page range displays two questions marks like this:

benefits 12-??

it means that the <$endrange> code was inserted incorrectly or not at all.

If entries seem to be out of order, it is probably due to incorrect typing or punctuation. For example, if you forget to type a colon to designate a subtopic of an entry, the complete text will be listed as an entry.

To return to the source of the index, press ALT+CTRL and click on the entry in the IX document. Then select Special, Marker to edit the text in the Marker Text box.

### Formatting an Index

When an IX document is generated the first time, the format of the file is copied from the source document. When you format this file and save it with the same name, the new format becomes a template for subsequent generations of the IX document.

Special codes on the Reference page of the IX document control the format of an index. Figure 11-4 shows the Reference page of an IX document. The line at the top controls the separators for the page numbers. If you want a space before and after the dash, add it on this line. If you want a semicolon between numbers, change the comma to a semicolon.

**FIGURE 11-4**

*Index codes on the Reference page*

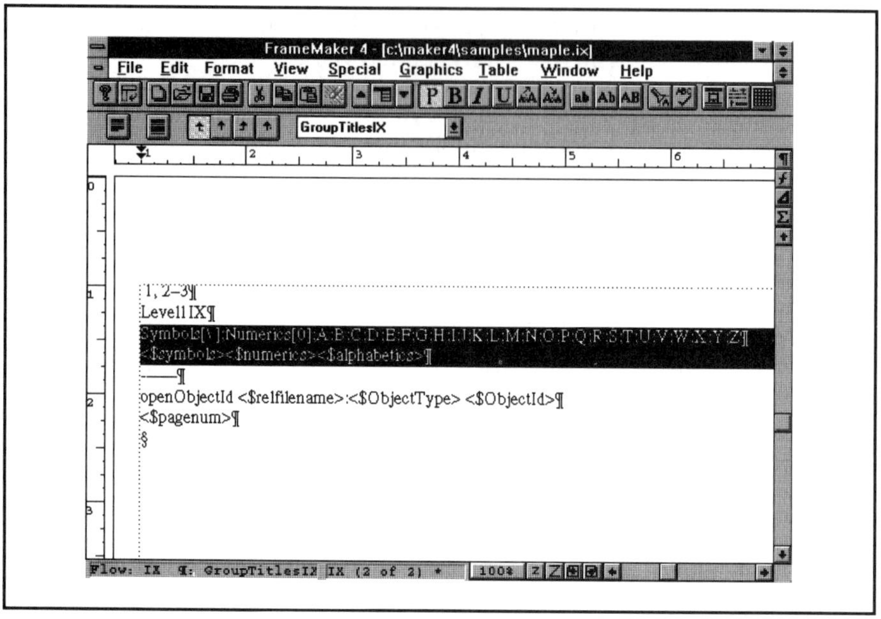


The two lines that are highlighted control the titles for the list of entries. If you want to group letters together, change the titles to something like this:

A-C[A];D-F[D];G-L[G];M-N[M];O-R[O];S-V[S];W-Z[W]

The letters in square brackets following the group titles indicate how the group titles themselves should be sorted.

The next line controls the order in which the groups of entries will be listed. If you want alphabetic characters to come before symbols and numerics, change the line like this:

<$alphabetics><$symbols><$numerics>

The next line lists the characters that should be ignored during alphabetizing. It is difficult to tell, since the hyphens run together on this line, but the line includes a hyphen, followed by a nonbreaking hyphen, an en dash, and an em dash. If you want FrameMaker 4 to sort by letter instead of by word, add a space to the beginning of this line.

The next two lines designate hypertext links, and the last line designates the index entry page number. You can add character tags to the page number if you want to use bold or some other attribute as in the following example:

<bold><$pagenum>

**Exercise**

Follow these steps to create an index:

1. In the history document on page 1, click the cursor before the word "History."
2. Choose Special, Marker.
3. Choose Index from the Marker Type pop-up menu.
4. Click New Marker.
5. Move the Marker window so it does not obscure the text. This window will remain open for several more steps.
6. Highlight "XYZ Industries."
7. Click New Marker.
8. Click the cursor before the word "increase."
9. In the Text marker box, type **<$startrange>increase.**
10. Click New Marker.
11. Click the cursor before the word "success."
12. In the Text Marker box, type **success: secret of;success: questions about.**
13. Click New Marker.
14. On page 2, click the cursor before the word "Future."
15. Click New Marker.
16. Highlight "XYZ Industries."
17. Click New Marker.
18. Click the cursor before the word "gain."
19. In the Text Marker box, type **<$endrange>increase.**
20. Click New Marker.
21. Click the cursor before "Product Development."
22. In the Marker Text box, type **<$nopage>development. See product development;<$singlepage>product development.**
23. Click New Marker.

24. Click the cursor before the number 20,000.
25. In the Text Marker box, type **20,000[twenty thousand]**.
26. Click the New Marker.
27. Close the Marker window.
28. Choose File, Generate/Book.
29. Choose Index (Standard Index).
30. Click Generate.
31. Move Index to the left box.
32. Select Create Hypertext Links.
33. Click Generate.
34. If you would like to make the headings for each letter stand out more, change the format for the paragraph tag GroupTitlesIX. You could use a larger font or bold and add space under the paragraph.
35. Save the document and close it.

## CREATING BOOKS

The Book feature in FrameMaker 4 treats multiple files just like a single file, making it easy to create a table of contents, generate lists, and create an index for all the files at once. Other functions like opening all the files, closing all the files, and printing all the files are also facilitated.

It is better to create a book that contains small files for each section than to create one large file with all the sections in it. Frame recommends splitting files that are more than 50 pages. Smaller files are easier and faster to manipulate. When designing a book, it is a good idea to put all the files in one directory reserved exclusively for the book.

To create a book, follow these steps:

1. Open a file that will be in the book.
2. Choose File, Generate/Book.
3. Choose New Multifile Book, Including.
4. Click Generate.

A window like the one shown here is displayed. The name of the file that is open is displayed in the window along with any files in the same directory that have been generated from the file.

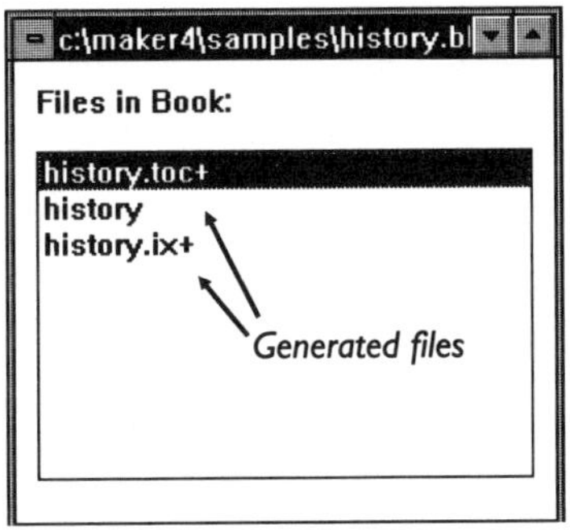


5. Choose File, Add File. This dialog box displays:

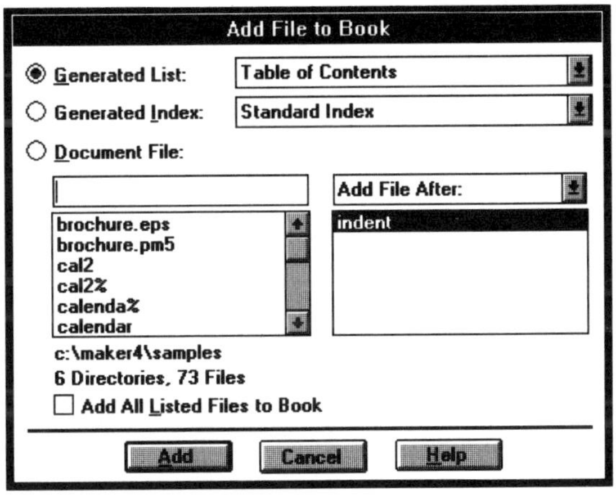


6. Choose a file that you want to add to the book from the list of files in the box on the left.

**NOTE:** *If you want to display files in other directories, type the path in the text box above the list of files on the left and press ENTER. For example, type* ***c:\maker4\book***.

7. To position a file correctly, select a file in the right box that the added file should come after. Or select Add File Before from the pop-up menu, and select a file in the box that the file should come before.

8. Click the Add button.
9. Repeat steps 5 through 8 to continue adding files in the desired order.

**TIP:** *You can select all the books in the directory by selecting Add All Listed Files to Book and clicking Add. Then you can delete any unwanted files and rearrange the order of the files later.*

10. When all the files are added, choose File, Save. (Be sure the book window is active when you do this step.)
11. Give the book file a name and click Save. Notice that the extension given to the filename is BK.
12. Close the book window.

### Adding Generated Files

If you want your book to have a table of contents and an index (or any other type of generated file), add filenames to the book list, and FrameMaker will generate them for you. Here's how you add the generated filename to the book list:

1. With the book window open, choose File, Add File.
2. Choose Generated List and specify the list type from the pop-up menu. Table of Contents is chosen in this example:

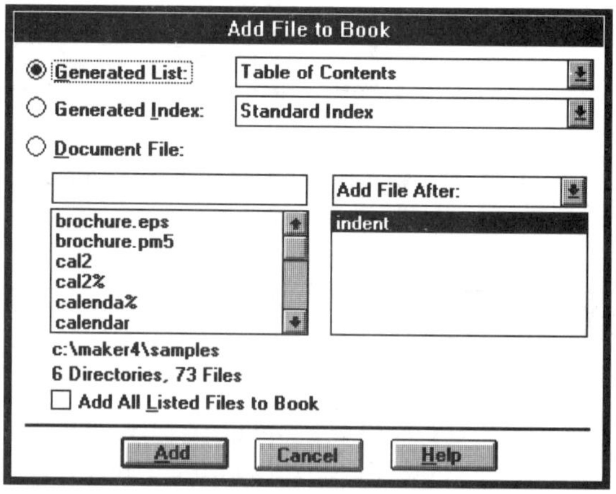

3. Click Add. This dialog box displays:

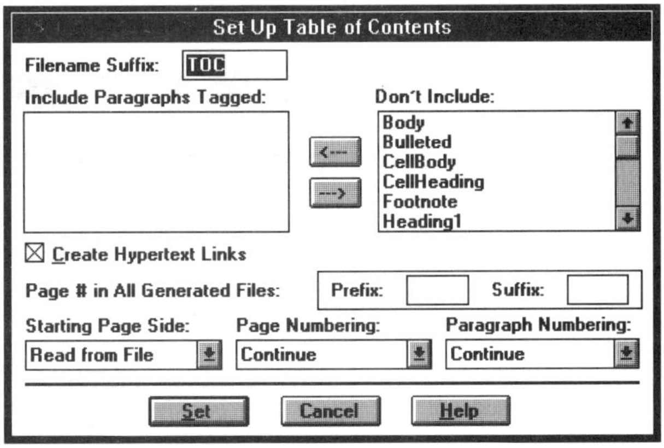


4. Choose the paragraph tags (or markers if you have selected a list type that uses markers) that you want to include and move them over to the left box.
5. Select Create Hypertext Links.
6. Enter a Prefix or Suffix for the page number if desired.
7. Specify a starting page (usually a right-hand page).
8. Specify Page Numbering.
9. Specify Paragraph Numbering.
10. Click Set. The name of the file displays in the list with a plus after it designating it as a generated file.

When you use the File, Generate/Update command, the file will be generated. This command is discussed later in this chapter.

## Rearranging and Deleting Files in a Book

Once files are listed in a book, the order might need to be changed, or a file may need to be deleted. This may be true if you have selected all the files in a directory when building the book. You will also have to delete a file if the filename changes. FrameMaker 4 cannot automatically update the file list when a filename changes, so you must delete the old filename from the list and add the new filename.

To rearrange or delete files, follow these steps:

1. Open the book file.
2. Choose File, Rearrange Files. This dialog box displays:

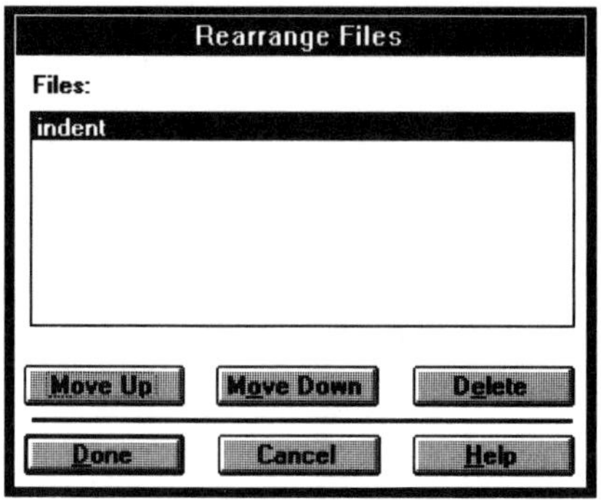


3. Select a file and click Move Up, Move Down, or Delete.
4. When finished, click Done.

## Setting Up the Book

It is common practice to start each chapter of a book on a right-hand page. Numbering in a book may be consecutive throughout the entire book; it may restart numbering in each section with something like 1-1, 2-1, 3-1, and so on; or it could be a combination of the two. A combination might number the front matter (copyright page, acknowledgments, table of contents) consecutively, restart the numbering in the body of the book, and restart the numbering in the index. Paragraph numbering can also be set up to restart or number consecutively.

To set up page and paragraph numbering as well as the starting page side, follow these steps for each file in the book:

1. Open the book file.
2. Select a filename in the list.
3. Choose File, Set Up File. This dialog box displays:

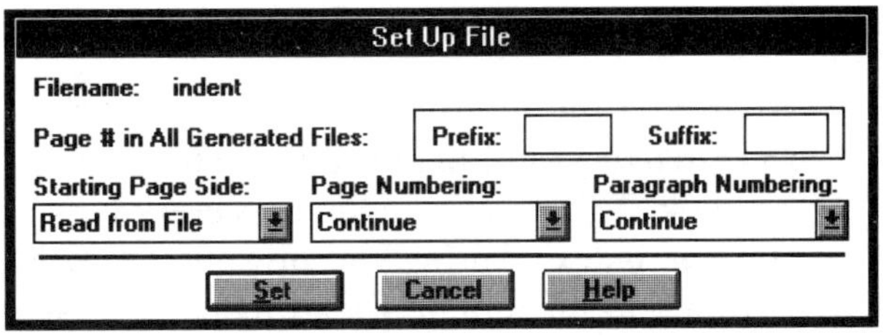


4. Enter a Prefix or Suffix for the page number if desired.
5. Specify a starting page. (Remember, this is usually Right, but you also have the choices of Read from File, Next Available Side, and Left.)
6. Specify Page Numbering. Your choices are Continue, which numbers consecutively from the last number in the previous file; Restart at 1, which renumbers the file starting with 1; and Read from File, which takes the page number from the file.
7. Specify Paragraph Numbering. (Your choices are Continue and Restart.)
8. Click Set.

## Creating Running Headers and Footers

A running header or footer is simply a header or footer that prints information about the contents of a page. The content of the header or footer changes when the content on the page changes. A system variable is used in the header or footer to accomplish the changing of data. The most commonly used variables are <$paratext> <$paranum> and <$paranumonly>. You should be familiar with these variables by now. If you need to review, refer to Table 11-1.

A running header or footer for a book would be set up on the Master page of the template that is used to create all the files in the book. If you think back to the first exercise in this book, you created a template that included a footer. You could have included a variable in the footer to pick up the number of the chapter title. Of course the chapter title paragraph would have to contain an autonumber.

## Generating and Updating

After all the files in the book have been listed for the book (including generated files) and all the files have been set up, you can generate and update the book. This process renumbers everything and generates the files like the TOC or index. During the process, FrameMaker 4 adds blank pages if necessary to maintain the starting pages as specified in the set up.

To generate and update the book, follow these steps:

1. Open the book file.

**TIP:** *Open as many files in the book as possible (you may be limited by RAM), and then save all the files. This will make the update process faster.*

2. Choose File, Generate/Update. This dialog box displays:

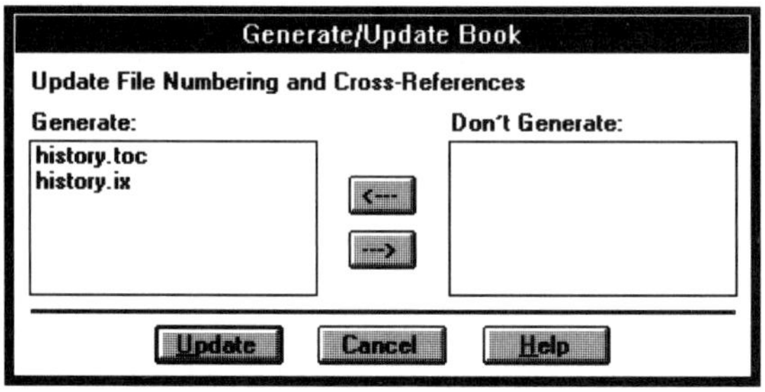


3. Select the files that you want to generate and move them to the left box.
4. Click Update.

**WARNING:** *If a file is open during the update process, be sure to save it afterwards or the updates will be lost.*

## Opening and Closing Files in a Book

When the book window is displayed, you can open a file by double-clicking the filename. To open all the files, hold SHIFT when you select File. Then select Open all Files in Book. To save all files and close all files, hold SHIFT and select File. Choose Save All Files in Book or Close All Files in Book.

### Printing Files

When the book window is open, choose File, Print to display this dialog box:

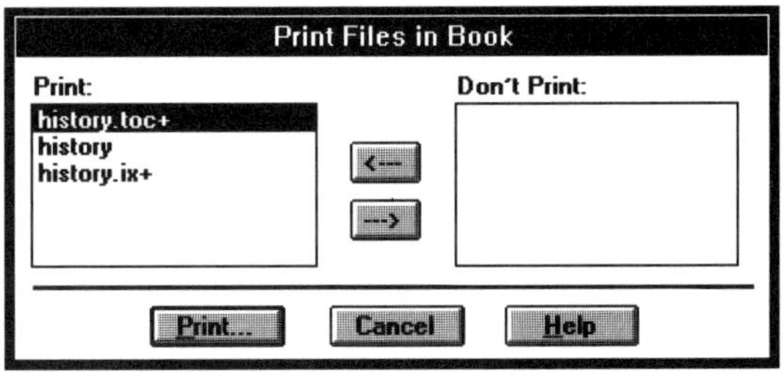


Select the files you want to print, move them into the left box, and click Print.

**NOTE:** *You can print only a complete file from this dialog box. To print selected pages, open the file and print as you normally would.*

### Changing the Format of a Book

Picture this—you have created a book with 25 chapters. All the paragraph tags, character styles, page layouts, Reference pages, and so on have been set for the whole book. You show the book to your boss for approval. Your boss hates it! (You should have reviewed it with the boss sooner!)

You have to make major changes to formats and page layouts. You see yourself working late every night for a month. Not so! FrameMaker 4 can solve your problems in a matter of seconds. What's the catch, you ask? Well, first you have to change the formats, layout, and so on for one chapter. How long will that take you? Not a month anyway.

After you have changed the format for one chapter (please get this chapter approved before you go any farther), follow these simple steps to update all the other chapters in the book:

1. Open the book file.
2. Open the file with the new formats.
3. Go to the book window.
4. Choose File, Import, Formats. The dialog box shown in Figure 11-5 displays.
5. Choose any of the Import and Update options you want.

6. If you want to remove format overrides, choose Manual Page Breaks and Other Format/Layout Overrides.
7. Choose the files you want to update.
8. Choose Import.
9. Heave a sigh of relief.

## CREATING CONDITIONAL DOCUMENTS

Conditional documents are used to create multiple versions of the document using text, tables, or graphics that can be included or excluded from the document. For example, you could create a welcome letter that describes the new employee orientation for hourly employees and for salaried employees. The parts of the letter that are different for each type of employee would be tagged as conditional text. Each type would have its own conditional text tag.

**FIGURE 11-5** *The Import Formats dialog box*

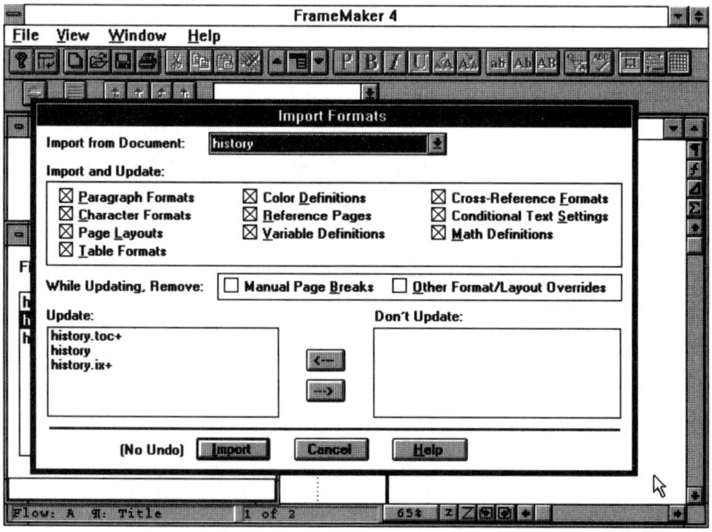

To create a conditional text tag, choose Special, Conditional Text, and click the Edit Condition Tag button. This dialog box displays:

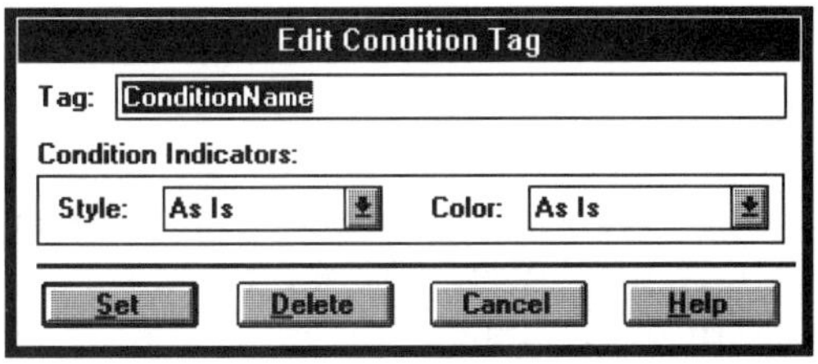


Give the tag a name and a style to identify it easily in the text. Style choices include overline, strikethrough, underline, and double underline. Also choose a color and click Set. After defining all the necessary tags, close the window.

To apply the conditional tag to text, select the text and choose Special, Conditional Text. Select the desired tag and move it to the box on the left. Click Apply. When finished, apply conditional tags, close the window.

The following illustration shows two conditional tags that will be used to produce two versions of the document:

Welcome. You are a valued member of the work force~~management staff~~.§

To make the document less confusing looking, you can change the view of the document and hide conditional tags so that only one version of the document is displayed like this:

Welcome. You are a valued member of the ~~management staff~~.§

Notice that the hidden tag is replaced with a marker.

To change the view of the document, follow these steps:

1. Choose Special, Conditional Text.
2. Click Show/Hide to display this dialog box:

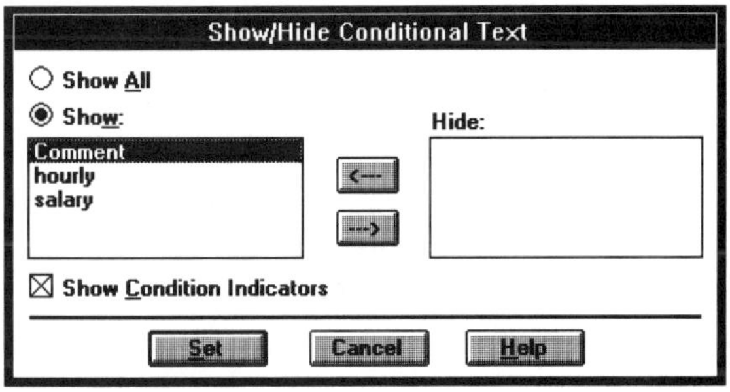

3. Move the tags that you do not want to see to the box on the right.
4. Click Set.
5. Close the Conditional Text window.

When you are ready to print the document with one version or the other, change the view of the document so the tag for the condition you want to print is displayed. Change the condition tag so that it is no longer strikethrough, double underlined, and so on. Change the color to black if necessary. Print as usual.

**NOTE:** *You can save the different versions of the document while the view is set for a particular tag.*

## THE EQUATION FEATURE

Although only a small percentage of users need FrameMaker 4's equation feature, those who do need it are provided with a full palette of math elements as shown here:

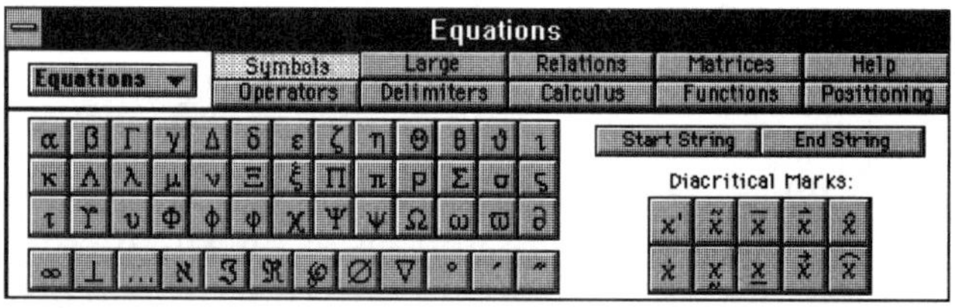


In this chapter, you will learn only the basic steps for creating equations. If you are a power user of equations, refer to the FrameMaker documentation for detailed information.

### Creating an Equation

An equation can be put in line with the rest of a paragraph, in its own paragraph, or in a frame. To create an equation, you must insert an equation object and then insert math elements in the equation.

To put an equation in line with other text, position the cursor, display the Equation palette (by clicking the equation button on the right border), click the Equations button, and choose New Small Equation, New Medium Equation, or New Large Equation. (The sizes refer to font size.)

Figure 11-6 shows the result of these steps. A marker is placed in the text, and a frame with a question mark is placed below the line of text.

Insert the desired math elements from the palette. Then, be sure the frame is selected, and click Equations. Choose Shrink-Wrap Equation. This shrinks the frame around the equation and puts it in the line of text like this:

First compute the area of the circle with this formula: $\pi r^2$¶
§

To create an equation in its own paragraph, follow the same procedure just described, but first position the cursor in a blank paragraph. To create an equation in a frame, first select the frame and then follow the same procedure already outlined.

**FIGURE 11-6** *An equation frame*

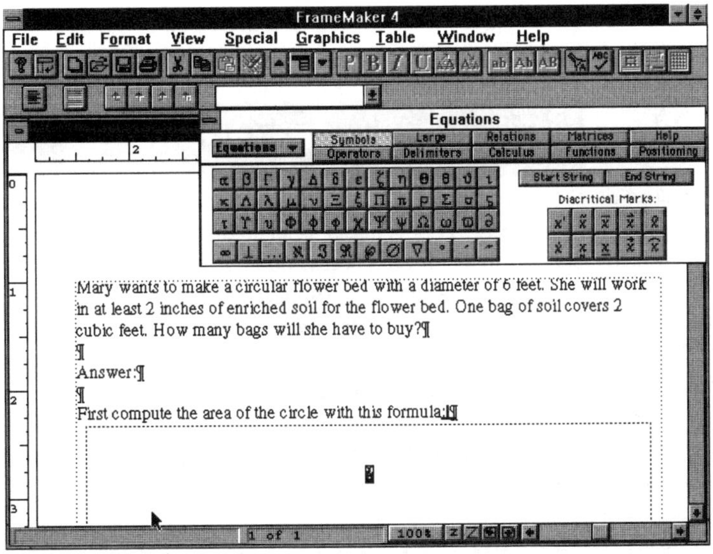

**Exercise**

Try this simple exercise:

1. Type this paragraph in a document:

   **The area of a circle with a diameter of 6 is**

   (Be sure to space after the last word.)
2. Click the Equation button on the right border.
3. Click Equations.
4. Choose New Medium Equation.
5. Click the symbol for PI (π) in the Equation palette.
6. Type **32**.
7. Highlight the 2 (this can be tricky) and click Positioning.
8. Click the upper arrow (under microposition) several times to raise the number above the baseline as an exponent.
9. Select the frame.
10. Click Equations.
11. Choose Shrink-Wrap Equation.

## About BrioPublish

*If you produce database documents, such as catalogs, directories, price lists, and even mail merge letters, you might be interested in BrioPublish. BrioPublish offers breakthroughs in database publishing through the seamless integration of data access and document formatting. BrioPublish is the first application to utilize FrameMaker 4's new API (Application Programming Interface), and it extends the capabilities of FrameMaker 4 by bringing extensive client/server database access capabilities to the program. Users can bypass traditional methods of database publishing that require extensive reformatting of updated data or are limited by export conversion formats. BrioPublish automatically generates fully formatted FrameMaker 4 documents directly from data stored in a database. BrioPublish runs on both Macintosh and Windows, and is available from Brio Technology for $795. Contact Brio Technology at (800)486-BRIO for more information.*

# 12

## Using Hypertext

*By Sandra L. Knox of Frame Technology Corporation*

BUSINESS, government, and education all depend on the smooth flow of information. Many FrameMaker 4 features already discussed in this book facilitate the flow of printed information. Hypertext, another FrameMaker 4 feature, reaches beyond printed media. Documents created with hypertext are used for onscreen viewing and online distribution.

With hypertext documents, you can set up instructional manuals, policy manuals, help systems, and guided tours for products and services. Readers can look at the contents page by page in sequential order or follow random paths by clicking an item in the text, a button, or a menu item. When a hypertext item is clicked, the link causes more information to be displayed. The additional information can be located in the same document or a different document.

With Frame's product called FrameViewer, the reader does not need FrameMaker 4 in order to view the online documents. To prepare a file for display, a FrameMaker author simply saves a document and it is immediately usable via FrameViewer. Since the same file is used for authoring and distribution, there is no need to keep two versions—an editable version and a noneditable, postprocessed version. Users save time and increase their productivity, and document authors can focus on document creation, not document or system administration.

Online systems can distribute information cost-effectively to thousands of users via traditional local area networks, hard-disk storage, and even compact disc, read-only memory (CD-ROM) media. Most systems can also print documents.

Frame has been providing online distribution and viewing products for more than four years and supports over a quarter of a million users. The growing list of companies that have adopted Frame's online viewing technology includes Claris Corporation, American Airlines, Cadence Design Systems, LSI Logic, Rolls Royce, Westinghouse, US West, PDA Engineering, and Rational.

## WHY VIEW DOCUMENTS ELECTRONICALLY?

Viewing documents electronically is one step toward the paperless office predicted by industry pundits shortly after the personal computer became so popular. With electronic viewing, information is more readily accessible, and navigation is faster. Printing and paper handling costs are reduced or eliminated, and documents can be changed in a more timely manner. For lively effects, multimedia such as sound and video can be included.

### Advantages

Online document distribution solves some of the problems associated with paper documents, and even offers significant improvements. For example, electronic documentation adds value by significantly reducing the time it takes to accomplish work, by offering reduced cost, and by providing capabilities not available through traditional methods. The savings associated with reducing printing and paper costs alone have often been cited as a primary reason to move to the paperless office. But that is not the whole picture. The hidden costs of paper are also staggering. Mailing, storage, and filing costs easily outweigh the original cost of printing the materials.

For documents such as catalogs, price lists, and policy guides that require periodic updates, online documentation is particularly appropriate. Several large firms and government agencies have subject matter experts whose sole job is to keep specific catalogs updated. Online distribution of this information could significantly reduce the direct costs associated with their efforts.

For many software vendors, printed documentation can easily be 50 percent of the total cost of goods. An average set of Unix software documents can cost $15 to $35 to print and $4 to $7 to mail. For software vendors distributing software on compact disc or magnetic tape, adding documentation on these media has a negligible incremental cost. Even adding an additional floppy disk or two to disk-based products can save $20 to $30 per unit.

Time to market is critical, transcending most other factors that determine the success of an organization. The faster and more effectively you can communicate information or produce a product, the greater your advantage over the competition.

The time-to-market savings of electronic documentation go beyond the obvious comparison between mailing a hard-copy document (even by overnight express) and the almost instantaneous transmission of electronic documents. Most importantly, electronic documents provide the flexibility to update small portions of larger documents without reprinting the entire manual.

## SUCCESS STORY #1

*The Strategic Engineering Department of the Process Control Division at Westinghouse designs process control hardware and software for a variety of different industries—everything from nuclear power plants to steel mills and chemical factories. The product documentation—manuals that range up to 450 pages in length—is vital to plant and factory owners who need to keep their operations running smoothly and efficiently. Any system failure could jeopardize factory productivity and mean the loss of thousands of dollars in goods. Recognizing the need to streamline the documentation process and distribute manuals quickly to customers, Westinghouse decided to use FrameMaker to achieve its goals.*

*FrameMaker makes it convenient to import illustrations from the in-house graphics department. And the integrated drawing tools are ideal for writers who generate their own illustrations, thereby eliminating the need for learning new programs. Screen captures and CAD drawings from the engineering groups are also easily imported, saving time and streamlining document production.*

*The move to FrameMaker solved a major publishing headache for the documentation group as well. Since both the documentation team and the engineers are on a network of Unix-based workstations, FrameMaker files can be shared and accessed by multiple contributors to a project. The writers produce the documentation in FrameMaker, make a copy of their file, and put it into a common directory. Engineers can access the files, verify editing remarks, and make changes directly into the document, eliminating the time lag inherent in hard copy review cycles.*

*Westinghouse has been able to extend the benefits of FrameMaker to their customers by providing manuals online. When a new factory opens up, it is imperative that customers have access to the process control documentation immediately. Westinghouse gets two values from FrameMaker: online documentation that can be used to interact with the engineers' comments, and online distribution of documentation to customers who need the information before the manual is finished. The process control documentation group is currently putting together an entire set of manuals on CD-ROM media. Using FrameMaker's unique hypertext feature, they are creating hypertext links and buttons for easy navigation and information retrieval between the manuals.*

**SUCCESS STORY #2**

*US West Enhanced Services delivers worldwide fax mail and other enhanced fax services to its customers. The company has adopted Frame as its official publishing standard and will soon distribute online service information to its 100 employees via FrameViewer. FrameMaker 4 is replacing word processing packages and batch mode software. FrameMaker's cross-platform compatibility was the initial attraction for Enhanced Services. It was the only package that could accommodate so many computer environments and could seamlessly incorporate data from so many different software applications.*

*One of the most innovative applications for Enhanced Services is the Online Reference System, a new approach toward the distribution of internal documents and forms using FrameMaker 4's hypertext capability and FrameViewer. A surprising benefit of FrameViewer has been its impetus to convince people to stay on schedule and to fill out required paperwork electronically. Documents are online, right in front of their faces, not sitting on a shelf somewhere; so it's a lot easier to get people to write.*

## DEVELOPING AN ONLINE SYSTEM

When planning an effective online system, you need to pay particular attention to the hardware on which the system will run, the monitor type and size, and fonts. The structure of the online documents should make information in the document accessible, aid navigation, provide for browsing, show readers where they are in the document, show relationships between ideas, and so on.

**TIP:** *Remember that, unlike printed documents, online documents are typically viewed in a nonlinear manner. You must provide adequate paths for the reader to navigate.*

### The Development Process

The following steps briefly outline the process of developing and using an online system:

- Plan, map, and organize the information.
- Design the page layout for the screen.
- Write the contents of the documents.
- Insert hypertext commands that create the navigational paths.
- Test the hypertext commands.
- Save the documents in View Only format.
- Distribute the documents to the readers.

### Tips for Creating Online Systems

Online systems work faster if you use several short documents rather than one long one. Frame recommends using documents of ten pages or less to minimize the time it takes to open a document if the reader clicks an active area to display a page from another document.

Use fonts that are readily available on many systems. Times and Helvetica are good choices because these fonts are available on most systems, and they print on all laser printers.

Store all the documents and graphics that make up the system in one directory. This eliminates the need to keep track of and specify path names.

## HANDS-ON EXERCISE

The following exercise develops a comprehensive online system for an employee handbook. When designing the system, keep in mind that the reader may begin by scanning a table of contents, but navigation "will jump all over the place" from there. The handbook will give access to a company organization chart, seating map, biographies on each employee, and the company phone list. The following illustration shows the possible navigation paths that the system will accommodate:

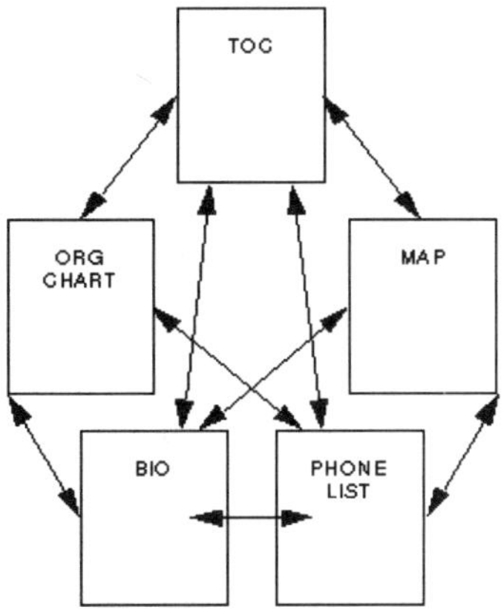


This exercise is divided into five sections—employee biographies, the phone list, the building map, the organizational chart, and the table of contents. You may wish to adapt the text in this exercise to your own company information so that you have an actual, real-life example to use or show to management at your company.

## Section 1: Employee Biographies

1. Create a new document using a page size that can be fully displayed on the screen at 100 percent zoom. For example, if the system will be used on Apple Macintosh PowerBooks, make the page 8.75 inches wide by 4.785 inches high.
2. Set the margins at .75 inches from the top, .50 inches from the bottom, 4.0 inches from the left, and 1.0 inch from the right. (The wide left margin will be used for graphics. You may have to use a different margin on the left to accommodate the page size that you have chosen for your monitor.)
3. Apply the paragraph style Heading1, type your name, and press ENTER.
4. Apply the paragraph style Heading2, type your title, and press ENTER.

5. Create a new paragraph style called Phone based on the Body paragraph style. Change the font angle to Italic. Type your phone number and press ENTER.
6. Create a new paragraph style called Job Desc based on the Phone paragraph style. Change the Space Above to 12 points, and change the font angle to Regular. Type your job description in a short paragraph.
7. Create additional biographies as needed, in alphabetical order. For the purpose of this exercise, try to create at least four more biographies.
8. Delete all paragraph styles except Heading1, Heading2, Phone, and Job Desc. (Choose Delete from the Commands list in the Paragraph Designer window.)
9. Spell-check the document.
10. Create a frame that is anchored to the Job Desc paragraph for each biography. If available, place a scanned photograph of the person in the frame. Use the following settings for the frame:

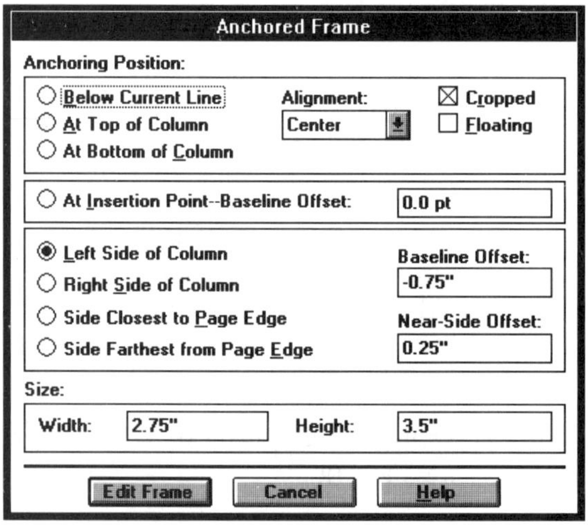


**NOTE:** *The frame size will have to be adjusted for the width and height you are using for your particular page size.*

11. Save the document with the name **biograph** but do not close it.

## Section 2: The Phone List

In this section you will generate a table of contents document for the file biograph that will be added to the documents in the online system.

1. With the file biograph still open, choose File, Generate/Book.
2. Choose Table of Contents from the List pop-up menu and click Generate.
3. Heading1 and Heading2 will already be in the Include Paragraphs Tagged box. Move Phone from the Don't Include box to the Include Paragraphs Tagged box.
4. Click Create Hypertext Links.
5. Click the Generate button.
6. Save this newly generated file as biograph.toc.
7. Delete the paragraph styles Heading1, Heading2, Job Desc, and Phone from biograph.toc.
8. Save, but do not close, this file.
9. Choose View, Reference Pages.
10. Go to the second Reference page named TOC.
11. In an online document you do not need to refer to page numbers, so delete all occurrences of <$paranum>.
12. Go to the Body page.
13. Save the file, without closing.
14. Close the file biograph. Click on Yes when asked to save before closing.
15. In the biograph.toc file, place the insertion pointer in the first line. This paragraph is tagged Heading1TOC.
16. Open the Paragraph Designer. Change the Space Above in the Basic Properties to 12 points. Click Update All.
17. Change the Default Font to Helvetica and the Weight to Bold. Click Update All.
18. Change the Pagination Properties to Keep With Next. Click Update All.

19. Place the insertion pointer in the next paragraph, tagged Heading2TOC. Change the Pagination Properties to Run-In Head with a period as the Default Punctuation. Also select the check box Keep With Next. Choose Update All.
20. Place the insertion pointer in the next paragraph, tagged PhoneTOC. Change the Autonumber Format in the Numbering Properties to "\t." Click Update All.
21. In the Basic properties, add a new, right-aligned tab stop at 3.75 inches (or a measurement that is appropriate for your page size). Choose dot leaders. Click Update All.
22. Change the Pagination Properties to Keep With Previous. Click Update All.
23. Save the file without closing.

### *Testing the Hypertext Document*

To test the hypertext commands, you must save the document in the View Only format or emulate the format. To emulate the View Only format without saving the document, press, ESC, F, l, k. To cancel the emulation, press ESC, F, l, k again.

**TIP:** *If you just want to test some of the links without using the View Only format or emulation, press ALT+CTRL when you click an active area (a hypertext link).*

To actually change a document to View Only format, choose File, Save As. Choose View Only from the Format menu and click Save. This locks the document so readers cannot make any changes to it.

If you need to edit a view-only document, you must first change it back to a normal document. Switching back to a normal document is done by pressing ESC, F, l, k , not by resaving the document in the Normal format as you might expect. A view-only document does not have a Save or Save As command in the File menu.

Readers will see the contents of a view-only document exactly as it appears when you save it as view-only, so be sure to set the View options before saving. You will probably want to turn off the display of the grid, the ruler, text symbols, and borders.

**NOTE:** *If the online system will be used on a network, set the file permissions to read-only so readers cannot make changes to a document even if they change it to Normal format.*

Follow these steps to test the hypertext links in the biograph.toc document:

1. Turn off the grid, the ruler, text symbols, and borders.
2. Save the document in View Only format.
3. Click your name in the locked, view-only biograph.toc document. The information about you in the biograph document should be displayed.
4. Click on Window and notice that biograph.toc is still open.
5. Press ESC.

When creating online systems, you might want a hypertext link to go to another document and close the one that is current. To accomplish this, you must change the code on the TOC Reference page. Follow these steps to change the code in the biograph.toc document:

1. Make biograph.toc the current document.
2. Go to the second Reference page named TOC. Change the openObjectID command to gotoObjectID.
3. Go back to the Body page and save and close biograph.toc.
4. The biograph file should now be the current document. Regenerate the table of contents using the same options you used earlier.
5. Close and save the biograph file.
6. Change the biograph.toc file to View Only format.
7. Click your name in biograph.toc. This will activate the hypertext command, but this time biograph.toc will be replaced by biograph.

## *Hypertext Navigation*

As discussed earlier, a reader navigates through an online hypertext system by clicking areas that contain hypertext commands. Hypertext commands can be inserted in text, a graphic, or different parts of the same graphic (on Body pages or Master pages).

Before you insert a hypertext command, you must first prepare the area. To designate a word or phrase as an area, select the text and change the character format to underline, superscript, subscript, color, or As Is (if you do not want to change the appearance).

To designate a graphic or a part of a graphic as an active area, draw a text column over the desired area of the graphic. Set the column's pen and fill patterns to None (to make the text column transparent) and bring the text column to the front.

**NOTE:** *An entire paragraph can be an area if there are no character format changes in the paragraph. FrameMaker will search the paragraph until it finds a hypertext command.*

To insert a hypertext command, follow these steps:

1. Click the insertion pointer in a prepared area.
2. Choose Special, Marker.
3. Choose Hypertext from the pop-up menu.
4. Type the hypertext command (in lowercase) in the Marker Text box.

**TIP:** *Make sure that the hypertext marker is placed inside of the text with the character format change. If this is not done, the hypertext area will be the text before the active area, not the actual active area.*

5. Click New Marker. If Text Symbols are on, a marker symbol (T) appears at the insertion pointer.

### *Inserting an Alert in the Employee Handbook*

In the next part of the exercise, you will insert a hypertext command that displays an alert dialog box. The alert is just one of the many hypertext commands you can insert throughout your documents.

1. The file biograph should still be open.
2. Select a word in the Job Description.

3. Apply the Character Style "Emphasis" from the Character Catalog to that word.
4. With that word still highlighted, choose Special, Marker.
5. Choose Hypertext from the pop-up menu.
6. Erase any marker text, and type: **alert This is an example of an alert. It can contain up to 250 characters. It is dismissed by clicking the OK button.**
7. Click the New Marker button.
8. Change the biograph file to View Only format.
9. Click the word you selected. You should see an alert box.
10. Click OK.

### *Inserting Navigational Buttons*

In the next part of the exercise, you will put buttons on the bottom of the page with hypertext commands to help the user navigate forward and backward throughout the document.

1. Change the biograph file to Normal format.
2. Go to the Master page and delete the header and footer columns.
3. Open the arrows file in the CLIPART directory.
4. Select an arrow style and copy it to the clipboard.
5. Close the arrows file.
6. Paste the arrow on the Master page of biograph. Before pasting, be sure that the insertion pointer is not in the text column.
7. Paste two more times so that you have three arrows. Arrange them on the page similar to the following image:

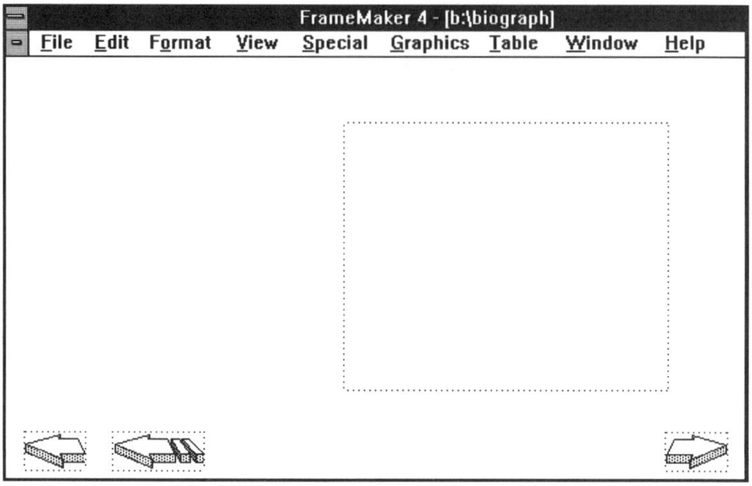


8. Display the Graphics Tools palette. Draw a text column over each arrow.

**NOTE:** *When you draw the text column on a Master page, FrameMaker asks whether you want to create a template column or a background column. Text columns for active areas should be background (untagged) columns.*

9. Place the insertion pointer in the text column over the far left arrow. Insert a hypertext marker with this command: **previouspage**.
10. In the text column over the middle arrow, insert a hypertext marker with this command: **previouslink**.
11. In the text column over the right arrow, insert a hypertext marker with this command: **nextpage**.

**NOTE:** *See Chapter 27, "Hypertext and View-Only Documents," in* Using FrameMaker *(Frame's user manual) for a list of hypertext commands.*

12. Turn off borders. Go to the Body page. Change the file to View Only format. Save.
13. Click the button on the far right side of the page. This will take you to the next page.

14. Change the document back to Normal format and go to the Master page.
15. Copy all three arrows and the text columns over them.
16. Open biograph.toc. Change to Normal format, if necessary. Go to the Master page.
17. Delete the header and footer columns.
18. With no insertion pointer, paste the buttons and text columns.
19. Turn off borders, go to the Body page, and change the file to View Only format.
20. Save the file.
21. Click your name in the biograph.toc file. FrameMaker 4 will automatically take you to the biograph file and highlight your name.
22. Click on the middle arrow at the bottom of the page. FrameMaker 4 will automatically take you back to your previous location. You can continue to jump to the previous location as many as 69 times.

**NOTE:** *You can override Master page active graphics on individual Body pages if you want to send the reader somewhere else. To override a Master page command on an individual Body page, put a graphic or a different hypertext command over the area on the Body page.*

### *Adding a Button to Close a File*

In the next steps, you will add a button to the biograph file that closes the file.

1. Change biograph to Normal format, if necessary.
2. Go to the Master page.
3. Open the dingbats file from the CLIPART directory.
4. Select a graphic you would like to use to represent "close" and copy it to the clipboard.
5. Close the dingbats file.
6. Paste the graphic on the Master page. Before pasting, be sure that your insert point is not in the text column.

7. Display the Graphics Tools palette and draw a text column over the close icon.

**NOTE:** *When you draw the text column on a Master page, FrameMaker asks whether you want to create a template column or a background column. Text columns for active areas should be background (untagged) columns.*

8. Click the insertion pointer in the text column over the Close icon. Insert a hypertext marker with this command: **quit**.
9. Click the New Marker button.
10. Turn off borders, go to the Body page, and change the file to View Only format.
11. Save the file.
12. Click the Close icon. This will close the document.
13. Open biograph again.
14. Change the document back to Normal format and go to the Master page.
15. Copy the Close icon and the text column over it.
16. Open biograph.toc. Change to Normal format, if necessary.
17. Go to the Master page and paste the Close icon and its text column. Before pasting, be sure the insertion pointer is not in the text column.
18. Turn off borders, go to the Body page, and change the file to View Only format.
19. Save the file.

### Section 3: The Building Map

In this section of the exercise, you will create a seating chart or building map. When the end users of this online document click an office area, they will automatically be navigated to the biography for that person.

1. Choose File, New.
2. Click the file biograph to use it as a template. This way you can reuse the paragraph styles and Master page that have already been established.

3. Change the new document to Normal format, if necessary.
4. Save this new file with the name **map**.
5. With the insertion pointer in the body text, choose Edit, Select All and press DEL.
6. Click the insertion pointer outside the body text. Choose Select All from the Edit menu and press DEL.
7. Display the Graphics Tools palette.
8. Using the rectangle tool, draw a box that is wider than it is tall.
9. Draw vertical lines to divide the rectangle like this:

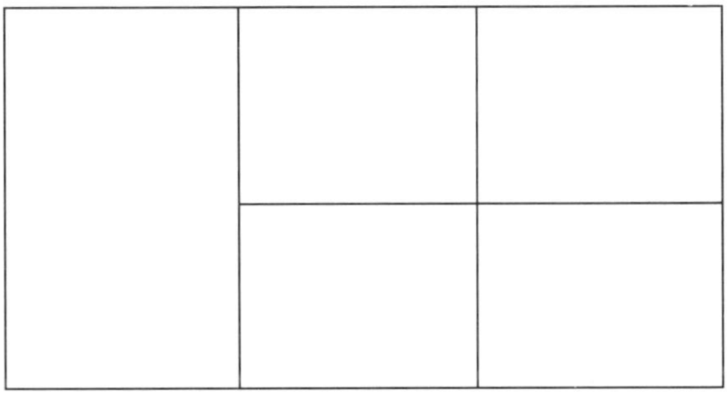

10. In the center of each small rectangle (office area), use the textline tool to type a name from your biograph file.
11. Draw a text column over the first, and largest, office area on the map. (Be sure the text column is transparent.) Go to the biograph file (it should still be open) and change to Normal format, if necessary.
12. In the map file, place the insertion pointer in the text column of the largest office. Choose Special, Marker.
13. Type the hypertext command: **gotolink biograph:***firstname* where firstname is the first name of a person in your biograph file. (Give yourself the largest office if you like.)

**NOTE:** *The exercise assumes that all the documents are stored in the same directory; therefore, you do not need to specify a path name in the gotolink command.*

14. Click the New Marker button.

15. In the biograph file, double-click the first name used in step 13.
16. Choose Special, Marker. The name will already be in the Marker Text edit box.
17. Before the name, type the hypertext command: **newlink**.
18. Click the New Marker button.
19. While still in the biograph file, change the file to View Only format. Use the Close icon you added in the previous exercise. Save the changes.
20. In the map file, change to View Only format. Click the largest office button. Save changes.
21. FrameMaker 4 will automatically navigate you to the biograph file and highlight the name.
22. Click on the previouslink arrow in the center bottom of the page that you added earlier to return to the map file.
23. Change the map file to Normal format.
24. Draw one transparent text column over the four-office area on the map.
25. Place the insertion pointer inside this new text column and insert a hypertext marker. Now type the following hypertext command: **matrix 2 2 map**. This matrix command specifies two rows, two columns, and the corresponding hypertext commands are in a text column with the flow tag (map) on a Reference page.
26. Click the New Marker button.
27. Go to the Reference page. Delete all the reference frames on the page.
28. Draw a text column 3 by 3 inches.
29. Place the insertion pointer inside this new text column.
30. Choose Format, Flow.
31. Type **map** in the Flow Tag box and click the Set button.
32. Place the insertion pointer in the text column and type the following commands, replacing the first names with names you used in your biograph file:

    **gotolink biograph:Dale**

**gotolink biograph:Ed**

**gotolink biograph:Mary**

**gotolink biograph:Janet**

**NOTE:** *Make sure that each hypertext command is on its own line, and that each command does not wrap to another line.*

33. Go back to the Body page.
34. In the biograph file, double-click the first name of the second biography.
35. Choose Special, Marker. The first name will already be in the Marker Text edit box.
36. Type the hypertext command **newlink** before the first name.
37. Click the New Marker button.
38. Insert the same type of hypertext marker for all the other first names.
39. While still in the biograph file, change the file to View Only format. Use the Close icon you added in the previous exercise. Save the changes.
40. In the map file, change to View Only format. Click one of the smaller office buttons. Save changes.
41. FrameMaker will automatically navigate you to the biograph file and highlight the first name in the biography for the corresponding office from the map.
42. Click on the previouslink arrow in the center bottom of the page that you added in the previous exercise.

### Section 4: The Organization Chart

In this section you will create an organization chart and use cross-references as hypertext commands.

1. Change the biograph file to Normal format.
2. Choose File, New.

3. Click the file map to use it as a template.
4. Change the new document to Normal format, if necessary.
5. Save this new file as orgchart.
6. Click the insertion pointer outside the body text. Choose Edit, Select All, and press DEL.
7. Display the Graphics Tools palette.
8. Draw five rectangles. Inside each rectangle draw a text column. Organize them to look like an organization chart. An example is shown here:

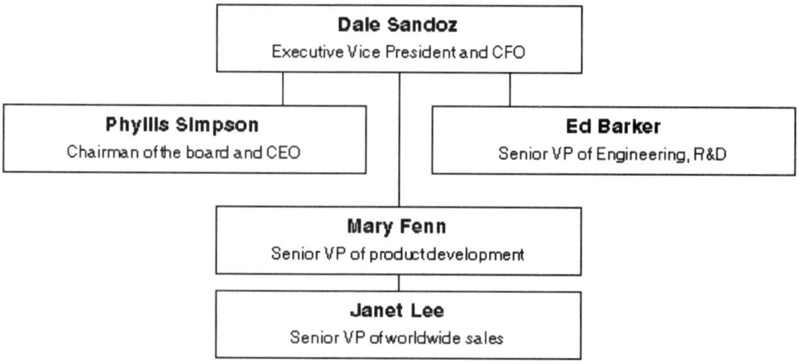


9. In each text column, apply the paragraph style Heading1. Change the Basic properties to 0 Below. Click Update All. Change the Default Font properties to 10 point Helvetica Bold. Click Update All. In the text column, type **name** and press ENTER.
10. Apply the paragraph style Heading2. Change the Basic properties to 9 above. Click Update All. Change the Default Font properties to 9 point Helvetica Regular. Click Update All. In the text column, type **title**. Do not press ENTER.
11. Double-click the first "name." From the Special menu, select Cross Reference.
12. From the Source Document pop-up menu, select biograph.

13. From the Source Type scroll menu, select Heading1. Select the first name in the Reference Source scroll menu. Click the Insert button.
14. Double-click the word "title." From the Special menu, select Cross Reference.
15. From the Source Document pop-up menu, select biograph.
16. From the Source Type scroll menu, select Heading2. Select the first title in the Reference Source scroll menu. Click the Insert button.
17. Repeat these steps until all the names and titles have been filled in using cross-references.
18. Turn off borders and Save in View Only format.
19. In the biograph file, turn off borders, if necessary, and Save in View Only format. Close the file.
20. In the orgchart file, click on any of the names or titles in the organization chart. FrameMaker 4 will automatically navigate you to the appropriate page in the biograph file.

## Section 5: The Table of Contents

In this section, you will create a table of contents for the online system. Follow these steps:

1. Choose File, New.
2. Click the file map to use it as a template.
3. Change the new document to Normal format, if necessary.
4. Save this new file as maintoc.
5. Click the insertion pointer outside the body text. Choose Select All from the Edit menu and press DEL.
6. Display the Graphics Tools palette.
7. Draw three rectangles as in the following example:

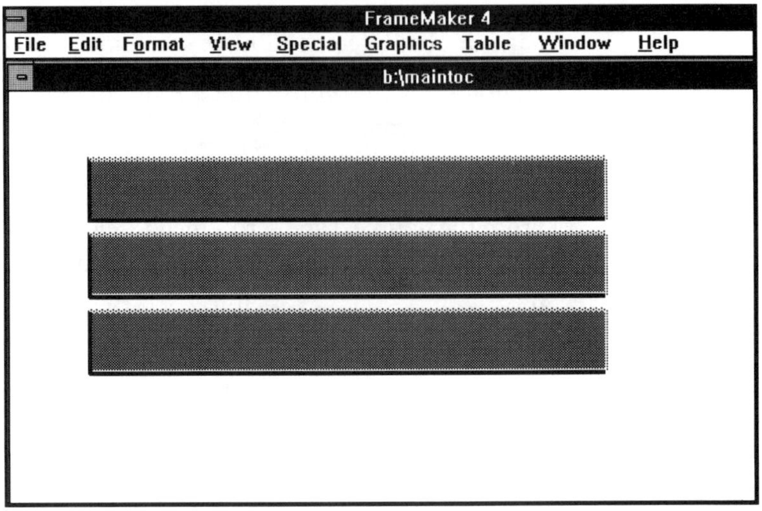


8. Open the icons file in the CLIPART directory.
9. Select a down arrow graphic and copy it to the clipboard. Close the icons file.
10. Paste the arrow on the Body page of the maintoc file. Reduce the arrow to .75 by .75 inches.
11. Copy, then paste, the arrow two more times.
12. Align the arrow on the page something like this:

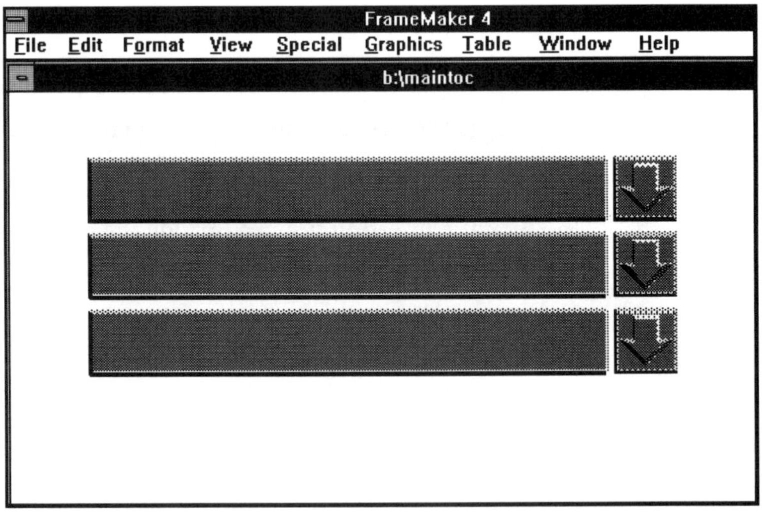

13. Display the Graphics Tools palette. Using the Textline tool, type **Organization Chart**, **Phone List**, and **Office Map** centered in each rectangle.
14. Draw a transparent text column over each rectangle and each arrow button.
15. In the first text column over Organization Chart, insert a hypertext marker with this command: **gotolink orgchart:firstpage.**
16. In the middle text column over Phone List, insert a hypertext marker with this command: **gotolink biograph.toc:firstpage.**
17. In the bottom text column over Office Map, insert a hypertext marker with this command: **gotolink map:firstpage.**

### *Creating a Pop-Up Menu of Hypertext Links*

If you have defined a pop-up menu with hypertext links, the user can display the pop-up menu by pointing to the active area and holding down the mouse button. In the table of contents document, you will define pop-up menus for the down-arrow graphics by inserting hypertext markers with the pop-up command.

The syntax for the pop-up command is

popup *flowname*

The items in the pop-up menu and the hypertext commands are defined on a Reference page in a text column specified by *flowname*.

**NOTE:** *The flowname cannot contain embedded spaces.*

Follow these steps to create a pop-up menu:

1. In the text column for the first arrow button next to Organization Chart, insert a hypertext marker with this command: **popup chart.**
2. In the text column for the middle arrow button next to Phone List, insert a hypertext marker with this command: **popup list.**
3. In the text column for the bottom arrow button next to Office Map, insert a hypertext marker with this command: **popup office.**

4. Draw three text columns on a Reference page, and assign a different flow tag to match the flowname in the pop-up command: chart, list, office.
5. Place the insertion pointer in the flow tagged "chart." Type the menu name **Organization Chart** in the flow, and press ENTER. This is the name that will appear at the top of the pop-up menu.
6. Type each name used in the biographies on a separate line. These names will appear as items on the menu.
7. Insert a hypertext marker in each line except the line that contains the menu name. The hypertext command should be **gotolink biograph:***firstname*, where firstname is the name of the person in each biography.
8. Since you will have the same information in each pop-up, complete the first text column with the flow tag "chart," then copy and paste into the other two text columns tagged "list" and "office."
9. Go back to the Body page. Turn off text symbols and borders, if necessary. Change the file to View Only format and Save.

### *Adding Additional Navigation Buttons*

It may be beneficial for the reader of these documents to have an easy way to go from one portion of the system to another. For the last part of the exercise, you will add additional navigation buttons. Follow these steps:

1. Change the biograph document to Normal format, if necessary.
2. Go to the Master page.
3. Copy a graphic from the icons file in the CLIPART directory that you would like to use for this button.
4. Paste the icon at the bottom of the Master page three times.
5. Draw a text column over each icon.
6. Add three hypertext markers with the following hypertext commands:

   **gotolink orgchart:firstpage**

**gotolink biograph.toc:firstpage**
**gotolink map:firstpage**

7. Once you have created and tested these buttons, copy and paste them to the other documents.

## Final Steps

After you have written the document and inserted the hypertext commands, it's a good idea to test the commands to make sure that all of your links are set up correctly, that the pop-up and matrix commands work correctly, and so on.

For troubleshooting suggestions, refer to Chapter 27, "Hypertext and View-Only Documents," in *Using FrameMaker*.

### SEYBOLD KIOSK

*Frame's online viewing technology was selected by Seybold for the San Francisco 1993 Conference to be used as an information kiosk. The kiosk provided an online, hypertext-based information system that allowed Seybold attendees to click graphics and keywords to find information on conferences, exhibitors, booth locations, and more. The guide incorporated some of the industry's leading technology, including QuickTime and FrameMaker 4's configurable user interface and automatic hypertext links.*

*The Seybold electronic information system was created entirely in-house at Frame using FrameMaker 4. Over 670 pages of information were presented, divided into four files, and navigated through cross references and automatically generated hypertext links. Updates could be made each evening during the Conference as times, locations, and titles changed. See Color Plate 8 for an example screen from the kiosk.*

# 13

# Tracking Your Progress

As a complex document develops, many features are used and many changes are made. Sometimes you may find it beneficial to know exactly what features have been used (such as paragraph tags and Master pages) and how the document has changed through successive revisions. All of this information can be obtained from FrameMaker 4 with these features:

- A report feature
- A list generation feature that lists the features used in a document
- Revision markings
- Revision pages that retain the original pagination
- A document compare feature that combines both versions of a document and shows the changes side by side

## THE REPORT AND LIST GENERATION FEATURES

FrameMaker 4 comes with one report that can be run to yield the word count in a document. This report is run by choosing File, Utilities, Document Reports. The following dialog box is displayed:

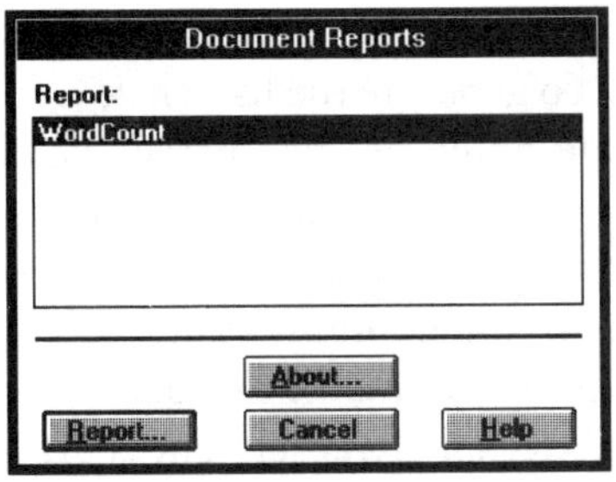


If you select the report called WordCount and click the Report button, the number of words in the current document will be displayed like this:

Click OK to return to the document.

To generate lists, choose File, Generate/Book. This dialog box is displayed:

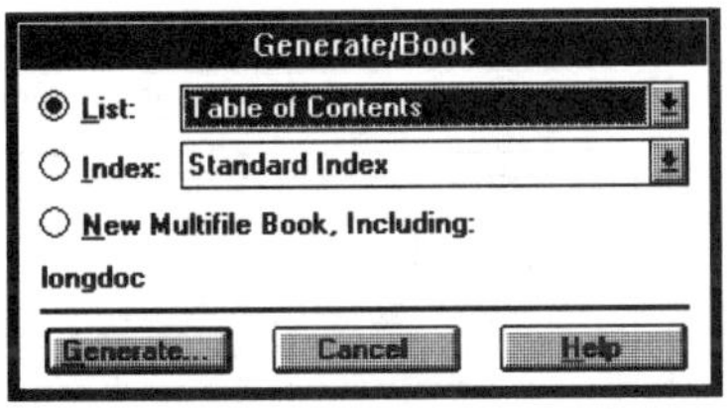


Choose List of References for List and click Generate. This dialog box is displayed:

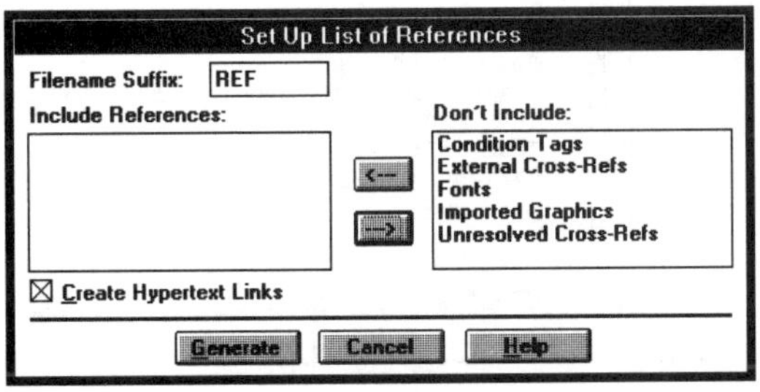


You can move all the options (Condition Tags, External Cross-Refs, Fonts, Imported Graphics, and Unresolved Cross-Refs) into the Include

References box by selecting one and pressing SHIFT while clicking the left arrow. To generate the list, click Generate. FrameMaker 4 creates a file with the same name as the current document and an extension of REF. The document is displayed on the screen as soon as it is generated.

Figure 13-1 shows an example of a file that has been generated for a document that contains many different elements. Notice that condition tags (MKT and Comment) are named and the pages on which they occur are listed. External cross references are listed with the source document names (including path if not in the same directory), the text of the cross-reference markers, and the page number on which the cross references are located. Font names, point sizes, and the pages on which they are used are listed. Imported graphics that were imported by reference are listed with the filenames (and paths if not in the same directory), the dots-per-inch (dpi) setting, and the page number on which they are located.

As you can probably see from Figure 13-1, the list is generated in the order in which features are encountered in the document. It may be more helpful to generate a list in alphabetical order or generate separate lists for each feature—a list of fonts, a list of cross references, and so on. To generate an

**FIGURE 13-1**

*A generated list of references*

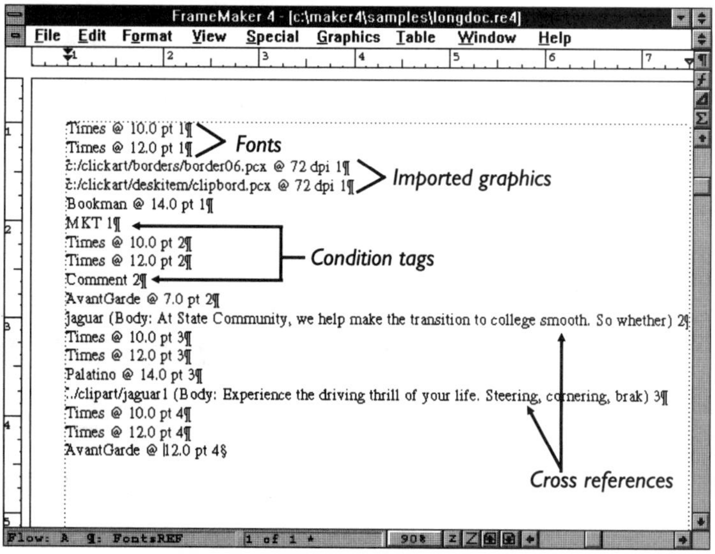

alphabetized list of features, choose Index: Index of References in the Generate/Book dialog box as shown here:

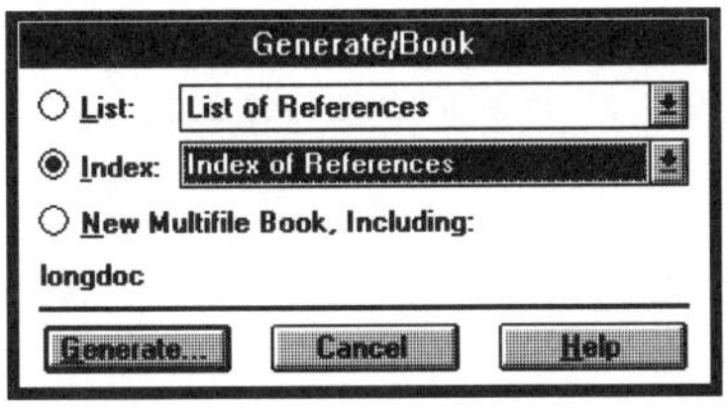


Then click the Generate button, select the features, and click Generate again. (FrameMaker 4 uses an extension of IOR for the generated file.)

To generate a separate list for each feature, choose List: List of References or Index: Index of Reference in the Generate/Book dialog box and click the Generate button. Choose one feature, change the filename suffix (the extension) and click Generate. Frame recommends that you use these extensions for the different lists: RE2, RE3, RE4, and so on.

## Creating Reports with API

Other types of reports about FrameMaker 4 documents can be generated if you create the reports with a companion program called Frame Developer's Kit (FDK). This program is not for the casual user or even the advanced desktop publisher—it is for programmers. The FDK program contains Frame's proprietary programming language called Application Program Interface (API).

With API you can create an application that takes control of FrameMaker 4 to do almost anything an interactive user can do. For example, an API application can create, save, and print documents; add and delete text and graphics; and perform many formatting and document-management tasks. It can also be used to create menus and display dialog boxes.

Two special kinds of API applications can be created—document reports, as mentioned earlier, and filters, used to import and export other file formats. When a document report is created with FDK, the name of the report displays in the dialog box shown earlier after the application has been "registered" with FrameMaker. To register the application, you must include the application name and other information in a special text file that FrameMaker 4 reads when it boots.

*The API represents everything in a FrameMaker 4 session as an object (not the same as object-oriented programming, though). Each object has a type, an identifier (ID), and properties (denoted by values). Lines of instructions using object ID, types, and properties are written in an application to accomplish certain tasks. When the application is compiled and registered, it is ready to use in FrameMaker 4.*

*Here is an example of a few lines of instructions (called code) that might be a part of an API application. The code opens a document called my.doc in the TMP directory and displays the document identification number (an internal number Frame assigns to keep track of documents). If it cannot open the document it displays the message, "Couldn't open."*

```
F_ObjHandleT docId;

UCharT msg[256];



docId = F_ApiSimpleOpen ("\tmp\my.doc", False);

if (!docId) F_ApiAlert("Couldn't open.", FF_ALERT_CONTINUE_NOTE;

else

   {

    sprintf(msg, "my.doc's ID is 0x%x", docId);

    F_ApiAlert(msg, FF_ALERT_CONTINUE_NOTE);

   }
```

## Marking Revisions with Change Bars

The special format style called change bars is used to mark revisions. This style creates a vertical bar in a specified color in the left or right margin of a document to identify new or revised text as shown in Figure 13-2.

**NOTE:** *Change bars can also be positioned to the right of a column, which would put the change bars for column one in the middle of the page if two columns are set up on the page.*

**FIGURE 13-2**

*An example of change bars in the left margin*

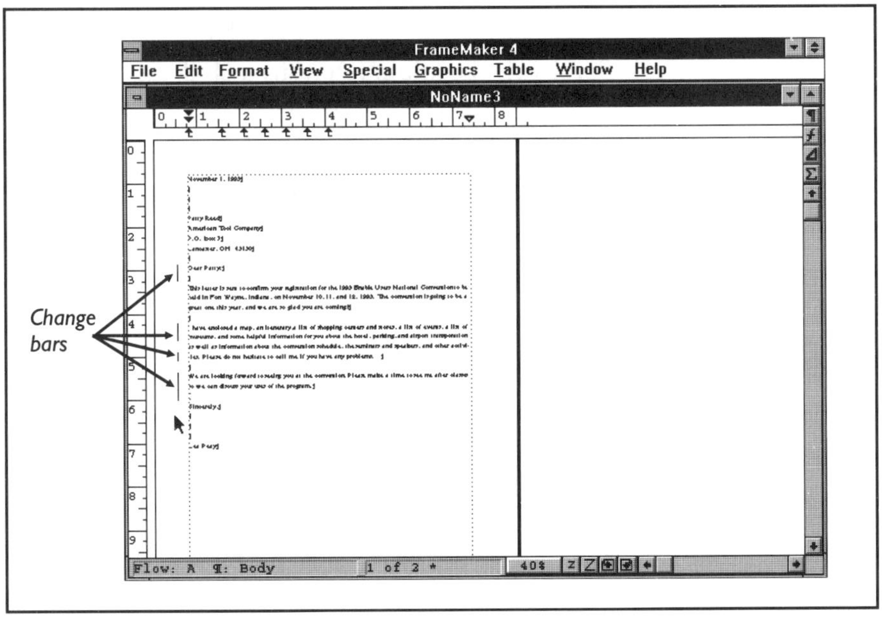


You can let FrameMaker 4 insert change bars automatically any time you insert, change, or delete text, or you can apply the change bar attribute to selected text yourself. FrameMaker 4 offers several ways to manually apply change bars.

## Using Automatic Change Bars

To use the automatic mode, follow these steps:

1. Choose Format, Change Bars. This dialog box displays:

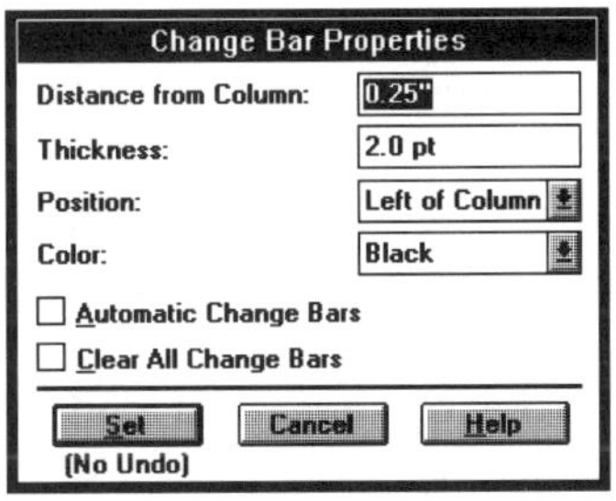


2. Specify a distance from the column (if the default 0.25" is not satisfactory).

3. Specify a thickness (if the default 2.0 pt is not satisfactory).
4. Specify the position. (Options include Left of Column, Right of Column, Side Nearest to Page Edge, and Side Farthest from Page Edge.)
5. Specify a color if black is unsatisfactory.
6. Select Automatic Change Bars.
7. Click Set.

### Manually Applying Change Bars

One way to apply change bars to text that you choose yourself is to apply a character attribute. To use this method, follow these steps:

1. Select the text.
2. Choose Format, Characters, Designer.

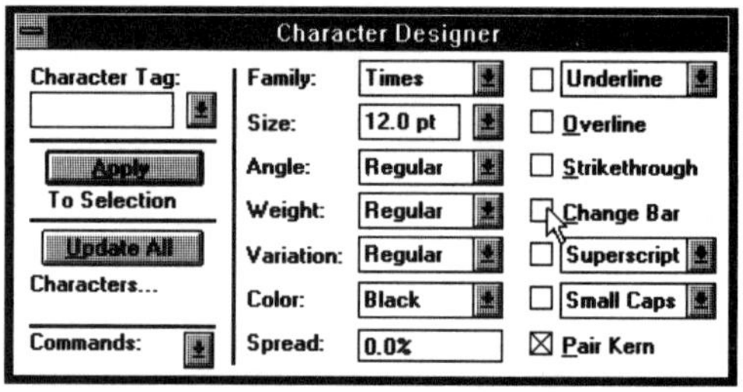


3. Turn on the Change Bar property and click Apply.

**NOTE:** *To manually apply change bars to complete paragraphs, regardless of which lines have changes, you can turn on the Change Bar property in the Paragraph Designer window and apply it to selected paragraphs.*

Another way to apply change bars is to create a character tag, store the tag in the catalog, and then apply the tag to selected text. (Remember that a character tag is created by displaying the Character Designer window, selecting the options, and choosing New Format from the Commands pop-up menu.)

### Removing Change Bars

Change bars can be removed selectively or all at once. To remove all change bars at once, choose Format, Change Bars, and select Clear All Change Bars. Then click Set.

To remove a particular change bar, select the text and choose Format, Characters, Designer, turn off the Change Bar property, and click Apply. If selected text has a character tag with a change bar, apply another character tag (usually the Default Font tag) to the text.

## REVISION PAGES

A revision page is a page that is inserted between existing pages that have had their pagination frozen. A revision page has the number of the previous page plus a period and a number or letter. For example, if the previous page is 5, the revision page could be 5.1 or 5.a. Revision pages can be used only in documents that have one text flow and no master page layout overrides on any body pages.

When revision pages are used, FrameMaker 4 inserts a revision page to accommodate any added text that causes text to move to another page. More revision pages are inserted as needed. When text is deleted on original pages, the document does not repaginate. For this process to work, however, one key setting must be made first. Pagination must be frozen.

To freeze pagination, press ESC, p, z. This dialog box is displayed:

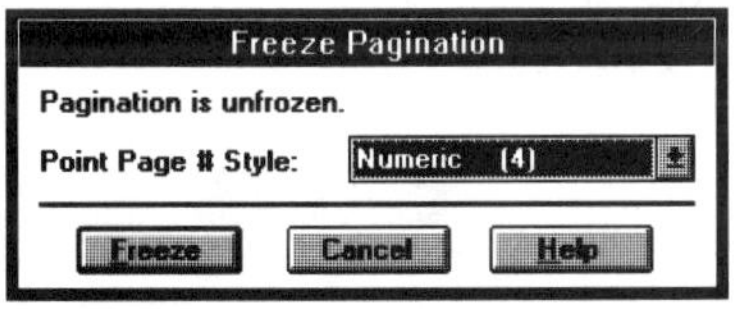


Choose a numbering style and click Freeze. Numbering styles include Arabic numbers, upper- and lowercase Roman numerals, and upper- and lowercase alphabetic characters. When you click Freeze, FrameMaker 4 warns you that what you are about to do cannot be undone. Click OK to continue.

When you want to repaginate the document with the revision pages included in the numbering sequence, unfreeze the pagination by pressing ESC, p, z. Choose Unfreeze and click OK to continue.

## DOCUMENT COMPARE

Have you ever had two versions of a file, and you could not tell which version was the most recent version? Usually the date and time the files were last saved is a good indication of which file is the most recent, but not always. Computers can lose time just like watches and system dates can be changed.

The document compare feature in FrameMaker 4 can assist you in this situation if the files you want to compare are FrameMaker documents or documents that can be read by FrameMaker 4. Of course, trying to determine which document is the most recent is not the only reason you would use this handy feature. Many times you simply want to trace the revisions that have been made.

When two documents are compared, FrameMaker 4 creates one or two documents (as specified by the user)—a composite document that shows the differences side by side and a summary document that lists the differences. You can choose to have both documents created during the process or just the summary document created.

To compare two documents, follow these steps:

1. Open both versions of the document.
2. Make the document that you think is the newer document, the active document on screen.
3. Choose File, Utilities, Compare Documents. This dialog box displays:

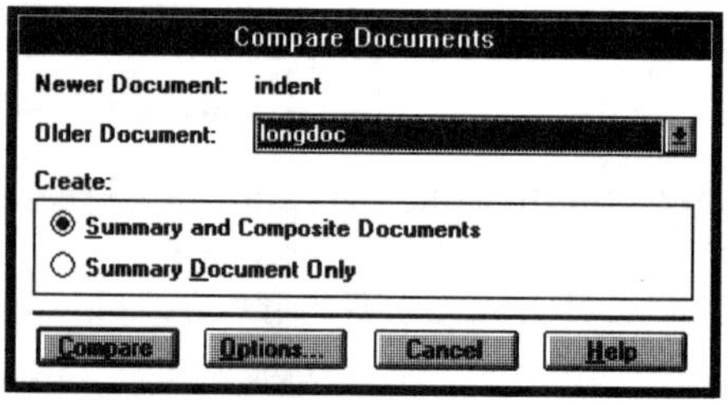


4. Choose the old version.
5. Select the type of documents you want FrameMaker 4 to create.
6. Choose Options. The following dialog box displays:

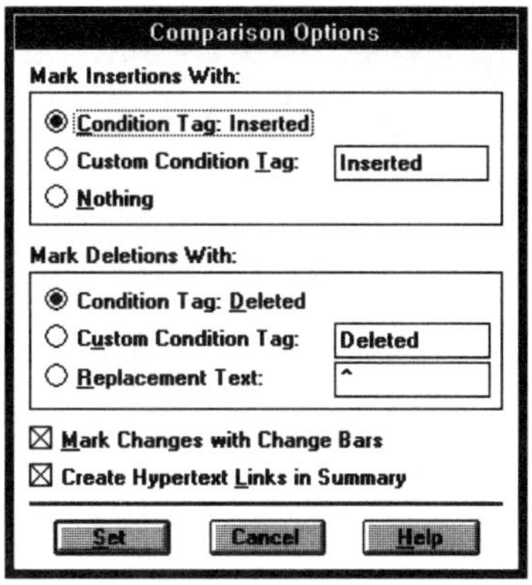


7. Choose the method by which you want FrameMaker 4 to mark insertions of text and deletions of text.
8. Select Mark Changes with Change Bars (if desired).
9. Select Create Hypertext Links in Summary (if desired).
10. Click Set.
11. Click Compare.

When the comparison is complete, the composite document displays on the screen (if there are differences in the two documents) and the summary document is open in another window. The composite document has the name of the newer document and an extension of CMP. The name the summary document is simply summary (with no extension).

In the composite document, insertions are shown in green text that is underlined. Deletions are shown in red text with a strikethrough. Change bars are shown in the margin where changes have been made (if this option was activated in the Comparison Options dialog box).

**NOTE:** *If the documents have no differences, the composite and/or summary documents are not created.*

The summary document looks like Figure 13-3. Notice that page numbers tell where differences are. If you have specified the option Create Hypertext Links in Summary (in the Compare Options dialog box), these page numbers are linked to the documents. By clicking a number you can go to the document page specified and look at the document and make changes if

**FIGURE 13-3**

*A summary document*

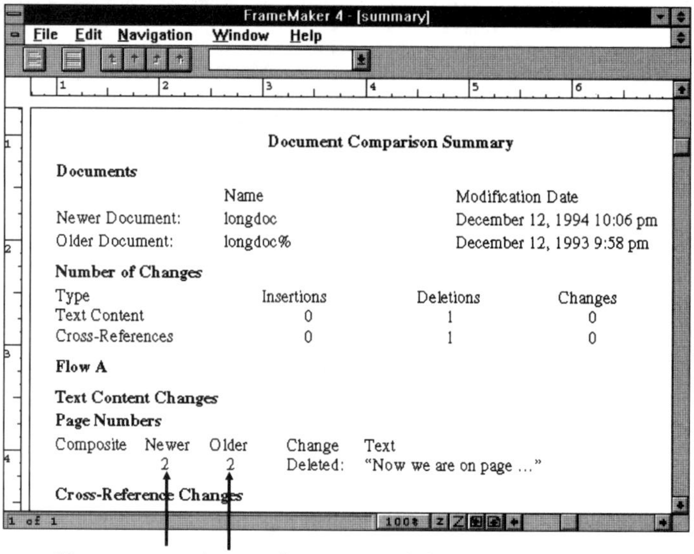


*These page numbers can be interactive links*

desired. If hypertext links are not created, the summary document is just a regular FrameMaker 4 document.

## COMPARISONS MADE

When FrameMaker 4 compares two documents, it compares the contents of flows that have the same name, anchored frames, imported graphics, equations, and tables.

When comparing text flows, it looks at the following:

- Inserted or deleted text
- Footnotes
- Anchored frames
- Tables
- Variables and their definitions
- Cross-reference formats and references
- Marker types and text

In anchored frames, it compares objects and their positions. If an object has been moved, sent to the front, or sent to the back, the frame is considered to be changed.

When comparing imported graphics, it checks to see if the graphic has been rotated, flipped, or resized. If the graphic has been imported by reference, it compares the path and filename.

Equations are checked for size, location, and math expressions. If a difference is detected, the entire equation is marked as changed.

The number of rows and columns in tables are compared as well as straddled and rotated cells. If more than 75 percent of a table has changed, the whole table is marked as changed. If only text is changed in the table, the text is marked as changed, but not the table.

## COMPARISONS NOT MADE

FrameMaker 4 does not compare flows on Master pages (including header and footer flows) or untagged flows. Graphic objects and text lines not contained in an anchored frame and anchored frame positions go unnoticed. These areas also remain unchecked: Character, Paragraph, and Table catalogs; text and table formatting; and footnote properties and their numbers.

# VI

## Getting to Press

# 14

## Producing the Final Piece

YOU have designed your piece, labored over a hot keyboard, and applied all your FrameMaker expertise. Now you are ready for the last phase of the project—getting to print. For the purpose of discussing the production of the final piece, three distinct types of print jobs will be addressed:

- Those jobs that can be produced adequately with 300 to 600 dots-per-inch (dpi) laser printers. This category, considered the low end of desktop publishing (DTP), includes business cards, letterheads, simple logos, newsletters, and simple three-fold brochures.
- Those jobs that can be produced with 300 to 600 dpi laser printers, but need supplemental services to provide halftones, more complex artwork, and color separations. This category could be considered mid-range desktop publishing.
- Those jobs that are so demanding that 1200 dpi resolution is a bare minimum for output. Laser printers are used for proofing these high-end jobs, but imagesetters produce the final output in the form of film.

Although producing the first two types of print jobs are discussed in this chapter, the primary focus is on the third type of print job, the high-end piece.

## LOW-END DTP

If you are creating a low-end piece, you can print the camera-ready copy on your laser printer and take it to a commercial printer, or you can print all the copies in house. Printing in house might mean printing all the copies

on your laser printer or printing one copy on the laser and duplicating it on a high-quality copy machine.

With the special papers that are now available for laser printers, you can even print business cards, letterheads and matching envelopes, and three-fold brochures in house. These special papers are even preprinted with vibrant color and design. For small print runs, you can have color at a very reasonable price by using these specialty papers. When print runs are large, however, it is more economical to go the conventional color route with a commercial printer.

Printed pieces that are produced in house sometimes need to be trimmed, folded, hole-punched, or bound. Fairly inexpensive equipment capable of dealing with small quantities is available for all these tasks; however, these services can also be purchased at a very reasonable rates from quick-copy shops. For example, Kinko's Copies, a global chain of quick-copy shops, charges 50 cents per cut to trim a quantity of 200 to 250 sheets. If you want to take care of your own needs in house, you'll need some or all of these:

- A paper cutter (just under $600 for a cutter that will cut a stack of paper 1.5 inches thick)
- A hole puncher ($15 for a manual three-hole puncher that can punch about 10 sheets of paper at a time)
- A folding machine (just under $300 for a machine that does a standard letter fold)
- A binding machine that uses plastic combs (about $400 for the popular GBC manually operated machine)
- An add-on to the GBC binding machine that inserts wire spirals in the pages cut by the GBC machine (about $125)
- A Velobinding machine that uses a manual or heat process to bind pages inside a plastic strip (from $600 to $2800)
- A pad-making press for making glue-backed note pads—a great way to recycle paper (about $125)
- A laminator that laminates sizes up to 12 inches (about $250)

## MID-RANGE DTP

When your printed piece includes multiple colors, photos, or other images with screens or gray tones, you will not be able to produce the final product on your laser printer. You may be able to produce the text portion, however, and obtain the other portions from other sources. Often a commercial printer can supply all the services you need for making halftones and color separations (although color separations are usually sent out).

## HIGH-END DTP

Few desktop publishers have their own $30,000 imagesetter, so high-end jobs generally require that you work with a service bureau. The question is, how do you work with a service bureau? To answer that question, let's look at the kinds of services offered.

### How the Imagesetter Works

*Based on the PostScript description of a page, the raster image processor (RIP) decides where to place tiny black dots. When a PC file is being processed, it is said to be "getting ripped." Then the RIP tells the imagesetter's laser beam where to etch those tiny dots on a piece of paper or film. The target medium is stored in a light-tight canister. After being imaged, the canister is removed for processing by the film-processing system. The processor develops the image captured on the photosensitive material and chemically stabilizes it. The processed medium emerges from the canister in a continuous sheet and is cut into pages or jobs by the operator.*

*A separate developer should be used for paper and for film because they have different requirements. Chemicals in the developer should be changed regularly.*

*Imagesetters should be calibrated often except for the newest and most expensive imagesetters, which maintain accurate calibration automatically. Accurate calibration is especially critical for color work.*

## Services Offered by Service Bureaus

Service bureaus come in all sizes and offer a wide range of services. More and more, services of a "service bureau" are being offered by copy shops and print shops that want to expand their services and consequently their profits. These services fit right in with the services they are already offering.

Services that might be offered include:

- Converting media (disk and file format)
- Renting equipment
- Making laser prints
- Providing imagesetter output to paper or film
- Scanning photographs (black and white or color)
- Making color separations
- Creating computer-generated slides
- Supplying proofs
- Making color prints
- Doing layout and design services
- Providing prepress services such as page imposition
- Providing artwork
- Making Optical Character Recognition (OCR) files

## Obtaining the Services

How you obtain many of these services from a bureau is pretty obvious. If you want a disk converted to another format, you take in the disk and pay the fee. If you want some documents scanned and turned into OCR computer files, you take in the documents and pay the fee. If you want a color separation of a photograph, you take in the photograph and pay the fee, and so on.

What is not so obvious is how you get a FrameMaker document output in high resolution on paper or film. This service is not quite as simple as dropping off a disk.

## Outputting FrameMaker Documents

Basically, you can give a service bureau two types of FrameMaker files for output—a FrameMaker document or a PostScript file. In either case, the goal is to supply a file that can be output successfully.

Outputting a file successfully the first time is a major concern because service bureaus charge anywhere from $7 to $15 per lettersize page for output on coated paper and $15 to $30 per lettersize page for output on film. At these prices, you do not want to output some or all of the same job twice.

### Getting the Files to the Service Bureau

*If files are small enough, they can be copied to a floppy disk (usually a 1.44MB, 3.5-inch disk). Larger files, which are usually compressed with a utility like PKZIP, can be sent by modem to most service bureaus. For really large files, the SyQuest removable cartridge (basically a removable hard disk) has become popular. A 44MB drive is now selling for about $300.*

When working with a service bureau, you will find that what you are able to print on your laser printer as a proof may not print on an imagesetter. Admittedly, this sounds impossible or at least ironic. You would think that a $30,000 imagesetter could print anything that a $1,000, 300 dpi laser printer can print. This is not the case, however. A long Bezier curve that prints on a 300 dpi laser may produce *limitcheck* errors on an imagesetter—errors that occur when an imagesetter has consumed more than it can digest. The reason an imagesetter might not be able to print a Bezier curve that will print on a laser printer is that the curve turns fewer corners at 300 dpi than at 1200 dpi.

**NOTE:** *Limitcheck errors are also produced if the file contains images that have been scanned at resolutions that are unnecessarily high or if you have used a TrueType font in a text-heavy document instead of a PostScript font.*

### *Providing a FrameMaker Document*

Working with a service bureau that uses FrameMaker may seem like the easiest way of getting successful output, but it does not guarantee smooth sailing. If the service bureau that you select uses FrameMaker (see the Frame publication *Frame Connection* for a list of service bureaus that do), you *can* simply give them the file. The service bureau can open the file and look for potential problems, but this method is fraught with potential dangers on top of being expensive. The system at the service bureau may use a different version of the printer driver or the system and application may be configured differently.

Another potential problem with this method is a mismatch of fonts. If the service bureau does not have the fonts that you used to create the document, substitutions must be made. This can cause realignment of text and ruin a layout.

### *Providing a PostScript File*

The most common way to deal with a service bureau is to provide a PostScript file of the FrameMaker document. The PostScript language describes *every* detail of the document including size, margins, color, layout, fonts, art, and so on. When the service bureau receives a PostScript file, it is not opened or looked at—a single command is issued to send the file to the imagesetter for output. This means that the burden of perfection is on you. No corrections or troubleshooting are done by the service bureau.

*PostScript is the key to working with a service bureau. When you use a PostScript printer driver with FrameMaker, you can create a file that can be read by any PostScript device, whether it is a 300 dpi laser printer or a 1200 dpi imagesetter.*

The PostScript file contains all the information needed to print the file, but this method again does not guarantee smooth sailing. Although there is no worry about matching fonts, since fonts are fully described by the file, other problems can arise.

One problem is the contrast of gray tones. What looks good when output by a 300 dpi laser may look dull and muddy when output by an imagesetter. Black-and-white laser printers cannot really print gray. They fake it by using black dots and white space to fool the eye. Gray tones must be carefully produced with the proper frequency and screen angles. (See Chapter 9.) These issues should be discussed with the service bureau and correctly implemented in the FrameMaker document before giving the file to the service bureau.

## CREATING A POSTSCRIPT FILE WITH FRAMEMAKER

The steps to creating a PostScript file are relatively easy. First, you must install a PostScript printer driver using the Windows Control Panel of the Program Manager. In the Connect dialog box, select File as the Port. See Figure 14-1.

> *The most current Windows PostScript driver is version 3.56. If you are not using this version, it is almost certain that the service bureau will have problems with your PostScript file. See Chapters 15 and 16 for questions and problems concerning PostScript.*

In FrameMaker, choose File, Print. In the Print Document dialog box, shown in Figure 14-2, choose Print Only To File and type a filename. Choose Print. The resulting file will contain all the PostScript language that describes the file.

**FIGURE 14-1**

*The Connect dialog box*

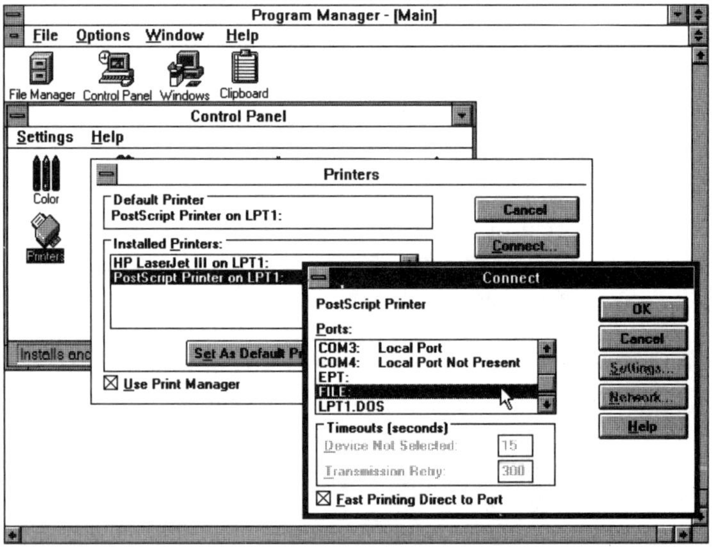

**FIGURE 14-2**

*The Print Document dialog box*

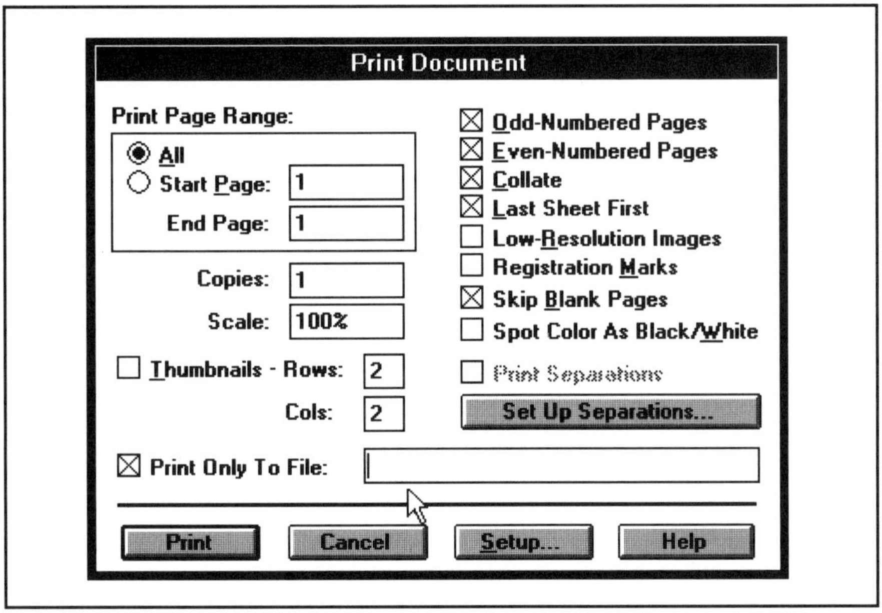


**NOTE:** *This file is not the same as an Encapsulated PostScript (EPS) file. To create an EPS file, choose Setup, Options from the Print dialog box and choose Encapsulated PostScript File. Give the file a name, click OK twice, and then click Print.*

## SELECTING A SERVICE BUREAU

When shopping for a service bureau, keep these two things in mind:

- The majority of service bureaus are solidly entrenched in Macintosh hardware and software. If you are using FrameMaker for Windows, look for service bureaus that are also versed in Windows products regardless of the hardware that is actually connected to the imagesetter. You need to be able to count on the expertise of your service bureau to point out hidden traps associated with preparing Windows files for printing. If possible, use an experienced Windows bureau that is also familiar with FrameMaker.

- Price is always a consideration, but it should not be your prime consideration. Service and expertise should be your first concern. Your final cost from a service bureau that charges less per page may be higher than one that provides you with better service. At the cheaper service bureau, you may spend extra money printing pages multiple times to correct errors that the more expensive service bureau might point out to you in the first place.

Naturally you will want to know the hours of business, the type of equipment being used (helium-neon lasers are preferred over infrared for quality of output), what fonts are available, what support is offered and how much it costs, what the turnaround time is, and so on.

## TIPS FOR WORKING WITH BUREAUS

These miscellaneous tips may help you as you seek to build a relationship with a service bureau:

- Once you have selected a service bureau, be the best customer you can be by knowing what you want and providing that information to the service bureau. Know the names and formats of all the files. Know all the fonts that are used. Include all the files in what you provide, and don't overlook graphic files that are linked to the file and not contained in the file.
- Provide the service bureau with a proof. The proof is usually a printout from a low-resolution laser printer.
- Use the cyan, magenta, yellow, black (CMYK) color model instead of the red, green, blue (RGB). Most service bureaus do not use RGB.
- Use the tagged image file format (TIFF) for bitmapped files. A widespread consensus holds that TIFF is the best format to use.
- Files that take a long time to print on a laser will take a long time to print on an imagesetter. Try to simplify the file to hold down your costs. (Although service bureaus may charge by the page, they will also charge by the hour, especially if a job is very complex and takes a long time to print each page.)

- Delete all unnecessary and extraneous material in a file. For example, do not cover a graphic with a white rectangle instead of deleting it. Also, make sure that nothing unnecessary is hidden underneath a stack of graphics. Even though these objects are not visible on the screen, they require processing time on an imagesetter and therefore cost more money.
- Stick with the standard Adobe Type 1 fonts as much as possible.
- Run virus checks on your disks before giving them to the service bureau and after receiving them back from the service bureau.
- When creating your file, use the exact printer driver for the output device that will be used by the service bureau.
- Create a test page of your job and print it on the imagesetter before running the complete job. Include graphics, fonts, gray scales, and other elements you might be worried about.
- To avoid delays, if some graphic will not print due to incompatibility, tell the service bureau to suppress or delete the problem graphic and have the commercial printer strip those graphics in manually.
- If you will be outputting to film, find out whether your printer wants emulsion side up or emulsion side down. (Most printers use emulsion side down.)
- Put your service bureau in touch with your printer so that line-screen frequency and angle can be discussed.
- Remember that service bureau employees have work to do, and they cannot sit around and answer 100 questions from you for free. You need to ask questions, but be prepared to pay for the consulting time. One hour of consulting can save you plenty of money in the long run.

## TAKING YOUR JOB TO THE PRINTER

The final step in producing a job that is not printed in house on a 300 dpi laser is taking the job to the printer. It is as important to choose the right printer as it is to choose the right service bureau. Three types of printers can be identified—quick-print shops, commercial printers, and specialty printers.

### Quick-Print Shops

Quick-print shops specialize in one-color jobs without solid images, two-color jobs without abutting colors, jobs with low-resolution halftones, and jobs smaller than 11×17 inches. The kinds of jobs that fall into this category are business cards, letterhead, forms, simple brochures, newsletters, and flyers.

### Commercial Printers

A commercial printer can usually handle a wide range of jobs—two to four spot color jobs, process color, jobs with large print runs, jobs larger than 11×17 inches, and jobs that are run on a web press. The kinds of jobs that fall into this category are unlimited, including posters, tabloid-style newspapers, catalogs, books, magazines, annual reports, product labels, and so on.

### Specialty Printers

A specialty printer can handle two to eight spot color jobs, jobs with complex registration, die cutting, embossing, foil stamping, varnishing, and so on. Think of any printed media that you have seen that is unusual, colorful, and glitzy—it was probably done by a specialty printer.

### Selecting a Printer

Look for several printers that fit your needs, and visit each one. Ask to see samples of their work, especially samples similar to what you want to print. Get at least three bids on your job, and don't take the cheapest bid if it is considerably lower than the other two unless you have asked for bids from different types of printers. Quick printers are much cheaper than commercial printers, but the quality is not as good.

**TIP:** *Beware of printers who claim they can print anything. They may be starving for business because their quality is poor and they have no repeat business.*

Once you take everything to the printer (camera-ready copy, photographs, art, film, and so on), the printer does whatever is necessary with what you have provided to make the plates for the press. Before the actual job is run, you should ask for a blueline proof. If printing color, ask for a press check.

A blueline is a blue (sometimes brown) proof produced by burning-in the film directly on paper. Changes are much less expensive to make at this stage than after the plates are created. A press check is an actual print made when your job is set up on the press and ready to run. Registration and color can be checked at this time and the final adjustments made.

When the piece is finally printed, check it carefully before accepting it. Occasionally a print job will be unacceptable for a variety of reasons. When trying to assign blame and cost responsibility for an unacceptable print run, it is best if you have all your specifications on a written form that the printer has signed off on. (This could be the printer's bid or a form that you have created yourself and submitted to the printer.)

# VII

## Support and Troubleshooting

# 15

# Technical Support Directly from Frame

This chapter features the Frame technical support staff's responses to users' questions. The questions have been alphabetized here by category and divided into the three platforms on which FrameMaker 4 can be used—Windows, Macintosh, and Unix. You may want to peruse the questions related to all platforms, even those you do not use, because you may glean some useful information that you might not otherwise see.

## WINDOWS PLATFORM

This section pertains to the Windows platform.

### Angle of Rotation

#### *Question*

I select an unrotated object and display the Object Properties dialog box. In the Angle box, I enter "1in" and click Set. I bring up the dialog box again and the angle is 72 degrees. Why doesn't the answer display in inches?

#### *Answer*

Object Properties expects degrees. When it gets a unit symbol that is valid in other places in the document, it translates the number to the unit in which FrameMaker internally stores measures—points. There are 72 points per inch, hence the value.

If you were to enter "2.54cm" in the angle dialog, it would convert that to points as well and you would also see a 72 degree rotation.

## Catalog Formats

*Q*

In FrameMaker 4, can I apply formats to the Paragraph or Character catalog only?

*A*

Not very easily. In FrameMaker 4, you have the opportunity to apply a format to the Paragraph or Character catalog only when you initially create the paragraph or character tag. After a tag has been created, FrameMaker 4 will not allow you to apply formats, for that tag, to the catalog only.

However, when you first choose New Format, if you create a new tag and choose not to store it in the catalog, but only to apply it to selection, the next time you click Apply you are once again given the pop-up with the choices of storing in the catalog and applying to selection.

There is a tricky workaround, which requires several steps:

1. In the Designer window, select the tag to be updated (only to the catalog)—Body, for example.
2. Erase the tag name in the text box and fill in a temporary name, such as "temp."
3. Click Apply and store "temp" to the catalog.
4. At this point, all temp properties are identical to Body.
5. In the Designer window, make any modification you need to temp and choose Update All.
6. Delete Body from catalog. Note that at this point, all existing Body paragraphs become Body paragraphs with overrides and have no catalog format.
7. In the Designer window, select temp from the tag pop-up menu, then rename temp to Body and click Apply to create the new tag Body with the properties of temp. STORE TO CATALOG ONLY, DON'T APPLY!
8. Delete temp from catalog. Updating Body in catalog only is completed.

## Color

### Q

Can I change the FrameMaker 4 for Windows document background colors? The white document background is hard on my eyes, and I can change the document background color in FrameMaker for Unix.

### A

FrameMaker for Windows follows the Microsoft Windows Multi-Document Interface (MDI) specification. MDI gives applications the ability to open multiple documents at one time. This is very important for FrameMaker 4, especially when working with multiple documents contained in a book file.

Following the MDI specification, there is no way to change the color of an application's document window without actually making that document black with white fonts. Doing so would cause the document to print black with white fonts also.

The only two applications that can display documents with background colors other than white are the Program Manager (a Microsoft application that cannot print), and Microsoft Word (a Microsoft application that looks like it uses MDI, but does not).

In the Windows 3.x environment, users can change the FrameMaker 4 application background, but not the document background itself. No Windows application that follows the MDI specification can change a document window background display color.

## Comparing Documents

### Q

I am running Compare Documents on two documents, but it keeps telling me that the documents are the same. They are NOT the same. What is wrong?

### A

The document compare feature will only work for text that has a flow tag. If you have text inserted in a text column that does not have a flow tag assigned, the document compare feature will report that the documents are the same.

**Q**

With the document compare feature, deletions are shown in magenta instead of showing deletions in green strikethrough. Why is this?

**A**

If your source document has condition tags named "Deleted" or "Inserted," the format overrides from those tags will be used in the CMP document.

There is an Options button that displays the Compare Options dialog box in the document compare feature. This dialog box lets you set the name of the conditional tags to be used, but not their overrides.

If you choose Custom Condition Tag, then your explicit settings will get picked up. However, if a condition tag in your source document has a name which matches that used by Compare Document, the tag will be used with the defined Format Overrides in the default report.

The workaround is to change the Format Overrides in the CMP document after the document is generated, or to define a new condition tag in your document expressly for the use of the document compare feature and specify that in the Report options dialog box. There is no way to specify another condition tag name to be used as the default. This is because the CMP document is a generated file, which uses much of the information from the source documents for its contents. The condition tags are one of the definitions that come into the new document. The tag has a property of a Character Override, which determines how the tag will be displayed. As the tag comes into the CMP document, the definition of the tag is applied to the text in the CMP document.

## Conditional Text

**Q**

How can I use the conditional text feature for text that should only appear when two conditions are both on?

*A*

If you want to do a "logical and" with two tags, you can create a new tag called "mac+maker" and use it for text that should only appear when the conditions "mac" and "maker" are both on. Then whenever you change the show/hide setting, make sure to set the "mac+maker" state as "shown" only if both "mac" and "maker" are shown.

## Dictionary

*Q*

How do I create and use my own dictionary instead of using the personal or site dictionaries?

*A*

You can quickly create your own dictionary in FrameMaker by writing your personal or document dictionary to a file (it is generally better to write your personal dictionary, as this file contains all of the words you have saved for ALL FrameMaker documents via the Learn command in Spelling Checker).

After creating your new dictionary, if you want to use this new dictionary (instead of your current personal dictionary or your current site dictionary) you can use the Change Dictionary command in FrameMaker (this affects dictionary usage only for the current FrameMaker session). To use this new dictionary permanently, edit your maker.ini file to reference this new filename in place of what FrameMaker currently references for the Personal or Site dictionaries as follows:

L 15.1

```
________________Files________________
UserDictionary=user.dct
SiteDictionary=dict\site.dct
```

(Replace "user.dct" or "dict\site.dct" with the new pathname and filename for your dictionary).

Often, newly created dictionaries are used as site dictionaries so that an entire workgroup can use the same dictionary while working on documents. You can replace the site dictionary with your newly created dictionary as noted above. This works well, since no user can edit the site dictionary via the Learn and Allow in Document commands in FrameMaker. Users can set up their network to reference this site dictionary over the network.

## EPSI Color File

*Q*

I've created a color EPSI (Encapsulated PostScript Interchange) image that I've imported into FrameMaker. I thought that it would display in color, but it displays in black and white. How can I tell if the preview image will display in color?

*A*

If you search for the string "BeginPreview" you should see something like:

5.2
```
%%BeginPreview: 256 192 1 192
```

The third field represents the depth, and in this example, since the depth is one, the preview image is not color. Values of 4 or 8 would imply a color preview image (16 and 256 colors, respectively).

## Equations

*Q*

Why don't my curly braces grow with my equation? When I insert a simple fraction, the curly braces are not the same height as my fraction. I thought that this problem was fixed in FrameMaker 4.

*A*

Unfortunately, this bug was not fixed in FrameMaker 4. FrameMath users will need to insert superscripts and/or subscripts to the quantity that should be enclosed within the curly braces.

These steps illustrate the problem you are having:

1. Insert an equation in a FrameMaker 4 document.
2. From delimiters, insert a curly brace.

3. Now insert a fraction.
4. Notice that the curly braces do not enlarge to the height of the fraction.
5. Select the entire equation.
6. Click on the toggle from the Delimiter menu.
7. Notice that the brackets and parenthesis are the right (large) size/height, but still the curly braces are too small.

Here is one way to solve the problem:

1. Select the numerator.
2. From Operators, click on superscript.
3. The curly braces should be the right size.
4. If they are not, select the denominator.
5. From Operators, click on subscript.
6. The curly braces will now be the right size.

Another way to accomplish this is to add more white space to the equation as described in Frame's documentation, *Using FrameMaker*, page 29-5:

1. Select the equation (or the equation and the curly braces).
2. From Positioning click the "+" on top of the B several times until the braces suddenly grow to the correct size.

The advantage of this workaround is that there are no extra question marks, so the equation is no wider than it needs to be.

## Fonts

*Q*

Why do I have fonts listed in my ATM (Adobe Type Manager) Control Panel that are not showing up in FrameMaker?

*A*

You may not have the fonts installed correctly, or you may be using the wrong printer driver.

1. Check to see if the fonts show up in any other applications, such as Write.
2. Make sure a PostScript printer is installed.
3. Do the following:
   a. Go to the Program Manager window and select ATM Control Panel.
   b. In the ATM Control Panel dialog box, select Add.
   c. The Add ATM Fonts dialog box displays. Under the Directories column on the right, double-click [psfonts]. This brings up a new directory listing. Double-click [pfm].
   d. In the left-hand column, the list of PFM files will appear. Make sure the font you want to add is in that list. If not, there was an improper installation and you need to reinstall that font onto the PC. At this point, the Add button is grayed out.
   e. Click the first font name in the left-hand list and with the left mouse button pressed, drag down the entire list, selecting it. At this point the Add button is black.
   f. Press Add. This takes you back to the ATM Control Panel dialog box.
   g. Click Exit and then log out of Windows for the changes to take effect.

## Footnotes

*Q*

If I insert a footnote in a paragraph that has small caps or uppercasing applied to it, and the numbering style for my footnotes is set to alphabetic or roman, the footnote reference uses a different font than the footnote number itself. Is there a workaround?

*A*

The workaround is to choose Format, Footnote Properties, and set the Numbering Style to one of the following:

- Numeric
- ROMAN (as opposed to roman)
- ALPHABETIC (as opposed to alphabetic)
- Custom (but do not include any lowercase characters)

**NOTE:** *The same problem occurs with table footnotes and the workaround is the same as described above.*

*Q*

I notice that it is possible to number my regular footnotes sequentially via the Format/Footnote Properties window, but there is not an automatic option to number my table footnotes sequentially from one table to the next. Is there a workaround?

*A*

The following steps will work around this problem:

1. Create an additional body row at the bottom of each table and straddle all the cells in that row. You will probably want to apply to this row a ruling of none for the left, bottom, and right outside edges via Table/Custom Ruling and Shading. This row is where you will insert your table footnotes.
2. Create a new paragraph tag for the non-FrameMaker generated footnotes. You can set up the same Properties as the regular table footnotes have except you will need to add an autonumber format something like F:<n+>.\t and apply it to your new paragraph tag. This will allow the footnote numbering to increment from table to table.
3. Create a cross-reference format to insert the footnote reference in your table cells. First you may need to create a character tag called Superscript. Then you need to create a cross-reference format with the following definition:

<Superscript><$paranumonly><DefaultParaFont>

You can now enter the footnote reference by inserting a cross-reference to the appropriate footnote using the format you defined above.

## Fractions

*Q*

With FrameMaker 4 for Windows, I created the characters 1/2, 1/4, and 3/4 using special ANSI numbers. Are these supported across other platforms? Can I see and print those characters in the Macintosh or Unix versions of FrameMaker?

*A*

The 1/2, 1/4, and 3/4 characters are not in the Unix or Macintosh FrameMaker character sets. The historical reason for the absence of these characters is that they did not exist in PostScript fonts at the time the character set was devised.

The slots that these characters occupy in the FrameMaker for Windows character set are reserved slots in the Unix and Macintosh character sets. Thus, there is no guarantee at all about their behavior onscreen or when printed out on other platforms. In fact, they display as random characters and do not print; Frame reserves the right to change this behavior in future releases.

To get the 1/2 character on the Unix or the Macintosh platform, either use micropositioning, or try using FrameMath. If you have a PostScript font with this character, you can install it as a NonTextFont and be able to access the 1/2 character.

## Hypertext

*Q*

In FrameMaker 4, can I create hypertext menus with nested pop-ups?

*A*

No. Although nested pop-ups worked in FrameMaker 3.x on the Unix and Windows systems, they were not a supported feature. Nested pop-ups never worked on the Macintosh platform because clicking a menu and having it stay open (called *sticky mouse*) is not supported on the Macintosh. To ensure compatibility between platforms, the ability to do nested pop-ups was stripped from FrameMaker 4.

## Importing Files

*Q*

Why do I see a graphic when I import an Object Linking and Embedding (OLE) object from Word for Windows, instead of the text I am trying to paste?

*A*

The graphic you are seeing is an object from object packager. Microsoft always sends a package when you try to cut/paste text as an OLE object.

EXAMPLE Open the RELNOTES in Word for Windows, and locate the small table on the first page. Using the mouse, highlight the cells in the table and copy them to the clipboard. Now invoke FrameMaker, and place the insertion point in the document where you wish to paste a copy of this table. Choose Edit, Paste Special, and select OLE as the Paste Special item. A color icon with the Word for Windows logo is pasted. If you click the logo, you see the contents of the package, the table that you copied from Word for Windows.

Since most people do not like this result, remember two things. In an OLE link, you have a client application and a server application. FrameMaker is a client application, which means that the link and its contents are controlled by the server application—in this case, Word for Windows.

At this time, there is no real way to fix this. You can copy the table from Word for Windows and then use the Paste Special feature of FrameMaker, but choose TEXT instead of OLE. This pastes the text and not the object. However, no link is created.

Microsoft has been notified of this odd behavior; they claim all is well. Microsoft says that you need Dynamic Data Exchange (DDE) to link text.

FrameMaker for Windows does not support DDE. (For related information, see the OLE heading in this section.)

## Installation

### Q

Are there any tools for troubleshooting an unsuccessful installation of FrameMaker 4 for Windows?

### A

The FrameMaker 4 installer will write to a log file, install.log, when copying the FrameMaker files to the user's disk. Install.log will reside in the FrameMaker destination path. If the installation is successful, the install script deletes install.log. If installation fails, then install.log should be in the destination directory and should provide some helpful information. If installation fails before the point of copying the files from a floppy disk to a hard disk, the install.log will not have been created.

### Q

I am installing FrameMaker 4.0 from 5.25-inch disks. I selected all the options, but I was not prompted for all the disks. What is wrong?

### A

When installing the 5.25-inch disks, even when all the options are selected, you will not use all the disks. For a complete US English install, you will use disks 1 through 9. For a complete UK English install, you will use disks 1 through 4 and 6 through 10.

## Master Pages

### Q

I have opened up a FrameMaker 3 document in FrameMaker 4. When I am on the Master page and try to go to the Body page, I get the Page Layout Warning asking me if I want to keep overrides or remove them. I choose to remove them, but the next time I try to go from the Master page to the Body page I still get the message. What am I doing wrong?

*A*

It's possible that you have overlapping text columns on the Master page. FrameMaker warns you that you have the overrides, but even if you choose to remove them, FrameMaker will not create an extra text column on the Body page, so the next time you try to go from the Master page to the Body page, you will still get the warning. To fix this, simply remove the extra text column from each Master page.

Another way to test for this is to choose Format, Pages, Master Page Usage. If you choose Normal Page Layout on Current Page you will probably see an alert that says: "Some Body pages to which you are assigning a Master page contain text flows not found on that Master page. This may result in overlapping text columns. Are you sure you want to do this?" Even if you check that all the flows seem to be matching, these two symptoms suggest overlapping text columns.

## OLE

*Q*

How can I link Windows applications to FrameMaker? Can I link FrameMaker to other Windows applications?

*A*

FrameMaker for Windows supports Windows Object Linking and Embedding (OLE). This support is handled as a client application in Windows OLE. A client application can receive links from other programs that support OLE as a server application. FrameMaker cannot create a link to another program, but another OLE program can make a link to FrameMaker.

To make a link to FrameMaker, select the object in the OLE server application (Windows Write is one example of a server application) and copy it to the Clipboard with the Edit menu.

Now go into FrameMaker. Open your document and place your cursor where you wish to anchor your object. Choose Edit from the top menu and select Paste Special, choosing OLE in the dialog box. If the application correctly supports OLE, you will receive a copy of the file. If the application does not support OLE, you will not see the OLE choice in the Paste Special dialog box.

To invoke the link, double-click the graphic to launch the server application. You will now be looking at an object in the application you created it in. You will not be editing the original file, as OLE lets you link objects, not documents.

When you are finished, save your changes or choose Update link to return to FrameMaker.

**NOTE:** *The method to return to the client application (in this case, FrameMaker) is different in each Windows server application. You may have to refer to the documentation of your Windows application to figure out how to return to FrameMaker or any OLE client.*

### *Additional Comments about OLE*

If you receive an object from a server application and it does not look as you expected, you will need to contact the manufacturer of the application that renders the OLE link. In OLE, the server application dictates how the link will look, how it will behave, and therefore how it will be updated. FrameMaker 4 has no direct control over the operation or display of an OLE link.

There have been some reported problems with links from the following programs:

- Microsoft Excel—Invoke the link and change nothing. When you return to the client application, you will see a different display.
- Microsoft Word—When you make a link, Word sends a packaged object. This results in a Word icon as the linked graphic. To alleviate this, choose Paste Special and select a format other than OLE. You will not have a link, but you will get the graphics or text you are trying to receive from Word.
- CorelDRAW! and Micrographix Designer/Charisma Ver. 3.*x*—These companies have seen problems with large graphics when you link them to other applications. These problems can result in FrameMaker 4 documents you cannot open, or perhaps a document that will occasionally crash for no apparent reason. To alleviate this, get the newest version of the program from Corel or Micrographix or choose Paste Special in FrameMaker and select something other than OLE.

Currently, FrameMaker 4 for Windows does not support Dynamic Data Exchange (DDE), which allows application programs to request and exchange data automatically.

## Printer Fonts

*Q*

What fonts go to the printer when I print in Windows? Do they all go?

*A*

When a PostScript printer is configured, Windows allows you to use the Type 1 fonts that would be in that printer, usually 17 or 35 typefaces. Windows has no method to verify this information, so the driver dictates what fonts show up. These same fonts would not have a display version without the Windows printer substitution table which is accessed by selecting Control Panel, Printers, Setup, Options, Advanced. The substitution table is a way you can tell Windows what to display when a printer-only font is used. When Windows creates the Encapsulated PostScript (EPS) output, it assumes that these printer typefaces are resident, based on the default printer driver, so the PostScript code only makes a "reference" to them.

In the case of a Type 1 font that is not printer-resident, the font information is essentially sent to the printer via the PostScript file. For TrueType fonts, the font metrics are converted to a Type 1 format and also sent with the PostScript file. If the printer driver does not match the printer, then the assumption about the printer-resident fonts will be incorrect, and you may get Courier or Times when those fonts are called.

The foregoing information is valid with any Windows application that completely leaves printing up to Windows. Since not all Windows applications do this, you may need to check with the manufacturer of the software you are using as to the models used to create print.

When using a software package that does not let Windows control the printing, you would get the best print performance if you used only printer-resident fonts. This way the system does not have to download them. Also, the Microsoft PostScript drivers will resend all fonts and page headers EVERY TIME you print. So again, using the printer-resident fonts may put a dent in your print times.

Some third-party printer drivers allow you to download the header and the fonts to the printer once, and the information stays in the printer until you power it off or reset it. Currently, Adobe has a driver version 2.1 for Windows 3.1 that has these abilities.

## Rotated Objects

### Q

I can only rotate frames (anchored or unanchored) 90 degrees. Is there a way to rotate them in other increments?

### A

An anchored frame in a text column will rotate with the text column. Insert the frame prior to or after rotation.

An unanchored frame created from the Graphics Tools palette is positioned in the base page frame. The page can only be rotated 90 degrees. Thus, the unanchored frame can only be rotated 90 degrees.

### Q

It seems that a user cannot access the Normal Page Layout command when a document contains rotated pages. This presents a problem if your document is single-sided and you want to make it double-sided or if you want to change the document page size. What is the problem?

### A

It is a very unfortunate limitation in FrameMaker 4.0 that you cannot change the sidedness, page size, or any other "Normal Page Layout" property of documents containing rotated pages.

The most direct workaround is to unrotate all of your pages, change the sidedness, and then rerotate things again as needed.

## Slides

### Q

How can I make a FrameMaker template for 35mm slides?

*A*

A 35mm slide is 35mm wide and 28mm high. So, as long as you keep your document size in this same proportion, you are fine. It has been suggested that a page setup of 7.33 inches high and 11.0 inches wide should produce an acceptable template for 35mm slides, but anything that has the same proportion as the slide will work.

## Smart Spaces

*Q*

When I copy text in from my xterm window, multiple spaces are preserved even though I have Smart Spaces on. However, when I go to delete any one of the "extra" spaces between a pair of words, all but one between the words delete.

*A*

This is designed behavior that enables you to get preformatted ASCII text into your Frame document without losing formatting. If you delete a space, FrameMaker assumes you are reformatting the text and forces it to conform to your document design (for example, with Smart Spaces).

If you do not want this behavior, turn off Smart Spaces in the Format/Document Properties dialog box before selecting the external text. Then paste in your text and edit. If you later turn on Smart Spaces, the extra spaces in your text will not collapse to one space.

## Tables

*Q*

How can I create two tables side by side?

*A*

The best way to make two side-by-side tables is to put them both in a single anchored frame. Each table is placed in a separate text column just below the first line of the column. Think of the text column as a handle for the table. Select each text column and drag them one at a time into the anchored frame.

**NOTE:** *If the space above the table is not wanted, just slide the text column up so that the space lies cropped above the top of the anchored frame.*

For autonumbering to work properly, connect the two text columns within the anchored frame. The table should be in the same text flow.

## MACINTOSH PLATFORM

This section pertains to the Macintosh platform.

### Adobe Illustrator

Q

How can I get Adobe Illustrator files to be editable in FrameMaker?

A

You need ARTery made by Docu-Net, Inc. ARTery converts Adobe Illustrator files (through version 3 only) into editable FrameMaker graphics.

ARTery translates the graphic into MIF (Maker Interchange Format), which can then be opened on any version of FrameMaker for Macintosh, Windows, or Unix. It works by displaying information including the file's compatibility level, header type, creation and modification date, and illustration's dimensions. ARTery then creates a new file in MIF format.

### Automatic Launching

Q

How can I set FrameMaker to launch automatically when I log in?

A

In the Workspace Preferences, you can specify applications that will launch on login as long as their icons appear in the dock. This usually means less waiting for FrameMaker to launch after you log in.

## Capitalization

Q

How do I get capitalization on text from the insertion point forward using a keystroke?

A

The keyboard shortcuts for capitalizing text (CTRL+OPTION+U, CTRL+OPTION+L, and CTRL+OPTION+C ) work from the insertion point forward, as well as on selected text. For example, to change Apple to APPLE, place the insertion point to the left of the first P and press CTRL+OPTION+U. FrameMaker changes pple to PPLE and moves the insertion point to the next word.

## DCS Graphics

Q

How do I import, separate, and print Desktop Color Separation (DCS) graphics?

A

You can import and print EPSF (Encapsulated PostScript Format) graphics from software (such as Letraset, ColorStudio, or Adobe Photoshop) that use the DCS standard. This feature allows you to print four-color graphics using a high-end prepress system.

A DCS graphic comprises five files, all of which must be present: a main file for the preview image, and four files for each of the color separations (cyan, magenta, yellow, and black).

Different applications use different names for the main file. The main file might include the word Main or Master in its name. In Photoshop the main file is the only one without a filename suffix: the separation files have a suffix that indicates their color. For example, if you save a graphic named Fish in DCS format, the main file is named Fish, and the separations are named Fish.C, Fish.M, Fish.Y, and Fish.K.

## Digital Librarian

*Q*

Can I use FrameMaker documents with the Digital Librarian?

*A*

FrameMaker binary files do not work with Digital Librarian. Because Digital Librarian cannot search a binary file, you will need to save a copy of your document in Text Only format for use with the Librarian.

## Graphics

*Q*

What graphic file types can I import into FrameMaker?

*A*

You can import TIFF (Tagged Image File Format), EPSI (Encapsulated PostScript Interchange), and MacPaint. By purchasing a utility such as Pixel Magician, you can convert nearly any image file into a NeXT-Friendly file type.

## Hypertext

*Q*

Even though I have properly locked my document, the hypertext features are inactive.

*A*

If your document was not saved before it was locked, the hypertext features will not be active. You need to save the document to disk before you lock it.

### Numbering

*Q*

How do I get my page variable to pick up my chapter number (for example, 1-1)?

*A*

The easiest way to do this is to edit the Current Page # variable so that it includes a building block that will pick up the paragraph number for the chapter paragraph tag.

Edit the definition of the Current Page # variable so that the definition reads as follows:

<$paranum[Chapter]> - <$curpagenum>

This variable definition tells FrameMaker that it needs to display the paragraph number of the paragraph tag Chapter - the current page number. This will result in:

1 - 1

**NOTE:** *"Chapter" can be substituted with whatever paragraph tag gives you the chapter number.*

### PostScript File

*Q*

How do I send a PostScript file to a service bureau without the fonts included in the file?

*A*

You will need to go into the system folder and remove the fonts before generating your PostScript file. This will stop the print drivers from downloading the fonts into the PostScript file.

*Q*

I am using FrameMaker on a Macintosh and import an EPSF graphic. I can turn on the "Save FrameImage with imported graphics" so that the graphic will be visible on the screen when I view the document on the Unix or Windows platforms. What happens when I print? Is FrameMaker for Windows intelligent enough to get the PostScript from the EPSF facet even though it is a non-native facet, or does it print the bitmap?

*A*

A little confusion needs to be cleared up. When FrameMaker for the Macintosh imports by copy, the EPSF file gets broken into two facets:

- Encapsulated PostScript, which is used by PostScript interpreters
- QuickDraw PICT, which is used for preview on the Macintosh

When you save with FrameImage, you get a new facet added to the list (now you have three). This new facet is a bitmap which all platforms can view on the screen.

All platforms still send the Encapsulated PostScript to a PostScript printer.

*Q*

Why are PostScript files created on FrameMaker for the Macintosh much larger than those created on FrameMaker for the Unix platform?

*A*

The difference is probably that the Macintosh file includes the PostScript versions of all of the fonts used in the document in order to do automatic font downloading, whereas the Unix version of FrameMaker does not. Right now, the only way to avoid this is to remove all Adobe Type 1 and TrueType (but not screen bitmap) fonts from the system before printing. This problem will be solved with a new Adobe print driver available soon, which will allow you to download fonts more selectively.

## Screen Display

**Q**

My update cross-references panel came up, but the bottom of the panel extends beyond the bottom of the screen. What can I do?

**A**

This is due to having a large default window size. You will need to kill FrameMaker from either the Processes window in the Workspace or from a terminal window. Open the Edit application. Choose Open from the File menu, and shrink the panel to about 2×3 inches. Click the Cancel button, then quit Edit. This action will write a new value to the Window Manager and prevent the extra-large panels from appearing.

## Stationary Document

**Q**

How do you create a stationary document?

**A**

Creating a stationary document is a convenient way of utilizing a popular template.

This is how you do it:

1. Create a single- or double-sided document with the desired page size.
2. Set up the Master pages.
3. Create Paragraph, Character, and Tables formats.
4. Set up variables.
5. Bring up the Save As dialog box and name the template. Choose Stationery in the Format pop-up menu.

Now, when you use the New or Open commands to launch this document, an untitled copy of it will open.

For more information on stationery documents, consult the *Using FrameMaker Manual for Macintosh*, pages 1-3 and *FrameMaker Reference for Macintosh*, pages 1-108.

## UNIX PLATFORM

This section pertains to the Unix platform.

### Color

*Q*

How can I change the screen display to reverse video?

*A*

You can customize your .Xdefaults file to have the "fmconsole" display in reverse video. To do this you need to add the following lines:

15.3
```
fmconsole*background: black
fmconsole*foreground: white
```

You can also customize the .Xdefaults file to have FrameMaker come up in reverse video by entering the following lines:

15.4
```
Maker*background: black
Maker*foreground: white
```

These two lines change the colors in the main FrameMaker window, menus, dialog boxes, and document window scroll bars.

This line changes the background color of the document window:

15.5
```
Maker*docBackground: black
```

This line changes the color of the text:

```
Maker.black: white
```

When you have FrameMaker in reverse video, the cursor defaults to a black cursor with a white border.

## Fax

Q

How can you set up the fax modem and software to use the FrameMaker fax capability to send a fax directly from the FrameMaker Print command? I notice in the FMlpr.fax script that we are sending the FrameMaker file to a mail alias fax (fax@faxmodem). What will happen after that?

A

The alias fax is a dummy user identifier that spools the fax document to the fax modem software. The user must have some sort of fax modem software to which he or she will send FrameMaker PostScript output. The method that the user chooses to send it to the fax modem software is mainly determined by the software. Here, for convenience, and because the fax modem software provides this means of input, Frame happens to use a mail alias. After the fax modem software receives the fax request from the dummy user identifier, it processes it and sends it to a fax machine.

The comments in the FMlpr.fax script explain the basics. This script is called by FrameMaker when a file is printed to # printername of fax: or FAX:. This script must be called FMlpr.fax and installed in the .fminit2.0 directory. This script assumes that you have a fax modem that receives send-fax requests from an e-mail alias called fax.

## Memory

Q

I run pstat -s before running and after exiting FrameMaker and do not get equal values. Why wouldn't the swap be the same after exiting if FrameMaker is finished using it? Is there a memory leak?

A

When a TNT application starts up, it brings TNT and other related processes into the NeWS Server. And this memory that is reserved on startup is never released. This is typical of any TNT application (although the amount of memory not returned might be different for other applications). So FrameMaker is behaving as any TNT application would. The user can start up other TNT applications to see how much memory those applications are not releasing upon exiting. The File Manager is a good example. The swap can be reclaimed by restarting the other applications that are using the memory left over from the FrameMaker session: ttsession and openwin, for example.

## Mouse

*Q*

How can you adjust the time interval in which FrameMaker interprets two mouse clicks as double-clicking?

*A*

Use this resource:

```
Maker*XmDialogShell*XmList*doubleClickInterval: 500
```

## Network

*Q*

What is Frame's definition of a "network" with respect to "networked" floating licenses?

*A*

Frame uses its own floating license mechanism to distribute FrameMaker licenses across the network. While it's hard to define the word "network" in general terms, here is a brief description of what Frame's Floating License Server (FLS) requires in order to share licenses.

Frame only supports the FLS in a local area network (LAN) environment. It is not Frame's intent that the FLS be used to support wide area networks (WANs). Frame distinguishes between a LAN and a WAN by requiring that all machines on a LAN must reside within the same building.

Furthermore, Frame only supports the FLS on a LAN that has reasonable network performance. As a guideline, if the LAN is used for Network File System (NFS), then it most likely fits the requirement for reasonable performance. The LAN must maintain a reasonable level of performance at all times.

What are reasonable network requirements for Frame's FLS to work? The main factors that influence the timing of point-to-point communication are

- Physical distance between the points
- Maximum speed and bandwidth of the carrier
- Volume of other traffic on the carrier that reduces the effective speed

In order for floating licenses to work, there must be a reliable connection between the FrameMaker client central processing unit (CPU) and the FLS CPU, where a Request/Acknowledge dialog can take place in less than 10 seconds; ping -s <remote_hostname> can be used to roughly determine if you have reliable communication between the current host and a remote host. If it takes longer than 10 seconds to send and receive a Remote Procedure Call (RPC), then that network will not support Frame's floating licenses. Many packets do not reach their target destination on Ethernet, so a retry mechanism is built in. Every 0.1 seconds, FrameMaker will continue trying to engage in the dialog, but will give up after 10 seconds of no response (100 tries).

## OpenWindows

*Q*

What is the easiest way to figure out which version of OpenWindows is being used?

*A*

At a Unix prompt type:

L 15.8

```
xdpyinfo | grep vendor
```

This will return:

5.9
```
vendor string: X11/NeWS - Sun Microsystems Inc. vendor
release number: 3000
```

Divide the vendor release number by 1000 to get the version of OpenWindows being used.

## Printing

*Q*

How can I print the word DRAFT on the background of every page?

*A*

On the Master page, create a new text rectangle. Add the following text:

5.10
```
(DRAFT) /Times-Roman /B -52 /UL .8
#include "$FMHOME/.fminit2.0.ps/docs/BigFill.ps
```

where $FMHOME is the pathname of your $FMHOME directory. Select the text rectangle and choose Format Flow. Select PostScript Code and choose OK. Go to the Body pages and print.

The arguments in the first line (i.e. (DRAFT) /Times-Roman /B -52 /UL .8) are:

- string to print in parenthesis, i.e. (DRAFT)
- font desired: /font, i.e. /Times-Roman
- mode code where /W = fill width, /H = fill height, /B = fill both
- rotate value from –180 to +180 where positive = counterclockwise, negative = clockwise
- starting corner: /LL /LR /UR /UL where LL = Lower Left, etc.
- gray scale value from 0 to 1 where 0 = Black, 1 = White

The size of the text is determined by the size of the text rectangle and the "mode code" argument.

*Q*

What is the printing performance of imported bitmaps/images?

A

Printing with integral scaling is much faster than nonintegral scaling. That is one reason why Frame has the Raster File Scaling Options dialog. If you are printing on a 300 dots-per-inch (dpi) printer, and you choose 300, 150, 100, or 75 dpi (all divide into 300 evenly), you get much faster printing than choosing something like 200 or 72 dpi.

A common problem is with screen captures. If you import the image at 72 dpi, it looks great on screen but takes a long time to print and can look a bit distorted (especially if there are gray patterns in the image). It is much better to import screen images at 75 or 100 dpi if the goal is a printed document. The images will look a bit distorted on the screen, but print much faster and produce cleaner-looking output. Unfortunately, it is not possible to import images that both look good on the screen and also print cleanly.

Similarly, if you manually stretch the bitmap to a dpi other than the ones listed above, you'll get slower printing. So avoid manual stretching if possible.

By the way, Frame tests suggest that FrameMaker achieves significantly faster bitmap printing than most popular PostScript-capable programs when the above procedures are followed.

## GENERAL TOPICS

This section pertains to any platform.

### Frame Bulletin Board

Q

What do I need to know to use the Frame OnLine Bulletin Board?

A

First, you will need to know a little about the software that you are using to call this bulletin board system (BBS). Almost all of the problems connecting to the BBS can be resolved by checking the following information:

1. Do I need communications software to call the Frame OnLine BBS?

Yes. The communications software allows you to communicate with your computer and the modem, and make configuration changes to your communications environment. Your communications software will allow you to set up some important parameters for use with Frame OnLine or any BBS.

2. What parameters does my communications software need to support?

   First is the terminal emulation. You need to be able to set a terminal emulation of ANSI or VT-100. VT-100 emulation will not allow you to use the color menus, so the ANSI emulation is preferred, as the color menus are easier to read. Next, you need to be able to set up a transfer protocol. Frame OnLine supports Xmodem, Ymodem, and Zmodem transfer protocols. If your communications software does not support one of these protocols, you cannot upload or download files to/from the BBS. You should know how to set up these parameters before you call any BBS.

3. How do I go about uploading a file?

   Before you call the BBS, you should know the name of the file you want to upload, the path to the file on your computer, and the keystroke to tell your communications software to start the upload. This is the most overlooked part of uploading a file. All communications software has a key or keys that tell the software to start sending a file. When you upload to any BBS, you first tell the BBS what the file will be named. Do not include the path when you tell the BBS the file name. Next you will be asked how you want to send the file. This is where you tell the BBS with which transfer protocol your communications software will send the file. Now the BBS and your computer can "speak the same language." Last, the BBS will show you the file, the time to upload, the protocol you have chosen, and a message that the BBS is ready to receive the file. At this point, you press the upload button for your communications software, answer all the pertinent questions, and the upload begins.

4. How do I go about downloading a file?

   Before you call the BBS, you should know the keystroke to tell your communications software to start the download. This is the most overlooked part of downloading a file. All communications software has a key or keys that tell the software to start receiving a file. When you download from any BBS, you first tell the BBS what the file is named. Do not include the path when you tell the BBS the file name. Next you will be asked how you want the file sent to you. This is where you tell the BBS with which transfer protocol your communications software will receive the file. Now the BBS and your computer can "speak the same language." Last, the BBS will show you the file, the time to upload, the protocol you have chosen, and a message that the BBS is ready to send the file. At this point, you press the download key for your communications software, answer all the pertinent questions, and the download begins.

5. How should I prepare the files to be sent to the BBS?

   This is another step that should be done before you call the BBS. Here are steps to follow for different platforms:

   - *Macintosh* Files should be compressed with Stuff-It. The resulting SIT file should then have BINHEX run on it so that it can be used with any of the Apple operating systems. Macintosh files that do not follow this setup may not work when sent to the BBS.
   - *PC/Windows* These files can have PKZIP, PKARC, ARJ, or no compression run on them. The BBS is DOS-based, so the files do not require compression or encoding.
   - *Unix* It is best if files are binary. UUENCODE and compress them. ASCII is OK.

6. The BBS is a DOS-based system. Do I need a DOS computer to use Frame OnLine?

   While PC Board is based in the DOS environment, it is NOT a requirement that a DOS-based system be used. Any standard modem communications package should be adequate, assuming that it supports the following parameters and protocols.

7. What are the recommended settings for the BBS?

   Generally, the BBS is set up to answer the line with either 2400 or 9600 baud, 8-bit word length, and 1 stop bit with no parity. If another setting is used, the modem will have to fall back and communication could be hampered if both modems do not support the same settings.

8. What is the baud rate?

This is the rate in which the modems communicate over the telephone line. Currently, Frame OnLine supports baud rates of 300 to 9600 BPS. 2400 or 9600 baud is preferred.

9. What is the word length?

   Frame OnLine supports one word length, 8 bits. 8 bits is the word length used by most BBS systems.

10. What are the stop bits and parity?

    The settings for Frame OnLine are 1 stop bit and no parity. A parity setting of even or odd will also work, but is not recommended.

11. What specific file transfer protocols are supported?

    File transfer protocols allow the BBS to receive files that consist of data, control information, and file-specific information. These protocols allow the computers to transfer this complex information at a rapid rate. For more information about the file transfer protocols that are supported by your communication program, check the documentation of your software package. Frame OnLine supports the following file transfer protocols, and new protocols can be added if necessary:

    - XModem
    - XModem 1K (1024 byte transfer with ECC)
    - XModem CRC (transfer with Cyclic Redundancy Check)
    - YModem
    - ZModem
    - ASCII

12. Is there graphics support on Frame OnLine?

    The BBS has two modes, graphics and nongraphics. To use graphics, the system calling Frame OnLine must have an ANSI driver loaded, and the terminal mode for the modem software should be set to ANSI or ANSI BBS. If the user cannot get the graphics to display, the "M" command can be used at any time while connected to the BBS to switch modes. Problems with graphics should be addressed via BBS mail directly to the systems operator (SYSOP).

## Dictionary

### Q

Why does the Spell Checker not check words longer than 24 characters?

### A

This is a limit imposed by the code licensed by Frame from Proximity, the creators of the dictionaries and spell search engine.

### Q

Why doesn't text flow to a page added with the Add Page option?

### A

The solution lies in connecting the text flows. This can be done with the Format, Pages, Layout commands. For documents with only one intended flow, here is a fast way to connect all the columns—invoke Freeze Pagination (ESC, p,z) and choose Freeze. Then invoke Freeze Pagination and choose Unfreeze.

## Footnotes

### Q

Is there a way to have two or more references to the same footnote?

### A

Yes. First you insert the footnote. That gives you the first reference and the footnote itself. To get the second reference to the footnote, insert a cross-reference to the footnote paragraph. The cross-reference picks up the <$paranum> of the footnote paragraph. Its format is something like:

L 15.11

```
<Superscript><$paranum><Deault Para Font>
```

You have to edit the footnote properties so that the footnote format has no prefix or suffix (otherwise <$paranum> picks up the prefix/suffix).

## Graphics

### Q

Very often when I create lines or objects in a frame they do not stick to the frame; instead, they stay attached to a page when the frame moves. I tried grouping these lines with the rest of the object in the frame to make them stick. This doesn't work either, as these lines refuse to be selected with the other objects. What am I doing wrong?

### A

FrameMaker lets you place objects inside anchored and unanchored frames, and also directly on pages. Objects drawn directly on pages can overlap the area inside a frame. This can make it hard to know where an object is. This can be a problem if you think an object is in an anchored frame, but it's really on a page. The frame moves as the text above it is edited, but the object doesn't move with the frame.

You need to think about this topic when you draw, stretch/reshape, move, and paste objects in or near frame edges. Here are some tips to help you understand and control this effect.

DRAWING OBJECTS The object will be placed in whatever frame or page you press the mouse button down in when you begin drawing the object. If you press down inside a frame and drag to draw, the object will be placed inside the frame, even if you drag outside the frame while drawing. It's easy to see that the object is inside the frame, because any part of the object that you draw beyond the frame's border will be invisible while you draw.

Conversely, if you start drawing directly on the page (outside of any frame), the object will be placed directly on the page, even if you draw it with a portion that overlaps a frame. This is harder to see, because the object lies in front of the frame, and is therefore completely visible.

RESHAPING AND STRETCHING OBJECTS Reshaping and stretching an object will not change the object's frame or page assignment. This can cause some confusion when you reshape an object that's directly on a page, so that it lies completely within the borders of a frame. FrameMaker thinks the object is still on the page, even though it sits "in front of" the frame. While this can cause confusion, it can also be a useful feature. If you need to get an object into a frame after it's drawn, move it or paste it (see below), but don't reshape it.

MOVING OBJECTS As you drag an object around with the mouse, FrameMaker places the object in whatever frame or page the mouse pointer is over as you drag. You must pay attention to the location of the mouse pointer when near frame boundaries.

It turns out that this is the easiest way to make sure an object is inside a frame. Just move it around a bit and then release the mouse button with the mouse pointer inside the frame.

If you move an object using the keyboard, it will not switch frame or page locations, even if you move a page-based object so that it sits in front of a frame.

MOVING FRAMES If you move a frame, all the objects inside the frame move with it. But the frame doesn't gather up additional objects as it moves. So, if a frame moves under an object that's on a page, that object remains on the page, even though it sits in front of the frame.

PASTING OBJECTS If you paste an object while a frame is selected, it will be placed in that frame. If you paste an object while another object is selected, it will be placed in the frame that contains the selected object. And if you paste an object with nothing selected, FrameMaker will paste the object onto the current page, and then check to see if the object happens to sit in front of a frame that entirely encloses the object. If so, it will place the object inside that frame. Otherwise it will leave the object on the page.

CHECKING WHETHER AN OBJECT IS IN A FRAME The quickest way is to move the frame and type ^L (to make sure the screen is up-to-date). If the object is in the frame, it will have moved with the frame.

Another check can be made without having to change the document at all. Select the object and use the Object Properties command. Look at the Top/Left offset values shown in that dialog box. If the object is in a frame, the offsets are measured from the top/left corner of the frame. Otherwise the values are measured from the top/left of the page.

## Languages Supported

Q

What languages are supported and what dictionaries are used?

*A*

FrameMaker's language support (spelling and hyphenation) is via Proximity:

| | |
|---|---|
| US English | Merriam-Webster |
| British English | William Collins Sons & Co/Merriam-Webster |
| Dutch | Van Dale Lexicografie bv |
| French | William Collins |
| Italian | William Collins |
| Portuguese | William Collins |
| Spanish | William Collins |
| Danish | Munksgaard Int'l Publishers Ltd |
| Norwegian | International Data Education a.s. |
| Swedish | International Data Education a.s. |
| Canadian French | Hachette |
| Finnish | IDE a.s. Swiss |
| German | Text & Satz |
| Catalan | Lluis de Yzaguirre i Maura |

## Math Coprocessor

*Q*

How does FrameMaker utilize a coprocessor, and is a coprocessor necessary?

*A*

Since FrameMaker depends heavily on math functions, Frame always requires the ability to have a math coprocessor.

- Equations: no coprocessor, no math.
- Graphics: Vector graphic formats would probably benefit from a coprocessor. What FrameMaker and many other applications do is to have a math emulator loaded in the absence of a coprocessor.

> This allows math calculations to go on as they would with a coprocessor, but in a system that has no coprocessor actually installed. Performance might be better on some systems with the coprocessor as opposed to the emulator, but not noticeably.

An 80386 processor needs an 80387 coprocessor—two chips, each in a different socket. An 80486 processor has a built-in coprocessor. An 80487 is a coprocessor for the 80486-SX. The SX version of the 486 chip has no coprocessor, so it needs this 80487 chip.

## Measurements

### Q

How do the different units of measurement compare to an inch? How can I determine this in FrameMaker?

### A

One inch is equal to:

2.54 cm
72 pts
6.0 pc
67.431 dd (didots)
5.619 cc (cicero)

An easy way to discern the differences is to give a paragraph a 1-inch indent in the paragraph format box, and then change the display units under View, Options. As you change to other units of measurement, the 1-inch indent will change to 2.54 cm, and so on.

## Merging Documents

### Q

How do I merge two FrameMaker documents?

*A*

Open both documents and place your insertion point in the document that contains the desired text. Select Edit, All In Flow, then Edit, Copy. Now place the insertion point in the destination document and select Edit, Paste.

## Nonprinting Comments

*Q*

How can I create comments in a document that show on the screen but do not print?

*A*

In version 2.1, a software bug with spot colors allowed text to be visible on the screen, but not print. Version 3.0 fixed that bug, so now there is a little more work involved. To allow nonprinting comments, follow these steps:

1. Somewhere in your document, type a couple of letters in black.
2. Apply a conditional text tag to them. This tag will later contain your notes. When editing the tag name, select an override of underline so you will be able to differentiate the notes on the screen at a glance.
3. Select and copy the text that has the conditional tag associated with it. This will copy your conditional text information to the Clipboard.
4. Open up the Find/Change dialog box.
5. Under Find, select Character Format. Set everything in the menu to the As Is setting (In Sunview press the Meta F8 keys). Set the color to white.
6. Under Change, select By Pasting.
7. Do a Change & Find until all instances of the notes bear the characteristics of the conditional tag.
8. Choose Special, Conditional Text. Highlight the tag and select Edit Conditional Tag. In that dialog box, change the color to black.

9. Hide the tag. With the text symbols turned on, there will be a "T" every place where you had a note.

This needs to be a document by document change. Unfortunately there is no global way of making these changes.

## Sharing Files

*Q*

Can I share FrameMaker files between different platforms?

*A*

Yes. FrameMaker files are completely interchangeable between different hardware platforms. To ensure complete integrity of your FrameMaker files, save the files out to MIF (Maker Interchange Format) (File, Save As... Maker Interchange Format MIF).

## TIFF Files

*Q*

Does FrameMaker support CCITT Group 4 tagged image file format (TIFF)?

*A*

Frame explicitly does not support CCITT Group 4 TIFF. It is not recommended for use in desktop publishing products (such as FrameMaker) in the TIFF specification standard. The real application of CCITT Group 4 is for fax machines.

# 16

# Avoiding Trouble Before It Starts

THIS chapter features troubleshooting tips from the Frame technical support staff. The questions have been alphabetized here by category and divided into the three platforms on which FrameMaker 4 can be used—Windows, Macintosh, and Unix.

## WINDOWS PLATFORM

The following categories pertain to the Windows platform.

### Dictionaries

PROBLEM An error message occurs when creating dictionaries.

SOLUTION If you get an error message when you try to create your own dictionary, the error is probably caused by the Share (SHARE.EXE) program, which comes with DOS 3.0 and above. The Share program prevents two processes from corrupting files by trying to write to them simultaneously. Microsoft and the *Windows 3.1 Secrets* book recommend running the program; however, you may see some strange anomalies with the program.

If you try to write your personal or document dictionary to a file via the Spelling Checker, Dictionaries dialog box and you get an error that FrameMaker cannot write to the file, go to the File Manager, select the file you just created, and check the Properties under the File menu in the File Manager. If the read/write access is set to Read Only, the Share program may be affecting your ability to create this new dictionary.

Edit your AUTOEXEC.BAT file. If you see an entry for SHARE.EXE, make it inactive by typing:

**REM share**

before the line entry. Save your changes to AUTOEXEC.BAT and reboot the system. Then re-enter Windows and FrameMaker, and try to create the new dictionary again. Check your work by opening the new dictionary in FrameMaker. You should see any words that have been saved to it in FrameMaker (including hyphenation for these words).

## Fonts

PROBLEM Screen fonts do not look good.

SOLUTION When you open a Frame document that contains unavailable fonts, FrameMaker must decide what font to use in place of the missing font. In most cases, the entry in the MAKER.INI file called "Default Font" dictates which font is chosen. This setting can be changed by modifying the MAKER.INI text file with a DOS editor, edlin or edit.

The current line in the MAKER.INI file is:

```
Default Font=Times, Times New Roman, Tms Rmn
```

If you change this line to:

```
Default Font=Helv, Times New Roman, Tms Rmn
```

FrameMaker will pick up most variations of Helv (Helvetica). This font is resident as a default Windows font in Version 3.0 and maps to another resident font in 3.1. The Helvetica type face is much better with its screen representation than Times. If Adobe Type Manager is installed, and/or you have a PostScript printer, it looks better when printed.

The entries after the Helv entries are alternate default fonts in the event that the first default option is not present.

## General Protection Faults

PROBLEM How can crashes be diagnosed?

SOLUTION In their infinite grace, Microsoft included an application called Microsoft System Diagnostics (MSD). This diagnostic program allows you to get a closer look at the system, and even get printouts of the system's configuration.

To use the MSD program, exit Windows completely and change directories to the Windows directory. Type **MSD** at the DOS prompt. A screen displays with these options:

```
Computer, Memory, Video, Network, OS Version, Mouse, Other
Adaptors, Disk Drives, LPT Ports, COM Ports, IRQ Status,
TSR programs, and Device Drivers.
```

You can choose one of these options to get information about the system.

For example, you want to find out why your system occasionally crashes when RELNOTES.DOC is opened. To find out whether your TEMP, Swapfile, SMARTDrive, or video environments were configured incorrectly, you need to find out about your system's memory, its allocation, and your video adaptor. To find out about your system's memory, choose Memory to display a screen that shows the total random access memory (RAM), extended RAM (HIMEM) XMS information, and UMB information. Selecting the Video option, you can get exact information on the installed video card, its manufacturer, model, driver version, and operating mode in pixels (800×600, and so on).

By checking the memory configuration, you may determine that the memory is not set up correctly, and conclude that this is causing the crash.

**NOTE:** *Information from MSD may be helpful if you have to call Microsoft with a Windows problem.*

PROBLEM Crashes occur for no apparent reason.

SOLUTION A general protection (GP) fault in Windows 3.1 (referred to as an unrecoverable application error [UAE] in Windows 3.0) occurs only in standard and 386 enhanced mode Windows. A GP fault signifies that something unexpected has happened within the Windows environment, usually an improper memory access. In other words, something running within the Windows environment has made a call to a location in memory that it did not have access to, potentially overwriting and corrupting other program code in that area of memory. More specifically, an application or Windows component might read or write to a memory location that it has not preallocated, or memory that it does not own. All memory management within Windows is handled by the Windows environment itself, and when applications and Windows components directly access memory, the result is often a GP fault.

Another situation where a GP fault may occur involves the passing of parameters between applications and the Windows environment. Invalid parameters affect the performance of Windows and its applications by forcing an invalid instruction. This is usually the result of an application's internal program code incorrectly passing specific data that could not be correctly interpreted for Windows or another Windows application. The result is often a GP fault.

If you have repeated GP faults, the following troubleshooting advice may help you:

1. Check for incompatible terminate-and-stay-resident (TSR) programs or unsupported device drivers in your CONFIG.SYS or AUTOEXEC.BAT file.

   Temporarily "comment out" all lines relating to suspect drivers and TSR programs to bring the system to a minimum configuration for testing purposes. (To comment out a line, use a text editor such as Notepad, open the AUTOEXEC.BAT or the CONFIG.SYS file, and type **rem** at the beginning of the line.) If this eliminates the problem, then the problem was related to one of the drivers or TSR programs that was commented out. Reinstate the removed lines one by one until the problem reappears, thus showing which line was loading the TSR program or driver causing the error.

2. A third-party Windows device driver may not be functioning properly. Run the MS-DOS version of the Windows Setup program and select the lowest level configuration of drivers for the listed hardware devices. Many video drivers have problems, so always try a lower resolution.

3. If you have a permanent swap file set up in Windows, it may be corrupted. If you do not have a permanent swap file, setting one up will increase performance and allow you to open a larger number of applications.

4. Upgrading to Windows 3.1 from Windows 3.0 has been known to cause corrupted files. Reinstallation of Windows will solve many inconsistent and unexpected GP faults.

5. Make sure you have the latest driver for your video and printer systems under Windows. Most of these drivers have been updated more than three times since Windows was released.

6. Most GP faults can be remedied by reading and understanding the concepts outlined in Chapter 14 of the *Microsoft Windows User's Guide*.

**NOTE:** *There are no bugs in FrameMaker that will cause GP faults. To date, all GP faults with FrameMaker running have been resolved by correctly setting up the Windows installation.*

## Graphics

PROBLEM Graphics do not display when moving to another platform.

SOLUTION If you set your document preferences incorrectly, your graphics may not display if you take the Frame document to another Frame platform.

For example, *before* importing the graphic on the PC or the Sun system, make sure that the Properties or Preferences (in the File pull-down menu) are set to Save FrameImage with Imported Graphics. Import the graphic by copying it into the Frame Document.

If the image imports and prints correctly, the document will also work the same way when you take it to another Frame platform.

Some XWD graphics and poor EPS graphics may not display due to differences in the platform's expectation of a "preview" or "display" header. For best results, test the document before you move it to another platform.

## Hard Drives

PROBLEM Miscellaneous problems arise with hard drives and controllers.

SOLUTION The following list describes known problems with known hard drives and controllers:

- Adaptec Controllers The Adaptec 1520 SCSI controller has problems with Windows 3.X. To resolve these problems, upgrade to the Adaptec 1542-X controller.

  Some Adaptec controller boards require that the double-buffering feature of Windows 3.0 SMARTDrive disk cache in 386 enhanced mode be disabled. If this is the case (contact Adaptec for a list of these controllers), add the undocumented /B- switch to the end of the line as follows:

  ```
  Device=c:\windows\smartdrv.sys 1024 512 /B-
  ```

  The /B- switch disables the SMARTDrive double-buffering feature that is the default with Windows 3.0.

- PS/2s and CORE Technologies Some PS/2s may have CORE Technologies CNT-MCK and CNT-MCA disk controllers. If this is the case, and you are experiencing excessive hangs, contact CORE Technologies at (407) 997-6033 for an update to the MCA driver. Again, the symptom will be an unexplainable hang in all Windows applications.
- IBM PS/2 systems (PS/2 models 70-041, 70-071, 80-041, and 80-071; PS/2 models 60-041 and 60-071; and PS/2 model 50-021 (the 20MB system only)) These systems can have problems with Windows 3.X. There is a fix already included with the systems that is not automatically loaded.

  Loading the file DASDDRVR.SYS into your CONFIG.SYS as a device will alleviate the problems. The file should be Version 1.03 or later. It is 734 bytes in size and resides on the IBM reference disks. The file looks at the system's BIOS rev. If the patch is needed, it is loaded. If not, it is ignored. You have nothing to lose by trying this. The symptoms are: intermittent General Failure Error reading Drive X: messages; Track 0 Bad, or Invalid Media messages; loss of system date and time with the #162 or #163 errors; and system request for a password where one never existed before.
- Plus Development Hard Card Since these drives use their own interface called the Cluster Disk Interface (CDI), two lines have to be added to the SYSTEM.INI file to keep the systems from hanging and running excessively slow. Add the following entries to the [386ENH] section of SYSTEM.INI.

  ```
  VirtualHDIRQ=off
  EMMExclude=C000-DFFF
  ```

  Plus HardCard II #40 and #80 drives need an updated driver to run with Windows 3.X. Versions up to 1.30 will not work correctly. Version 1.31 fixes the problems and can be identified by the text you see when the driver is loaded, or by looking at the Driver disk. If the Driver disk has Revision C on the disk label, you have the 1.31 driver and you are OK.
- Double Disk by Vertisoft This must be Version 2.14B or higher to run with Windows 3.1.

- Western Digital WD 1007A ESDI Controller This controller requires the following line in the SYSTEM.INI file of Windows 3.X in the [386Enh] section:

  ```
  VirtualHDIRQ=off
  ```

  This slows performance somewhat, but alleviates unexplained hangs.

## Installation

PROBLEM FrameMaker for Windows displays the message, Invalid Registration Number.

SOLUTION

1. Windows must be running in 386 enhanced mode. To check the mode, open the Program Manager. On the top bar, click the Help option then click the window option About Program Manager to see the program operating mode.
2. Make sure that the NUMLOCK key is off. Check to see if you are using the numeric keypad to enter the numbers. The installer will not recognize these numbers. Use the numbers over the alpha part of the keyboard. Capital letters in the registration number do not have to be entered in uppercase.
3. Include the dashes in the number.
4. Be sure you have not misread the number. All reg numbers use the following syntax: 00-5-01-01-3-XXXXX-YYYYYY (notice the syntax has five Xs and six Ys).

The Xs and Ys will be any hexadecimal combination; that is, numbering between 0 and 9, and A through F. Many users get a 6 confused with a G. Since G is out of the hexadecimal range, 6 would be the correct digit.

## Math

PROBLEM Certain characters misalign or print incorrectly.

SOLUTION FrameMaker for Windows has had problems with some of the characters in the Math palette. These problems are not peculiar to FrameMaker, but can be found in all Windows applications.

Certain characters (tilde, circumflex, and umlaut) may appear to be misaligned over the character they accompany. This occurs when using the diacritics in the Math palette.

If you notice that the diacritic is not properly aligned (perhaps it is left aligned as opposed to centered), change the character format for the diacritical character until the proper alignment is achieved. Since FrameMaker has no control over the fonts, the diacritics will be aligned differently based on the font used.

Additionally, certain diacritical marks (circumflex and tilde) display correctly, but print the wrong mark. This occurs if you are printing with Microsoft PostScript printer drivers, which do not correctly map the characters that Math is using. To alleviate the problem, print to a PCL or HP LaserJet printer and make sure you are using the latest drivers for these printers. New drivers can be downloaded from the Microsoft Windows Driver Library at (206) 637-9009 (2400 baud or higher).

## Memory

PROBLEM In trying to boot FrameMaker for Microsoft Windows, the following messages come up: Out of memory, or Insufficient memory to launch application.

SOLUTION These messages occur because of Windows' inability to get enough virtual resources. The virtual resources include the following: the TEMP variable in AUTOEXEC.BAT, SMARTDRV.EXE in AUTOEXEC.BAT, swap file or virtual memory, virtual machine size, and space on the Windows global heap.

If any one of these resources comes up with a goose egg (zero) when you try to run (or install) FrameMaker (or any other Windows application), you will get an Out of Memory or Insufficient Memory message.

To fix the problem:

1. Make sure that the TEMP variable is assigned in AUTOEXEC.BAT and it is set to an empty directory that is not used by any other variable (like TMP). Do not set TEMP to a RAM drive or network drive.
2. Make sure SMARTDrive is running (SMARTDRV.EXE for Windows 3.1 and SMARTDRV.SYS for Windows 3.0). Do not run SMARTDrive with any other disk cache program.
3. Make sure that your system has at least a 5MB permanent swap file. A temporary swap file is not the same as a permanent one. If a

permanent swap file cannot be set up, set the swap file to temporary and have as much space on your drive as possible. Without a large permanent swap file, the error messages may never subside. If a swap file exceeds 15MB permanent, and you still get error messages, your swap file is probably not a problem.

4. Make sure that only the HIMEM memory manager is used. Third-party memory managers are difficult to configure. The misconfiguration of the third-party memory manager causes the Windows 386 enhanced mode to be highly unstable.
5. If any font manager is present, such as Adobe Type Manager (ATM), disable it and try the install or startup again. Sometimes the Windows global heap gets trashed and ATM seems to be a rather large "heap hog." If this works, reload Windows and ATM.
6. When this all fails, it seems that reloading Windows solves the problem. It is not necessary to reload FrameMaker if it has installed successfully. Move the /WINDOWS/SYSTEM.INI and /WINDOWS/WIN.INI to any other directory. Reload Windows in its original place. The idea is to rewrite the data files, and have the installer re-create the WIN.INI and SYSTEM.INI files. Do not use the old WIN.INI and SYSTEM.INI files until you see if the memory errors have subsided. After this, you can add the FrameMaker lines to the WIN.INI file.

This problem is especially prevalent for users who have loaded Windows 3.1 over Windows 3.0. To fix the problem, reload Windows 3.1 with no WIN.INI and SYSTEM.INI so the current settings in these files are not overwritten.

## Mouse

PROBLEM A three-button mouse does not work in Windows the same way it does in Unix.

SOLUTION This happens because Windows drivers control the mouse and FrameMaker. If you wish to use a three-button mouse, you must purchase a mouse that is designed for use with Windows. Then you must be able to map, or set up, the functions for the different buttons if you wish to use mouse conventions like those in the Unix version of FrameMaker.

## Printing

PROBLEM FrameMaker displays the message, Cannot Print, SoftRIP Error.

SOLUTION This is due to an out-of-memory situation in your Windows environment. Some printers (such as HP DeskJet, HP PaintJet, and so on) do not have an internal buffer; the job has to be turned from an instruction into a bitmap. Since this is normally done in the printer's buffer, the lack of a buffer and Windows resources will cause the process to die resulting in the message referred to. This can also happen if you have a PCL (HP LaserJet) printer that has an incorrect memory setting in the Control Panel, Printers dialog box. Close some windows, and even wait for a few minutes and try again.

This message is usually simple to alleviate. First, you can get this error if you try to print to a file and something goes wrong with the file at the DOS level. The system may think it is out of memory, so you get the error. Make sure you have plenty of disk space if you are going to print from any Windows application.

When all else fails, check the printer memory against what is set in the Windows Control Panel. If you are not sure of the memory amount, choose the lowest setting.

PROBLEM Printing is too slow and sometimes imcomplete pages are printed.

SOLUTION Verify that your default Windows printer is either a PCL or PostScript printer. To check the setting, follow these steps:

1. From the Windows Control Panel, select the Printers icon to reach the Printers window.
2. Note the default Windows printer in the box labeled Default Printer. The printer has to be one of the following types:

   PCL HP LaserJet, HP DeskJet, or any non-PostScript laser printer.
   PostScript Any laser printer with PostScript printing abilities.

If a correct printer type is specified, check the TEMP directory. Any time a Windows application prints, Windows puts temporary files into the directory that is specified as TEMP in the computer's AUTOEXEC.BAT file. This directory must exist, be empty, and not be set to a RAM drive. RAM drives limit the size of the TEMP variable, and when Windows stops making TEMP files, your print job will abort or crash.

### Setting Up PCL Printers

If you are using a PCL printer, follow these steps:

1. Choose Connect from the Printers dialog box.
2. In this dialog box, make sure that Fast Printing Direct to Port is disabled. This feature will bypass Windows and DOS and attempt to write directly to the hardware on your computer's communication port. This will cause many errors, slow print times, and usually result in crashes on long or complex documents.
3. Set the Transmission Retry value from 45 seconds to 250 seconds. This will allow Windows enough time to send the whole page and not multiple pieces.
4. Choose OK from the Connect dialog box to return to the Printers dialog box.
5. Choose Setup from the Printers dialog box.
6. Choose About from the Setup dialog box. Note the version of the current driver.
7. Choose OK from the About dialog box.
8. Look at the value for the Memory in the Setup dialog box. Make sure this is set correctly. If this is set too high or too low, your print jobs will occasionally crash. If you are not sure of the memory in your printer, use the printer's internal self-test to verify the amount (see the printer documentation for information on running this self-test).
9. If you have a newer version of the PCL printer driver (Universal Printer Driver Version 2.0 or later) you will have an option to Print TrueType As Graphics. This option will circumnavigate a bug in the Windows TrueType font management. This option must be selected if you use TrueType fonts in any of your Windows applications.

See the Notes section at the end of the Windows platform section in this chapter.

### Setting Up PostScript Printers

1. Choose Connect from the Printers dialog box.

2. In this dialog box, make sure that Fast Printing Direct to Port is disabled. This feature will bypass Windows and DOS and attempt to write directly to the hardware on your computer's communication port. This will cause many errors, slow print times, and usually result in crashes on long or complex documents.
3. Set the Transmission Retry value from 90 seconds to 250 seconds. This will allow Windows enough time to send the whole page, and not multiple pieces of the page.
4. Choose OK from the Connect dialog box to return to the Printers dialog box.
5. Choose Setup from the Printers dialog box.
6. Choose About from the Setup dialog box. Note the version of the current driver. Choose OK from the About dialog box.
7. Choose Options from the Setup dialog box.
8. At the bottom of the window is an option labeled Send Header with Each Job. This option must be selected.
9. Choose Advances from the Options dialog box.
10. In the center of the dialog box is the Virtual Memory. This is a very important value. Never guess the number for this value. Leave the default for now.
11. Choose OK on all the dialog boxes until you are back at the Printers dialog box. Choose Close to get back to the Control Panel, and exit Windows completely.
12. Change directories until you are in \WINDOWS\SYSTEM. Type the following command to run the Microsoft Windows PostScript printer test:

    ```
    copy testps.txt "printer port"
    ```

13. This copies the file to the port that the printer is plugged into. Substitute your port name for "printer port" in the preceding example (for example, LPT1:, COM1:, and so on).
14. You will get a printout that will tell you two things. The first line is the maximum virtual memory that Windows can access from that specific system, and the second line is the suggested virtual memory. This suggested virtual memory goes into the advanced

printer setup for the PostScript printers. If you do not use this value, your system will not print reliably.

See the Notes section at the end of the Windows platform section in this chapter.

### *Printing to a Linotronic Typesetter EPS File*

Before you can successfully print to the Linotronic typesetter, you must download the latest driver from the Microsoft Windows Driver Library by calling (206) 637-9009 with a 2400-baud modem.

You must have Version 3.56 or later of the Microsoft PostScript printer driver and the newest Linotronic WPD (Windows Printer Driver) files. These are all included in the program you can download from Microsoft's driver library.

Only the following Linotronic devices are supported:

100, 200/230, 300 ver. 47.1, 300 ver. 49.3, 330, 500, 530, 630

If the specified Linotronic model is not listed here, Linotronic 90 for example, there is no Microsoft-approved driver for that model.

To print to an Encapsulated PostScript (EPS) file, follow these steps:

1. Once the driver is installed, go to the Control Panel, select the Printers icon, and select the specific Lino model as the default Windows printer.
2. Now select Setup, Options, and choose Print to Encapsulated PostScript File. This option will force the Windows printer driver to create an EPS file. For the filename, leave the space blank. This will force Windows to prompt you for a filename and path when you try to print. This output is not formatted for use in a Unix environment or Unix printer server; it is formatted for a Linotronic Soft RIP (Raster Image Processor) system.
3. From the Setup, Options dialog box, choose Advanced. Near the bottom of the Window, note the line Conform to Adobe Document Structuring Conventions. Select the box on this line. For more information on this switch, look in the help file provided with the 3.56 PostScript driver from Microsoft.

**NOTE:** *If you put a filename in the "name" box, Windows will print the first EPS file with a header, and then append the subsequent print jobs to the same file.*

### Printing Thumbnails to a Lino Printer

Not all the Lino models support thumbnails. Please test the thumbnail ability to find the best settings. Some Linotronics will print 1×2 thumbnails OK, while a setting of 2×2 may yield insufficient results.

### Printing Registration Marks to a Lino Printer

In Windows, you must place registration marks off the printed page. To do this, the page size in FrameMaker must be smaller than the page size in the printer driver. As an example, if you have a page size of 8.5×11 in FrameMaker and a page size of 9.5×12 in the Lino printer driver, the registration marks will print. If the page sizes are not different, you will get a message from Windows that the registration marks will not fit on the printed page. Some Lino models automatically put registration marks on the page. Check with your service bureau to see if you need to use the Registration Marks setting when you print from any of your Windows applications.

See the Notes section at the end of the Windows platform section in this chapter.

### Printing to an HP LaserJet 4

Before you can successfully print to the HP LaserJet 4 printer, you must download the latest driver from the Microsoft Windows Driver Library by calling (206) 637-9009 with a 2400 baud modem.

You must have Version 31.V1.08 or later of the Microsoft LaserJet 4 printer driver.

Be sure the LaserJet 4 is set up according to the instructions for setting up a PCL printer. Try the print job. If it fails, go into the Control Panel, Printers, Setup dialog box and change the graphics option from HPGL-2 to Raster. The Print TrueType as Graphics option will become available; and you should select it.

Exit the Control Panel and try the print job again. If it fails again, then go to the front panel of the HP LaserJet and set the Page Protect option to ON. Put the printer online, and go back to the Windows Control Panel. In the Control Panel, Printers, Setup option, select on for the Page Protect option. Do not set this option if you have not set it at the printer first.

Try the print job again. If it still fails, then you must set the printer to 300 dots per inch (DPI) to print.

Hewlett-Packard has reported some problems with the HP LaserJet 4 printing vector file formats. In some tests, a 15K vector file would not print in any Windows application. If you are having trouble printing and you have followed all of the steps above, then try to print without any vector files in your documents.

HP reports that adding memory to your printer may help the problem, but Frame Technology has not seen an improvement when printer memory is upgraded.

This problem can potentially occur in any Windows application.

See the Notes section at the end of the Windows platform section in this chapter.

### *Printing to a File*

You can make Windows create Encapsulated PostScript (EPS) or PostScript files out of your document by correctly setting up the printer driver and then following these steps:

1. Go into the Windows Control Panel and select the Printers icon.
2. Note the default Windows printer in the box labeled Default Printer. The printer has to be a PostScript printer to print an EPS or PS file.
3. Select Setup from the Printers dialog box, then select About from the Setup window. Note the version of the driver. This must be Microsoft PostScript Version 3.5, 3.52, 3.53, or 3.55 to print the files correctly. Any other drivers are not supported.
4. Exit the About dialog box, and you will be in the Setup dialog box. Select Options.
5. In the Options dialog box, note the button for Print to Encapsulated Postscript File. This option will force the Windows printer driver to create an EPS file. For the filename, leave the space blank. This will force Windows to prompt you for a filename and path when you try to print. This output is not formatted for use in a Unix environment or Unix printer server.

**NOTE:** *If you put a filename in the "name" box, Windows will print the first EPS file with a header, and then append the subsequent print jobs to the same file.*

A second method of outputting to EPS files is also available. In the Connect window you can choose the port FILE:. When you print, you will be prompted for a filename, but the output will be less likely to print on all printers. This output may be better suited for the Unix environment.

### Notes

To get the latest drivers for Windows, contact Microsoft at (206) 637-9009 via modem. All video and printer drivers have been updated at least three times since Windows 3.1 was released. The latest drivers are faster, more robust, and support true "what you see is what you get" (WYSIWYG) better.

The Print Manager should be enabled to make sure that Windows will not crash when you print.

Since FrameMaker for Windows prints a page description to the Windows Graphic Device Interface (GDI), Frame has no control over the abilities or limitations of any printer driver. Frame Technology can only support printer drivers that have been approved by Microsoft.

## Stacker Disk Compression

PROBLEM Frame, Microsoft, and other vendors of Windows 3.1 applications have seen problems when using the Stacker Disk Compression program. The problems that can occur are a result of improperly configuring the system with the Stacker utility. The following are guidelines from the *Microsoft Windows 3.1 Resource Guide*. If these guidelines are not met, the reliability of the Windows environment is compromised, and Frame will be unable to correct any problems therein.

SOLUTION

1. Stacker should only be run with Windows 3.1. If Windows 3.0 is being used, Frame cannot fix any apparent anomalies with the Windows 3.0 environment and/or FrameMaker.
2. Stacker must be Version 2.0.
3. Never use SMARTDrive or any disk-caching software to cache a stacked volume.

4. Make sure that SMARTDRV.EXE is loaded after SSWAP.COM. This will ensure that SMARTDrive is caching only the physical drives, and not the logical stacked volumes. Frame recommends using the "−" and "+" drive switches for SMARTDrive. (See the *Microsoft Windows User's Guide*, Using the Smartdrv Command Line.) Caching a stacked volume can cause file corruption.
5. If you encounter the message Insufficient Disk Space when adding applications to a stacked volume, it is possible that the disk is full even if the MS-DOS chkdsk command reports significant disk space. The only accurate check of disk space on a stacked volume is to use the MS-DOS dir command.
6. Stacker installation deletes empty subdirectories. If Windows is already set up, prior to the Stacker installation, your Windows TEMP subdirectory will be deleted. Re-create the TEMP subdirectory prior to using Windows again.
7. Do not attempt to create a permanent swap file on a stacked volume. Permanent swap files can only be created on uncompressed volumes.
8. Hard disk defragmentation utilities such as Norton's Speedisk and PCTools' Compress should never be used on a stacked volume. Stacker includes a utility called SDEFREG.EXE that is safe to use on a stacked volume. Do not run SDEFRAG.EXE while Windows is running.

Combining Stacker with QEMM or 386Max memory managers will compound problems. When you can, remove Stacker and the third-party memory managers to achieve the most reliable system, and achieve the maximum system performance.

## Printing

Undocumented feature: PostScript printers under Windows now have the ability to use virtual memory for the PostScript print device.

This virtual memory can be configured in the Control Panel, Printers, Setup, Options, Advanced dialog box. Setting this memory amount correctly will help printing performance greatly and can also alleviate some unexplainable print anomalies. How do you know for what amount to set the PostScript virtual memory? Use an undocumented feature in Windows 3.1. Connect the PostScript printer to Windows, and use the NotePad to verify that it is working. Next, use the DOS prompt icon to get a DOS window. At the prompt, type the following:

```
COPY C:\WINDOWS\SYSTEM\TESTPS.TXT LPT1
```

You may substitute the path to your Windows directory for the one above. If not printing from LPT1, put the device into the line (LPT2, COM1, COM2, etc.). You will get a result on the printer that looks like the following:

| | |
|---|---|
| Max Printer VM(K): | 1500.0 |
| Max Suggested VM(K): | 1105.0 (This is the value you need, never use the first value.) |
| Baud Rate: | 300 |
| Data Bits: | 8 |
| Parity: | None |
| Stop Bits: | 1 |
| Flow Control: | Xon/Xoff |

According to our little PS utility, we should allocate about 1100K (1.1MB) to the Virtual Memory option in the Advanced printer setup for this printer. Do not worry about the baud rate and parity if you are not printing to a COM (Serial) port. This information is only useful when you are printing serially. If the user is printing serially and the print times are slow, the baud rate entry reports how fast the data is coming. Increasing the baud rate can be done with the Ports option of Control Panel.

## Video Drivers

PROBLEM Crashes occur that seem to be caused by video drivers.

SOLUTION With the introduction of Windows 3.0, Microsoft began to deal with the issue of a device independent bitmap (DIB). Before 3.0, all bitmaps were device dependent. This meant that a bitmap created in one environment might have trouble imaging correctly in another environment or even on a printer. Also, the old bitmap format was not extensible or robust—it would not support future enhancements. So, Microsoft has encouraged all application developers, such as Frame, to use the new DIB format instead of the old bitmap format. FrameMaker for Windows uses this new representation, the DIB, exclusively.

Unfortunately, not all device driver manufacturers have been as quick as Frame to embrace this new and positive way of representing bitmaps. Specifically, device driver writers were required to write a new function with Windows 3.0 to support the DIB. This function is called StretchDIB, and it enables the driver to image a DIB. This is a new and fairly complex function, and many device drivers are still having some trouble with it causing program crashes.

**NOTE:** *DIBs are the only spec that will be supported in upcoming versions of Windows, Win32, or Windows NT.*

## MACINTOSH PLATFORM

The following categories pertain to the Macintosh platform.

### Crashes

PROBLEM Some customers have been complaining about FrameMaker crashing or other font problems within applications while running under System 7.0 with 32-bit addressing turned on. The problem is actually within Adobe Type Manager (ATM); there is a bug between ATM pre-2.0.2 Version and System 7.0. You should get a 2.0.2 upgrade.

SOLUTION Version 2.0.2 and later of ATM are System 7.0 compatible. It fixes two problems. First, it's 32-bit clean, meaning that it will work with System 7.0's 32-bit addressing mode. Second, it looks for outline fonts in the Extensions folder as well as in the System folder, which is where the new Finder likes to put them.

This version of ATM also shipped with PhotoShop 2.0.

### Crossing Platforms

PROBLEM When transferring from the Macintosh to the Sun platform using Gatorbox or TOPS, additional "%file" filenames result or a .RSRC directory is created.

SOLUTION Macintosh files have two parts: a resource fork and a data fork. They are just two parts of the same file, like a left side and a right side.

Other platforms do not manage files this way, so various cross-platform server software deals with this two-part file in different ways. For GatorShare, it looks like the following:

%foo.doc (resource fork)
foo.doc (data fork)

For TOPS, Sitka puts the resource fork in a subdirectory, and it looks like:

foo.doc (data fork)
.rsrc/foo.doc (resource fork)

Other vendors do it differently. The examples just given are examples of Apple Double format, where a Macintosh file is split into two pieces. Apple's own A/UX saves files on Unix servers as Apple Single, where they have wrapped the Macintosh file up into a single opaque entity. FrameMaker cannot read Apple Single format files.

The resource fork is a collection of container objects, like CODE (machine executable code), DLOG (dialog layout), STR# (string resources), and so on.

The data fork is where you are supposed to put user-visible data. A simple text file has most of the data in the data fork, but may have Macintosh-specific information (such as tab spacing, font, etc.) stored in the resource fork.

When a file is saved in FrameMaker, all the information needed by all FrameMaker ports goes in the data fork. Macintosh-specific information (such as Macintosh print dialog settings) goes into the resource fork. So, in reading a FrameMaker file across platforms, use a binary transfer mechanism and read the data fork of a file saved as Apple Double.

## Error Messages

PROBLEM When a limited amount of disk space is available and a Microsoft Word file is being filtered, this error message is displayed: "Could not read the temporary filter file. Unable to open another window. Close some other windows and try again."

SOLUTION The temporary filter file is the Maker Interchange Format (MIF) file that is created and then imported into FrameMaker. This file is stored in the System folder. After the new FrameMaker document appears on your screen, the last step of the filtering process is to delete this MIF file, so it is transparent to the user that the file was even created. If you are interested in looking at the MIF file that is created from the filtering process, you can hold down the OPTIONkey at the last part of the filtering process (when the clock is spinning rapidly), and it will not get deleted.

If you get the error message, Unable to open another window..., and you do not have many windows open, it may be that FrameMaker ran out of memory. Try closing all other applications that were running under Multi-finder, or closing other Finder/File windows that may be open. You may even need to split the Word file into two separate files and filter these individually.

If you get the error message, Disk is full..., you will simply have to create more room on the hard disk. In general, an MIF file is big. We also keep two copies of the MIF data around when filtering a Word file. Here is the filtering process:

```
Word File --> Temp File 1: MIF of Text flow + Temp File 2:
MIF of Table data
```

Combine these two files into a third; this is the final MIF file that is imported into FrameMaker. At this point, there are two copies of the MIF output on the disk. That's a lot of data. Then the first two temporary files are deleted. Then FrameMaker reads Temp File 3, creates a document, and then deletes Temp File 3.

If a 500K Word file makes a 5MB MIF file (possible if it contains tables), then at least 10MB of hard disk space would be needed. Also, the free space needs to be on the hard disk that holds the System folder.

If you are filtering Microsoft Word files that contain many tables and/or graphics, you can expect the resulting MIF files to be large. A one-page table with many rows and columns can actually be a fairly large MIF file since many MIF statements are needed for each part of the table.

PROBLEM In loading FrameMaker, the error message Symbol Font not Installed is displayed and the program does not start.

SOLUTION This means that you do not have the Symbol font installed on the Macintosh. If you are running System 7.0.x, you merely need to open the Fonts suitcase included with FrameMaker, select all in the folder, and drag the selection on top of the System folder. Under 6.0.x, you must run the Font/DA Mover utility, which is included on the system installer disks. The Font/DA Mover can also be obtained from Apple Authorized dealers and most online services, such as America Online, CompuServe, GEnie, Delphi, and AppleLink.

## Excel Imports

PROBLEM When importing Macintosh Excel 4.0 information into FrameMaker with the SHIFT key/Copy Picture option in Excel 4.0, the pictures have jagged lines.

SOLUTION Excel does not copy hairline information to the Clipboard.

## PostScript, EPS, EPSF, and EPSI

There are three distinct encapsulated Postscript formats:

- EPS (Encapsulated PostScript) binary usually from PC and scanner applications These binary files have either a TIFF (Tagged Image File Format) preview image or a Windows metafile preview image.
- EPSF (Encapsulated PostScript Format) from Macintosh applications such as Adobe Illustrator These files have a QuickDraw PICT in the resource fork. Only Macintoshes know how to read a PICT file. This is the preview image.
- EPSI (Encapsulated PostScript Interchange) interchange format These files have a bitmap embedded in the PostScript as comments for a preview image. (Sun Maker reads these.)

There are two relevant differences between an EPSF file and a standard PostScript file. First, the EPSF file is set up in a way that makes it easy to stick the PostScript in the middle of some other PostScript (much like an anchored frame). A few things make it easy, including the fact that there is information at the beginning of the EPSF file to allow the entire PostScript image to be scaled easily. Second, a Macintosh-generated EPSF file can contain a non-PostScript representation of the image. Instead of being PostScript, it is a Macintosh PICT format. That lets a Macintosh application display the image on the screen using the PICT data and lets the image be printed on a PostScript printer using the PostScript data. So the EPSF file can contain two representations of the image, one for the screen and one for the printer. That double representation is needed if you use a system that does not have display PostScript capability. On a system with display PostScript, the special screen image is not needed.

The EPSF functionality that Frame has added lets the EPSF file be imported into FrameMaker, just like a raster file (by reference). On the screen, you see a rough (bitmap) representation of the image. Frame uses the real PostScript on printout.

On the Macintosh:

1. FrameMaker can import EPSI supported by the Sun (ASCII EPSI 2.0).
2. FrameMaker can import EPSF generated by Macintosh applications such as Illustrator.
   a. If you import by copy, and choose Save FrameImage Facets, by the time you get over to the Sun, you will have three facets: PostScript (called EPSI by Sun), FrameImage, and QuickDraw PICT. Sun will use the FrameImage to display to the screen and the postscript to print. The Macintosh will use the QuickDraw PICT to display to the screen and the postscript to print. If you do not choose to save FrameImage facets while on the Macintosh, you will get a gray box on the Sun's screen, but you should print just fine.
   b. If you import by reference, the Sun does not understand Macintosh EPSF files and you should run the converter utility. Then, both Macintosh and Sun Versions of FrameMaker should be able to continue to use the graphic as referenced artwork (an external file).
   c. The converter utility is for the Sun product, and so is not included in the Macintosh product.
3. FrameMaker can import binary EPS files generated by many DOS applications and will show a preview image if it uses TIFF.
   a. If you import by copy, same as 2.a above.
   b. If you import by reference, Sun can't read the file. the suggested route is to read the file into Illustrator and save as EPSF, then run Frame's converter utility.

Regarding EPS that does not import and does not print:

EPSI files can be directly printed; depending on the application that generates it, you may have to add a single line to the bottom of the file that says: show page if there isn't one already there (the EPS spec says it's optional, although most applications put it in so you can in fact print directly as a test).

## UNIX PLATFORM

The following categories pertain to the Unix platform.

### Booting Problems

PROBLEM Every time FrameMaker is launched it asks for a license number.

SOLUTION The home directory contains a folder called .NEXT, which has a file named .NEXTDEFAULTS. This is where the license number is written. If the file or its folder do not have write permissions enabled for the owner and group, the license number will have to be re-entered every time FrameMaker is launched. Please do not attempt modifications to these files yourself. Ask your system administrator for assistance.

PROBLEM When FrameMaker is launched, error messages such as the following are displayed—maker: No type Kayna in fontlist; substituting default values.

SOLUTION This means that you are probably launching International FrameMaker and do not have the proper fonts installed. In this case, purchase the necessary fonts.

### Color

PROBLEM Spot colors print out as black on a black-and-white printer instead of shades of gray.

SOLUTION Print your document to a file. Edit the PostScript file:

```
line 15: % Uncomment this line to force b&w on color printer
line 16: % /FMPrintInColor false def
```

Change these lines to read:

```
line 15: % Uncomment this line to force b&w on color printer
line 16: /FMPrintInColor true def
```

Notice that the "%" is removed in line 16 and false is changed to true.

If you simply uncommitted the original line, you would force black-and-white output on a color printer. To create the gray spot colors, you want to force color output on a black-and-white printer. So, to do this, you change the true to false.

To change this for all output, you can edit the $FMHOME/-.FMINIT2.0/POSTSCRIPT_PROLOG file.

**IMPORTANT:** *Before you edit the POSTSCRIPT_PROLOG file, be sure to make a backup copy!*

PROBLEM Color information in a screen capture that is done on a color X terminal changes to a black-and-white bitmapped image when imported.

SOLUTION The color information is still there, and the document will print in color on a color printer. To see the color onscreen, start Frame-Maker like this:

```
install_dir/bin/maker +colorImages
```

The default behavior is to not display full-color images because that causes other windows on the screen to change colors. This is because there are a limited number of colors available on the display, and when Frame set the color map up to use Frame's colors, other windows will have their colors altered, sometimes drastically. If you really want to have color images turned on all of the time, set up a resource in your ~/.XDEFAULTS file like this:

```
Maker.colorImages: TRUE
```

## General Troubleshooting for Color

Here is a good set of resources to use for troubleshooting color mapping problems while importing gray scale and color images. Sometimes imported graphics do not appear to be using all the colors or grays they should be. It is possible that colors set up for FrameMaker (such as for the vertical scroll bar, document background, and so on) are using part of FrameMaker's color map, and thus imported graphics cannot use all colors necessary. Back up your .XDEFAULTS file and put the following resources alone in your .XDEFAULTS file to ensure all colors will be utilized by imported graphics:

```
*Maker*foreground: White
Maker*background: Black
Maker.colorDocs: True
Maker.colorImages: True
Maker.useDps: False
```

**NOTE:** *If you are using OpenWindows or other Window managers described in the release notes that need "focus" resources in the .XDEFAULTS file, also add those resources.*

## CorelDraw

PROBLEM An imported CorelDraw graphic displays fine on the Unix platform, but will not print. There is an empty space where the graphic should be.

SOLUTION Search for EPSI (Encapsulated PostScript Interchange) in the Maker Interchange Format (MIF) file and look at the line endings in the inset. Each line should end in \n rather than \r or \r\n. Since the file was transferred to the Unix workstation from a PC, the line endings were inappropriate. You must edit the file, replacing the current line endings with \n. This problem is not limited to CorelDraw files.

## File Transfers

PROBLEM Transferring files between FrameMaker platforms using the Kermit transfer protocol does not work well.

SOLUTION When transferring files across platforms, remember that FrameMaker files are binary and compatible with the Maker Interchange Format (MIF) on all platforms. This cannot make up for differences in the hardware and operating systems, however. Since the various machines are different, so is the structure that the machines manipulate the various files. Kermit is a transfer protocol that can be used to send a file to another platform without having to consider these differences in the systems. Kermit can send two type of files, an ASCII file (like MIF) and a binary file (like FASL). As a default, Kermit is set up to send ASCII files. As a default, FrameMaker is set up to save binary files. This is where any problems may lie.

If you have a standard FrameMaker binary file (FASL) you will need to set up Kermit to send (on the Unix side for instance) in binary mode, and to receive (on the PC side for instance) in binary mode. Both sides of the transfer need to be in binary mode. The exact command to do so depends on the platform and version of Kermit you are running, but the key factor is that you are running two Kermits, one on each side of the transfer, and they both have to explicitly be told to go into binary mode.

In some cases, the two Kermit protocols are slightly different. This is not rare as there are many flavors of Kermit. When all else fails, you can save the FrameMaker file as MIF (ASCII) and send it to another system with the standard default Kermit mode.

The MIF file is not as good, since it is many times bigger, and therefore many times slower to transfer. The preferred method of moving FrameMaker document files among the Unix, Macintosh, and Microsoft Windows (DOS) platforms is a binary transfer of the file. Only when your file transfer method is unable to move binary files without modifying the file between systems would you want to use MIF through a line-oriented ASCII text file transfer.

### *Advantages of Binary Transfer Over ASCII Transfer*

FrameMaker binary files are much smaller than FrameMaker MIF files; thus file transfer time is much shorter. Transferring a MIF file may cause changes to FrameMaker variables such as Creation Date and Modification Date that are within the document. It may also change the printer settings for the document. These are all maintained, however, if you transfer the file in binary format.

### *Stripping Line-Ending Characters*

If you get a corrupted file when transferring a binary file, the file transfer software you are using may not be set up for binary transfer. This means that certain line-ending characters will be stripped off. In binary files, every character is used, and stripping off any character corrupts the file. The possible line-ending characters are character 13 (Carriage Return-Macintosh), character 10 (Line Feed-Unix), or a combination of both (DOS). If a file transfer software is set up for line-oriented ASCII text transfer, it may automatically convert the line ending characters it is set up for in the transfer, thus corrupting the binary file.

### *Setting to Binary Mode*

By default, many file transfer software packages are set up for line-oriented ASCII text transfers. In order to send a binary file, you need to change the settings or issue a command to put them in binary transfer mode. In some file transfer packages (most notably Kermit), this must be done on both machines involved in the file transfer.

## Saving with FrameImage

When importing graphics into a FrameMaker document that you intend to transfer between platforms, you may want to import the graphic by copy, not reference, so the graphics are completely contained in the document. When transferring files from either FrameMaker for the Macintosh or FrameMaker for Microsoft Windows, you need go to File Preferences and turn on the Save FrameImage with Imported Graphics option to ensure graphics will be viewable on other platforms. If you do not select Save FrameImage and your graphics are EPSF format, the images may not display but they will still print. For EPS graphics, Save FrameImage only affects the preview image. Other graphics such as TIFF and PITCH will not display or print from FrameMaker on the Unix platform unless FrameImage is turned on.

## Opening FrameMaker Unix Files on the Macintosh

When bringing files from a Unix workstation to a Macintosh, you will not immediately be able to double-click the document from the desktop to open it. Because the file originated in a Unix environment, the file type will be text and the creator Unix. You can open the file one of two ways. You can use the Open command from FrameMaker's File menu, or you can change the file type to FASL and the creator to From using ResEdit or a similar application. Some files may not show up in the Open dialog box after a transfer. Because FrameMaker looks for and lists the files that it owns, it won't list the files that were just transferred because the file type and creator were set to TEXT/Unix. To list all available files, hold down the Option key when you select Open from the File menu. This will list all files in the current folder/directory.

## Graphics

PROBLEM A document created on a Macintosh and moved to a Unix platform shows all graphics as gray boxes.

SOLUTION Make sure that the graphics were imported by copy, not reference, into the FrameMaker Macintosh document. Also on FrameMaker for the Macintosh, under the File/Preferences menu, make sure to check the box Save FrameImage with Imported Graphics, then resave the document.

PROBLEM An Encapsulated PostScript (EPS) file created by Micrographix Designer will not import into FrameMaker for Unix platforms. A message appears stating that this is not an importable file. If it is imported into a FrameMaker file on the PC and that file is then sent over to a Unix machine, the file will display but not print.

SOLUTION Micrographix Designer has the capability of saving in many different formats, notably Paintbrush (PCX) and Computer Graphics

Metafile (CGM). You can choose one of those formats (the FilterPak will be needed if CGM is chosen).

Micrographix Designer does not generate proper EPS. However, if you remove lines 51 and 52, it seems to get it into good enough shape to print.

The PostScript file is creating and downloading its own fonts. The EPS file also contains an illegal lettertray command. This command is not valid in an EPS file.

To complicate matters, not only does it illegally use the lettertray command but it also goes to great length to contravene any error handler you might try to use (such as EHANDLER.PS) to track down the problem, making it difficult to troubleshoot these files.

PROBLEM If you start FrameMaker on one machine and create a document with images imported by copy, then start FrameMaker on another machine that uses the same home directory as the first machine, the FrameMaker on the first machine will lose its imported by copy images! The images are lost from the document. You will have to re-import, or revert to an earlier saved version of the file.

SOLUTION The reason is that FrameMaker temporarily stores imported-by-copy images in ~/.makerswapXXXX, which is a directory off your home directory. The second maker on the other machine sees the ~/.makerswapXXXX directory already there, thinks that it is a stale swap directory, deletes the first maker's ~/.makerswapXXXX directory and then proceeds to create its own ~/.makerswapYYYY. When FrameMaker on the first machine tries to save, ~/.makerswapXXXX is no longer there and things go haywire at that point. The workaround is to save all your documents and quit FrameMaker before starting the new maker on the new machine.

If you were not running on two machines at the same time, then lost graphics may be the result of a previous FrameMaker crash.

**NOTE:** *Imported-by-copy images live in the ~/.makerswap directory until you save and quit the document. In other words, the *.inset files stored in the ~/.makerswap directory will remain after you have executed a save but will be removed once you quit the document. The ~/.makerswap directory itself remains until you exit the FrameMaker session.*

## HP-VUE

PROBLEM Opening a document on a color HP workstation running HP-VUE is fine. Opening a document or template on a monochrome workstation and document is white text on white background. Changing Maker.winrectForeground doesn't work.

SOLUTION HP-VUE creates a color map where the color definition gets mapped to white in gray scale. You must go to the Style Manager in HP-VUE (an icon that appears as a painter's palette). In the Style Manager, select Color and choose "Gray scale" from the list of color palettes. If applied, this becomes the default color map on that workstation. If you object to some gray choices, use the "Modify" command in the Color selector to change some colors individually.

A gray scale X display is really a color display, with all of the colors in the range from white to black. The color maps are translated into a ramp from white to black, with each color mapping to a shade of gray. In the default installation, the color of the document background and the color of the foreground are mapped to nearly adjacent grays. The gray scale map is chosen by HP to have the greatest contrast between colors as viewed in gray. It is merely an unfortunate coincidence that the colors Frame has predefined get mapped to an invisible white when displayed to a gray scale monitor.

## Platform

PROBLEM Running OpenLook Window Manager (OLMW) on an NCD Xterminal results in the error, Cannot connect to NeWS server. The host is a SPARC system running OpenWindows. Xterminals are connected to SPARC.

SOLUTION FrameMaker for OpenLook will not run on an Xterminal.

OpenWindows is a Window server that contains three personalities: X11, NeWS, and SunView. These three window services work together to run X, NeWS, and SunTools clients. This is why all three versions of FrameMaker will run under OpenWindows. FrameMaker for X runs in OpenWindows attaching to the X server, FrameMaker for OpenLook needs the NeWS server, and SunView FrameMaker uses the SunTools capabilities.

The FrameMaker for OpenLook product is kind of a misnomer; it is really an OpenWindows/NeWS product. It uses the server to do things like PostScript rendering on-screen via calls to the NeWS-server inside OpenWindows.

OpenLook, however, is a window *manager* (distinct from the window *server*). It does things like control the shapes of buttons, layer windows over each other, arrange menus, buttons, and check boxes.

To complicate matters, The OpenLook Window Manager will run on X11-based servers—it doesn't need to have NeWS. X-terminals, to my knowledge, only run the window server "Xdm". Xdm is an X11 server, not a NeWS server. So, you are running an Xterminal, an X11-based window server, and the Open Look Window Manager. FrameMaker is looking for the OpenWindows NeWS server on the Xterminal and cannot find one.

To demonstrate this is not just a FrameMaker problem, try running the OPENWIN/BIN/PAGEVIEW program, which views a PostScript file. This program also requires NeWS services, and will not display on an Xterminal running an Xserver.

The short and long of it is that FrameMaker for OpenLook will not run on Xterminals, because, though they may be running the OpenLook Window Manager, they are not running OpenWindows with the NeWS server.

## PostScript

PROBLEM In running Display PostScript, an imported PostScript file shows up on the screen as PostScript code.

SOLUTION When running the X Version of FrameMaker with the Display PostScript option, you will only be able to view Encapsulated PostScript files, with or without preview images. Raw PostScript will still appear as PostScript code. Only the FrameMaker for OpenLook product has the ability to interpret the PostScript code and display an image on the screen.

## Printing

PROBLEM It's possible to print to a file, but not to the printer. How does FrameMaker print?

SOLUTION The following describes how FrameMaker prints:

- FrameMaker generates an IPL (intermediate printer language) file, which describes the document.
- FrameMaker runs the FMPRINTDRIVER.PS program, passing it a number of arguments, one of which is 0 or 1 depending on whether or not you clicked the Print Only To File button.
- FMPRINTDRIVER.PS reads the IPL file and generates a PostScript file. Then it looks at the Print Only To File option it got from FrameMaker. If Print Only To File was 1, then the program copies the generated PostScript file to the filename you entered in the Print dialog. If the Print Only To File option was 0, then the program runs the shell script $FMHOME/.fminit2.0/FMlpr. This shell script calls the Unix program "lpr" with different options.

If you can print to a file, then FrameMaker is doing its part of the job. If you cannot print directly to the printer, then perhaps something differs about the lpr options that FrameMaker uses versus the lpr command you are using. In the FMlpr shell script, you can add a word "echo" in front of every lpr statement. This would not run the command, but would print it to the window where FrameMaker was started. Then compare the two lpr commands and see what differs. Try running the command manually on the .PS files and see what the result is. You may have to modify the FMlpr script in order to have it work correctly on his system.

## Resources

PROBLEM Setting the maker.Visual and maker.Depth X-Resources in $FMHOME/.fminit2.0/xresources/Maker, does not make resources available for running FrameMaker on a 24-bit machine.

SOLUTION The .visual and .depth resources cannot be set in $FMHOME/-.fminit2.0/xresources/Maker. The code to set these up is in XtInitialize, which is called before the local resource database has been read. The current workaround is to set them in each user's .XDEFAULTS file, /usr/lib/X11/app-defaults/Maker, or one of the other standard resource files.

## Screen Display

PROBLEM FrameMaker disappears from the screen.

SOLUTION This is usually caused by low memory situations. Disappearing applications are a common occurrence on the NeXT when memory is low. Your NeXT computer should be configured as follows:

A monochrome NeXT should have at least 12MB of random access memory (RAM).
A color NeXT should have 16MB of RAM at the bare minimum.

# VIII

## Appendixes

# A

## Glossary of Terms

THIS appendix lists common terms used in the publishing industry.

**ASCENDER** The part of a lowercase letter that extends above the x-height.

**BASELINE** The imaginary horizontal line on which type rests.

**BEZIER CURVE** A curve that has adjustment points so it can be redrawn and rendered correctly by moving the points on the curve.

**BINDING** The way in which pages are joined together. Types of bindings include perfect, saddle-stitched, case, comb, and so on.

**BITMAP** A format used to create fonts, art, or images with a dot pattern. When bitmap images are enlarged by graphics programs, the screen is divided into a grid (map), and each square is filled with a color or left blank to form the image.

**BLEED** A method of letting ink reach the edge of the page without gumming up the press or interfering with the grippers that hold the paper. This is accomplished by printing on a piece of paper that is larger than the final size. The ink crosses the trim line but does not reach the edge of the paper. Then the paper is trimmed.

**BLUELINE** A proof copy generated by the negatives used to produce the printing plates. This proof is usually sent to the client for approval before the plates are made.

**CALLOUT** Text that describes various parts of an illustration. Usually the callouts are referenced to the illustration with arrows.

**CAMERA-READY COPY** The completed layout of text, graphics, and so on, that is ready to be photographed for printing.

**CLIP ART** Illustrations, line drawings, designs, borders, and other graphic elements that are cut from printed sheets or imported as graphic files. An inexpensive alternative to custom-made art, clip art is copyright-free.

CMYK An abbreviation for cyan, magenta, yellow, and black. See color model.

COLOR MODEL A system that explains how one color relates to another. FrameMaker uses the CMYK (cyan, magenta, yellow, and black), RGB (red, green, and blue), and HLS (hue, lightness, and saturation) models. The CMYK model is used for four-color process printing; the RGB model is used for on-screen color; and the HLS model is traditionally used by artists.

COLOR SEPARATION The process of creating four halftone transparencies from a full-color original. The colors are separated into cyan, magenta, yellow, and black (the CMYK model) for the purpose of printing process color.

CONTINUOUS TONE Continuous shades of gray as found in a photograph.

CREEP The problem incurred by saddle stitching in which middle pages in a folded signature extend beyond the outer pages.

CROP To trim portions of a visual.

CROP MARKS Small marks on a mechanical showing a printer where to trim the printed paper for the final size.

DESCENDER The lower part of a lowercase letter that extends below the baseline.

DIGITIZE To convert to a digital format or bitmap.

DISPLAY TYPE Type that is used generally as a headline or attention-getter rather than body text.

DROPPED CAP An oversized first letter of a paragraph.

DPI An abbreviation for dots per inch, a measure of resolution. The greater number of dots, the sharper the image (the higher the resolution).

DUMMY A rough layout showing the placement of text and graphics. Also a folded and trimmed mock-up to show the size of the final printed piece.

DUOTONE A halftone separated into two negatives and printed in two colors.

EM DASH A dash equal in length to the size of the font. Called an "em" dash because it is approximately the width of the letter "M." It is used to show a break in thought.

EM SPACE A space equal in length to the size of the font. Approximately the width of the letter "M."

EN DASH A dash equal in length to half an em dash. Called an "en" dash because it is approximately the width of the letter "N." The en dash is used to show a range, like 1–4.

EN SPACE A space equal in length to half an em space. Approximately the width of the letter "N."

EPS-ENCAPSULATED POSTSCRIPT A format used for storing a PostScript description of a page or image. Also called EPSF.

FEATHERING A method of adding space evenly between all lines in a column.

FLAT Holds all the negatives of the pages that will print on one side of the paper. Printing plates are created from flats.

FOLIO A page number.

FONT A single size and typeface. For example, 12-point Times Roman and 14-point Times Roman are two different fonts. The word *font* is sometimes used interchangeably with *typeface*, but this is not technically correct.

FOUR-COLOR PROCESS The process of overprinting four halftone images that have the colors separated into cyan, magenta, yellow, and black to produce a full-color graphic that simulates virtually the entire color spectrum.

FPO For Position Only. Used to designate an item as a mock-up and not a final piece to be printed.

GALLEY In typesetting, a section of type output on paper for the purpose of proofreading or paste-up.

GRID Horizontal and vertical lines that intersect to form a visual framework to aid in the placement of copy and graphics.

GUTTER The space between two columns. Called the gap in FrameMaker 4. In printing, also refers to the inside margins of pages that are connected to the spine.

HALFTONE A continuous-tone image that has been photographed through a screen to produce an image formed with dots.

HLS An abbreviation for hue, lightness, and saturation. See color model.

KNOCKOUT The removal of one color when one color would normally print over the other color. This knockout allows the second color to print directly on the paper instead of on the first color of ink. When one color ink prints on a second color ink, the resulting color is not the same as it would be if printed directly on the paper.

IMPOSITION The arrangement of pages on a flat so they will appear in proper sequence when printed and folded.

KERN To decrease the space between selected pairs of letters.

LAID Paper with parallel lines running though it in the same color as the paper.

LEADER DOTS Evenly spaced dots (or other characters) used to guide the eye between two text items. Often used in a table of contents.

LEADING The vertical space between lines of type. Usually measured from baseline to baseline.

LIGATURE A single character made by combining two letters like "fi" and "fl."

LINEN A textured paper usually with a high cotton content.

MECHANICAL See camera-ready copy.

MOCK-UP See dummy.

OFFSET PRINTING A method of printing whereby the page is photographically reproduced on a plate that is placed on a cylinder. Ink is transferred from the plate to a rubber blanket and then to the paper.

ORPHAN A single line at the bottom of a page that has been separated from the rest of a paragraph. See also widow.

OVERPRINT Printing one complete color object over another. FrameMaker 4 uses this method instead of trapping to avoid registration problems.

PANTONE MATCHING SYSTEM A system of specifying colors of ink. Each color has an assigned number and can be selected from a swatch book. Printers then use a specific recipe to mix the ink to match the color.

PERFECT BINDING Assembling signatures of a book by gluing them along the spine and attaching a cover.

PHOTOSTAT A photo copy of a black image. The photostat can be an enlargement or a reduction of the original. Photostats are often pasted directly to mechanicals.

PICA A unit of measure equal to 1/6 of an inch.

PLATE A metal or plastic image used on printing presses to transfer the image to paper. Metal plates are superior to (and more expensive than) plastic plates and are used for large print runs and color work.

POINT A unit of measure equal to 1/12 of a pica and 1/72 of an inch. (There are actually 72.27 points in an inch, but most desktop publishing programs round this off to 72.)

PMT Same as photostat and velox.

PMS See PANTONE MATCHING SYSTEM.

POSTSCRIPT A page description language devised by Adobe and used by many laser printers. PostScript can be used on many computer platforms and output devices.

PROCESS COLOR See four-color process.

PULL QUOTES A quote pulled from a body of text and enlarged or emphasized to attract the reader's attention and pique his or her interest.

REGISTRATION MARKS On a mechanical, circular marks with two intersecting lines in the middle used to ensure the proper alignment of printing plates. Generally used for four-color printing.

RGB An abbreviation for red, green, and blue. See color model.

SADDLE STITCHING Assembling pages of a book by stapling them in the fold of the spine, so called because the pages are laid under the staple head like the saddle on a horse.

SANS SERIF Typefaces without small strokes at the end of lines that form the characters.

SCALE To change the size of a graphic.

SCREEN FREQUENCY The number of dots or lines per inch on a halftone screen.

SERIF Small decorative strokes at the end of lines that form the characters.

SEPARATION See color separation.

SERVICE BUREAU A business that provides desktop publishing services and high-quality output (usually from imagesetters). Typically service bureaus charge for time on the imagesetter by the page or by the minute.

SIGNATURE A section of pages in a book or long publication that have been printed on the same piece of paper, folded down to size, and trimmed.

SPOT COLOR A nonprocess color that is added to a page, usually a PMS color.

STRIPPING The process of positioning negatives in flats for the purpose of making a plate for printing.

TAG In FrameMaker 4, the name that identifies a group of characteristics that are applied to a paragraph or a character. Also the name applied to a flow.

TEMPLATE A previously designed document that used a specific layout, paragraph tags, visuals, and so on.

THUMBNAIL A printed image of a page in reduced size. FrameMaker 4 can print a maximum of 256 thumbnails per page.

TIFF (TAGGED IMAGE FILE FORMAT) A file format used for paint-type images.

TRAP A slight overlap of ink along the edge where two colors meet to prevent white from showing between the colors when printed. Trapping is used to enhance registration.

TRIM To cut away the excess paper so the final size is achieved. Crop marks show where the cuts should be made.

VELOX A screened, black-and-white print of a halftone. Same as PMT or photostat.

VISUAL A graphic (photograph, illustration, drawing, graph, chart, and so on).

WATERMARK A mark put in paper during the manufacturing process. When held to the light, the mark can be read. It is usually the name of the paper, such as "Classic Laid."

WEB PRESS A press that prints on paper from a roll that is called a web. Newspapers are printed on web presses.

WIDOW A single line at the top of a page that has been separated from the rest of the paragraph. See also orphan.

WOVE A paper surface with a soft, smooth finish.

X-ACTO KNIFE A sharp scalpel-like tool used to cut copy and visuals during paste up.

X-HEIGHT The height of a lowercase letter without its ascenders or descenders; roughly equivalent to the height of an *x*.

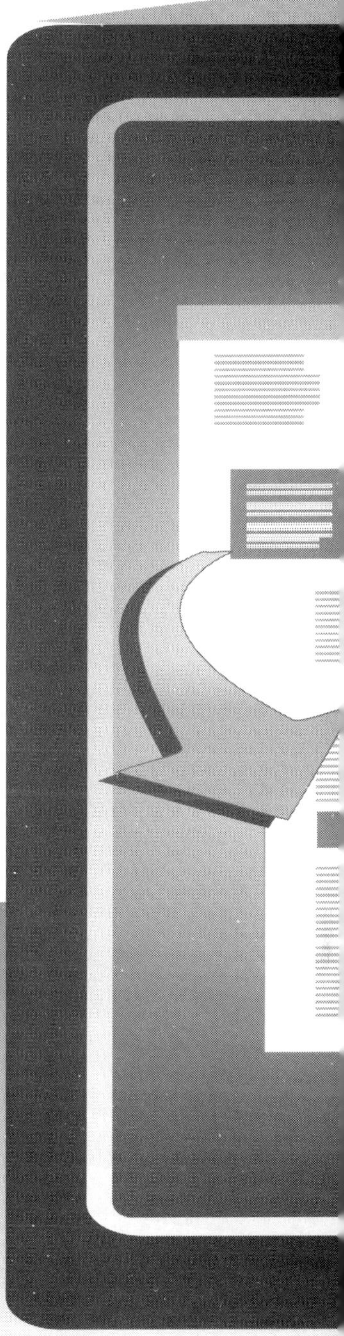

# B

# Installing FrameMaker 4

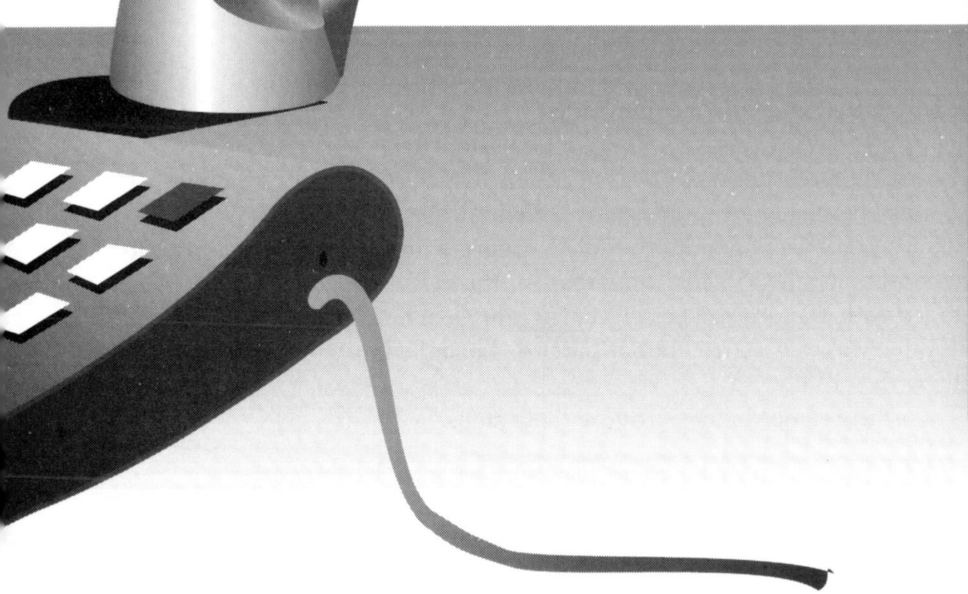

To install FrameMaker 4, you need the following hardware:

- 80386 central processing unit (CPU)
- 8MB of random access memory (RAM)
- 10MB free space on the hard disk
- Video graphics array (VGA) monitor and adapter
- Mouse

The following software is also required:

- DOS 3.3 or higher
- Windows 3.1 (running in enhanced 386 mode)

Adobe Type Manager is recommended.

FrameMaker 4 supports TrueType fonts, which come with Windows 3.1, and fonts managed by a program called Adobe Type Manager (ATM). FrameMaker 4 also includes the ATM program and a standard set of fonts that can be installed if, for some reason, the ATM program has not been installed with Windows. The ATM program must be installed before installing FrameMaker 4. After FrameMaker 4 is installed, it will work automatically with ATM.

To install FrameMaker 4, follow these steps:

1. Start Windows.
2. Choose File, Run from the Program Manager window.
3. Insert FrameMaker 4 Disk 1 in the floppy drive.

4. Type **a:setup** (or **b:\setup**) and press ENTER. The FrameMaker 4 Installation dialog box displays as shown in Figure B-1.
5. Choose the Type of Installation, the FrameMaker Language Interface, and click Continue. The FrameMaker 4 Registration dialog box displays as shown in Figure B-2.
6. Type the user name and press TAB to move to the next line.
7. Type the company name (if appropriate) and press TAB to move to the next line.
8. Type the Registration Number (including the dashes) and press ENTER. The FrameMaker 4 Installation Options dialog box displays as shown in Figure B-3.
9. Select the desired options in the FrameMaker 4 Installation Options dialog box and click the Install button. FrameMaker 4 is installed in a subdirectory called MAKER4. If a different directory name is desired, click the Set Path button, specify the desired path, and click Continue. If limited space is not a problem, install everything. After the training files and sample files have been used, they can be deleted to free space. If space is limited, install the program files and selected filters. To select filters, click the Select Filters button. All filters are selected by default. Click the filter names that you do not want to install to deselect them.

**FIGURE B-1** *The Installation dialog box*

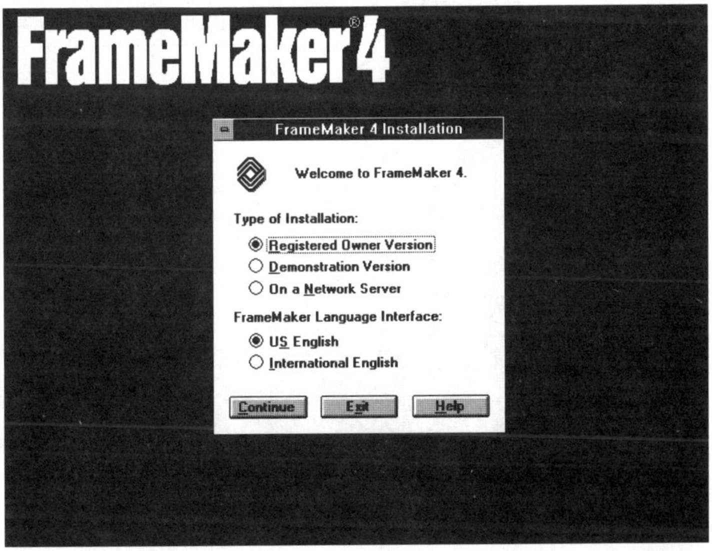

**FIGURE B-2**

*The Registration dialog box*

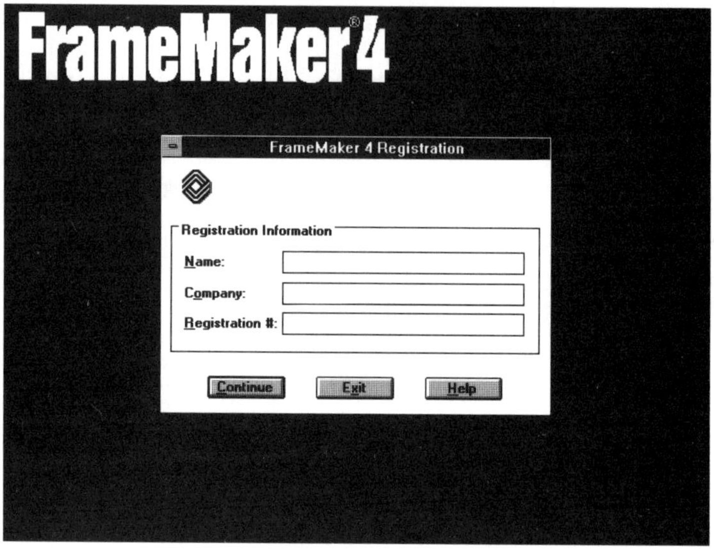


**FIGURE B-3**

*The Installation Options dialog box*

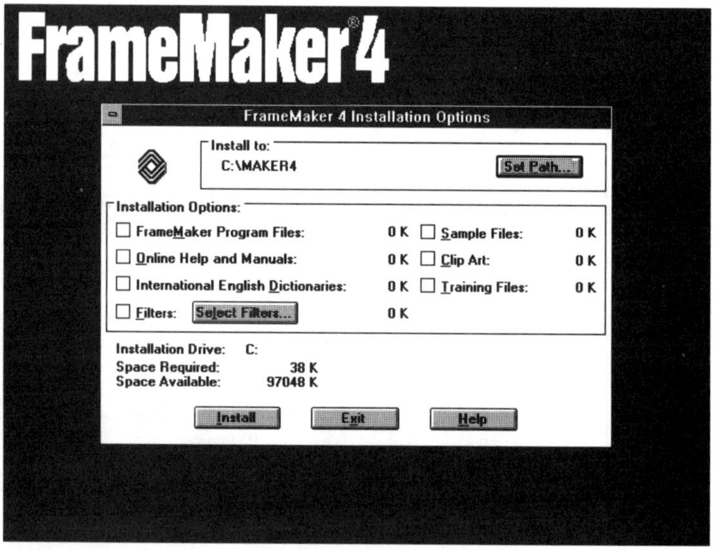

10. The files from the first disk are decompressed and installed.
11. When prompted, insert the second disk and click OK.
12. Continue inserting disks as prompted and clicking OK. During the process, FrameMaker 4 shows the percent of completion in a bar graph.
13. When the last disk is installed, the Frame Products window will be displayed briefly in Windows and then the FrameMaker 4 Installation-Exit Message is displayed telling you that FrameMaker 4 has been installed successfully. Click OK to return to Windows.

## Starting FrameMaker 4

To start FrameMaker 4, first start Windows. Then open or go to the Frame Products window and double-click the FrameMaker 4 icon.

**NOTE:** *The first time FrameMaker 4 is started, three files are automatically opened. The first file (welcome) is a welcome document that takes approximately 10 minutes to tour. The second file (demodoc) is a demonstration document, and the third file (relnotes) is a document that contains last-minute information and tips. It is a good idea to print this third document.*

# C

# Review of Basic Functions

THIS appendix contains the steps to perform some of the most common FrameMaker functions. These functions are covered in the tutorial that comes with FrameMaker, but are not covered in any detail in this book. Use this information as a quick reference or to review your knowledge. At the end of this appendix is a table that summarizes the control-key shortcuts associated with menu commands.

### *Apply a character format*

Select the text, then use one of the following methods:

- Display the Character Format Catalog and select a format.
- Choose Format and select a font, size, or style.

### *Apply a paragraph format*

Select the paragraph(s), then use one of the following methods:

- Select a format from the pop-up menu in the formatting bar.
- Display the Paragraph Catalog and select a format.
- Choose Format and select a font, size, or style. (This method only works if the complete paragraph(s) is/are highlighted.

### *Cascade windows*

Press SHIFT+F4or choose Window, Cascade.

### *Close a file*

Press CTRL+W or choose File, Close. If you have unsaved changes, FrameMaker 4 will ask you if you want to save before closing the file.

### *Copy text or object(s)*

Select the text or object(s). Click the Copy icon or press CTRL+C or choose Edit, Copy.

### *Create a new file*

Click the New icon or press CTRL+N or choose File, New. A dialog box is displayed. If you choose Portrait or Landscape, the new file will be opened immediately. To specify the paper size, margins, columns, and pagination, choose Custom, make selections, and choose Create.

### *Create a table*

Choose Table, Insert Table. The Insert Table dialog box is displayed. Make the desired selections and then choose Insert.

### *Cut text or object(s)*

Select the text or object(s). Click the Cut icon or press CTRL+X or choose Edit, Cut. The text or object is stored on the Clipboard and can be retrieved with Paste.

### *Display/Hide the formatting bar*

Choose View, Formatting Bar.

### *Display/Hide the graphics tools*

To display the tools, click the Graphics tools icon in the right border or choose Graphics, Tools. To hide the tools, double-click the control menu in the upper-left corner of the tools window or press ALT+F4.

### *Display/Hide the QuickAccess bar*

Choose View, QuickAccess Bar.

### *Display/Hide the rulers*

Choose View, Rulers.

### *Display/Hide the window borders*

Choose View, Borders.

### *Exit FrameMaker 4*

Choose File, Exit. If you have unsaved changes in the file, FrameMaker 4 will ask if you want to save before closing.

### *Find or find and change*

Choose Edit, Find/Change. The Find/Change window is displayed. Select text, character format, paragraph tag, etc., from the Find pop-up menu. If you select text, enter the text to find. If you do not want to change the text, paragraph tag, etc., click Find. If you want to change the item searched for, make a selection from the Change pop-up menu and choose Change, or Change & Find, or Change All In. When finished, close the window.

### *Go to a Master page*

Choose View, Master Pages.

### *Go to a specific page number*

Press CTRL+Gor choose View, Go to Page. Enter the desired page number and choose Go.

### *Go to another window*

Click on the window if part of it is visible or choose Window and select the desired window.

### *Import a graphic file*

Choose File, Import, File. The Import File dialog box is displayed. Enter the file name, and choose Import by Reference or Copy Into Document. Choose Import.

### *Help (display contents)*

Click the Help icon or press F1 or choose Help, Contents. For context sensitive help, press SHIFT+F1 or choose Help, Context Sensitive.

### *Open an existing file*

Click the Open icon or press CTRL+O or choose File, Open. A dialog box is displayed. Select the desired file from the list box and choose Open.

### *Paste text or object stored on Clipboard*

Click the Paste icon or press CTRL+V or choose Edit, Paste.

### *Print a file*

Click the Print icon or press CTRL+P or choose File, Print. The Print dialog box displays. Make desired selections and choose Print. To change the printer, choose File, Print Setup, specify the desired file, and click OK.

### *Save a file that has been saved before*

Click the Save icon or press CTRL+S or choose File, Save.

### *Save a file that has not been saved*

Click the Save icon or press CTRL+S or choose File, Save. The Save Document dialog box displays. Be sure the path is the one you want. Type a filename and choose Save.

### *Save a file with a new name/path*

Choose File, Save As. The Save Document dialog box displays. Be sure the path is the one you want. Type a filename and choose Save.

### *Select text*

Drag the mouse cursor through the desired text or position the insertion cursor in a word and double-click the mouse to highlight the word.

### *Select paragraph(s)*

Drag the mouse cursor through the desired paragraph or paragraphs or position the cursor anywhere in a paragraph and triple-click to select the whole paragraph.

**NOTE:** *For some tasks, like applying a format from the Paragraph Catalog, it is not necessary to highlight a single paragraph. You can click the cursor anywhere in the paragraph.*

### *Spell check*

Choose Edit, Spelling Checker. The Spelling Checker dialog box is displayed. Choose Document or Current Page. Choose Start Checking. FrameMaker 4 starts checking from the point of the insertion cursor. To spell check only selected text, follow the same steps, but press CTRL when you click Start Checking. When finished, close the window.

### *Start FrameMaker 4 from Windows*

Double-click the FrameMaker 4 icon.

### *Thesaurus (use to find synonyms)*

Highlight the word in the text. Choose Edit, Thesaurus. Choose Look Up. Click the desired synonym. Click Replace. When finished, close the window.

### *Tile windows*

Press SHIFT+F5 or choose Window, Tile.

### *Zoom in*

Click the Zoom In button until the desired zoom percentage is displayed in the status bar.

### *Zoom out*

Click the Zoom Out button until the desired zoom percentage is displayed in the status bar.

## KEYBOARD SHORTCUTS

The following table lists the keyboard shortcuts associated with some of the options on the pull-down menus.

| **Function** | **Shortcut Keys** |
|---|---|
| Cascade windows | SHIFT+F4 |
| Copy the selected text or object | CTRL+C |
| Create a new file | CTRL+N |
| Cut the selected text or object | CTRL+X |
| Design a table | CTRL+T |
| Find text or find/change text | CTRL+F |
| Go to a page | CTRL+G |
| Help (display contents) | F1 |
| Help (context sensitive) | SHIFT+F1 |
| Open an existing file | CTRL+O |
| Paste the text or object on the Clipboard | CTRL+V |
| Print a file | CTRL+P |
| Refresh the screen | CTRL+L |
| Save a file | CTRL+S |
| Select all text and objects on the page | CTRL+A |
| Tile windows | SHIFT+F5 |
| Undo the last command | CTRL+Z |

# D

# Special Characters and Symbols

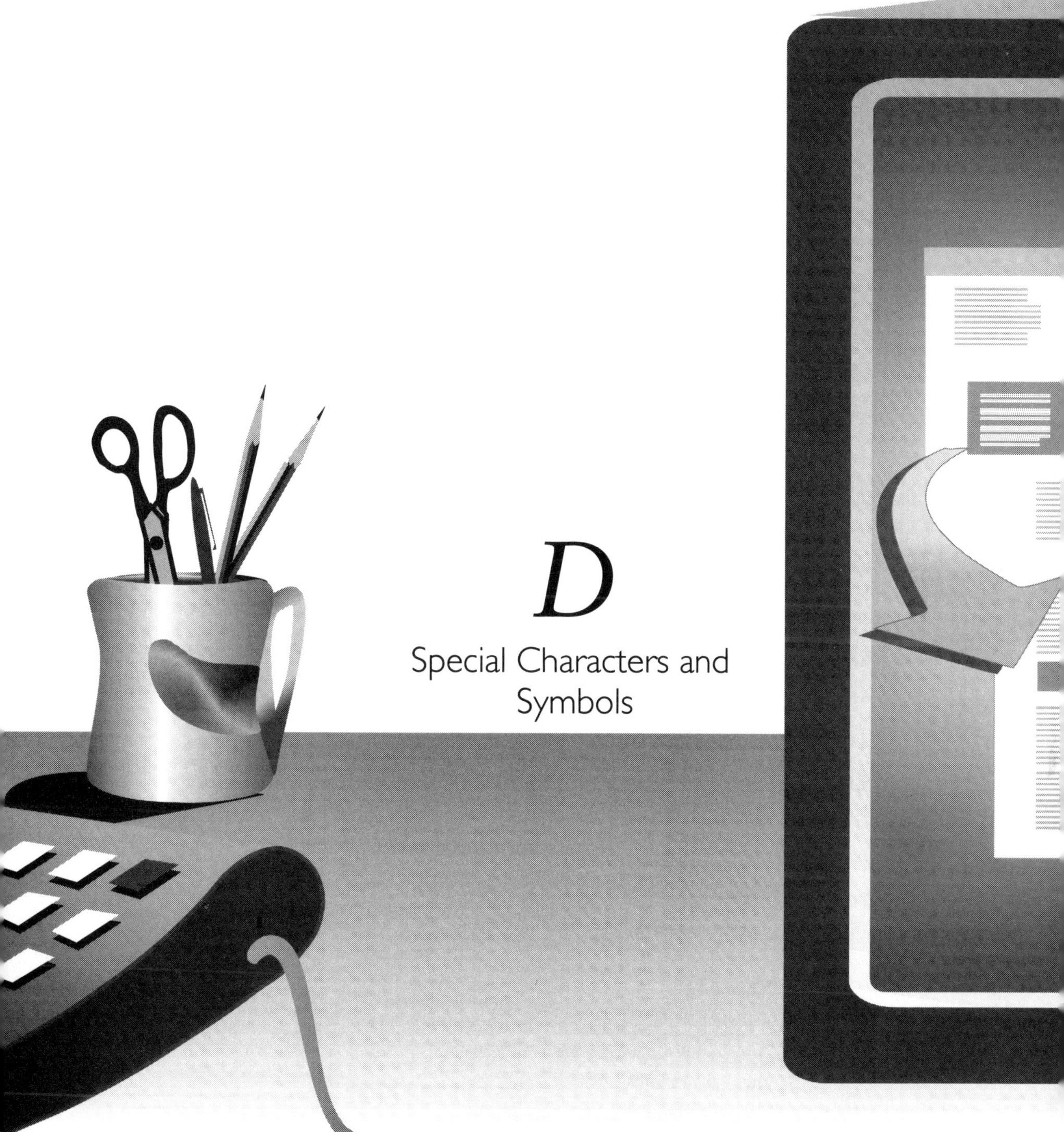

THE codes listed in this table are used with the Find command to search for the special characters or symbols. For example, to find a bullet, you would enter **\b** in the Find text box. Only the most commonly used special characters are listed.

| **Special Character** | **Code** |
|---|---|
| • (bullet) | \b |
| ^ (circumflex) | \@ |
| † (dagger) | \d |
| ‡ (daggerdbl) | \D |
| … (ellipsis) | \e |
| – (en dash) | \= |
| — (em dash) | \m |
| < (guilsinglleft) | \( |
| > (guilsinglright) | \) |
| " (quotedblleft) | \` |
| " (quotedblright) | \' |
| ~ (tilde) | \~ |
| ™ (trademarkserif) | \TM |
| ` (grave) | \{ |
| ' (quotesingle) | \" |
| Tab symbol | \t |
| Forced return | \r |
| End-of-paragraph symbol | \p |
| Start of paragraph | \P |
| Non-breaking space | \space |
| Thin space | \st |
| En space | \sn |

| Special Character | Code |
|---|---|
| Em space | \sm |
| Numeric space | \s# |
| Discretionary hyphen | \– |
| Nonbreaking hypen | \+ |
| End-of-flow symbol | \f |

# E

## Recommended Reading

*Author Law and Strategies,* Brad Bunnin and Peter Beren; Nolo Press: 1983. Includes advice for authors who want to negotiate their own contracts.

*Beyond the Desktop, Tools and Technology for Computer Publishing,* Barrie Sosinsky; Bantam Books: 1991. A detailed book on all aspects of desktop publishing.

*The Careful Writer*, Theodore M. Bernstein; Atheneum: 1965.

*The Chicago Manual of Style*; University of Chicago Press: 1982. A handbook of styles for various kinds of printed material, especially books.

*Color Publishing on the PC*, Kim and Sunny Baker; Random House: 1993. A guide to all aspects of color production.

*Computer Graphics, Principles and Practices*, James D. Foley, Andries van Dam, Steven K. Feiner, and John F. Hughes; Addison-Wesley: 1990. Covers all aspects of graphics and theory.

*Copyediting: A Practical Guide*, Karen Judd; William Kauffman, Inc.: 1982.

*A Desktop Publisher's Guide to Pasteup*, Tony Middleton; Plusware, Inc.: 1987.

*Desktop Publishing Type & Graphics*, Deke McClelland and Craig Danuloff; Harcourt Brace Jovanovich: 1987. A guide to fonts with examples of text set in each style.

*Editing Your Newsletter*, Mark Beach; Coast to Coast Books: 1988.

*The Elements of Style*, William Strunk Jr. and E. B. White; Macmillan Publishing Co., Inc.: 1978. A handbook of techniques to produce effective, concise writing.

*Everyone's Guide to Successful Publications*, Elizabeth W. Adler; Peachpit Press: 1993. A start-to-finish guide covering the publication process.

*The Gray Book*, Michael Gosney, John Odam, and Jim Schmal; Ventana Press: 1990. A guide to computer design in black and white.

*Looking Good in Print*, Roger Parker; Ventana Press: 1988. A guide to basic design. Many before-and-after examples.

*The Makeover Book*, Roger C. Parker; Ventana Press: 1989. Before-and-after designs of flyers, newsletters, advertisements, and many other types of printed material.

*Pocket Pal: A Graphic Arts Production Handbook*; International Paper Co.: 1983. A reference on typesetting, printing, binding, and papermaking.

*A Practical Style Guide for Authors and Editors*, Margaret Nicholson; Holt Rinehart, and Winston: 1967.

*Understanding Desktop Publishing*, Robert Harris; Sybex: 1991. A design handbook for PC users.

*Windows 3.1 Secrets*, Brian Livingston; IDG Books: 1992. This book could be very helpful with the proper set-up of Windows which is critical to the operation of FrameMaker 4.

# Index

## Q



## R



## S



## T